Conducting the People's Business

UNIVERSITY OF OKLAHOMA PRESS : Norman

CONDUCTING THE PEOPLE'S BUSINESS

The Framework and Functions of Public Administration

Edited by:
William G. Hills
Voyle C. Scurlock
Harold D. Viaille
James A. West

Library of Congress Cataloging in Publication Data

Conducting the people's business: the framework and functions of public administration.

Includes bibliographies.

1. Public administration—Addresses, essays, lectures.

I. Hills, William G., 1937–   comp.
JF1351.C59   350   73-7417

This book is dedicated to administrators and managers everywhere who direct public programs that serve people. If, perchance, they find between these covers a thought or an idea that makes their task a little easier and more effective, it will have been worth all of the time and effort involved in putting it together.

The idea for this publication grew out of the experiences of the people associated with twin programs operating at the University of Oklahoma: the Rehabilitation Management Training Program and the Regional Rehabilitation Research Institute.

THE EDITORS

PREFACE

The idea for this book came from our collective experience in research, consulting, training, and administering human service agencies. From our experience we have come to know intimately the great need for administrative training in these agencies. We have also become aware that few, if any, works are being compiled or written with the goals of the practicing public administrator in mind. We feel that many state and federal agencies share a common need for training in administration. Much of this need stems directly from the common practice of promoting administrative personnel from practitioner ranks to executive responsibility with no special preparation for their new tasks.[1]

We are convinced that the solution to many of the complex problems of our times depends as much upon administrative competence as on technological capacity. In all human services, the standards of professional service are inextricably bound up with the prevailing level of administrative ability and maturity. Indeed, in many medical organizations, the quality of administration may be more crucial than even the quality and quantity of the professional staff to the delivery of health care.

While this book is oriented toward practicing administrators, it by no means bypasses the college student—graduate or undergraduate. Indeed, we see it as being relevant and meaningful for these future administrators in a variety of courses in public administration, supervisory principles and practices, and applied administrative management. It is also designed for specialized courses in administration of social services, vocational rehabilitation services, hospitals, police, and health care organizations.

A NOTE ON SELECTION

In the selection of these readings we have tried to break new ground in several ways. We have selected many articles from smaller publications which the practitioner might not ordinarily see, we have sought out materials of special interest to state government administrators, and we have emphasized the experience of human resource agencies. These criteria of selection have necessitated a comprehensive search that has

---

[1] For but one example, see Katherine Kendall's remarks in the preface to *Social Work Administration: A Resource Book* (ed. by Harry A. Schatz, New York, Council on Social Work Education, 1970).

led far beyond the standard categories and indexes. We hope the selections will introduce the user to publications which contain valuable new sources of materials and professional practice relevant to his own work. There is a great diversity in the contributions included, both by author and by source. We have intentionally brought together articles by scholars and by practitioners. It was our intention to include as many good sources as possible, and we have fulfilled this purpose in the thirty-seven journals and papers used.

We agree with Churchill that short words are best and the old words when short are best of all, and with Urwick that the development of communication as a primary social skill should not be retarded by the "jerrybuilding of imposing façades" of polysyllables. Thus we have attempted to keep the book as free of unnecessary technical terminology and jargon as possible. Our purpose has been to present a wide range of topics briefly and succinctly, and this purpose has eliminated many excellent pieces that have dealt at length with specific details of organization and administration. We have also emphasized more recent contributions, although occasionally an older article has been included where it seemed particularly apt. Except for adjustments for consistency of format, omissions of extraneous material, and correction of obvious typographical errors, the articles are reprinted as they appeared in the original sources.

In fairness, we must warn the reader that this is not a difficult book to read. It is intended to be straightforward and to the point. This conciseness was a requirement for inclusion of an article, and this, we feel, contributes to effective learning.

ACKNOWLEDGMENTS

A book is inevitably the product of the efforts of many people in addition to the authors. This book is no exception. The editors, however, assume full responsibility for its shortcomings.

We thank the various publishers, journals, and authors for permission to use their articles and to quote from their works. Special appreciation is due the following persons: Professor Hugh G. MacNiven, University of Oklahoma, who read the entire manuscript and provided much helpful advice; Richard J. Dunsing, Management Center, University of Richmond, and Dr. Donald Galvin, Michigan Division of Vocational Rehabilitation, who provided helpful criticism and suggestions; Mary Llewellyn and Theresa MacMillan, who did much of the necessary library work; and Lana McFarland, who performed the typing and directed the mechanics essential to completion of the manuscript.

This publication was supported in part by the Vocational Rehabilitation Administration, Department of Health, Education, and Welfare, Washington, D.C., Grant Nos. 44–P–81004–6–01 and 15–P–55226/6.

Norman, Oklahoma
January 15, 1973

WILLIAM G. HILLS
VOYLE C. SCURLOCK
HAROLD D. VIAILLE
JAMES A. WEST

CONTENTS

Contents

Conducting the People's Business

OVERVIEW

Formal organizations (or *cooperative systems*) have existed since earliest times. They have been formed for various reasons—all, in essence, variants of these two: men form organizations to do what they cannot do at all as individuals, and men form organizations because together they can perform better, easier, quicker, cheaper, and so on, than they could singly. Impressive products of such cooperative systems in earliest times include the fabled seven wonders of the ancient world, the Great Wall of China, Hammurabi's Code, the empire of Alexander the Great, and Caesar's Roman legions. For each of these massive achievements there were countless lesser organizations to help man cope with an uncertain and hostile environment; to hunt and harvest food; to construct clothing, shelter, and tools; to placate the gods; and to vanquish enemies. Families, clans, and tribes, whether settled or nomadic, are species of organizations; they are cooperative systems with identifiable purposes. It is no exaggeration to say that culture and civilization —down through the ages and still today—depend upon organizations both for their creation and for their continuation.

Organizations existed before the dawn of history, and the importance of organizations has been appreciated over the centuries. Indeed, a library could be formed of treatises written before 1900 which deal with various aspects of organization and management. One would note that a large proportion of the earlier works discussed warfare and other affairs of the state. Later publications, especially those since the Reformation, have dealt increasingly with the management of private enterprises.[1] Despite these numerous and often perspicacious writings, it is fair to assert that organization and management have become a field of systematic and comprehensive study only in this century. The management literature of the last seventy-five years constitutes an enormous compilation.

The beginning of modern management theory is commonly associated with the works of such persons as Henri Fayol and Frederick W. Taylor. Henri Fayol (1841–1925) was a brilliant French industrialist whose book *General and Industrial Management* was published in 1916.[2] This

---

[1] Examples of the earlier writings include Sun-Tzu's *The Art of War* (ca. 200–300 B.C.) and Niccolo Machiavelli's *The Prince* (1513); in the vanguard of later students of organization are two officials of the East India Company: Thomas Mun, *A Discourse on Trade from England into the East Indies* (1621), and Sir Josiah Child, *Brief Observations Concerning Trade and the Interest of Money* (1668).

[2] *General and Industrial Management* (trans. by Constance Storrs, London, Pitman Publishing Corp., 1949).

pioneering work was not translated into English until 1929 and was not printed in the United States until 1949. Fayol described management in terms of six categories of activities which he considered universal; that is, activities found in every type of enterprise, whether private or public, industrial or service-rendering. His six categories were technical, commercial, financial, security, accounting, and managerial. In addition, he identified five functions of management: planning, organizing, commanding, coordinating, and controlling. A review of present-day literature will reveal the continuing impact of this pioneering classification effort. The theories of Fayol and those who followed in his wake—L. Urwick, Mooney, R. C. Davis—have been denoted "classical," "traditional," "principles," and "mechanistic."

Frederick W. Taylor (1856–1915) was an American contemporary of Fayol who has often been called the father of scientific management. Taylor was an engineer and experimenter. His presidential address to the American Society of Mechanical Engineers in 1895, "A Piece-Rate System," set forth the principles of time and motion study and the first modern incentive wage plan. He conducted some of the first systematic studies of management methods in this country, as evidenced by the titles of his works; his magnum opus was the *Principles of Scientific Management* (1911).[3] Taylor and his good friends Gantt and the Gilbreths, and their disciples, constituted the core of the early scientific management school of thought. These pioneers could be considered forerunners both of a continuing group which has been interested in the quantification of important organizational variables and of those who support the present-day systems approach to management.

Elton Mayo's classic experiments at the Hawthorne Works of the Western Electric Company from 1927 to 1932 mark the entry of the social scientists into the systematic study of organizational life. The lineal descendants of this fruitful study include an assembly of diverse viewpoints represented by Chester Barnard, Chris Argyris, John Gardner, Rensis Likert, Abraham Maslow, Frederick Herzberg, and Douglas McGregor. In one way or another, all of these scholars emphasize the psychological and social dimensions of organizations; they are "people-minded." In contrast to the classical school, these authors see an organization as being more akin to a living creature than to a machine, and they recognize the importance of such factors as environment, change, and uncertainty.

Another group conceives management as a decision-making process

---

3 Taylor's other publications, in order of copyright, were *Shop Management* (1903); *A Treatise on Concrete, Plain and Reinforced . . .* (1905); *On the Art of Cutting Metals* (1907); and *Concrete Costs: Tables and Recommendations for Estimating the Time and Cost of Labor Operations in Concrete Construction and for Introducing Economical Methods of Management* (1912).

and sees organization as a system through which various inputs are combined and transformed to produce the desired outputs. This group is composed of such personalities as Herbert A. Simon, Ray E. Brown, and others.

Finally, perhaps the largest group of contemporary theorists could not properly be assigned to any of the foregoing categories and would themselves resent any such assignment. (This group might include some who were named above and consigned to certain groups.) These are the eclectics who, each in his own way, build their theories of organization and management by selecting particular parts of others' formulations.

As far back as 1961, Harold Koontz characterized the state of management theory as a "jungle,"[4] and subsequent issues of numerous publications have contained articles seeking a way out of that jungle. They would find that way by identifying the essential elements of a general theory of organization and management. No one knows whether, how, or when such a general theory can be developed.

In light of the above discussion, a manager of a government agency might wonder why he should read about organization theory and the history of management thought. His doubts might be increased when he realizes that the authors of such writings are mainly academicians and executives whose interest has focused on business and industrial organizations. Before his interest is turned off entirely, however, he would do well to consider the following three points. First, management is conceived, in some circles, as being universal; that is, the basic principles of organization and management are valid whatever purposes are to be achieved. Whether the organization seeks to manage a city, rehabilitate clients, prevent pollution, produce goods, or vanquish an enemy, the manager's job is essentially the same. It is in detail, not in basic concepts, that the differences are found. In the final analysis, the principal responsibility of the leader of a cooperative system is to facilitate the maximum contribution of all participants. An understanding of the problems faced by managers of other kinds of organizations will demonstrate this universality of management. Second, the views of those who have studied and experienced management problems will help the reader to identify and understand his own problems (even though there may be some variance) and see possible solutions. We can learn from the mistakes and successes of others. Finally, not all authors see the same problem exactly the same way. The diverse views of thoughtful men will help the reader formulate his own philosophy of management and his own style of leadership—to the great benefit of his organization, his associates, and himself.

4 "The Management Theory Jungle," *Academy of Management Journal*, Vol. 4, No. 3 (December, 1961), 174–88.

If it is profitable for a manager of a public agency to become familiar with various organization theories, it should also prove advantageous to him to be informed about actual management practices. He should know how these practices developed, how they have been influenced by changing conditions, and the direction of current trends. There are, and have been from the beginning, certain essential differences between the management practices carried on in the private and industrial sector and those of government. These differences lie primarily in purpose—either profit or service. There are also many similarities in practices and in the ways in which those practices developed.

Many, perhaps most, of the industrial organizations in this country had small beginnings, often limited to a single individual, a family, or a partnership. In time, the shop or store moved from the home to the market place, and gradually the operation grew and expanded to involve the services of more and more people. These private and industrial organizations were proprietary and authoritarian in nature. Their authority derived from ownership. The owners reserved the right to do as they liked with what was theirs. Often, those in charge were much more adept as craftsmen than as managers of people and resources. These features directly affected employment practices, wages, working conditions, and production, frequently leaving much to be desired by all concerned. Later, the small private and industrial organizations that were able to survive grew and expanded, some of them becoming huge corporations with thousands of stockholders. This growth was accompanied by increasing management problems. Many of these problems were unforeseen, and for many the organization was unprepared. Growth tended to shift the management responsibility from one or two people to a group, and thus the organization tended to become less authoritarian and more people-minded.

The modifications mentioned above came as a result of several factors and developments. First, the constantly increasing emphasis on profit in a competitive field forced management changes in the interest of better overall performance. These changes tended to demand more consultative services and greater group involvement in policy and decision making. Second, the labor movement, concerned primarily with working conditions and wages, forced management to become more aware of employees as people and to give greater consideration to their welfare. Finally, the fact that many employees became stockholders in the corporation meant that they were no longer just employees but part owners of the enterprise and, as such, were entitled to a voice in its operation and management. Today's trend is toward better performance through increasing personnel participation. This trend is accompanied by a constant review and evaluation of management practices in an effort to make the best and most innovative use of the management knowledge and tools available. Perhaps the most notable change that has developed in management in the private sector has been the shift in emphasis from profit, as such, to the concept of service to the buying public.

Government agencies, by comparison with their present size, were mere infants in the early history of this country and had barely reached the "crawling" stage at the beginning of this century. Too often, administrators were appointed as a reward for political support, with little concern for administrative ability. Under the spoils system, government management was proprietary and authoritarian in nature. Authority was derived from the party's political success at the polls, and the primary consideration in management decisions was political expediency, often dictated by political bosses. Not unlike private and industrial organizations, government agencies grew and expanded. Much of this growth was in keeping with the growth of the nation and its need for services, and these services at first were minimal. They were limited to such things as national security, defense, and housekeeping chores, including collection of taxes and handling of mail. In time, poor services and scandals of one kind or another resulting from maladministration brought demands for government reforms. Out of these demands came the establishment of civil service at the federal level (Pendleton Act, 1883) and merit systems in many of the states. This development tended to place increased emphasis on ability and integrity in the selection and retention of employees.

The greatest periods of growth in government activities followed the two world wars and were made possible by increased federal grants to the states. Enactment of the grant-in-aid that established the state-federal program of vocational rehabilitation was the first of its kind in the social service field.[5] Grants-in-aid were greatly expanded with the passage of the Social Security Act during the depression years of the 1930's.[6] The basic understanding was that the federal government would aid the states in providing needed services in certain areas which, at that time, the states were unable to provide for themselves. The federal government was to provide leadership and some "seed-corn" funds to get the programs started. Eventually, the states would take over the programs and assume all the cost.

The results of the grant-in-aid programs have been both good and bad. They have been good in that needed services became available in many areas earlier than would otherwise have been possible. Also, federal controls require certain standards to assure desirable emphasis on performance in spite of the political climate in which such programs

[5] Smith-Fess Act, Public Law 236, August 2, 1920.
[6] Public Law 271, August 14, 1935.

7

operate. On the bad side, the results, in terms of the states assuming financial responsibility for the grant-in-aid programs, have been almost totally negative. The increasing availability of federal funds has been accompanied by an increasing shift of responsibility from the states and the local communities to the federal government. Grants-in-aid were accompanied by the entry of the federal government into all sorts of social and welfare programs aimed at providing more and more services to more and more people at the local level. These programs today extend into and directly affect such things as education, research, housing, criminal justice, pollution control, flood control, agriculture, highways, airports, and small business administration, to name a few.

In the years following World War II came rising and widespread demands for government reorganization in the interest of both efficiency and effectiveness. The tremendous increase in the number of government agencies, often with kindred and even overlapping missions and responsibilities, brought consumer and public demand for better coordination and less fragmentation of services. A few examples will indicate the continuing trend. The army, navy, and air force were brought together in 1946 under the new Department of Defense. In 1965 and 1966, two new cabinet departments were created to coordinate and give new emphasis to federal functions in their respective fields. The Federal Housing Authority and the Bureau of Urban Affairs were brought together under a new Department of Housing and Urban Development, and a number of transportation agencies, the Coast Guard, the Federal Aviation Agency, and the Federal Highway Administration were combined to make up the new Department of Transportation. In 1953, the Department of Health, Education, and Welfare was created with cabinet status to administer a whole host of social, educational, and medical services. These included the Office of Education, the Department of Health, the Social Security Administration, the Institute of Mental Health, and a number of others. In 1967, the Department of Health, Education, and Welfare itself was reorganized by the establishment within the department of the Social and Rehabilitation Service, aimed at a better grouping of services for operation and at a greater emphasis on these services. Reorganization remains a critical concern of federal government, and the present national administration gives this activity highest priority on its list of urgent program activities.

The variation in organization structure at the state level is notable in that there are almost as many different kinds of structure as there are states. Nevertheless, reorganization at the federal level has been and is being followed in many of the states, and this trend promises better overall government in time. However, the reasons for reorganization advanced by some states may be open to question. In practically every case, economy and efficiency are promised by the proponents of reorganization. Observation indicates that much more is involved in attaining cooperation and coordination of services than the creation of large umbrella agencies or the drawing of new organization charts. It is also doubtful if such reorganization has resulted, or will result, in huge savings of funds. What is looked for is the better delivery of services to citizens.

Between 1946 and 1966, state and local government employment more than doubled. Since 1946, state and local government employment has increased more rapidly than employment in any other sector of the economy in both absolute and relative terms. Regarding this growth, Senator Edmund Muskie of Maine has said:

The striking fact is that this growth in manpower and public programs at state and local levels has not been accompanied by improvement in the quality and professional caliber of administration.[7]

For the past three decades, state governments have not been in a position to compete effectively with the federal government and with the private sector for professional and technical manpower.[8] Other studies of public employee training have pointed out the need for greatly expanded programs of supervisory and management training on a continuing basis, particularly for first-line supervisors and middle-level managers.[9] Training at the state government level is currently not highly coordinated or directed toward meeting any defined overall manpower needs of the state government.[10] It has even been suggested that manpower problems of state and local governments are more critical than their fiscal woes, although the two issues cannot be separated entirely.[11]

Recently, the Department of Labor proclaimed that the manpower shortage which exists in state and local government threatens to get worse during this decade.[12] A compounding factor is the indication of

[7] "Problems, Programs, and People," mimeographed (Speech given at Boston College, Boston, Massachusetts, April 22, 1967), 8.

[8] Eli Ginsberg, "Challenge of the 70's: Professional Manpower for State Governments," *Personnel Administration*, Vol. 34, No. 6 (November–December, 1971), 28–32.

[9] Clayton Ringgenberg, *Local Government Training Programs: Problems and Needs* (Iowa City, Iowa, University of Iowa Institute of Public Affairs, 1968), 27; Charles E. Moan, Jr., *Public Employee Training on the State Level in the United States*, Research Series Number 8 (Kingston, Rhode Island, 1964); Earl Planty and George Kanawaty, "Training Activities in the State Governments," *Personnel Report* (Chicago, Public Personnel Association, 1962); and Lytton K. Caldwell, *Improving the Public Service Through Training* (Bloomington, Indiana, Indiana University Institute of Training for Public Service, 1962).

[10] *State and Local Government Training in Wisconsin: A Summary of Status and Issues* (Madison, Wisconsin, University of Wisconsin Institute of Governmental Affairs, February, 1970).

[11] Robert P. Fairbanks, "Manpower Needs of State and Local Governments" in *Manpower for Illinois Governments* (ed. by Joseph P. Pisciotte, Urbana, Illinois, the University of Illinois Institute of Government and Public Affairs, 1968), 13.

[12] *Manpower in State and Local Government, 1965 and 1975* (Washington, D.C., U.S. Department of Labor Bureau of Labor Statistics).

high retirement rates during the 1970's. A recent inventory of administrative professional and technical personnel in one populous state revealed an agency bureaucracy with nearly half of the executives being fifty years of age or older.[13]

The Department of Labor has projected that the 1970's will witness an increase in state and local government positions of over 50 per cent, while federal government is slated to increase by only 10 per cent. The 9.6 million employees in state and local government in 1970 will increase to 13.5 million by 1980. The 1970's will also see a dramatic increase in the number of young adults coming into the work force. This group increased 16 per cent in the 1960's, but is predicted to increase 50 per cent in the following decade as the baby-boom generation, which got a toe-hold position in the labor force of the 1960's, moves into full maturity.[14]

With the single largest growth in employment about to occur in the area of state and local government, with state agencies having a disproportionate number of employees at the administrative level who will soon be retiring, and with the labor force becoming much younger during the 1970's, we can expect a corresponding increase in the demands for training in public administration. While the complexity of modern life has created demands for public employee skill and sophistication of high level, public management at all levels of government has faced and continues to face a problem of employee recruitment and development. Public management has, in many cases, turned to colleges and universities for management training help. In the future, agencies will have to develop their own resources to more nearly take care of their needs. This development, however, requires money, a commodity no state seems to have in adequate amounts, and as everyone knows, money comes from Washington.

Congressman Henry Reuss of Wisconsin, while finding revenue sharing through unrestricted bloc grants to be a panacea for the states' fiscal problems, ties to it one big string—the states must prepare for fiscal and organizational modernization of themselves and their local governments.[15] This preparation would be the condition for the states to receive bloc grants. Senator Muskie and Representative Mills, as well as others, have taken similar positions. Sundquist and Davis[16] agree that unless and until state governments are vastly improved or upgraded,

[13] Robert D. Lee, *et al.*, "A Profile of State APT Manpower Resources: Preliminary Findings," *Public Administration Review*, November–December, 1970, 602ff.

[14] J. D. Hodgson, "The Future World of Work," *Conference Board Report*, February, 1971.

[15] Henry S. Reuss, *Revenue-Sharing: Crutch or Catalyst for State and Local Governments?* (New York, Praeger Publishers, Inc., 1970), 146.

[16] James L. Sundquist and David W. Davis, *Making Federalism Work: A Study of Program Coordination at the Community Level* (Washington, D.C., The Brookings Institution, 1969).

revenue sharing with them will have to occur along the lines enunciated by Congressman Reuss.

In the meantime, some help has come in the form of the Inter-governmental Personnel Act of 1970, the purpose of which is to reinforce the federal system by strengthening the personnel resources of state and local governments. The act is to perform this strengthening by providing grants for the improvement of state and local personnel administration, by authorizing federal assistance in training state and local employees, and by authorizing interstate compacts for personnel and training activities. The Intergovernmental Personnel Act of 1970 will increase the amount and availability of training as well as the need for relevant training materials.

Books about public administration have primarily been prepared for the college audience, and if they are applicable to or can somehow be used by the practicing public administrator, so much the better. As a result, administrative personnel in state government have found themselves with a scarcity of learning materials, and, as seen by the practitioner, much of what they have had to use is often not relevant or meaningful. Generally, books on public administration pursue the politics and process approach to administration while tending to ignore the "stuff" that most individuals working in public agencies must contend with throughout their careers.

In conducting the people's business, much of public administration for the practitioner is not arguing the merits or demerits of weighty issues such as welfare reform, national education priorities, or a national comprehensive health program, but rather maintaining the integrity of a relatively small operation not unlike a small business. Only a small percentage of public administrators eventually rise to the position of agency head. For these top-level decision makers, the study of politics and process is essential and appropriate. However, it makes little sense for the great majority of middle- and lower-level administrators who need the basic skills of public management to continue using learning materials designed for agency heads.

To date, our society has experienced difficulty building bridges between the world of school and the world of work. With its focus on the practicing administrator, this book may help strengthen the bridge between education in administration and the practical application of that education. Our approach is to deal with the separate functions of administration, being satisfied that materials for studying policy are already available. For this reason we have compiled a book of readings consisting of material that is both relevant to the public problems of the 1970's and appropriate for application by middle- and lower-level administrators in public agencies.

Notwithstanding the pronounced need for attention to administrative matters, it would be shortsighted and a disservice if we were to attempt to present a straightforward set of "how-to-do-it" techniques. Organization problems are not essentially mechanical, and administration is not a precise science. Hence, mechanical or scientific rules do not exist which can be applied to solve administrative problems.

It is important for administrators to take a long, hard look at who they are and where they are in this value-oriented society as well as at their goals and priorities. It is also essential that they be prepared to do their job by having proper training. The administrator who fails to orient himself to, sympathize with, or understand the value and purpose of specific rules of administration will, of course, frustrate, if not totally destroy, their potential for good. Effective administration and problem solving call for the right kind of person as much as the right kinds of rules. The ability to anticipate problems and to size up situations requires the incorporation of specific skills into an appropriate personality. Practical solution of a problem is dependent upon the values, knowledge, skills, and attitudes of the individual decision maker. An administrator with an understanding of how his environment relates to his function, and how he can mold the environment relates to his function, and how he can mold the environment to meet his functional needs, is equipped to act upon his environment rather than simply react to it, as do so many managers. Conceptual skills aid the individual to know his environment and to shape it for greater job effectiveness. They also arm him with alternative solutions.

"Principles" of administration are at best fundamental truths of general validity; at worst they are "little more than mutually contradictory proverbs."[17] Nevertheless, the government manager can benefit much from a rudimentary knowledge of basic "principles" of administration if he recognizes their situational applicability. Because it remains the administrator's task to use his judgment in determining when to apply a certain principle, it does not follow that certain principles are, per se, invalid. Rather than spend much time searching for universal principles of administration, we need to concern ourselves with the different situations and environments which decision makers face.

The question is often posed whether public administration is a science or an art. George Alexandris answers well that

Administration cannot be considered solely as a science or solely as an art. Neither, in practice, has anybody ever maintained either extreme view. Principles, i.e., universal rules, cannot by themselves serve as a background for administration unless their application is supplemented, supported and

17 Herbert A. Simon, "The Proverbs of Administration," *Public Administration Review*, Vol. 6, No. 1 (winter, 1946).

corroborated by the specific art, based on experience and knowledge, of putting them into practice. The creative force of an ideal administration resides in that art.[18]

Public administration is a science in the sense that it consists of a body of knowledge arranged in an orderly manner, and it is an art in the sense that many practitioners apply this knowledge in the course of their work.

Most studies in public administration in the past can be classified in three categories: (1) the legal, classical tradition, concentrating upon definition of jurisdictions and development of rules and responsibilities; (2) the political science tradition, focusing on politics and administration and the effects of centralized administration on the functioning of democracy; and (3) scientific management, stressing management principles and normative statements on conditions promoting efficiency. None of these approaches utilize the tools and analytical methods of modern organizational analysis, with its concepts and propositions rooted in the behavioral sciences. Newer concepts of organization and administration emphasize that administrative success depends on many skills, including the effective use of groups; interpersonal competence; development of explicit executive, legislative, and judicial systems in the organization to induce into it a democratic culture; and psychodiagnostic understanding of the leader by the leader himself.[19] This book of readings, while not presenting the detailed research studies from which the newer concepts and propositions have sprung, does present an array of articles based on the newer behavioral research.

Though claiming to be practical and not really interested in theory, many self-confident people in management are slaves of the classical management theory of two or three decades ago. While organizational behavior as a school is more recent and more soundly based in rigorous scientific investigation, it has not yet had the impact that the principles-of-administration school has enjoyed among practicing managers.

Richard Hodgson has pointed out organizational behavior studies which show that the application of much of what scientific management and principles of organization tell us should produce effective performance actually produces ineffective behavior.[20] Likert has found that the traditional theories of management are based on an inadequate motivational assumption and that the principles and practices of high-producing managers are deviating in important ways from those called for by

18 George Alexandris, "Public Administration as a Science or an Art" (English summary, original in French), *International Review of Administrative Sciences*, No. 1 (1961), viii.

19 Ishivar Dayal, "Some Dilemmas in Newer Concepts of Administration," *California Management Review*, Vol. 13, No. 1 (fall, 1970), 51–58.

20 Richard C. Hodgson, "Viewpoint . . . Toward More Effective Management: A Behavioral Science Viewpoint," *Business Quarterly*, fall, 1966, 10–25.

present-day theories.[21] Likert has demonstrated that a leadership style based on participation by groups is more productive than the traditional authoritative style. He argues that the supervisor should be employee-oriented and practice general supervision rather than close supervision. The supervisor's role, as he sees it, is to support and nurture groups and allow them to function while serving as a link between them. While McGregor's work supports Likert's on the effectiveness of groups, McGregor thinks it is the leader's self-knowledge, his activity as influencer of the group, rather than his role of linking pin that accounts for the groups' effectiveness.[22]

Argyris has pointed out the incongruity between the demands made upon an employee by the organization and his personality as an adult. Only a part of the psychological energy or skills of the individual is used, resulting in the individual withdrawing from the task or using other defense mechanisms.[23] He suggests an employee's involvement can be attained by designing a job to use more of the employee's mental energy. All this contradicts the isolated job station and piecework practice so common in assembly-line business, industrial, governmental, and educational institutions with their division of labor and cult of specialization.

This book is divided into eight parts, each containing articles selected for their insight and relevance to the needs of public management. Instead of merely presenting a collection of articles, each of the eight parts includes an introductory comment by the editors that contains materials not included in the articles. Thus, each introduction is also a complete article.

Part One is an introduction to public administration in that it gives the backdrop and setting—the environment. Management in any of the public realms, be it health care, education, law enforcement, the military, or one of the myriad federal, state, or local agencies, is in the public arena. This setting poses special difficulties for the administrator. He is expected to operate efficiently among the conflicting pressures of many power centers, always keeping in mind an elusive "public interest." He must be concerned not only with what the public sees of government operations, but also of the meaning it attaches to what it sees. In a political society that still responds to the Jacksonian myth of the best government being the least government, it is not startling that a large segment of our populace is quite thoroughly convinced of the sickness

---

21 Rensis Likert, *New Patterns of Management* (New York, McGraw-Hill Book Co., 1961), and *Human Organization: Its Management and Value* (New York, McGraw-Hill Book Co., 1967).

22 Douglas McGregor, *The Human Side of Enterprise* (New York, McGraw-Hill Book Co., 1961), and *The Professional Manager* (New York, McGraw-Hill Book Co., 1967).

23 Chris Argyris, *Personality and Organization* (New York, Harper & Row, Publishers, 1957).

of government. In this mileau, the public administrator labors with few defenders. The terms *bureaucrat* and *bureaucracy* have taken on a sinister meaning to the citizen, who must relate to the complex activities of modern organizations, both public and private. Some fundamental characteristics of public administration in general, and bureaucracy in particular, are examined in Part One from the point of view of various schools of administrative theory.

The second major divisions of the book, Parts Two through Six, proceed with the elements of the administrative process: planning, organizing, developing human resources, directing, and controlling. In developing these respective areas, we have kept the old acronym *posdcorb* in mind. In our discussion we have included *coordinating* under the category *controlling*, and *reporting* has been dealt with as the other side of *delegating* and under *directing*.

Evaluation is one major process of administration that the public administration field has largely ignored. Poland found in his examination of four widely used textbooks in public administration that none included a chapter on evaluation.[24] While the economists have monopolized evaluation with their cost benefit models, and while public administrators have ignored it, our experience leads us to conclude that the evaluation of social programs will become increasingly important.

Of those writers who feel that the heyday of planning-programming-budgeting systems (PPBS) is already over,[25] we can only ask, Over where? In the journals? While PPBS has had some of the aspects of a fad, the concern with program evaluation which it engendered will necessarily continue, even though the activities may be carried on under some name other than PPBS.[26] New York, Massachusetts, Wisconsin, Pennsylvania, Hawaii, and Michigan, as well as other states and, of course, the Office of Management and Budget (OMB) and the federal government continue to push for a systems analysis program integrated into the total administrative and operational structure of agencies.[27]

24 Orville F. Poland, "Why Does Public Administration Ignore Evaluation?" *Public Administration Review*, Vol. 31, No. 2 (March–April, 1971), 201–202.

25 See Heinz Eulau's review of Suzanne Farkas' *Urban Lobbying: Mayors in the Federal Arena* (New York, New York University Press, 1971) in *Western Political Science Review*, December, 1971, 809.

26 A number of states are pursuing PPBS under different titles due to the sour reception that an often-rigid academically flavored "quickie" approach brought about. See Stephen M. Fletcher, "From PPBS to PAR in the Empire State," *State Government*, summer, 1972, 198–202; for the Massachusetts experience, see Robert C. Casselman, "An Old State Takes a New Look at Public Management," *Public Administration Review*, Vol. 21, No. 4 (July–August, 1971).

27 For an excellent operationalization of PPBS, see Paul Brown, "An Operational Model For A Planning-Programming-Budgeting System," paper presented to the Post Audit Seminar, Lexington, Kentucky, June 17, 1970, condensed and reprinted in *Planning-Programming-Budgeting: A Systems Approach to Management*, 2d ed. (ed. by Fremont J. Lyden and Ernest G. Miller, Chicago, Markham Publishing Co., 1972).

Because of this continuing interest we have selected five of the ten articles in Part Two to cover PPBS and evaluation.

Organization development is handled in Part Three, "Organization for Administration," rather than in Part Four, "Developing Human Resources," because we did not want organization development to become confused with staff development or human relations. Organization development requires organization-wide cognizance and commitment. It is a total-organization approach to solving an organization's problems. It cannot be separated from the entire organization involvement, for it is not an end in itself, as was so often the case with human relations. The concept of organization development applies to work groups and large organizations as well as to the individual. It requires thinking in the systems terms of planning the tactics and strategies of change, including, if necessary, the restructuring of an organizational unit. As organization development is interdependent rather than dependent, it is fitting to place it within Part Three. Regardless of the wisdom involved, personnel departments—engaged in human resource development—have rarely been included on an equal footing with other departments in the executive council's decision-making process. The location of organization development elsewhere than within this area should strengthen the organization's potential for development.

The term *staffing* we viewed as old-fashioned and as too limited in both meaning and matter; hence, the part was entitled "Developing Human Resources." As the reader can see, both the wider philosophical and conceptual approach and a systems or whole-goal approach are taken on staffing. For years the idea that an organization's most valuable asset is its people has been extolled. Yet we see spacious data-processing machine rooms that are spotless and air-conditioned while many public employees continue to work in cluttered, crowded, un-air-conditioned, and even dingy quarters. Equally demeaning and stultifying is the practice of using biased tests and adhering to overly rigid, irrelevant, and unrelated job requirements in the recruitment, selection, and promotion of personnel. If personnel are the greatest asset of the organization, a comprehensive and systematic program for further developing all personnel seems to be in order. To develop human resources, physical, structural, philosophical, psychological, and cultural needs have to be reckoned with in appraising all personnel and working with them in balancing their self-actualization with the self-actualization of the organization.

To direct, one must communicate to others both a direction to be followed and a sense of urgency in pursuing that direction. There must also be delegation of responsibility and accountability by the superordinate to the subordinate for the organization to be effective. Function, responsibility, and authority are inseparably concomitant. Given a specific function to perform, the employee must be given authority commensurate with his responsibility for performing the function, and only then should he be held accountable for performance. This delegation distributes authority throughout the organization, and "responsibility for" replaces "responsibility to."

The opposite side of delegation is reporting—giving evidence that responsibility and accountability have been handled. As the evidence of results is passed up the organization in the form of reports, those reports must be clear and usable. The idea of completed staff work must be kept in mind.

Over-all controls are used to monitor the progress of the entire organization and its major departments toward meeting objectives. Control should be focused on the process and not on the creative man. Some overall control systems are procedural manuals, budget summaries and reports, staff control, and the monitoring of key result areas. An unquestioning compliance with instructions, together with an overriding compulsion to regulate and control minutia, are unsatisfactory to the modern organization's needs.

The last sections of the book deal with what we term "the new public administration"; Part Seven takes up employee relations, while Part Eight looks at the individual and changing bureaucracy. The focus in this section is on the present and the rapidly approaching future.

By overviewing the whole span of public administration applicable to the federal, state, or local government administrator, we have necessarily been restricted in the depth of treatment possible for a given topic. Because of this, we have included, at the end of each chapter, a selected list for further reading.

PART ONE. Introduction to Public Administration

The public administrator who would do his job well needs a clear understanding of both the conceptual framework and the environment of public administration.

While the trend in American management literature is towards treating public, private, and voluntary organizations as being generically similar, there are those who hasten to point up some weaknesses, if not fallacies, in this treatment. Sherwood is one of those who believes that there are significant differences between the public and the private organization. He points to two clear examples. The first is in the area of local government, "where the multiplicity of decision-making points, each seemingly independent of the others, exercises a pervasive influence on behaviors."[1] The second is in the area of developing nations (which include most of mankind). In such countries, the government is the major source of investment, employment, and profit. Economic development is a political process to the extent that it is dependent upon economic policy making. Given such circumstances, we must take politics for granted in government administration. And are we not being asked to buy a dream when it is implied that United States governmental organizations can be run like private organizations? Surely it is a myth when we think of insulating governmental organizations from politics while attempting to build and retain a democratic society. Politics must go on, or we have to call our political system something other than democracy. While there is nothing wrong with dreaming that we can run government organizations just like business organizations, public

---

1 Frank Sherwood, "The Relationship Between Public and Private Organizations," *Public Administration Review*, Vol. 23 (September, 1963), 248.

servants must always remain responsive to the individual citizen, his representatives, and his organized interest groups. This by no means lessens the responsibility of the public servant for improving the effectiveness of his services.

While public administration and business administration are undoubtedly part of a single broad art and science of administration, public administration is much broader and more complex than many business persons realize. As to the common characteristics of administration in business and government, Paul Appleby wrote:

> Public administrators can learn a great deal by studying business administration—but not as much as most businessmen believe, and no more than business executives can learn by studying public administration.[2]

While this statement implies business administration and government administration have certain common characteristics, it also implies that there are dissimiliarities between them, the understanding of which is helpful to the understanding of the administrative process. The culture or subculture dominating the particularized environment distinguishes public administration from business administration.

Using efficiency—that axiom of good administration so singularly praised in business and administration—as an example, we clearly see the implications. The impact of supremacy of law, public interest, and democracy in public administration is distinctly different from that in business. More than a few city managers have learned too late the priority the public gives to accessibility over efficiency. The business of government takes place in a different environment from the business of business.

A question public administrators have to deal with is, Should the same standards and criteria used to evaluate private business enterprise be used to evaluate public administrators and their work? Public administrators may have to aid their superiors—the politically elected chief executives—in setting forth policies requiring business to really begin measuring intangible social costs. These costs have always been with us, but society was not really supposed to add up any cost for environmental pollution and contamination although it often had to pay for remedial action.

At no time in American history has the civil servant, that employee who works for government, been thought of very highly. We have no tradition, as have many other countries, in which it is an honor for a family to have one of their own in the civil service of the country. Indeed, employment, especially long-term employment, in the civil service, be it

---

[2] Paul Appleby, "Administration in Big Business," *Public Administration Review*, Vol. 5 (summer, 1945), 255.

federal, state, or municipal, gains one the reward of being denigrated as a "payroller" or one of those "feeding at the public trough." The low esteem in which the American people hold their civil servants does nothing to improve the civil service, but it does increase the difficulty of recruiting and hiring as well as running the business of government. We have not progressed, as yet, to the point where many of our young people enter university with a definite career of life-long government service as their goal; this despite the fact that the largest, most complex, oldest, and perhaps most challenged and challenging business in the world is the United States government as it grapples with the gargantuan problems of a highly mobile, urbanized, technological society.

In his article "The Public Image of Government Agencies," Sidney J. Levy points out that Americans want to be able to criticize their government; that they prefer to believe that their government is bureaucratic, lazy, and authoritarian; and that government agencies cannot do much to improve their image or gain recognition for their accomplishments. An example of a source of some of the myths of government inefficiency and business efficiency is provided by the statements of a distinguished professor of economics in testimony to a government subcommittee. In "Economic Analysis and Efficiency of Government," Milton Friedman flatly states that it is impossible for government to be efficient.

In "The Sickness of Government" an anonymous civil servant reviews a book chapter entitled "The Sickness of Government."[3] He strongly disagrees with Drucker's position that government is not only sick, but almost dead. The author points out that those who wish the state would wither away refuse to acknowledge such effective government undertakings as the Department of Agriculture's programs, which have produced an overabundance of food rather than a shortage.

Bureaucracy is a phenomenon appearing in all industrialized countries and all kinds of political systems. It applies equally to private and public organizations. It is simply the ordering of institutional life. The term *bureaucracy* should have special meaning to a public administrator, for it is a central concept in his professional life. He performs his job within a legal-rational structure, with accountability and open information as prevailing criteria.

The widespread use of the terms *red tape* and *bureaucracy* to denote government agencies ignores the extent to which red tape and bureaucracy are also typical of large private businesses. The very function of public administration and the sensitive milieu in which it operates may make red tape a legitimate and even desirable component of administration. Many governmental procedures are intended to safeguard the citizen against arbitrary misuse of power. Essential red tape allows a

3 Peter F. Drucker, *The Age of Discontinuity* (New York, Harper & Row, Publishers, 1969).

system of professionals to dispense services in a systematic, reliable manner with arbitrary, whimsical, or unjust decisions and procedures minimized.

Bureaucracy has been defined as the institutional manifestations which tend toward inflexibility and depersonalization and as the state of society in which institutions overshadow individuals and wherein division of labor, specialization, organization, hierarchy, and regimentation of large groups of individuals are the order of the day.[4] On the other hand, rules and regulations are directly related to the accomplishment of objectives, and, like objectives, they must be formulated in advance. Rules and regulations are but means to an end and nothing more. It is the keeping of laws and rules of organizational behavior to a minimum that will help avoid rigid bureaucracy and help ensure goal attainment.

In "Bureaucracy: Characteristics and Problems," Chester A. Newland clarifies some of the confusion that public administrators face with the twofold meaning of bureaucracy. Newland analyzes the main characteristics of a bureaucratic structure by using the precise social science concepts derived from that classifier of bureaucracy, Max Weber. He concludes by reminding us that even in a well-rationalized bureaucratic organization, a tendency exists to displace ends with means. In any organization, there exists at all times the possibility that the organization will lose sight of its goals and allow elements of administration to exist and function for their own sake.

The article "The Characteristics of Public Administration," from John C. Buechner's small book *Public Administration*, provides an account of the historical development of public administration. Paul J. Gordon, in the article "Transcend the Current Debate on Administrative Theory," categorizes the various approaches to the theory of administration. Individual practitioners need not be troubled over what school they should subscribe to. Gordon maintains that what is needed is a "take it and leave it" approach based on demonstrated applicability rather than on purely theoretical debate. The ideas and concepts which are found in each school contribute to the total body of knowledge comprising modern management.

---

[4] Marshall E. Dimock, "Bureaucracy Self-Examined," *Public Administration Review*, Vol. 4, No. 3 (1944), 198.

1. The Nature of Administration and Management*

The terms *administration* and *management* are more and more being used synonymously. While the term *administration* has been applied more to the conduct of public affairs and the term *management* more to that of business enterprise, there has been a tendency in recent times for *management* to be used to a greater degree in public affairs. This is probably because of the increasing application of business management practices in the field of public administration. Sometimes a different distinction is made, in both public and private undertakings. The term *administration* is used to comprehend the processes both of policy formulation and of *management*, in the limited sense of getting things done, within a given framework of policy. This distinction is useful to keep in mind, but it is difficult, if not impossible, to define it precisely. The fact is that policy-making and getting things done react upon one another, and the one continuously causes modifications to the other.

The term *management* is used in this document in its broadest sense, to include not only the achievement of objectives with the optimum use of limited resources in manpower, money, materials and time, but also the active and continuous role of contributing to the clarification and reformulation of policies and objectives to make the former more effective and the latter more realistic. In this sense the terms *administration* and *management* may be considered synonymous.

In any enterprise, public or private, which requires the co-operative effort of a number of people to achieve a common objective, there must be a focal point of leadership, authority, responsibility, and motivation for the achievement of this objective. There may indeed be a series, or hierarchy, of these focal points, which indicate the location, within the network of the organization, of managers, or administrators, who to a greater or lesser degree perform management functions.

The nature and scope of administration or management continues to be the subject of much study and debate. However, while administration or management was regarded as a natural art some hundred years ago, its various aspects have now been intensely studied to the point where the terms *scientific management* or *administrative science* are used and *principles* are enunciated. These *principles* do not stand such rigorous tests as those of the natural sciences and perhaps fall more accurately

* From *The Administration of Organization and Methods Services* (New York, United Nations, Department of Economics and Social Affairs, 1969).

23

into the categories of *concepts* and *techniques*, arrived at by the application, as far as possible, of scientific method.

SPECIALIZED FIELDS OF ADMINISTRATION AND MANAGEMENT

Administration and *management*, when used synonymously, are intended to indicate a special field of study, and some attempt is necessary to clarify their scope. The first necessary clarification arises from these terms being used loosely in conjunction with the different activities, which are being *managed* or *administered*. For example, such terms as *hospital administration, city management, library administration, military management* and so on, refer to highly specialized and professional fields. It is obvious that these require not only specialized knowledge of management or administration, but also specialized knowledge of the activities being managed. To deal with administration or management as a field of study in itself, it becomes necessary to define what all these specialized phases of management have in common.

DIVISIONS OF ADMINISTRATION OR MANAGEMENT

A second clarification is necessary because the terms *administration* or *management* are freely applied to certain fields of activity such as finance, personnel, production, distribution, records, forms and so on, which are, in themselves, merely sectors, or divisions, of management or administration. All these fields of activity are involved, to a greater or lesser degree, in the management of the specialized and professional activities mentioned above, but they also tend to become regarded as specialized and professional fields in themselves.

LEVELS OF ADMINISTRATION OR MANAGEMENT

The achievement of the major task in any large organization is usually so complex and onerous that it is beyond the capacity of any one manager. It is necessary to divide the task into carefully delineated parts, so that authority and responsibility may be delegated for the bulk of the administration or management of each part. Hence the series or hierarchy of focal points, mentioned above, where sub-managers or junior administrators, to a greater or lesser degree, perform management duties throughout the organization.

It is the complexity of this hierarchical network of administrative or managerial relationships, and the increasingly specialized processes of management, which create the need, in a dynamic organization, for the constant review of the whole process, both as a total system and in detail, to ensure the most effective and economic achievement of the objectives of the organization as a whole.

ADMINISTRATIVE AND MANAGEMENT PROCESSES

Certain continuous processes can be identified, within any organization, as common to the administration or management of all its activities at all levels. They may be briefly summarized as follows:

1. *Clarification of objectives*: continuously making clear to all who work in the organization and in its subsidiary parts the precise objectives or goals that are to be achieved and the general conditions and policy guides which must be observed in work performance;

2. *Planning and scheduling*: the continuous prediction and specification of the requirements and use of resources (manpower, money, materials, time and so on) that will ensure the achievement of the objectives effectively and economically;

3. *Organization*: the continuous division of work into parts, which will lend themselves to greater productivity, by the grouping of particular activities and functions in order to gain the greatest advantage from specialization, and the delegation of authority and responsibility for the management of these parts;

4. *Co-ordination and control*: the continuous process of ensuring that all parts of the organization work together in a harmonious and balanced way, so that each makes its optimum contribution to the achievement of the main objectives;

5. *Motivation*: the continuous process of ensuring that working conditions are such that each employee is motivated to make the maximum contribution to the achievement of the objectives;

6. *Decision-making*: ensuring that relevant data are continuously available for the making of decisions, and that these decisions are made soundly and promptly to expedite the flow of work; and

7. *Communication*: continuously ensuring the availability and flow of information, to ensure effective processing of work and control by higher authority in adequate, clear, concise, timely and economical fashion.

Whilst the administrator or manager should possess identifiable and assessable qualities, such as initiative, intelligence, ability to see things in perspective, capacity for leadership, and so on, he cannot, even at the most senior level, be expected to have detailed knowledge of the full range of social and natural sciences, from which are derived the principles and techniques, which contribute to the economic and effective achievement of his objectives. However, he must be aware of these potential resources, and it is his responsibility to ensure that they are drawn upon as far as possible, and synthesized to make the optimum impact on the achievement of the objectives of his organization. He does this

25

through the processes, summarized above. These processes and their subsidiary elements tend to become identified as *principles*, concepts, techniques and practices of management or administration.

For example, in the *planning and scheduling* of the work to be done, each manager or sub-manager will, in varying degrees, have to use, and promote the use of, a wide variety of planning techniques. These will include budgeting techniques for financial, material and manpower resources, and each of these techniques has its own complexities. The application of these resources in programmes of work must be planned in advance, and this again requires the use of a variety of techniques. Relatively routine work may require techniques of processing analysis, time and motion study and work flow analysis. More sophisticated mathematical techniques may be applicable to more complex work planning such as, for example, operations research, linear programming, queueing theory, simulation and the use of mathematical models.

Similarly, in the process of *organization*, the administrator should use the *principles*, or concepts, of organization, which have been developed, and in recent years redeveloped to reflect the contributions made by such sciences as psychology, sociology, anthropology and biology. These are analysed in the works of a great number of specialists, who have studied this subject over the past hundred years. Only by drawing upon this knowledge can the administrator achieve arrangements of work and people which are conducive to optimum productivity. Only in this way can he effectively divide the major task into subsidiary and logical parts to be delegated to sub-managers with appropriate authority and responsibility for effective and economic accomplishment. Through this process the administrator will determine the functional divisions, which must be specifically provided in his organization, to allow for specialization in different activities. Each of these will involve its own background knowledge and its own range of principles, concepts and techniques. For example, specialization in financial activities involves background knowledge of economics and public finance and the application of a variety of techniques in accounting, cost accounting, budgetary control, investment appraisal, cost benefit analysis, discounted cash flow and techniques of programme evaluation and review. Specialization in personnel activities involves background knowledge in economics, sociology and psychology, as well as the application of principles and techniques in labour relations, manpower planning, recruitment, selection, rating, training, promotion, career planning, job analysis, classification and pay, personnel relations, health, welfare, incentives and the use of pension plans and other fringe benefits.

The administrator must ensure the *co-ordination and control* of all activities so that all parts work harmoniously, effectively and economically in the achievement of the major objectives of the organization. This calls for the use of a variety of techniques, some of which involve personal relationships, as for example the judicious use of meetings and committees; and it also calls for a well-developed system of management reporting. These techniques should give the administrator the most economic, effective and timely method of applying restraints or stimulation, when and where they are needed to maintain the highest productivity of the whole organization under his control.

Maintaining high *motivation* is of special concern to those who may be specializing in personnel matters, but it should also be of prime concern at each administrative or managerial level. To obtain the maximum contribution from each worker requires the continuous application of techniques designed to improve individual and group personal relationships and to stimulate job interest through incentive plans, suggestion schemes and self-sustaining systems of work simplification, whereby each individual is encouraged to devise and put into effect methods of improving work performance. Motivation requires the application of techniques, designed to make the working environment fully conducive to the optimum productive capacity of the individual worker.

The process of *decision-making*, closely related to the process of planning, is a specialized field of study which draws upon a variety of mathematical, statistical and other techniques, such as operations research, mathematical programming, programme evaluation and review techniques, econometrics and so on. Their aim is to reduce the scope for errors of judgment.

The process of *communication* involves not only provisions for systematic and clear oral communications, but also knowledge of a wide range of techniques, ranging from the effective and economical design, control and use of all kinds of written communication such as forms, records, directives and so on, and the effective and economical processing of data through mechanization, to the more sophisticated study, now called cybernetics, of information processing and automatic feed-back of data, essential for management or administrative control.

THE PRACTICE OF ADMINISTRATION OR MANAGEMENT

The above outline gives some idea of the complexities that surround the task of administration or management. The professional civil engineer, who is often appointed manager of a construction project, may become dominated by the scientific and technical problems of the project, to the exclusion of the problems of management as such. The professional functional specialists in personnel, finance and production, who are often appointed as managers or administrators, may continue to be dominated in their thinking by their own specialties. There is, as yet, no clearly established profession of administration or management, as such, in spite of the very extensive research and literature of recent years.

For the most part, the practice of administration or management lacks the advantages which could be derived from the development of theory. In practice, managers or administrators are the busiest of people and are invariably overloaded but, under close observation, their overload often reveals weakness in their balanced performance of management functions as such. Often they are not themselves clear about their objectives. Often they have not made use of the necessary planning and scheduling techniques. Often they are unaware of the inadequacies of the organizational framework within which they work. Often they have a meagre notion of the many co-ordinating and controlling techniques which could eliminate day to day problems. The necessity and the means for the motivation of employees escape them. Their decision-making capacity is slowed down or impaired by the lack of relevant data or by the lack of knowledge of the nature of decision-making. Communications are often inadequate, lacking in relevancy, flow, clarity, conciseness and timeliness.

These are the circumstances that give rise to the inevitable demands for more and more staff and the ever-increasing budgetary estimates for administrative or managerial overhead expenses, the wastage of materials, inordinate delays, or even failure in attaining objectives. These conditions, in turn, draw attention to the need for improving management. Basically this means getting better administrators or managers. The improved recruitment, selection, appointment, assessment, training, development and, above all, the most effective use of administrators should therefore have the highest priority in any administrative improvement programme. This is not only a difficult but a time-consuming task, often spreading over generations before spectacular results can be achieved. In the meantime, it is well to explore every other source for expediting the improvement of administration.

2. Sources of Administrative Improvement*

Public administration differs from business administration or industrial management. In the two latter, the sphere of activity in most enterprises is relatively limited in scope. The objectives and policy may be relatively easily defined. The line of authority and responsibility may be comparatively simple and clear-cut. The emphasis can be placed on judicious risk-taking, productivity and financial returns. The final results can be forecast and achieved in a relatively concrete and measurable form.

Public administration, on the other hand, is more complex. It is an integral part of government. Its ultimate source of authority and responsibility for an extremely wide range of activities is in the people it serves. Public will is formed and expressed through complex social and political processes and, eventually, through legislation which, in turn, is subject to the interpretation of an independent judicature.

The objectives laid down in legislation are, for the most part, in very general terms, and the precise objectives may not become evident until the legislation has been interpreted in the courts. The executive, which usually has, through legislation, delegated powers of regulation to define still further the scope and nature of objectives, and the civil service administration which operates under the executive, must, in all detailed policy formulation and administration, constantly observe the essence of the will of the people as expressed in legislation and must be subject to the rule of law.

The civil service administrator, or manager, although he may operate to a great extent in a similar manner to the manager in private enterprise, must not only try to achieve the objectives with the optimum use of limited resources in manpower, money, materials and time, but must also perform an active and continuous role in contributing to the clarification and reformulation of policies and objectives. However, the process by which he does this is far more complex and time-consuming than it is in private business.

PUBLIC SUPPORT

Public support is essential for the improvement of public administration because in the long run it is the public's multiplicity of wants that has to be satisfied. Whatever is done to use limited resources in one way rather than another must have public sanction. Efficiency in the ad-

* From *The Administration of Organization and Methods Services* (New York, United Nations, Department of Economics and Social Affairs, 1969).

ministration of public business must have public sanction. Efficiency in the administration of public business does not necessarily demand the technical efficiency inherent in each scientific and technical discipline, or the economic efficiency with which the economist is concerned. The public may be quite ready to settle for something less, if its needs can be satisfied to a limited degree and more quickly.

The best interests of the public in both the long and short run can only be decided upon by the public, if it is well informed of the consequences of alternative choices, when making its multiplicity of demands. Similarly, the public can be made aware of the advantages of administrative improvement only by knowing the disadvantages of poor administration. Though this may be difficult to achieve, the fact remains that public education is the first requirement for administrative improvement.

POLITICAL LEADERSHIP

Political leadership and support are the next essentials for administrative improvement, and they are just as essential in the party in power as in the political opposition. The representative in the legislature knows the needs of his constituents, and although these may be so numerous and varied as to be unattainable, he should at least know the priorities and should endeavour to secure legislation for their achievement. His knowledge of the administrative implications of legislation can be of equal or greater significance than his knowledge of the social economic or technical implications.

LEGISLATIVE FOUNDATIONS

The machinery of government in the legislative field can be an important source of administrative improvement, for it is here that the broad objectives are debated and decided. It is here that the estimated revenue and expenditure are scrutinized and the final accounts presented. Here the reports of achievements are received, and here the cost and benefit relationships of the various government activities may be assessed if there are adequate and appropriate reporting procedures. It is here that checks may be made on the effectiveness of the administration of programmes. Such checks may be made through discussion or debate or through specially constituted instruments of the legislature such as public accounts, or other standing committees, *ad hoc* committees or specially constituted offices such as that of Auditor General.

MACHINERY OF GOVERNMENT BELOW THE LEGISLATIVE LEVEL

The structure of government below the legislative body may also be a source of administrative efficiency. The creation of ministries, appropriately divided into departments, may have a significant bearing on

30

the effective direction, control and co-ordination of the various governmental activities. The establishment of inter-ministerial agencies and committees for the co-ordination of the work, or certain aspects of the work of different ministries, may be an effective means of expediting government business. A special agency may be created under the Prime Minister or President for the development of common administrative policy and practices which should be applicable throughout the whole range of the activities of government.

Within the machinery of government the establishment of a semi-autonomous and non-political public service commission and, associated with it, the development of a soundly based career civil service may be a significant source of administrative improvement. There are recognized criteria for a career service. These include open entry, based on academic competition; permanency of tenure irrespective of party political change; division of staff into grades or classes according to the nature and importance of the work and the degree of responsibility involved; a regular, graduated scale of pay; and a system of promotion, based on a combination of seniority and merit.

3. The Public Image of Government Agencies*

Sidney J. Levy[1]

Many federal executives are concerned with the public relations of their agencies. They want to do a good job and to have this recognized by the public; but often they find themselves in the position of feeling damned if they do and damned if they don't. Where this is the case it seems as though some sturdy public viewpoints are at work, leading to the thought that it might be useful to study elements in the public image of government agencies, to analyze what complex of goals and feelings characterizes the American attitude.

This paper discusses a small tentative exploration of this problem. The assumption is that beyond the stances of political divisions or formal social philosophies, and putting aside for the moment the peripheral (even if not unimportant) views held by extreme groups in this country, there is a general and typical public outlook that sees American government agencies as having certain purposes, to which they may relate in certain ways.

To formulate a hypothesis on this topic, a small group of people were interviewed about their attitudes toward government agencies. They were asked to recall the names of government agencies, to define their purpose, to evaluate the kind of job they do. They discussed specific contacts with government agencies, telling what occurred, how it came about, their treatment and feelings, the outcome, their reactions, etc. Then they commented more generally on the kinds of people who work in government agencies.

The interviews were focused, open-ended conversations; the people interviewed talked fully and freely. Intensive analysis of this tiny sample is offered in no sense as the results of a formal survey or research, nor as "representing" the conceivable range of experiences and attitudes among American citizens. Rather, the aim was to acquire some expressive data for thinking about the problem, to stimulate ideas and further study of the relationship of the public to government agencies.

THE NATURE OF PUBLIC IMAGES

It may be useful, first, to comment on the nature of public images. Since 1955, the concept of public images has gained widespread interest. Developed in earlier studies and reported[2] at Social Research,

* From *Public Administration Review*, Vol. 23, No. 1 (March, 1963), 25–29. Reprinted by permission.

[1] I am grateful for the assistance of Miss Shirley Greene and Mr. Horst Finkemeyer.

[2] Burleigh B. Gardner and Sidney J. Levy, "The Product and the Brand," 33 *Harvard*

Inc., this concept grew in value to people in advertising, marketing, and management because it provided a coherent, focused way of thinking about products. It put forth the idea that people are governed in their behavior and attitudes toward products by a constellation of pictures and thoughts that sum up for them what the product means to them. Known brands have a kind of identity made up of central conceptions and impressions to which consumers characteristically respond.

Any public object—product, person, institution—has an image for the publics, audiences, or consumers who know of it. Since knowledge always falls short, and is always filtered through the capacities and special circumstances of the people who experience an institution, what they know of it is always an abstraction to some degree. But this does not mean that an image is a false, invented projection on a screen[3]—although some images may be less accurate than others. An image is a dynamic relationship between a public and an object, one that takes on persisting qualities through time which determine how the participants in the relationship will behave toward each other. It is a relationship that may not readily change; in some cases it is remarkably stubborn and tenacious. Once people develop a set of ideas and impressions about a product, company, institution, it is part of their characteristic outlook; the more they feel it characteristic of themselves to have the image they do, and the more basic an observation it seems to them to be, the more firmly they will stick to it. They do not yield easily, even, at times, in the face of new or contradictory evidence, because it conserves energy not to change their minds and because they are prone to believe themselves to be correct and right in the first place.

The public image of government agencies is compounded out of many sources. It is influenced by people's conception of American government, by what they seek from it and expect to get from it; by concrete experiences with it and the personnel who represent it. As they discuss these things, people convey a sense of how government agencies loom in their minds, how they want to define and relate to them. The view that comes across is a selective one, with some agencies standing out more than others, with people differing in how strongly or clearly they perceive agencies as impinging on them. And in addition to individual variations due to personal temperament, political philosophy, etc., there are differential outlooks that grow out of social class position (e.g., higher status people are apt to have broader and more educated knowledge of governmental realities).

Business Review 33–39 (March-April 1955); Burleigh B. Gardner and Lee Rainwater, "The Mass Image of Big Business," 33 *Harvard Business Review* 61–66 (November-December 1955).

[3] Leo P. Crispi, "Some Observations on the Concept of Image," 25 *Public Opinion Quarterly* 115–120 (Spring 1961).

IDENTIFYING AGENCIES

In naming government agencies, people show the readiest awareness of two main governmental functions; these are tax collection and law enforcement. The Internal Revenue Service and the FBI stand out in people's minds, followed by "Social Security" and the Veterans Administration (or Selective Service). That is, after the broad, central perception of government agencies as fiscally demanding and policing, thoughts go in more individualized directions. Older people are quicker to associate to social security, younger people (especially male), veterans, and parents of boys are apt to think about the draft or veterans' benefits.

After this most significant quadrant of taxes, police, security, and military, associations spread in miscellaneous directions, tending to be comprised of a group of service and regulatory agencies. Prominent among them are the Post Office, Agriculture, FHA, and the FCC. Then, in the general context of thinking about "government agencies," thoughts radiate to the apparently more remote groups that reflect international or foreign emphases: State, "Immigration", Defense.

Government agencies loom in a natural progression from those of most immediate concern to the individual, to those that impinge less directly. Views are modified by this perspective. Government agencies tend to mean federal government; and self-interest and experience are important in directing attention. This is not an inflexible process. The FBI is renowned less through personal contact than via publicity, the widespread respect given J. Edgar Hoover, and via the personalization he affords his agency over many years. In addition, the FBI seems impressive in its earnest dealing with serious crime, arousing mixed feelings of awe, excitement, and admiration. The broader the individual's horizon, the more likely he is to think of government abstractly, and to give more attention to problems of foreign relations. But the average citizen tends not to do this except under pressure of specific crisis.

CONTACTS WITH GOVERNMENT AGENCIES

Contacts with government agencies do not stand out in people's minds. They are inclined to be matter-of-fact about those they have had. Any given contact may have been important or significant to the individual—they do not underestimate the potential or actual influence government actions or decisions can and do have on their lives. Nevertheless, there is a casual tone, as though government agencies are either a minor, integrated part of daily life (such as the Post Office, hardly requiring mention), or they remain mostly in the background to be dealt with as occasional instances arise. The feeling is one of "of course" —it was "natural" to have dealt with the agency in the normal flow of events. For the typical citizen such contacts as they reminisce about usually came to them as requirements, so to speak, including particularly such matters as social security numbers, filing of income tax, immigration or customs contact, military experience. In such contacts as these they felt themselves to be ordinary people, fulfilling the law whether they liked it or not, with no undue sense of aggravation. These are essentially routine contacts.

Other contacts have a more individual flavor. They are sought out by the individual to further his own goals. People mention such matters as insurance, counseling for education, requests for information from the Bureau of Standards, from the Government Printing Office. These are essentially voluntary contacts.

The contacts that are apt to be most threatening are those which single people out. The implication of negative personal attention is potentially disrupting and alarming, arousing thoughts of punishment and coercive dealings. Internal Revenue checks, variations in agricultural controls, security checks have this quality of being essentially arbitrary, involuntary contacts.

REACTIONS TO GOVERNMENT AGENCY CONTACTS AND PERSONNEL

In talking about specific dealings with government personnel about specific matters, people tend to express themselves positively. The personnel handling the situation are regarded as courteous and polite in manner, as showing consideration and reasonable interpersonal attitudes. The matter at hand is described as handled helpfully and satisfactorily. Delays are not blamed as a problem; the contacts were said to take an appropriate amount of time. Some quotations will convey the complimentary tone of these descriptions.

They were courteous, considerate, and prompt.

I was treated very nice . . . very nice, everybody was most helpful.

Was very fast.

The information was very good and I would have done a hell of a lot of fumbling and wasted a hell of a lot of time tracking it down on my own.

I was treated very well.

She was very softspoken and very nice and she explained in detail what we had to do . . . I was a little bit nervous but they were so very lovely, they are used to nervous people, I guess.

They were satisfied and so was I. It took about an hour, I guess that was all right.

I didn't feel I waited too long, in fact they were faster than I thought.

Of course, not all incidents are favorable ones; as in any volume of human interactions, there are angry, complaining occasions. When such a negative experience has occurred, it stands out in the person's mind as a source of great indignation. An example is a man whose agricultural practices are controlled, and whose land is periodically and unpredictably flooded.

You can't raise what you want . . . I felt hard against them, for putting the limits on us. . . . They built this dam . . . about six miles upstream. All we got was indifference to our situation. . . . For example, two years ago they threw the gates open during the night and during that time a wreck from the railroad dumped oil into the river. We were irrigating at the time. Being as how it was night we could not see the oil in the river water, the oily water was pumped into the field and the crop totally destroyed . . . it's just that they *won't*, they just don't care about the farmer and his problems. We could have some warning to move our irrigation machinery up, but we can't get any satisfaction.

This man seems to have some grounds for resentment, since he suffers from a prime form of arbitrary involuntary contact. As might be expected, when he is later asked the more general question, "What kinds of people do you suppose choose to work for government agencies? Why?," he does not evaluate them kindly.

People who don't want to put in an honest day's work or those who can't get an honest job." Elsewhere he elaborates: "There are too many payrollers, featherbedders, political plums handed out, and there's a lot of buck passing.

However, the dominating imagery of other average citizens also derogates government agency personnel. The same individuals who provided the array of complimentary remarks listed earlier when talking about their specific experiences (at times the only contacts they could recall) provide this array of comments to characterize "the kinds of people who choose to work for government agencies."

Only average intelligence.

90 per cent Negroes.

People who are interested in pensions and security.

They don't want to work too hard.

I think the government employee may not be loaded with initiative.

Conservative people

Well, I hope they're morally and intellectually honest, but I have my doubts.

They have a tendency to get wrapped up in rules and regulations rather than efficiency.

Further, when asked to say how dealing with a government agency differs from other kinds of business dealings, despite the favorable experiences described, people tend to see the government agency as rigid, complicated, demanding, unknowing, and unconcerned.

Too much red tape, too many departments it must go through, too much time killing, ages pass before anything gets settled. . . . In a private concern they strive to please.

They are stricter, everything must be done properly, they don't stand for mistakes [although in her reported experience, she said, "They are very helpful, they realize that there is always room for error in making out the tax"].

One thing that comes to mind is the lack of flexibility.

It's difficult when people do not know what they are doing, this is the trouble with people who get the job with politics. There's always this in government agencies.

Stiff regulations, too much paper work.

When you go to an office on business where you pay for what you want they take care of you.

Along with these remarks on personnel and agencies are attempts to be rational and reasonable, to point out that "well, anybody, really," might work for the government, and that how one is treated depends on how one behaves. But, generally, it seems difficult for people to avoid the heavily stereotyped images of government agency people as motivated by laziness, security, and inadequacy, in a setting that is both careless and rigid.

Various explanations might be offered for the tenacity of these views. Some realism may enter in; to the extent that government agencies offer easier havens to people discriminated against in private industry, some selection occurs in favor of those seeking this haven. The fact of civil service protections, benefits in "sick leave the government allows," retirement pension, etc., imply an interest in rewards less certain or less distinctly perceived as part of the situation in non-government work. Further, despite the growth in fringe and security benefits in private industry, there are the general historic and cultural values placed on the willingness to compete, on the striving for distinctive individual advancement, on the energy and the daring to take a chance, on the autonomy and self-direction of the man in business for himself. These values, not regarded as generally part of government employment, make "havens" seem too nurturant:

Negroes, because they are strongly protected from prejudice and discrimination—too much so, I think.

THE PURPOSE OF GOVERNMENT AGENCIES

It may be useful to think of this view of government agencies and personnel as reflecting the way the public *wants* to see them, as growing out of a larger necessity. This larger necessity results from the public's conception of the purposes of government agencies.

More literal-minded individuals explain these purposes in instrumental terms. They perceive the agency's purpose as one of carrying out its *concrete defined functions.*

Inspection of meats.
To collect income tax.
Manufacture money and apprehend counterfeiters.
Support of prices on farmers.

Others step up the level of generalization, referring to the more formal regulatory mandate of the agency, where the function implies *service to broader governmental goals,* or to the impersonal implementation of general responsibilities.

They administer the services.
Supervise.
In a very broad sense, to carry out law enforcement, by that I mean laws made by Congress.
They perform necessary national functions . . . standardization.

The largest reiterated aims refer to *service to the public.* This fundamental view is repeated in various ways.

For the good of the people.
To aid primarily.
To protect the rights of individuals.
To take care of people.
To take care of things that the individual couldn't take care of by himself.
Service of the taxpayer mostly, well, service of all citizens.
They are supposed to protect you.

That is, the basic wish is to have a benevolent, protective government, one that safeguards persons by rendering routine or "necessary" services without otherwise impinging too strongly. The idea is "When I am not thinking of the government, the government should not be thinking of me." Americans do not *want* to be singled out by the government (except for meritorious recognition); also, they do not *expect* to be singled out, nor to have much to do with it other than in the most generalized and matter-of-fact ways.

This feeling of relatively minor active contact with government agencies and its appropriateness as characteristic of American philosophy was reflected in the casual, poised (even if inaccurate) comment of a

45-year-old, college educated, married, upper middle class woman who said, "I have never had personal contact with a government agency."

This attitude is highlighted in comparisons with foreign practices. Even in European democracies there seems to be greater emphasis on registration, on police authority, on face-to-face subservience of the public to bureaucratic officials, on restraint of and governmental knowledge of individual activities and mobility. A French war bride noted, "I thought the ability of calling on the phone was better than having to go there several times for information." And a German visitor remarked, "In Germany the bureaucratic official demands you appear and stand before him, to show he has authority, prestige, and strictness. Here everything is by mail."

THE WISH FOR INEFFICIENCY

In an ideal world a government might be benevolent and efficient. Normally, however, the belief is that efficiency, accuracy, system, etc., come about through severity of discipline, unmerciful application of impersonal principles, and indifference to individual variations and needs. Conversely, we associate indulgence with permissiveness of discipline, adaptation to human pressures, and sloppiness. The hypothesis is suggested that Americans prefer to believe their government agencies are lazy and security seeking, too involved in their own paper work and internal rigidities and carelessness to be authoritarian and punishing to the public. They want to be able to criticize this authority, as soldiers lambaste the food regardless of its quality, to show their security as citizens. It is safer to have a government that is an irritating old uncle who has trouble getting things right, hires too many people for anybody's good, but withal, is a lovable old shoe who means well.

If this interpretation is correct, it suggests that federal agencies cannot easily find generalized approval regardless of the actual merits of their accomplishments, that citizens are made anxious by too much zeal if it smacks of efficiency without heart. Federal executives must reconcile themselves to the negative image that makes people feel safe. Probably the efficiency that will be best received is that which enhances and reassures about bureaucratic intentions by emphasizing service, comfort, courtesy, attention to needs, and patience with the fears of those who would rather not be dealing with the government at all.

4. Economic Analysis and Efficiency of Government*

... MR. [MILTON] FRIEDMAN. The problem, Senator Proxmire, is the definition of cost. In terms of budgetary cost, in terms of what goes down in your books, a voluntary army may cost more, though I am not sure even of that. But the true cost to the society will be less.

The trouble is that part of the cost is now hidden. Part of the cost is hidden in the form of the unduly low salaries being paid to the people who are conscripted. The present pay and benefits of first-term men in the military is roughly one-half of that of their civilian counterparts. The men serving their first term are, in effect, paying a tax—in the form of compulsory service—equal to about half of the money they could earn. A proper calculation of costs would include this implicit tax.

In addition, we now use men very wastefully. A draftee who is in the military for 2 years spends 6 months being trained or being sent somewhere. He spends the last few months waiting to leave the military. He ends up finishing at most a year's service. In addition, much time of other men has to be devoted to training him. The result is that for each man-year obtained by conscription, the Armed Forces get a good deal less than a half-year of effective service.

I should not speak so much at length on this, but I happen to be a member of the President's Commission on an all-volunteer Armed Force. We have been meeting this weekend. One of the interesting facts we have learned is that a voluntary army would require adding to the army each year only two men for each three you now have to add under conscription, because conscription is a wasteful method of manning a military force. In terms of true social cost, the cost of manning the military would be greatly reduced by shifting to a voluntary basis.

When you turn to the other aspects of the military, it is impossible for a dog to meow or for a cat to bark, and it is equally impossible for Government activities to be efficient. Unfortunately, we have found no way in which we can turn the business of defending this country over to private activity. We do have a Government program and it is going to be inefficient. How do we keep that inefficiency down?

One answer is insofar as possible, to require all military procurement to be on the open market, through auction, through bidding, through trying to maintain competition, and of course, through the surveillance

* From *Report* of Joint Economic Committee (Washington, D.C., U.S. Government Printing Office, 1970).

which Members of the Senate and the Congress impose upon it. Beyond that, I have no easy cure for the reduction of military expenditures.

CHAIRMAN [WILLIAM] PROXMIRE. Our studies indicate that the private contractor, the defense contractor, is inefficient, grossly inefficient.

MR. FRIEDMAN. Yes.

CHAIRMAN PROXMIRE. We have had testimony that has not been disputed that when you procure on a negotiated basis rather than a competitive basis, it costs 30 to 40 percent more. This is in the private sector. At least, it is a privately owned corporation that has these high costs.

MR. FRIEDMAN. You have the problem that you need competition, not only among producers, but also among buyers. In the defense area, there is no way, unfortunately, of getting that competition.

5. The Sickness of Government*

Anonymous Civil Servant

Tucked inconspicuously away in the middle of his new book *The Age of Discontinuity*, Peter F. Drucker has thrown in a chapter 10 subtitled "The Sickness of Government." The book itself has drawn rave reviews in such forums as *Fortune* magazine and other periodicals that share the Marxian wish that—somehow or other—the State ought to wither away. Such a notion has a gut appeal to many taxpayers, citizens, and scholars, and even at times to bored or combat-weary bureaucrats.

What makes Drucker's chapter 10 reading for all judges, legislators, public servants, and professors of political science is not so much his thesis, which certainly is not original, but rather the audacity with which he carries out his diagnosis and the recklessness of his proposed "cure."

Government, according to Drucker, is not only sick, it is almost dead. It is overweight, flabby, sterile, lazy, unproductive, long on promises, and short on delivery. It shows a negative benefit/cost ratio, and is just one big sink for scarce talent and money that could better be applied elsewhere. Practically everybody, young and old alike, "digs" this fact.

Citizens lack respect for government. They don't believe in government. They are disenchanted with government. They balk at paying taxes. They doubt and distrust government. They no longer expect results from government. In short, government is no damn good. Or nearly so.

Drucker concedes in an unguarded moment, on p. 217, that there are two things that government can effectively do: wage war and inflate currency. Quite possibly he means this as a compliment. But by all other tests Uncle Sam's record is either unimpressive or incredibly incompetent.

What's more, and even more frightening, government has become ungovernable. It stalks our lovely land like an insatiable monster, with a big stomach and a mini-mind, virtually out of control, menacing all that cross its path.

Severe though Drucker's indictment of domestic government is, he saves his most devastating adjectives when he surveys the world scene. At the international level whatever is bad, wrong, or ridiculous is exponentially increased to the point where the very reason for the existence of government is wiped out.

* Originally published as "Dr. Drucker: The Great Healer," in *Public Administration Review*, July–August, 1969, pp. 386–88. Reprinted by permission.

By now, p. 225, you might be slipped into the notion that Drucker hates government. Not so. We desperately need it. But *not* to plan, or to innovate, or to set priorities, or to transfer resources from rich to poor, or to build, or to manufacture, or to render social and health services, because it is such a clod in all these things. Nor is it to manage, because all bureaucrats are mediocracies who have been attracted to public service as a haven for sloths. In summation: The government is not, cannot, and should not be a "doer."

If you think doing covers a lot of ground and sort of narrows the field, don't be alarmed. There is a residual role for government. It is to govern!

In searching around for a model of governing that will work, Drucker has discovered the big "decentralized" business corporation. According to him the guys at the top don't "do" anything. Except think and clip coupons.

They act like concert masters, waving their batons and gesticulating seriously to make sure that each instrument player follows the notes and lines instead of just doing their own thing, thus ruining the orchestral effects by improvising.

This is what government ought to do. Be a conductor. Hand off all "doing" to private business, or something like private business. Drucker is open minded about quasi-private and semisocialistic firms, and is very receptive of heavy subsidies or tax incentives, if the economic facts of life so require. In other words, if the normal or natural market situation cannot yield a profit, he has no objection to taxing (or not taxing, which can be the same thing) in order to underwrite "reprivatization." Just how he squares this with his assertion that risk and the right to go bankrupt is what keeps private firms healthy, competitive, and efficient is not made clear, or even referred to as a possible internal contradiction of his model.

In any event, all the President needs is a podium, a baton (and a checkbook), and he can run the entire country better than he does now with all those millions of civil servants, and those numerous procurement officers and their ream after ream of red tape.

What is so fascinating about Dr. Drucker's prescriptions for our current illness is that: (1) so many people take him seriously; and (2) his analysis so completely ignores reality.

He starts ignoring the real world of observable events and behavior right at the beginning—or perhaps one could say that he ignores causality entirely. Drucker fails to take on the embarrassing question as to *why* we have so much government intervention in the first place. Is it possible that the private sector—I mean the original virgin private sector, not his reprivatized sector, messed things up so badly that legislatures had to act? Is it possible that the mysterious and sacred forces of the market place often produce fiscal success for the few along with social failure for the many?

How high should interest rates go without escaping public concern? How much longer will we suffer under the lunacy of "marketing promotion games" and other forms of business imposed gambling? Are we to let paper conglomerates blight entire sectors of independent enterprise? As for inflating the currency, I commend to Mr. Drucker the front page of the *Wall Street Journal* (any recent copy will do) so that he may find out for himself whether there exists any true discipline or constraint in pricing in the corporate sector these days. The list of private firms putting inflationary pressures on the economy, in the face of extraordinary profit after taxes, is most impressive.

On the question of whether the government can "do," or can perform, or produce, or deliver, Mr. Drucker acts as though he has been cut off from his own senses. TVA produces and delivers more electric power than any private utility in the U.S. The Interior Department built, owns, and runs one of the world's largest water collection and distribution systems and a magnificent set of national parks. The intervening of the USDA has been so fantastically successful that we suffer from over-abundance of food and fiber, not failure to deliver. Vast dollar resources redistributions, both interpersonal and interregional, are being made daily by HEW and HUD and the VA. Are there market-oriented, for-profit firms that can do anything other than concentrate wealth and siphon resources upward through the economic hierarchy into the hands of those persons already in a strong capital accumulation position? At best they must resort to the foundation dodge to get their charitable urge out of their system. This has the effect, for all practical purposes, of creating many (mostly small) private, pseudo-governmental "do-good" agencies beyond the reach of the voting citizens.

The maps of the USGS, the precise time of the Bureau of Standards, the statistics of the Census Bureau, the FCC's allocation of the radio spectrum, HUD's massive underwritings, the Forest Products Laboratory's timber fastening systems, the BPR's national concrete specifications, the FAA's enroute and tower control of air traffic, the Corps of Engineers' flood reduction operations on the Mississippi, the NSF's support of doctoral students in hard science—the list is many times larger—are all realities ignored by Drucker. Has he a combine in mind to take over ESSA? Or the mint? Or control of nuclear materials?

What is even more remarkable is Drucker's lack of candor as to the genius of our present mixed system, with its massive mutual interdependencies and tightly symbiotic relationships between government and industry. Trying to draw the line between force account or "in-house" operations and functions, and those "external" to government is almost impossible in many public mission accomplishment systems today. The permutation of effective inter-institutional combinations is already large and still expanding.

One might just as well argue for resocialization as reprivatization if a doctrinaire rather than an empirical approach is to be taken. For the facts show that public enterprise in the extra-market portion of our socioeconomic environment has been very effective indeed. The fact that gaps exist, and that short falls have occurred says less about the capabilities of government as an executive and doing agent than it does about the costliness of our great Druckerian myth, i.e., that when government acts it is bad, but when private business *fails* to act it is good.

To attribute our national housing shortage, the large number of unemployables, or the existence of millions in poverty to the failure of *government* to perform is a piece of intellectual slight of hand that may fool some of the people all of the time, but is obviously illogical to many people most of the time.

The analogue of government as orchestra leader leaves out the most significant part of the equation. Who writes the musical score? Are we to conduct jazz, soul, rock, or classical music? Who is our audience, and are they listening? How are the musicians paid, and is admission to the concert free?

I have, in a sense, been unfair to "The Age of Discontinuity" thesis as laid out by Drucker, for there *are* 16 other chapters, some of them— shall we say—insightful. But chapter 10, if it can be taken as a measure of Drucker's objectivity, certainly gives one pause to wonder about the rest of his tome.

Fortunately the management consulting profession is at this time in a rich state of productive ferment.

There are medicine men for sick companies. And there are those who are expert in the pathology of government. We owe Drucker a debt of gratitude for proving once again, if such proof is needed, that what is good for General Motors has little relevance to what is good for the country. Meanwhile the quest for an omni-pill will probably go on unabated. If and when it is discovered one can be certain that life will suddenly become dangerously disinteresting.

6. Bureaucracy: Characteristics and Problems*

Chester A. Newland

The words "bureaucracy" and "bureaucrat" are nouns (both proper and improper, it might be said). They are frequently used as names and may therefore possess peculiar importance for public personnel people at this time when their field is emerging as a profession. For, regardless of other choices, public personnel people will be lumped together by friends and critics in a category with other public employees and be called "bureaucrats." That much is certain about your future name, and that much needs to be understood as basic in the future development of the public personnel profession.

TWOFOLD MEANING OF THE TERM BUREAUCRACY

For public personnel specialists, the term "bureaucracy" has significance both as a name with a double meaning which is applied to them and as a bundle of concepts which help to explain their complex environment. It is possible to begin an analysis with a simple definition: "Bureaucracy is the administrative machinery of large organization." That definition would probably win general approval on most grounds except that of adequacy. It will suffice only for a beginning.

Adequate definition will require consideration of two usages of the term bureaucracy. First, there is a popular, emotional usage to connote "bad" characteristics of administrative organization. Second, there is a more precise, analytical usage to denote qualities of "good" (rational) administrative organization.

The existence of these two widespread meanings of the term contributes to difficulties in communication. Partisan interests take advantage of these difficulties to promote confusion. Also, organization and management analysts find it difficult to communicate with laymen about administrative organization with adequate precision to satisfy technical interests. But despite the problems which result from the widespread existence of two usages of the term bureaucracy and conflicting interests in promoting either one or the other meaning, understanding of administration in large organizations may result from examination of both the popular and the analytical meanings of bureaucracy.

In this analysis of bureaucracy, I shall first examine the popular use of the term, referring particularly to a classic comment by Harold Laski as an example. Second, I shall examine the precise, social science usage

* From *Public Personnel Review*, Vol. 24, No. 1 (January, 1963), 24–29. Reprinted by permission.

of the term, as analyzed by Max Weber. Third, I shall briefly note the salient features of public administrative organization in the United States. Fourth, I shall note some problems of bureaucracy and personnel administration today.

POPULAR USAGE OF THE TERM BUREAUCRACY

The popular indictment of bureaucracy and bureaucrats may be readily illustrated by quotation from an amusing paper which was circulated by United States Civil Servants in Washington, D.C., a few years ago.[1] It was titled "A Service for Bureaucrats" and included the following:

Prayer: O Lord, grant that this day we come to no decisions, neither run into any kind of responsibility, but that all our doings may be ordered to establish new and quite unwarranted departments, for ever and ever.

Hymn:

> O Thou who seest all things below,
>   Grant that Thy servants may go slow,
> That they may study to comply
>   With regulations till they die.
>
> Teach us, Lord, to reverence
>   Committees more than common sense,
> Impress our minds to make no plan
>   But pass the baby where we can.
>
> And when the temper seems to give
>   Us feelings of initiative,
> Or when alone we go too far,
>   Chastise us with a circular.
>
> Mid war and tumult, fire and storms,
>   Strengthen us, we pray, with forms,
> Thus will Thy servants ever be,
>   A flock of perfect sheep for thee.

Benediction: The peace of Washington, which passes all understanding, preserve your mind in lethargy, your body in inertia, your soul in coma, now and evermore, Amen.

The excessive but witty condemnation above has been supplemented by numerous critics, but the most popular today is probably C. Northcote Parkinson, whose well-known "law" asserts that administrative personnel in bureaucracy increase at a rate of 5.75 per cent per year, regardless of work load.[2]

[1] Quoted in *The Washington Post*, "The Federal Diary," by Jerry Kluttz, July 7, 1959.
[2] C. Northcote Parkinson, *Parkinson's Law* (Boston: Houghton Mifflin, 1957).

47

Harold Laski contributed more significantly, however, to the indict-ment of bureaucracy in his brief article in the influential *Encyclopedia of the Social Sciences*, published in 1930. Laski's definition of bureau-cracy was: "a system of government the control of which is so completely in the hands of officials that their power jeopardizes the liberties of ordi-nary citizens."[3] Included among the characteristics of bureaucracy, according to Laski, are: (1) passion for routine in administration, (2) sacrifice of flexibility to rules, (3) refusal to experiment, (4) delay in decision-making, and (5) manipulation of the organization (govern-ment) to the bureaucrats' own advantage.

Among other frequently repeated contributions to the "bad" conno-tation of the term bureaucracy is that of Ludwig von Mises, the noted economist.[4] Writing in 1944, he distinguished "business management" from "bureaucratic management," asserting that the latter has no *money profit* as an incentive and measure of efficiency. According to this view, because bureaucracy has no cash value on the market, it is inefficient and bad. The conclusion is that, although bureaucracy is a necessary evil in public and service organizations, it should be restricted to the narrow confines of such necessity.

In summary, the popular usage of the term bureaucracy to connote that which is "bad" in large-scale administrative organization involves (1) the identification of undesirable characteristics with bureaucracy, such as mediocrity, inertia and stagnation, arbitrariness, formalism and impersonality, and officiousness; and (2) a recommendation that bu-reaucracy be destroyed and/or limited. (Interestingly enough, popular indictments of governmental bureaucracy in the United States rarely accuse it of dishonesty, recklessness, or tyranny.)

ANALYTICAL USAGE OF THE TERM BUREAUCRACY

In the analytical usage of most social scientists, particularly sociolo-gists dealing with organization theory, "bureaucracy denotes rational-ized administration in large-scale organization." In this sense, the term is not restricted to government.

Theory of bureaucracy as an aspect of formal organization was first formulated by the German sociologist, Max Weber, at the turn of the present century. So far as extent of influence, Weber's analysis remains the most significant contribution to the subject. A summary of his con-ceptual formulation is essential. Currently, research on *informal factors* in organization is adding greatly to understanding of bureaucracy. That research will be noted following comment on Max Weber and formal organization.

[3] *Encyclopedia of the Social Sciences*, Vol. 3, 1930, p. 70.
[4] Ludwig von Mises, *Bureaucracy* (New Haven: Yale University Press, 1944).

According to Max Weber's analysis, the following are typical characteristics of bureaucracy:

1. A defined jurisdiction with legal authority.
2. Rules and regulations to govern administration.
3. Impersonal detachment: administration which is impersonal and objective—formalistic.
4. Hierarchy: levels of graded authority.
5. Expertise and specialization of job tasks (role specificity).
6. Career personnel system staffed by full-time people selected by merit.

Bureaucracy of the above type, according to Weber, possesses certain advantages. These include:

1. Expertise (promoted by specialization).
2. Coordination for goal attainment (promoted by hierarchy).
3. Rationality (promoted by detachment).

In Weber's own words: "The decisive reason for the advance of bureaucratic organization has always been its purely technical superiority over any other form of organization. The fully developed bureaucratic mechanism compares with other organizations exactly as does the machine with the nonmechanical modes of production."[5]

Critical analysis of formal organization since Weber has produced numerous significant contributions. One leading social scientist today, Herbert Simon, has described administrative organization as a "decision-making structure."[6] According to Simon's analysis, organizations limit the scope of decisions required of each member by defining goals and responsibilities (for guidance); and setting up mechanisms, such as formal rules, training, and channels of communication (to promote rationality).

Besides conceptual formulations of what bureaucracy is, various types of bureaucracies may be identified. For example, bureaucracies may be classified as public and private, production and service, and so forth. Bureaucracy is a characteristic found in private businesses, churches, lodges, and other large organizations as well as in government.

Recent investigations of large-scale organizations have produced increased understanding of the need to consider informal factors which are present in bureaucracy. Knowledge of these aspects of administration is essential for personnel specialists. Some factors that currently command interest are:

[5] H. H. Garth and C. Wright Mills (eds.), *From Max Weber: Essays in Sociology* (New York: Oxford University Press, 1946), p. 214.
[6] Herbert A. Simon, *Administrative Behavior* (2nd ed.; New York: Macmillan, 1957).

1. *Personal relationships.* Individuals and social groups within bureaucratic structures greatly influence the organization.

2. *Communications.* We know that communication within a bureaucratic organization does not (and for certain conditions must not) follow rigid lines of hierarchical authority. Today, communications systems are expected to contribute significantly to coordination of large-scale organizations.

3. *Decision is a process.* The concept of decision as the function of a god-head to be implemented by command is generally rejected today. The value of "democracy within administrative organization" and group decision structures has been demonstrated as important in effective, dynamic organization. Understanding of this approach to management is essential to effective manpower utilization.

4. *Scientific knowledge.* Science and technology are climbing to positions of critical importance in bureaucracies. The bureaucrats must be meshed with vast systems of machines and other organizations at the same time that they are treated as people. No one who has observed the recently publicized efforts of the United States Government in space research can be ignorant of this complicated aspect of bureaucracy.

5. *Professionalism.* As personnel specialists increasingly gain professional status, they may encounter possible conflicts which will provide increased understanding of problems of professionalism in government generally. Professors Peter M. Blau and W. Richard Scott have recently suggested the following conflicts between bureaucracy and professionalism which personnel specialists must deal with:

Professionalism is characterized by
a. First duty to clientele
b. Authority based on knowledge
c. Limits imposed by profession
Bureaucracy is characterized by
a. First duty to organization
b. Authority based on hierarchy
c. Limits imposed by management[7]

PUBLIC ADMINISTRATION MODELS OF BUREAUCRACY

In actual practice governmental organization in the United States is characterized by diverse administrative types. Theoretically, however, it is possible to identify several concepts (or principles) that are generally advocated for organization. Wider knowledge and understanding of these concepts are needed today to promote rationality (and efficiency, economy, and responsibility) in government. These concepts of public administration are:

[7] See Peter M. Blau and W. Richard Scott, *Formal Organizations: A Comparative Approach* (San Francisco: Chandler Publishing Co., 1962).

1. Hierarchical conformation and executive leadership. (Various types of hierarchy exist, such as job, rank, skill, and pay.)

2. Boards are useful for advice, but their use for administration as such should be restricted. (Note how this basic concept of administrative theory is generally ignored as in state government.)

3. Coordinated staff services under a chief executive. These include:

a. Budget and finance (with an executive budget, performance type budget, and internal cost and accrual accounting).

b. Personnel (with a career merit system under management direction, but with civil service or labor-management contract protection).

c. Planning (administrative and policy).

d. Housekeeping (purchasing, stores, property management).

4. Departmentalization according to functions.

5. External policy direction and control.

a. The "politics-administration" dichotomy is rejected today, but the concept of separation of powers remains vital in public administration.

b. An independent or legislative post-audit of functions and finances is essential.

c. Judicial checks are retained, consistent with the basic political value of a "rule of law."

6. Internalized checks must be encouraged:

a. Reliance on facts, information, science, etc.

b. Sensitivity to public demands (individual and group).

c. Respect for basic cultural values of (1) dignity of man and (2) rule of law.

As noted, numerous deviations from the bureaucratic model above exist since the growth of government has been subject to diverse forces. The Executive Office of the President and Executive Departments most nearly resemble the model above so far as the federal government is concerned. City manager government is closest to the "ideal model."

EXTENT AND PROBLEMS OF BUREAUCRACY IN THE UNITED STATES TODAY

Bureaucracy, in the analytical sense, is a dominant feature of modern civilization. It could only be eliminated by reversion to small-scale organization in every field of social endeavor—political, economic, religious, educational, scientific, and artistic.

However, the extensiveness of bureaucracy in the denotative sense of Weber does not mean that the conditions which he described are universal in large-scale organizations today. To the contrary, county and state government in most of the United States can best be described as "organizational hodge-podge." Here we often find:

1. Ill-defined, irrational, or overlapping jurisdictions.
2. Unsystematic and unpublicized rules and regulations.
3. Attachment to little publicized but powerful individual and group interests.
4. Uncoordinated or practically nonexistent staff services.
5. Functional disintegration and an undisguised hodge-podge of boards and commissions.
6. Personnel selection by monstrously long ballots and spoils instead of by merit.

The last two characteristics especially cripple state and local government. State government is somehow expected to operate without any real executive branch. Even today, some political leaders advocate weakening of the position of the practically non-existent state "executive" even further by adding more limits to the Governor's powers and terms of office.

Special Problems for Personnel People

Deviations from a theoretical model are even sharper in the area of public personnel administration where, in actual practice, no single "model" can be identified. Elements persist from successive periods of emphasis on a quality public service, spoils, protective civil service, and personnel management with a human relations orientation. While some personnel specialists seek to introduce rationality into that inheritance of conflicting traditions, other pressure groups and policy makers continue to contribute still more conflict to the "system." For example, policemen and firefighters busy themselves at state capitals seeking "civil service protection" that would virtually free them from management control, and police and fire supervisors often lead in this effort. Municipal leagues then apply counter pressures under the banner of personnel management. Finally, the personnel specialist is handed a barely recognizable hodge-podge of legal provisions and told to avoid politics and practice his profession. That may not be bureaucracy in the analytical sense, but it is politics of a sort which is challenging (if not discouraging) to public personnel men.

While public personnel specialists must work as staff-level employees within existing organizations that are sometimes scarcely rational—and never ideal—professional aspirations require that they not be satisfied with unsatisfactory conditions. Among the obligations of a profession are promotion of improved practices, refinement of basic concepts, and group enforcement of defined standards compatible with the public good. Public personnel specialists may better meet such obligations if they understand both their actual and theoretical places in bureaucratic organization, as noted above. But they must also keep pace with rapid

52

changes in over-all management practices and in society as a whole. This requires constant attention to trends and formulation of acceptable alternatives for solution of public personnel problems. For example, public personnel specialists today are confronted with a problem of increased governmental utilization of the contract device for employment of specialized personnel and problems of reconciling a generally shorter work week and work year with the long hours required to maintain standards of professional competence at a time when professional services that are in short supply are increasing in demand by government. Add to these the large problem of constant redefinition of the role of public employees in American society and politics, as the size of government continues to increase. Finally, add the lesser problems which already occupy practicing personnel specialists, such as official relationships with public employee unions; supposed and real conflicts in merit and career concepts; and the overriding daily consideration of getting the job done even in the limited sense of populating the bureaucracy.

SUMMARY

Other large problems remain which are common to bureaucrats in general. Even in a well-rationalized bureaucratic organization, to which the social science usage of the term is applicable, *a tendency exists to displace ends with means.* That is, in bureaucracy, there is a constant danger that the organization will lose sight of its original goals (or whatever goals are established by policy-makers) and permit elements of administration to exist and function for their own sake.

A large problem of our society today is to reconcile bureaucracy and democracy while successfully meeting the challenges of competing political ideologies and of fantastically rapid change. It seems too obvious for argument that administrative machinery in large-scale organization is with us to stay so long as our civilization survives. Bureaucracy, so far as it refers to that aspect of rational organization, is essential.

At the same time, bureaucracy, even in that "good" sense, is only a means to other ends. Bureaucrats, and particularly personnel specialists, must not forget this. The values of our democratic society which constitute the basic goals sought are, in brief, *the dignity of man* and *a rule of law.* Americans today need better understanding both of these high values of democracy and of the necessity for the rational administrative organization which is called bureaucracy.

7. The Characteristics of Public Administration*

John C. Buechner

Ever since man formed governments to develop public policies, he also cared about how these policies were administered. Sometimes the administration of governmental policies has made the difference between success or failure of governmental actions. Thus, students of administration are often inclined to subscribe to Alexander Pope's famous dictum that "for forms of government let fools contest; whatever is best administered is best." But, of course, it is naïve to conclude that the structure or form of government has no relationship to the administrative process. Rather, the effects of administration are dominant throughout a governmental system, and the structure of a government may well determine the nature of the administrative system, the methods of conducting administration, and the success of administrative activity.

Because of the rapid growth of the apparatus of the modern state, there is a tendency to believe public administration is a phenomenon of recent origin. Although we cannot determine the exact date when administration became a concern of those in governing positions, it is known that such administrative tasks as the recruitment of officials, the financing of governmental programs, and the supervision of policies and subordinates existed before the birth of Christ. A brief review of the evolution of administration clearly illustrates the close relationship between governing and administration.

SOME HISTORICAL CONCERNS

The historical base of public administration probably rests on the administration that was practiced on a large scale in ancient Egypt as early as 1300 B.C. It was necessary then, as now, to arrange and plan programs, to procure materials and personnel, to supervise and coordinate decentralized programs, and to carry out the policies that had been decided by those in authoritative governing positions. Similar activities were undertaken in ancient China where the doctrine of Confucius stressed, among other things, the need for good housekeeping in government and the need to select honest and capable public officials. The Han Dynasty of 202 B.C. to A.D. 219 also emphasized such goals.

The concerns of public administration were not prominent in the minds of the ancient Greeks. Historical writings show that most of the Greek scholars and leaders, such as Aristotle, were primarily concerned

* From *Public Administration* (Belmont and Encino, California: Dickenson Publishing Company, Inc., 1968), 1–4. Reprinted by permission.

with clarifying and implementing forms of government and with merging popular power with the concept of democracy. Even the apostle
Paul noted that the Greeks spent a considerable amount of time "in
nothing else but either to tell or to hear some new thing." Still, there
were those Greeks who were at least cognizant of the importance of administrative matters. Pericles, in his famous funeral oration, called upon
the Greeks to devote energies toward planning and asked for more discussion about the affairs of government. Although Socrates and Plato
were chiefly concerned with the relationship between the state and
society, even Socrates discussed the role of managers in his discourse
with Nicomachides.

In the short period from the middle of the third century to about the
middle of the first century B.C., the Romans, like the Greeks, experienced
the problems of finding governmental solutions for economic and social
needs. In addition, they were faced with the task of obtaining and governing an enormous territory which embraced a variety of cultures. The
institutional arrangements the Romans established—a system of executive offices, assemblies, courts, and the senate—compounded such administrative problems as leadership, coordination, and control. Unlike
the Greeks, the Romans were much more systematic and methodical in
testing and perfecting techniques of political management.

The Middle Ages were also characterized by the development of
large-scale management problems, and the administration of large
domains was a crucial issue necessitating continual attention and study.
In A.D. 812, for instance, Charlemagne discussed the need for strengthened and improved administration of fiscal affairs, the supervision of
officials, the need for reporting systems, and the recruitment of good
workers. The medieval Church also had an impact on the conduct of
administration since, among its many activities, it served as a system of
government. Even during the Reformation, Calvin, unlike Luther, for
example, stressed the need for a church-society which would be effective
only if an institutional structure could be established. Calvin thought the
church needed strong leadership and direction, and as an alternative to
papal authority he devised an administrative scheme in which policy
formulation was relegated to the leadership, and congregational ratifi-
cation or rejection was within the province of the membership.

The Cameralists (German and Austrian professors and administrators whose activities dated from 1550 to the 1700's) included administration in their discussions of economics. Cameralists such as Frederick
William I of Prussia and Maria Theresa of Austria called for systematic
administration even though their primary interest was the physical
wealth of the state. Simply conceived, Cameralists adhered to the notion
that if the good life was to be achieved, good management must also

55

prevail. For the state to flourish and for the people to have the means of existence available to them, good management must be emphasized and executed.

The historical experience in America also illustrates the growth of interest in administrative matters. Before 1776, poor administration in the colonies led to numerous problems, some of which later influenced the separation from the motherland. Colonial management was often disorganized, confused, inefficient, and inequitable. To the colonist, administration was an imposition from England. To Parliament, the conduct of administration posed problems of managing colonies which were semi-autonomous in character. The concepts and practices of administration which were prevalent in England were not always applicable in the colonies, and after independence Americans were faced with the task of establishing a governmental and an administrative system suited to their particular needs. Unfortunately, the Articles of Confederation did little to improve administration in America. Because the confederation produced a loosely knit system of government and a corresponding diffusion of governmental power, conflicts between governmental units and inequities between and within governmental bodies developed, and the general problems of administering a new nation without commensurate power were magnified.

The struggle to adopt the Constitution of 1787 involved questions of how the national government would be administered. In arguing the benefits of the presidential system, for example, Alexander Hamilton noted in *The Federalist*, No. 70, that a "feeble executive implies a feeble execution of government" and, reminiscent of Alexander Pope, "a government ill executed, whatever it may be in theory, must be, in practice, a bad government."

Later, in 1831, Alexis de Tocqueville, an astute observer of political practices, described how administration was conducted in America. De Tocqueville studied the American system within the context of democracy; he concluded that American administrators did not possess sufficient administrative knowledge. Administration was a science, he reasoned, but in America those conducting public administration were not in a position to instruct others in that science. Thus, in the early years of the United States, there was a general concern about public administration but it was not studied or clearly understood.

As the population of the United States increased, as new units of government in the states were formed, and as the problems of governing the country became more complex and extensive, a greater knowledge of the conduct of administration was developed. Thomas Jefferson, with his agrarian ideals, his philosophy of decentralized government and administration, and his views on national-state relationships, epitomized the American approach to public administration in the early nineteenth century. The advent of Jacksonian democracy in the 1800's also influenced attitudes toward the administration of government, especially the employment of persons for public office.

Because administration has a history and because in theory and practice it has assumed many forms and approaches, it is necessary for the student of American public administration to follow some categorization, such as that outlined by Paul J. Gordon. The four approaches which can be distinguished in the United States today are: (1) traditional, (2) behavioral, (3) decisional, and (4) ecological. In many respects, they are not mutually exclusive, nor do they necessarily follow any chronological order. They are neither schools of thought nor philosophies, but may be considered simply as emphases in public administration.

8. Transcend the Current Debate on Administrative Theory*

Paul J. Gordon

Far too much of the recent literature on administrative theories has been dedicated to scuffling over which of several schemes of classification of a complex terrain might be better. The battle, if one is to be conducted and useful, should be on grounds other than classification alone. One system is better or worse than another only because it has more use in achieving the purposes intended. This gets down to whether it helps or hinders insight, verification and communication.

What is far more important for the practicing executive is the recognition that any particular approach to administration carries a number of assumptions, recognized or not, that can lead to both intended and unintended consequences.[1] Currently competing approaches can be classified in a manner to help thoughtful executives consider the uses and limits of each.

At least four approaches to administration can be distinguished in America today. The distinctions are not as compartmentalized as any scheme for analytical purposes might suggest. Each is really a perspective or a relative emphasis more than a separate school of thought. At different times among people of various backgrounds one perspective or another has been in the ascendency; others have been relatively subordinated. Brief elaboration may provide perspective and a framework for fitting together theories, research and practice useful for continued study and improvement. For convenience, we shall use the labels: *traditional, behavioral, decisional* and *ecological*.[2]

TRADITIONAL

The approach that has recently been called traditional represents the accumulation that has passed along from: the *mother sciences*; *rationalized views of administration*, frequently of European origin; and, the *scientific management movement*, with its development attributed at least partly to North Americans.

Mother Science Emphasis

During the period and among institutions and individuals when the *mother sciences* constituted the dominant perspective, the activity of

* From *Academy of Management Journal*, Vol. 6, No. 4 (December, 1963), 290–302. Reprinted by permission.

1 This would apply to the practicing professor, researcher, consultant and writer as well.

2 The term "traditional" is meant in no slighting sense. Both the traditional approach and the newer decisional one are based on a necessary rational core. The traditional has simply been around longer.

organizations was seen as principally economic in the case of business, political in the case of government and social for institutions such as hospitals. Early teaching in business administration was heavily influenced by the ideas of classical economists. The movement for better teaching and practice in public administration made relatively little headway until the overpowering preoccupation with political theory and law were eased. Writings on hospital administration only recently emphasize administration more than medicine and technology. Literature for practitioners early in this century was heavily influenced by principles and analogies drawn from various branches of engineering. Only gradually was fuller recognition given to economic, political, social, technological and moral aspects of administration and behavior that cut across organizations.

In fields such as business administration, public administration, educational administration, military administration, church administration, institutional and hospital administration and international administration, in general, policy and program were conceived to be uppermost. Policy was seen as the province of boards and chief executives. Administration was viewed more as a kind of housekeeping, record-keeping, maintenance of physical plant and routine supervision. Policy and administration were conceived to be related but separate entities, each treated at the correct level of hierarchy in larger organizations. Only later did writers describe policy and administration as joined and reciprocal, each setting premises and limits for the other. Eventually, the term administration came to cover both.

Broad Rational Emphasis

The *rational view of administration,* as represented by Henri Fayol, Luther Gulick and Lyndall Urwick, was a break with the mother science approach.[3] Administration was perceived as a separate and recognizable field of human activity. Administration was perceived as what administrators do. What they do was seen as a function—called administration —and composed of highly interrelated sub-functions such as planning, organizing and controlling. These people were concerned with the total task of administration applied to the total unit of organization. They were concerned with administration at all levels of sizeable organizations in all kinds of enterprise.

They sought to develop universal theories and principles that would explain and prescribe guides for planning, organization and control in any kind of administrative situation. Although not always specified, it was assumed that wise administrators would know enough to adapt these

---

[3] Deliberate choice to hold footnotes to a mimimum should make this paper more readable especially for an audience well equipped to supply those that pertain.

guides to particular situations. Emphasis was more at the top policy level of the organization with the subdivision and specialization of work in a rational way below. Administration was perceived as based on principles that could be deduced and applied in a rational, orderly and systematic way. Many of the currently discussed theories and principles of administration can be traced to the writings of Fayol, Gulick, Urwick and their colleagues and predecessors.

Early Scientific Management

The *scientific management movement,* as represented by Frederick W. Taylor, Frank and Lillian Gilbreth, Henry L. Gantt and others, was also concerned with rational study and improvement in administration. These people were advocates of knowing what work had to be done and getting it done in the most effective and efficient manner. They were concerned with division and specialization of work; the measurement of work and effort; and, the efficient and humane expenditure of effort. More recent focus on the individual in the work situation and his relationships with members of a group has suggested shortcomings in the earlier scientific management activities. In practice, the emphasis of the scientific management movement may have been more on the physiological than on the psychological and sociological aspects of behavior in the work situation. The writings of the pioneers for a scientific management movement, however, indicate interest in broader aspects of the well-being of people at work.

In contrast to the rational view of administration as posited by Fayol and others, a great part of the experimentation and writing of the scientific management group was more at the shop level. Emphasis was on engineering the most efficient arrangement of means to ends to get work done at the foreman and worker level. Applications were especially in manufacturing and construction. Many of the current uses of job analysis, motion and time study, work flow and plant layout, work simplification, process charting, production scheduling and the like had their beginning in the scientific management movement. These are residuals of a larger concept.

Traditional Summarized

According to the traditional view, the task of administration is that of planning relationships among the work, the people and the workplace; establishing organizational relationships with suitable authority and responsibility so that work can be directed; then measuring and controlling to be sure that specifications are met. That is, rationalizing and engineering an efficient means to ends relationship.

The anatomy of administration, that is the framework for exposition and analysis, is made up of certain administrative functions. These have been most elaborately articulated as planning, organizing, staffing, directing, coordinating, reporting and budgeting. For these, the perceptions and semantics among writers have varied. Some of the recent literature has amended this functional outline with the inclusion of more emphasis on motivation, communication and leadership; and, by conceiving of these activities as sub-processes that combine to make up a larger and integrative process of administration.

The goals of administration are to promote effectiveness (achieving desired organizational objectives) and efficiency (doing so without waste). The ways of dividing work at each level of organization involve combinations of decisions on the basis of: major work functions to be performed by the organization (for example, in business—marketing, production and finance); the processes involved (for example, the stages of refining oil in continuous-flow equipment); professional groupings (for example, economists in one organizational unit); and, the products, the clientele or the area most to be developed or served. The criteria to be used in designing and regulating organizations for the accomplishment of work are certain well-established "principles" such as unity of command (one boss), span of control (not too many subordinates), and homogeneous assignment (like activities put together). These are found on concepts of authority and responsibility arranged in a hierarchy from top to bottom of an organization.

The traditional view, compared with those that follow, is more work-centered. Administration is treated more as a technical problem to be solved on a highly rationalized and programmed basis with formal arrangements and guidelines. The ends are frequently taken as given; means are to be engineered to produce desired outcomes with maximum efficiency. Fundamental ideas include those of hierarchy, authority, function, specialization, measurement and efficiency. The influences that have shaped the traditional view are more those of classical economics, engineering and law.

BEHAVIORAL

Following the traditional approach with its work-centered emphasis, increasing but not always approving attention was directed to the emerging behavioral approach. In contrast, the emphasis of the behavioral approach was more on the people and the way that live people behave in live organizations. Through their writings the behavioralists have frequently appeared as opponents of rationalization. Likewise, they have often been questioned as critics who cast doubts on an established order but provide no firm edifice in its stead. (The objective view may be neither as black nor as white as one might suppose in reading the extremist positions of either school.)

61

Argument over Evidence

Advocates of the behavioral approach, still somewhat in formative stages and less neatly classified, have claimed not only that the traditionalists have neglected many aspects of administration; but further, that the traditional propositions were frequently wrong. The behavioralists complained that the traditional approach prematurely generalized in order to formulate principles too often based on personalized experience and limited evidence. The experience, they contended, was not sufficiently perceptive of behavior in live organizations and not adequately verified. Misconceptions, they argued, were conveyed through preoccupation with abstraction, rationalization and technique. These, they said, caused trouble through focusing on the physiological and mechanical attributes of men and machines while ignoring observable evidence of how people really behave. Such a mental set, they suggested, might lead the traditionalist into the hazard of wanting to bend reality to fit into his own mentally conceived model of the real world. (Modernists of various sorts are not entirely free of this hazard.)

In contrast, the behavioralists sought to compile as proof for their contentions empirical studies, characteristically more inductive than deductive. Many of the earlier studies were limited in the number of cases examined. Occasionally the implications were misinterpreted, especially through premature effort to find answers to meet operational problems. Fairly early in the behavioral approach, evidence was developed with which to refute some of the traditional propositions. Yet there appeared no systematic body of theory and evidence fully to replace the old with the new.

The traditionalists countered with charges that the behavioralists were gnawing away at existing beliefs without offering any substantive additions or replacements. They claimed that really perceptive behavioralists might recognize that wise administrators in practice took note of phenomena not detailed in the traditional principles. The traditionalists intimated that the behavioralists were making unwarranted claims for new discoveries. The behavioralists countered that their contribution was one of opening for public inspection their use of evidence and research methods to arrive at findings and conclusions.

Hallmarks of Behavioralists

One of the essential characteristics of the behavioral approach is the insistence on observable and verifiable phenomena that may serve at least in part as evidence for anything to be recognized as knowledge, principle or finding. For example, instead of asking about a man's traits (abstractions not easily to be observed and verified), the behavioralist is more likely to ask—what does he do—what does he say—what does he not do—what does he not say?

If one recognized the foregoing as the hallmark of the behavioralist, one will also perceive that various social scientists do not necessarily equate on a one to one basis with the behavioralist approach. Psychologists, sociologists, anthropologists, political scientists, biologists, economists and even mathematicians outside the conventional view of so-called social sciences may or may not be behavioralists.

Whether they are behavioralists or not can best be judged by the evidence of how they themselves behave in pursuing and disseminating knowledge. Some behavioralists might consider their research more "pure" under conditions of controlled laboratory experimentation. But, one may well use a behavioralist approach, even to some extent clinical and experimental methods, without insisting on "pure" science at every point. It seems only a matter of common sense to declare that the call for completely aseptic research technique and conclusions completely validated on a mathematical basis in fields such as administration is one way to stifle any progress at all.

Early behavioral contributions, publicized under what came to be the much-abused "human relations" label, were sometimes fragmentary, inconclusive and preoccupied with the plight of the misunderstood man at the lowest end of the hierarchical totem pole. Also, the legitimate concern with non-rational aspects of behavior led to preoccupation in some instances with psychotic behavior, hardly one of the cornerstones on which to build administration. Some behavioralists viewed the task of organizing, for example, as that of establishing relationships among individuals, groups and somewhat ominous things called formal organizations and bureaucracies.

More recently there has been more concern with what may be called normal behavior at all levels of organization. Increasingly, misinterpretations of earlier findings have been corrected through the work of the behavioralists themselves and through others. The swing in favor of the totally permissive and supportive climate with rule only by consent and emphasis only on rewards (never on penalties) may have been overdone. Insofar as there is any consensus, behavioralists currently seem to view the goals of administration as those of—facilitating suitable combinations of support and constraint—in order to achieve whatever degree of conformity and coordination may be essential for accomplishing the main activities of the enterprise.

Behavioral Summarized

Organization is viewed primarily as a social system—one that develops interactions, conflicts and cohesions not always within the power of the administrator to understand and control. Organizational decisions are perceived to involve various combinations of individuals, groups, social structures, bureaucracies and institutions. Administration is infused with individual and group feelings, sentiments, perceptions, identifications, motivations, inducements and sometimes culturally patterned responses and interactions. Questions of influence, the distribution and control of power and reconciliation of diverse interests both internal and external in relation to the organization are also involved. These are further conditioned by the development of informal patterns of leadership and group interaction that do not show on the official organizational chart but may either advance or hinder the achievement of official purposes.

According to the behavioral view, the task of administration is to choose those arrangements, broadly speaking, that are most likely to evoke a system of cooperative relationships among the people who are to achieve the mission of the organization. In contrast to other approaches, the behavioral view centers more on the people, their interactions and cooperation. It emphasizes, more than the traditional approach, the development of insight and understanding based on empirical investigation. It challenges administrators and students to understand non-rational as well as rational and informal as well as formal aspects of organizational behavior. The contributions of psychology and sociology to this approach are generally recognized; less often cited are those of political science and anthropology.

DECISIONAL

The perspective taken in the more recently stressed decisional approach is that the task of administration is that of decision-making. The organization is viewed as a decision-making unit and the administrator as a decision-maker. Rational analysis of utilities desired and the outcomes, probabilities, risks and uncertainties related to each set of alternatives under postulated conditions is characteristic of current developments. The design of models and the testing of quantitative techniques are further indicative of the nature of the effort that is going forward in trying to advance a "new science of managerial decision-making."[4]

Concepts and Tools

Differences in relation to other approaches are founded on the relative emphasis accorded decision as such and on the greater use of new and powerful tools for quantitative analysis. One of the recognized operational utilities of the decisional approach, as a way of conceiving

[4] Since the wording is the title of the Herbert A. Simon (Harper and Bros., 1960) book, the exception to the no-footnoting guide is in order.

of administration, is that it provides a better integrating device than some of the earlier approaches. One of the current limitations, at least as used by some proponents, is the relative omission of the qualitative and non-rational factors that are recognized to be present in some of the most crucial executive decisions. To include within the view of decision-making only the aspects that can be readily quantified and programmed may cut the most important parts. This many others have noted.

Nevertheless, this approach has barely begun and the universal requirement to make decisions or see that they are made provides a nexus for the integration of many approaches. The decision emphasis, more than some of the others, seems to get one up to the point of commitment involving subsequent action. Action as such cannot be cut altogether from the view of the executive task.

As with the earlier approaches, there is no fixed point in time that can be cited as the precise starting point of the decisional approach. Neither is it nicely segmented conceptually and semantically from the others or within itself. In the market place today, one may find material of recent publication treating decision as: an exercise in "common sense," sound thinking and logic; an integrated process of problem solving; and the application of "scientific method" in thinking through administrative issues. Recent material on learning theory, information theory, innovative behavior and heuristic programming can be related to both the behavioral and the decisional approaches. Decisions, of course, cut across the other approaches as well. Some writers have a scheme of thought that subordinates other aspects of administration to decision-making. Others view decision as no more than a monetary phenomenon among interdependent processes of thought and action.

Systems and Processes

The conceptualization that is involved here is one that some have viewed as a systems approach. That is, provided that we reject the older image of systems as a bundle of office procedures. The newer view relates administrative systems to unified arrangements of interdependent factors such as the solar system. The total input and output and processing of information and action by men and machines, for example, can be conceptualized as the integration of many sub-systems into a larger total system not unrelated to the decisional view.

The concept of administration as a process, which is at the core of the decisional approach, provides a framework for analyzing dynamic relationships among several variables. The concept of a process, decisional or any other kind, has not been the unique contribution of the decisionalist. The traditionalists have described planning, organizing and the like as a series of interdependent processes all adding up to a larger concept of an administrative process. The behavioralists have examined interaction, communication and learning as processes and the process of fusing people and organizations. But the concept has been more fully and widely characteristic of contributions by the decisionalists.

Once administration is conceptualized as decision-making, then the processes of making decisions assume major importance. The decisional (systems) view of administration is more sharply concerned than the earlier ones with the establishment of relationships among objectives, strategies and competition—whether political, social, economic or technological—internal to the organization or external.

Decisional Summarized

The goal is achieving objectives under competitive conditions. The function of administration is to facilitate the flow of information and the making of appropriate decisions. Persons faced with decisions must choose among combinations of ends, means, strategies, tactics, and information inputs and outputs. The anatomy of decision-making includes, not necessarily in this classification and sequence, but by some name: information, objectives, strategies, alternatives, probabilities and consequences.

This approach is decision and systems centered: information, including that about competitive forces, is regarded as a central problem. Certain aspects are more highly analytical, frequently involving quantitative expression. What we have summarized as the decisional approach is currently close to what has been included under the recently popular term—managerial sciences. That term, however, embraces some of the other approaches.

Mathematics, statistics, econometrics, engineering and quantitative programming techniques have already provided the basis for important contributions to this approach. The economic and marketing environment of the firm, for example in business, and the theory of games as applied to decision-making in war-time and peace-time have been prominent. Political science, which includes concern with relative power position, representation of diverse and competing interests and ultimate accountability, is still relatively untapped as an important well-spring for administrative theory. The last observation fits equally well the ecological approach.

ECOLOGICAL

The ecological approach is concerned with relationships among: the organization; its internal and external environment; and, whatever forces regulate interdependent adaptation, innovation and change. The term is taken from biology. Ecology is that branch of biology that deals with mutual relations between organisms and their environments.[5]

Adaptive Behavior

In the case of business, one might center attention on the relationship between the economic and marketing environment and the internal productive, distributive, financial and managerial capacities of the individual firm. The scope might be confined to one activity or extended to encompass an industry. In public administration, a focus of continuing interest is the relationship between the environment in which any governmental program must operate and the internal views, resources and administration of the agency. The importance of examining the reciprocal activity of simultaneously adapting to environment and effecting innovation in new environments should be self-evident in international administration.

The ecological view, as defined here, is that the task of administration is to build and strengthen organizations that will have the capacity to respond to changing environment and to create opportunities for growth. Growth here does not have to mean increased size. It could mean diminished size with greater strength, competitive ability and return on the investment. The latter would fit most clearly the case of business.

The goals of administration are survival and strengthening of the integrity and resources of the organization as a corporate unit amid the pressures of external, internal and organizational change. The administrator would seek the optimum mix between frequent organizational changes that might harm desirable relationships, one the one hand, and undue concern for stability in relationships that might lead to atrophy, on the other.

Ecological Summarized

This view is more eclectic than those already cited (it borrows from all of them) and more heuristic (ready for readjustment of ends, means and behavior anywhere along the line in the light of new discovery). To put the matter less abstractly, here we have an approach that starts with the grass roots (the customer for business administration, the voter for public administration or the patient for hospital administration), and then adds the necessary operational elements. It borrows along the way from the so-called principles of the traditionalists, the cooperative ideas of the behavioralists and the competitive strategies of the decisionalists. According to this view, administration functions as a catalyst in order to facilitate the direction and rate of growth and change most suitable for a viable organization.

The ecological approach, as defined, is growth-centered; regards viability as the key issue; and, is environmentally—even culturally and

5 Since compartmentalization is usually somewhat artificial at best, readers will recognize that the "life sciences" approaches to "systems" could fit here but is not divorced from "systems" as treated technologically and sociologically.

cross-culturally oriented. The last point especially has significance in a world increasingly sensitive to the international aspects of almost every major human endeavor. The basic underlying studies on which one might draw more fully in developing this approach would include, as a minimum, biology and anthropology. Viewed as an issue of responsiveness, political science is also relevant.

MULTIPLE APPROACH

The foregoing adds up to a multiple approach to a complex matter. The approach is at least four-pronged, with the four major headings serving as a convenience to house many more detailed considerations. The practical implications for continuing education, research, and practice are several.

First of all, it avoids getting caught up in the current debate on administrative theory—trapped within one set of assumptions or another without profit and without a larger view of the possible consequences. It should be evident that each of the four major approaches has a special perspective founded on certain assumptions and leading to certain possible consequences. It should be evident that each of the four major approaches has a special perspective founded on certain assumptions and leading to certain possible consequences. The executive who views primarily the work with little regard for the other aspects may lose sight of the objectives and the social consequences of his activity. The executive who views more exclusively the people and social interaction may be entirely too preoccupied with internal cooperation and lose sight of the ultimate decisions, the competition, and the kind of profit and capital that his organization is supposed to build. The executives who are preoccupied with the fascinating game of making decisions may lose sight of the action and the follow-up necessary to assure the result. Others can be so involved in the attention to adaptive behavior that they fail to assess and strengthen the character and the integrity of the enterprise for which they are responsible. So the whole relationship involving assumptions, perspectives, and consequences is worthy of examination. There are other uses as well.

The framework provides a fairly easy way to join in an educational setting the contributions of: the traditionalists who have dealt with processes such as planning, organizing and controlling; the behavioralists who have analyzed various processes of social and political interaction; the decisionalists who have emphasized different perceptions of decision processes; and, the ecologists who have stressed processes of adaptation and accommodation between organisms and environments. The content of an executive or graduate program might be cut in different ways. Yet, the probabilities are that increasingly all four views will have to be clearly presented, appraised and synthesized if the better programs are to set the stage for continued learning.

The framework should facilitate evaluation and use of research findings. Ideally, researcher and practitioner should share a concern to discover and verify the existence of similarities, differences and patterns under stated conditions with stated probabilities. The aim of research generally is to establish bases for prediction and therefore bases for better decisions for the future. The framework set forth has the flexibility and the "openness" in no way to close off advance of knowledge in the field; yet it can be treated as "closed" in order to establish commitment and assure delivery in executive work. As others have said, the need is for material that is both theoretically connected and empirically tested.

Finally, administration has come to mean taking decisions and actions to achieve organizational objectives. More than others, the administrator is *responsible for setting the character of the organization, the goals for the future and the direction and rate of change that may anticipate or mold future conditions. What most distinguishes administration is responsibility—responsibility to see that decisions and actions necessary to achieve organizational objectives are taken—and, responsibility for strengthening the total resources on which the future of the organization must be built.* Ultimately, the administrator is responsible for integrating the activities of a total unit of organization in relation to its total environment over time. How can such responsibilities be discharged except through applying the best of the old and the new to the aspects of administration that are environmental, organizational and personal as a minimum?

AN ACADEMIC EPILOGUE

In these pages, we have presented four viewpoints, each of which is an important and yet only a partial perspective. One does not have to make a forced choice and then cast the others aside. The distinguishing features have been emphasized in order to highlight the perspectives and contributions of each. Entering into any new field of study, one of the important guides is to learn the orientation of the field. Orientations change from time to time. At any particular point, however, knowing the orientation will help in recognizing what issues are considered important, what kinds of data are accumulated and what methods of analysis are used.

Building a Useful Framework

One important aspect of building a conceptual framework for administration is the idea of a number of variables related differently under differing circumstances. Precisely what the key variables may be, what their relative importance may be and how they may be related under different circumstances are not settled matters. Nor can they be conceived as settled and remain settled in this kind of a field. So, if one is not sure what the key variables may be and not sure of their relative importance, postulations must be made, subject to continuing discovery, learning and correction.

The idea that there are such variables, however, is fundamental. They provide the substance of administration without which processes, techniques and viewpoints in a vacuum can be sterile. The differences in relative importance among the variables under differing circumstances are also important. They account, at least in part, for significant differences in business, public and institutional administration in different settings. As a beginning, one can say that some of the key variables will be those in the external environment in which the organization conducts its activities and those represented in the internal programs of the organization itself. Further, one may include the external and internal attributes of organizational behavior and the techniques for qualitative and quantitative analysis. In addition, there can be little question that administrators themselves may be among the key variables in any administrative situation.

Another important aspect of building a conceptual framework is to provide for the inclusion of values, especially those related to the choices of ends and means for the organization and behavior for members. While advocating one set of values or another may not represent an addition to scientific knowledge, the analysis of values among organizations and their apparent relation, if any, to decisions and actions is highly important. Persons responsible for administration and the preparation of administrators cannot put aside, as unscientific, questions related to values.

The different purposes for which organizations are established and the different purposes conceived and advanced, consciously or not, by the members are but one of several factors related to value. Others include the estimate of worth attached to economic, social and political philosophies and the moral and ethical standards of administrators themselves. These also account for significant differences in administration among diverse institutional, national and international settings. In brief, in purposive organizations, purposes are important. They must be part of the conceptual apparatus of the administrator and part of the study of administration.

A third important aspect of building a conceptual framework is to decide on some unifying concept that will help in picturing the ways in which substantive aspects and value aspects may be combined and related for effective administration. For this purpose, the concepts of a series of sub-processes of decision and action joined into a larger process of administration provides a framework as satisfactory as any other, provided its utilities and limitations are recognized.[6]

The process concept is a mental tool for conceptualizing how to put the parts of administration together. The idea of sub-processes joined into a larger process of administration has the utility of providing the structural aspect of the framework so that it can be visualized, so that it can be communicated, so that the parts can be related to the whole and so that the contributions of many related fields can be brought into focus within one framework.

The utility of the process concept in administration is similar to that of the "scientific method" in the physical and biological sciences. It has been said that the unity of all science is in the method. The emphasis on method permits the transfer of learning from one substantive field to another in the sciences. The emphasis on process provides a sorting rack that permits comparative studies and therefore the transfer of learning and the accumulation of knowledge in administration. Once understood and retained, the process concept also helps the practitioner put his knowledge to use. In both instances, there is more accord on the need for a central unifying concept than there is in delineating the parts and agreeing that things actually get done that way.

Provisional Working Theory

A final aspect of building a conceptual framework for administration is to define the major orientation or point of view. For the purposes of this discussion, each of the four broad approaches (traditional, behavioral, decisional and ecological) is perceived as incorporating sub-processes all of which, combined and fused, join into the larger process of administration. As with evaluative work in the field of anthropology, we have chosen to establish a framework which is in itself subject to continued testing, refinement and possible future replacement. The framework permits the incorporation and comparison of many approaches as well as the joining of values, substance and processes.

It points the way to a synthesis that transcends the currently competing approaches while at the same time building on the significant contributions of each. It permits the degree of structure necessary to give order to a field to be studied and mastered while at the same time avoiding orthodoxy. In effect, this whole approach constitutes a provisional working theory of administration.

6 The conceptualization of "processes" used here, it should be said explicitly, is not solely linear but closer to a general systems network (both open and closed and heuristic on occasion).

SELECTED READINGS

Books

Achieving Excellence in the Public Service. Philadelphia, The American Academy of Political and Social Science, 1963.

Blau, Peter M. *Bureaucracy in Modern Society.* New York, Random House, Inc., 1956.

————. *The Dynamics of Bureaucracy.* Chicago, University of Chicago Press, 1955.

Buechner, John C. *Public Administration.* Encino, California, Dickenson Publishing Co., 1968.

Caldwell, Lynton K. *Selected Papers on Public Administration.* Bloomington, Indiana, Indiana University, 1960.

Dimock, Marshall Edward, and Gladys Ogden Dimock. *Public Administration.* New York, Holt, Rinehart & Winston, Inc., 1966.

Henderson, Keith M. *Emerging Synthesis in American Public Administration.* New York, Asia Publishing House, Inc., 1966.

Macy, John W., Jr. *Public Service.* New York, Harper & Row, Publishers, 1971.

Modernizing State Government. New York, Committee for Economic Development, 1967.

Mosher, Frederick C. *Democracy and the Public Service.* New York, Oxford University Press, 1968.

Mouzelis, Nicos P. *Organization and Bureaucracy.* Chicago, Aldine-Atherton, Inc., 1972.

Pfiffner, John M., and Robert Presthus. *Public Administration.* New York, The Ronald Press Company, 1967.

The Theory and Practice of Public Administration: Scope, Objectives and Methods. Monograph #8. Philadelphia, The American Academy of Political and Social Science, 1968.

U.S. Civil Service Commission. *Self Development Aids for Supervisors and Middle Managers.* Personnel Bibliography Series No. 34. Washington, D.C., Government Printing Office, 1970.

U.S. Department of Agriculture. *Guides for Supervisors.* Washington, D.C., Government Printing Office, 1969.

Articles

Anderson, Desmond L., Kent M. Lloyd and Kendall O. Price. "Crisis in Education of American Public Executives," *International Review of Administrative Sciences*, Vol. 32, No. 2 (1966), 145–52.

Argyris, Chris."The Individual and Organization: Some Problems of Mutual Adjustment," *Administrative Science Quarterly,* Vol. 2, No. 1 (June, 1957), 1–24.

Bailey, Stephen K. "Ethics and the Public Service," *Public Administration Review,* Vol. 24, No. 4 (December, 1964), 234–43.

Bendix, Reinhard. "Bureaucracy: The Problems and Its Setting," *American Sociological Review,* Vol. 12, No. 5 (October, 1947), 493–507.

Bennis, Warren G. "Organizational Developments and the Fate of Bureaucracy," *Industrial Management Review,* Vol. 7, No. 2 (spring, 1966), 41–55.

Boise, William B. "The Education of Public Administrators: Innovative Approaches," *Public Personnel Review,* Vol. 33, No. 2 (April, 1972), 96–99.

Constas, Helen. "Max Weber's Two Conceptions of Bureaucracy," *American Journal of Sociology,* Vol. 63 (1958), 400–409.

Corson, John J. "Distinguishing Characteristics of Public Administration," *Public Administration Review,* Vol. 12 (1952), 120–25.

Davy, Thomas J. "Public Administration as a Field of Study in the United States," *International Review of Administrative Sciences,* Vol. 28, No. 1 (1962), 63–77.

Fornataro, J. V. "Administrative Competence in Social Welfare," *Canadian Welfare,* Vol. 41, No. 5 (September–October, 1965), 218–24.

Ginsberg, Eli. "Professional Manpower for State Governments," *Personnel Administration,* Vol. 34, No. 6 (November–December), 1971, 28–32.

Hanlan, Archie. "Counteracting Problems of Bureaucracy in Public Welfare," *Social Work,* Vol. 12, No. 3 (July, 1967), 88–94.

Jaques, Elliott. "Too Many Management Levels," *California Management Review,* Vol. 8, No. 1 (fall, 1965), 13–20.

Kaufman, Herbert. "Emerging Conflicts in the Doctrines of Public Administration," *American Political Science Review,* Vol. 50 (1956), 1057–74.

Kindig, Fred E. "Management in Perspective," *The Journal of the Academy of Management,* Vol. 4, No. 1 (April, 1961), 59–66.

Klekamp, Robert C. "The Behavioral Approach in Management," *Advanced Management Journal,* Vol. 33, No. 4, (October, 1968), 54–58.

Koontz, Harold. "The Management Theory Jungle," *Academy of Management Journal,* Vol. 4, No. 3 (December, 1961), 174–88.

Lawlis, Don C., and Preston P. LeBreton. "Meeting the Manpower Requirements of a State Government," *Public Personnel Review,* Vol. 21, No. 1 (January, 1960), 33–35.

Litchfield, Edward H. "Notes on a General Theory of Administration," *Administrative Science Quarterly*, Vol. 1, No. 1 (June, 1956), 3–29.

Martin, Roscoe C. "Political Science and Public Administration: A Note on the State of the Union," *The American Political Science Review*, Vol. 46, No. 3 (September, 1952), 660–76.

Massie, Joseph L. "Management Theory," in James G. March, *Handbook of Organizations*, 387–422.

Meij, J. L. "Management, a Common Province of Different Sciences," *Management International*, No. 5 (1962), 37–46.

Miller, Glenn W. "Manpower in the Public Sector," *Public Personnel Review*, Vol. 33, No. 1 (January, 1972), 50–55.

Millett, John D. "The Values of Public Service," *Public Personnel Review*, Vol. 17, No. 1 (January, 1956), 28–33.

Price, Don K. "The Future of the Public Service," *Public Personnel Review*, Vol. 24, No. 2 (April, 1963), 83–87.

Sayre, Wallace S. "Premises of Public Administration: Past and Emerging," *Public Administration Review*, Vol. 18, No. 2 (spring, 1958), 102–105.

Schollhammer, Hans. "The Comparative Management Theory Jungle," *Academy of Management Journal*, Vol. 12, No. 1 (March ,1969), 81–97.

Smith, Michael P. "Alienation and Bureaucracy: The Role of Participatory Administration," *Public Administration Review*, Vol. 31, No. 6 (November–December, 1971), 658–64.

Stanley, David T. "Excellence in Public Service—How Do You Really Know?" *Public Administration Review*, Vol. 24, No. 3 (September, 1964), 170–74.

Urwick, L. "Public Administration and Business Management," *Public Administration Review*, Vol. 17, No. 2 (spring, 1957), 77–82.

Waldo, Dwight. "Administrative Theory in the United States: A Survey and Prospect," *Political Studies*, Vol. 2, No. 1 (February, 1954), 71–86.

Walker, David B. "Administrative Federalism," *The Federal Accountant*, Vol. 16, No. 1 (fall, 1966–67), 30–41.

SECTION I: PLANNING

Managerial planning is the deliberative activity leading to decisions concerning future courses of action. It involves knowledge of strategies employed in the past as well as the conditions which dictated their use and the results attained. It is forward-looking and requires analyses and weighing of the probable effects of trends and forces that indicate change. Planning assumes the establishment of objectives and the setting of goals for the organization. It is also concerned with the steps to be taken to realize those objectives and goals, including the assurance of acceptance of the objectives and goals by members of the organization. It is concerned with resources and with the relative commitment of the various resources to the attainment of the goals.

Planning, of necessity, is concerned with evaluation of the organization's performance and application of remedial measures when they are indicated. Evaluative judgment may be based on the findings of task force studies and pertinent information from other sources as well as feedback from employees at various organizational levels. An adequate informational system should provide the necessary information for that corrective action essential to the realization of organizational objectives and the attainment of goals. Evaluation as a part of planning must be continuous in nature.

One of the most obvious and useful forms of planning is budgeting. Usually the word *budgeting* is used in connection with the use of funds; however, it may also apply to the use of other resources. Budgeting is related to work to be done within time limits as well as to goals and

75

objectives. There is the need in planning and budgeting to work from the bottom up, beginning with the smallest unit and securing full participation in setting goals and determining priorities. Such procedure assures full agency participation in the planning process rather than making planning the responsibility of a small staff unit. Budgeting is closely related to forecasting, which is particularly difficult in public administration on a long-range basis because of the uncertainties surrounding legislative appropriations.

To some extent, planning has a necessary role to play in all functions of management. For this reason, the idea has sometimes been expressed that planning is the most important of the various management functions. The following well-known quotation from Benjamin Franklin's *Poor Richard's Almanack* illustrates how the most insignificant factor may influence the overall performance of the organization and its success or failure in reaching its objectives:

> For the want of a nail the shoe was lost,
> For the want of a shoe the horse was lost,
> For the want of a horse the rider was lost,
> For the want of a rider the battle was lost,
> For the want of a battle the kingdom was lost—
> And all for the want of a horseshoe nail!

Admittedly, the interrelationship of the various functions of management is such that no one function can operate without the others. Goal setting and the implementation of plans, emphasized by the idea of the primacy of planning, must be done before intelligent attention can be directed toward organizational relationships, staffing, directing, and controlling. Too often, executives involve themselves in short-term planning because of a crisis or from necessity while they postpone planning of a long-range nature. Neglected planning is the ghost that is certain to return to haunt the manager who was too busy to plan until too late.

Effective program action begins with effective planning. *Planning*, like many other management terms, is confusing because it is generally assumed that everyone knows what it means. However, the scope of activities that can be included or excluded under the term *planning* is great. As a result, planning, in spite of its common dictionary definition, has come to mean different things to different people. For that reason, commitment to planning by public administrators ranges from doubt that effective planning can be done in relation to rapidly changing circumstances and fluctuating political pressures to the feeling that the only way to consistently deal with these situations is through long-range planning efforts. The concept of the planner also varies from the idea that almost every person in the organization should be involved in the planning process to the belief that planning is a very specific professional function best left to a staff unit within the organization. There are also those who feel that planning is, in fact, policy making and should be restricted to top management and board functions. Other areas of disagreement exist. Perhaps these illustrations will serve to indicate the complexity of trying to determine what should be the content of a book of this type.

In keeping with the overall purpose of the book, selections have been made on the basis of what is practical and useful for first-line and middle managers in public organizations. This, too, is an area of judgment. The articles selected for this section are directed to the problems and factors peculiar to planning in a government agency and to some of the strategies and tools appropriate in such a setting. The first article, "Nature of Planning and Plans," by Robert G. Murdick, deals with some concepts and types of planning and the question, What is a plan? In addition to a discussion of objectives, goals, and missions, the article deals with policies, procedures, and regulations as well as tactics and strategies. The article distinguishes between planning and decision making and between planning and implementation. In theory, these distinctions may be clear-cut and definite; in practice, they tend to become more ambiguous.

Edward A. Lehan's article, "Programming: Its Role in Organization Theory," discusses the many uses of the words *program* and *programming* as they relate to planning. It deals with programming as a concept and points out some problems in program implementation which go beyond organizational lines. In spite of these problems, the author advances the idea that programming provides ways of "overcoming rigidities and partial viewpoints of men organized in normal bureaucratic patterns."

"Planning and the Management Information System," by Jonathan A. Cunitz and Ronald B. Lee, examines information systems in a period of rapid change and analyzes their importance in enabling top management to appraise thoroughly both the current and the expected planning environments. The authors point out that planning must reconsider its goals more frequently than in the past. To do this, it is imperative that the information system, whatever form it may take, provide reliable information for policy making and the setting of goals.

The tools and techniques of planning have increased and become more sophisticated since World War II. Mary F. Arnold, in "Use of Management Tools in Health Planning," points out the difficulty of using some of the tools which require rigid quantification and calls for clear specification of objectives. She illustrates how some of the problems that arise in the use of the new tools and techniques lie in the manner in which they are used.

PPBS has been a catchword since the middle 1960's. It has received increasing attention by the federal government, which has taken the initiative in urging the use of PPBS at other levels of government. The influence of federal funding of state and local government projects provides encouragement and incentive to the states and cities to follow recommendations from Washington in matters of this character. Because PPBS has not been fully understood at the state and local levels, and because it promises much greater use in the future, four articles have been selected relating to PPBS, each with a different focus. The first of the PPBS articles, by Samuel M. Greenhouse, "The Planning-Programming-Budgeting System: Rationale, Language, and Idea-Relationships," in a sense provides background for the other three. This article deals with basic concepts, particularly that of accountability and language, in an effort to make PPBS more understandable to the manager with limited knowledge of this approach to planning. The second of the four articles, "PPBS in Fairfax County: A Practical Experience," by Robert A. Luther, outlines some of the problems faced by counties in many parts of the country due to changing environmental factors and the approach taken to these problems in one such county through the use of PPBS.

The third article, by William M. Capron, "PPBS Re-examined—PPB and State Budgeting," takes up the question of whether state governments should follow the lead of the federal government in introducing planning-programming-budgeting. The author discusses the extent to which PPBS is applicable and advantageous to state government and expresses the view that one of the virtues of PPBS is the encouragement and opportunity it gives to innovation.

The last selection dealing with PPBS is "PPB: The View from the States," by Allen Schick. Schick discusses the experience of various states in instituting PPBS and claims that the strategies used by many of the states were self-defeating because of inadequate integration of planning and budgeting. He shows that in states that "took PPB seriously and furnished PPB with resources and support commensurate with the difficulties that had to be surmounted," PPBS was successfully implemented.

"Planning for Manpower Utilization," by Burckhardt Wenzel, speaks of determinants, internal and external, which affect manpower utilization in the private sector. It would appear that there are also many external determinants in the public sector, perhaps even more than in private industry.

Disenchantment of many citizens with the cost of government and its performance can easily be translated into decreasing appropriations or increased difficulty in financing. One cannot plan for manpower utilization without regard to objectives. A public-supported agency is forced to predict probable developments and base its planning and budgeting on these predictions. Rapidly changing political and economic conditions can radically change the most carefully planned operation or project, requiring changes in plans and priorities of a far-reaching nature. The last article in this section, by Clarence C. Sherwood, "Issues in Measuring Results of Action Programs," deals with the all-important problem of evaluating the performance of social action programs. While admitting a general lack of demand for "a hard accounting of the effects of social interventions" in the past, the author believes that more and better evaluation studies of social action programs are now required to provide the quality of accountability that legislatures and the public expect as well as to form a base for better planning in the future.

9. Nature of Planning and Plans*

Robert G. Murdick

UNIVERSALITY OF PLANNING

Plans are the means by which objectives are ultimately achieved. Planning, as the term is usually understood, is carried out daily by almost every human being. In our personal life we think of certain things we must do for the coming day, for this week, or for this month. We do not randomly make decisions for our next action after we have just completed our current activity. In general, human beings seek goals and objectives within some conceived time limits, not by cut-and-try processes or random motions, but usually by thinking in advance of acting.

We plan our personal activities and affairs most often in an informal way without usually documenting the plan. In business, the professions, or governmental administration, planning, planning is more thorough, more complex, and more formal. Risks and gains are relatively large. The consequences of plans of an executive or leadership group may affect the lives of many people. It is in these areas that good planning is highly important. Therefore, the theory and techniques of executive planning deserve careful study.

WHAT IS "PLANNING"?

Concepts of Planning

Planning is a process. Planning is concerned with the future, but planning is not the same as forecasting. "Planning is intellectual in nature; it is mental work. Reflective thinking is required; imagination and foresight are extremely helpful."[1]

Planning, it is generally agreed, depends upon the selecting and relating of "facts." Facts are objective, verifiable objectively, and measurable. But, facts as used by people depend upon people's perception of facts. It is in the process of this perception that facts become different things to different people. Psychologists today have proposed that there is no fixed correlation between data in the environment of the perceiver and data as they are perceived. Thus, attitudes, beliefs, sentiments, and values are treated as facts upon which the planning process is structured.

The planning process also is structured upon a sequence of decisions extending into the future. How closely planning is related to decision

---

*From *Advanced Management Journal*, Vol. 30, No. 4 (October, 1965), 36–46. Reprinted by permission.
[1] George R. Terry, *Principles of Management* (3rd Ed., Homewood, Illinois: Richard D. Irwin, Inc., 1960), p. 123.

making depends mainly upon the definition of decision making. If an individual concludes that he likes milk better than coffee, is this a decision? If we are to attempt to construct a logical theory of planning, we would not call the process by which we arrived at this conclusion a decision-making process. It is rather a crystallization of a belief, a recognition of a sensory discrimination, or at most, an evaluation.

Decision making must represent a choice of future actions. One author defines "decision" as follows: "We shall think of a decision as a course of action chosen by the decider as the most effective means at his disposal for achieving the goals or goal he is currently emphasizing—for solving the problem that is bothering him."[2] If planning consists of creating alternative courses of action for the future, then we conclude that decision-making is an evaluation and selection process which terminates a phase of planning and eventually the complete planning process. Since "decide" is derived from the Latin meaning to "cut off," the concept of decision making as the process of rational evaluation terminating in selection of one of two or more alternatives appears to be reasonable.

How, then, for the purpose of scientific inquiry, do we distinguish planning from decision-making since both relate to future action? First, we note from what we have said above that decision-making is basically the termination of an evaluation and selection procedure. Decision making results in a course of action, but a specified time is not necessarily involved. Planning is a much more comprehensive process. It consists of establishing objectives, determining various (and possibly numerous) lines of action to achieve the objectives, determining decision points through the pattern of alternative actions, and, finally, selecting a single primary pattern for action based upon sequential decisions and a decision among total possible patterns of action. Further, timing of action is a necessary requisite of planning. Planning may also include establishing a list of plans and their priority. The highest ranked plan is considered to be the plan which stipulates the action. Before the first ranked plan is put into action, however, conditions may have changed so that an alternate plan will be substituted instead. We can see that planning involves complex relationships among decisions.

From the above discussion, we may now define planning as follows:

Planning is a conscious intellectual process characterized by (1) identification of a need or reflection of a stimulus, (2) accumulation of information, (3) relating of bits of information and beliefs, (4) establishing objectives, (5) establishing premises, (6) forecasting future conditions, (7) structuring alternative chains of actions based upon sequential decisions, (8) ranking or selecting total plans which will achieve the best

[2] Manley Howe Jones, *Executive Decision Making* (Homewood, Illinois: Richard D. Irwin, Inc., 1957), p. 5.

balance of ultimate objective and subsidiary objectives, (9) establishing policies and (10) establishing standards and means for measurement of adherence to the plan of action.

Types of Planning

Since planning may apply to practically any activity, it will be useful for analysis to determine the basic types of planning. We find that there are six main classifications of planning.[3]

One type of planning is physical planning. Physical planning deals with spatial arrangements of objects. Office layout planning, city layout planning, building location, and equipment location are examples. While other considerations may enter into physical planning, this type of planning is distinguished by its primary objective of spatial arrangement.

Organizational planning is concerned with the grouping of activities, development of a pattern or structure of working relationships among people in the enterprise, establishment of channels of communication and lines of authority, staffing of positions in the organization, and development of the people.

Process planning has as its major objective the development of a method or process which may be required. The process might be a manufacturing method, a procedure for operating a chemical plant, or a procedure for firing a satellite into space. Process planning might be thought of as operations planning. It is concerned primarily with sequences of motions, rather than arrangements of things or relationships among people. Physical distribution of goods might be considered mainly process planning although considerations of spatial planning, organizational planning, and financial planning are interwoven.

Financial planning, like the previous classifications, may occur in nearly a pure form or in combination with other types of planning. Financial planning is concerned only with obtaining the right amount of money at the right time, the management of money available so that it does not lie idle, the investment of money in terms of risk-return ratios, and the preservation of money from waste and other forms of loss. In short, financial planning is directed towards providing a service in terms of dollars to other people, parts of an organization, or the organization as a whole. Financial plans, in other than purely financial institutions or estate management, are usually closely tied in with other functional plans of an organization.

Functional planning is directed towards a major type of work which the organization carries out, usually on a continuing basis. For example,

3 See also George R. Terry, *Principles of Management* (3rd Ed., Homewood, Illinois: Richard D. Irwin, Inc., 1960), p. 130.

in an industrial firm, major functions are marketing, manufacturing, and engineering. Functioning planning represents a slice of physical, organizational, and financial planning applied to functional objectives.

General planning is total planning. It is the master planning for the firm, institution, or organization as a whole. It is the summation and integration of functional plans in another sense. General planning is a combination of all four preceding types of planning. General planning is the process by means of which the organization adapts to its environment in time to insure its existence. General planning solves and prevents present and future problems, internal and external in nature.

WHAT IS A "PLAN"?
Definition of a Plan

A plan is a predetermined course of action over a specified period of time which represents a projected response to an anticipated environment in order to accomplish a specific set of adaptive objectives. Since a plan describes a course of action, it must provide answers to the questions of what, when, how, where, and who. The details of the course of action may or may not be spelled out in a plan. The plan may consist of a bare outline of the course of action to be taken. This outline may be filled in by others than the original planners and at a later time. "A plan is nothing more than an ordered sequence of events (or activities) necessary to achieve a stated objective. To be complete, this ordered sequence of events must show *all* significant interrelationships that exist among those events beyond simple sequence."[4]

Whereas planning is a process, the immediate result is an entity, namely the plan. The plan is intended to be an intermediate event between the planning process and the implementation process. If the plan is not implemented, the plan becomes the end result (a somewhat sterile result, perhaps) rather than an intermediate event. "All plans have a common purpose: the forecasting, programming, and coordination of a logical sequence of events, which, if successful, will accomplish the commander's mission."[5]

What if several over-all "plans" are developed, but only one is considered feasible? Are the rejected "plans" which do not represent the action to be taken really as plans? For the purpose of definition, they should be included within the meaning of plan on the basis that they outline a course of action. This idea of plans which are never put into effect is common to military operations. A vigilant country during peace time will have available plans defining action to be taken in case of assumed

[4] *Summary Report, Phase 1*, Special Projects Office, Bureau of Naval Weapons, Dept. of the Navy, July, 1958, p. 3.

[5] Colonel Jack D. Nicholas et al., *The Joint and Combined Staff Officer's Manual* (Harrisburg, Pa.: Stackpole Press, 1959), p. 105.

threatening events. As conditions change, such plans will become obsolete and new plans must be developed. Yet we would certainly consider the discarded outlines for action "plans" even though they are not put into effect.

The view is sometimes taken that "no plan" is also a plan. By definition, however, a plan is a predetermined course of action over a period of time. If action is not predetermined for some specified time in the future, then *ad hoc* decisions cannot be said to constitute a plan.

Plans and Forecasts

While forecasts are necessary for the process of planning, a forecast does not constitute a plan. A forecast is a prediction of anticipated future external events. Normally, forecasts of future conditions are first made without considering the effect or consequences of the action to be taken by the planner. It may be that the action prescribed by the plan will have only an infinitesimal effect on the environment forecasted. On the other hand, revised forecasts may have to be made when the effects of alternative plans are considered. In the latter case, plans may have to be revised in the light of revised forecasts and an alternative process employed until a stable point is reached.

Plans are concerned with lines of action to be taken by the executor of the plans, while forecasts are passive in that they are purely predictive. Plans are predictive in that the course of action laid out represents a prediction of future action by the executor of the plans. Thus, plans consist of specified courses of action for the future and, in a sense, represent a forecast of the executor's actions. Forecasting predicts environmental conditions at future times based upon the actions, nature, external actors in the environment, and the effector of the plans.

Forecasts are derived from facts, assumptions, creativity and deduction. In turn, forecasts become assumptions upon which the plans are based. Forecasts and plans, while distinct, will often interact with each other. Plans may be such that they will, when implemented, affect the environment in which they act so that the forecast needs to be revised in this light. Under a revised forecast the plan may need revision. This dynamic relationship is typical of planning where conflicting participants are acting.

Formal, Written, and Undocumented Plans

A proposed sequence of actions may be set down in a highly formalized and systematic manner. The more complex the plan, the more important that the plan be expressed in such a formal manner. Otherwise, for complex plans, part of the plan may be forgotten or may be changed unknowingly, or may lack many other characteristics necessary for a plan to be effective. If a complex plan loses form and changes because it cannot be recalled by those implementing it, it is doubtful if it can truly be identified as a plan.

Plans may be written out in general terms and in an incomplete and informal fashion. Such plans may be in the form of notes or memoranda. For simple plans, this may be adequate to define the course of action.

For even simpler, short range plans, particularly those of individuals in their everyday activities outside of business, plans may not be written down at all. Because of single objectives involved in each plan and because of few alternative courses of actions available at decision points, these plans can be easily stored in the memory. Yet the courses of action are presumed to be formulated mentally in a clear manner based upon forecast conditions, and these undocumented courses may represent true plans.

Objectives, Goals, Events, Milestones, and Missions

Part of the planning process is the establishment of objectives and goals. Hence part of the plan is the statement or recognition of specific objectives and goals. For purposes of definition, we will take "objective" to mean the ultimate end result which is to be accomplished by the overall plan over a specified period of time. The objective represents a state or condition which we desire to exist when the plan has been completely implemented. The objective may be a rather complex statement describing the desired situation. For example, a business objective may be to achieve a certain sales volume at a specified future time, to make its name known to a percent of the population, to be a leader in its field, and to expand its product line. The objective may be considered, in discrete terms, to represent a set of goals to be achieved.

Objectives may be either tangible or intangible. A tangible objective may be the development and construction of a nuclear reactor, a space vehicle, or a chemical plant. On the other hand, an intangible objective might be the achievement of a certain market position, an established brand image, a new social security system, or a favorable balance of world power. Whatever the objective is, it must be completely defined and identified with a point in time in order that a meaningful plan may be developed.

A goal is defined as an intermediate result to be achieved by a certain time as part of the grand plan. A plan can therefore have many goals. For large engineering projects employing modern management planning techniques, goals are usually called "events" or "milestones." The latter term, in particular, provides the flavor of meaning to the term 'goals" as we will use it to distinguish it from "objective." "Event" emphasizes the occurrence of a situation in the real world.

The word "mission" is sometimes used to denote "objective." The military writers have adopted this term to designate various assignments of people or special projects. In fact, according to some reports, it has been stated that inanimate objects have "missions." A mission is, according to the dictionary, a sending forth, a group of persons or envoy sent to perform some task, or an errand or commission. A mission may be considered to be a statement of a task and its objective assigned to an individual or group of people.

Policies, Regulations, Procedures, and Methods

Is a policy a plan or only part of a plan? The view we take here is that a policy is *not* a plan. A plan is directed toward achievement of specific objectives over a specified period of time. A policy is a guide which delimits action but does not specify time. It is open-ended in that it is not a plan of action leading to specific objectives over a given period of time; rather, policies are timeless. This view has been stated simply: "A policy is not a plan but a guiding cannon of interest."[6]

A policy is a definition of common purposes of an organization which establishes guidelines and limits for discretionary action by individuals responsible for implementing over-all plans. Policies may be written or implied. Policies may be identified by the following criteria:

1. Does it permit discretionary action and exercise of good judgment?

2. Are the provisions positive but permissive within clearly defined limits so that exceptions need not be made in implementing over-all plans?

3. Is it timeless? That is, does apply without any specification of how long it is to be in force?

Sometimes, for the sake of achieving uniformity of action in some area, an organization may issue a directive policy. A directive policy states a specific obligatory course of action which does not require interpretation by those who may be called upon to implement it. Despite the greater specificity, the directive policy is not a plan since it is designed to limit a process, not to reach a specific goal within a specific time.

Some organizations are guided by "regulations." When a question arises as to what should be done or how to do something, we would look in a book of regulations. Regulations may be policies which must guide actions. Some regulations constitute plans since they define sequences of actions or methods for achieving objectives within a limited time period.

Procedures, as the term is commonly understood, are plans. A procedure is a series of detailed steps telling how to accomplish a task or reach a goal contingent upon the decision being made to accomplish the

---

[6] John G. Glover, *Fundamentals of Professional Management* (New York: Republic Book Company, Inc., 1954), p. 71.

particular task or goal. Thus procedures are really subplans to larger plans. Procedures, because of their detailed nature, are ordinarily written down and made available to those who may use them. Actually, for a procedure to be a plan according to our definition, the procedure must be one that is accomplished within a specified time period once it has been started.

A "method" describes the process of performing one step of a procedure in terms of facilities, manpower and time available. Since a method describes an action thought out in advance, a method may be considered to be a plan of action. Actually, it is a sub-plan of a procedure.

In summary, a plan may consist of many sub-plans with different degrees of detail. Policies, which are necessary for the accomplishment of a series of plans, are important to the accomplishment of plans. They are a part of the plans, but they are not plans or subplans themselves. Procedures and methods, on the other hand, constitute detailed plans which are usually part of general plans. The general plan provides the time element for the procedure or method. A distinguishing feature of a plan is that a definite time limit is involved.

Tactics and Strategies

There are other terms in common use which relate to a plan and which need to be examined. Tactics represent a short-range plan for operations where an element of conflict is involved. Tactics represent a plan which has emphasis on counter actions of other players or actors in the environment. Tactics are adroit devices for achieving a goal. Thus tactics represent a special type of short-range plan.

The term "strategy" is founded upon military science which still has the greatest claim to the concept. Strategy in the military sense means "the art of the general" and is derived from the Greek *strategos* formed from *stratos* (army) and *agein* (to lead). In the military sense, strategy is the overriding long-range plan. Strategy in the military sense is said to have direction, compass point, or intent. This direction is known as the "Strategic Concept."

Shelling gives the most elegant discussion of the meaning of strategy:

Among diverse theories of conflict—corresponding to the diverse meanings of the word "conflict"—a main dividing line is between those that treat conflict as a pathological state and seek its causes and treatment, and those that take conflict for granted and study the behavior associated with it. Among the latter there is a further division between those that examine the participants in a conflict in all their complexity—with regard to both "rational" and "irrational" behavior, conscious and unconscious, and to motivations as well as to calculations—and those that focus on the more rational, conscious artful kind of behavior. Crudely speaking, the latter treat conflict as a kind of contest, in which the participants are trying to "win." A study of conscious, intelligent, sophisticated conflict behavior—of successful behavior—is like a search for rules of "correct" behavior in a contest winning sense.

We can call this field of study the "strategy of conflict."[7]

A recent definition of strategy has been developed in the theory of games, and while different authors give slightly different flavors to the term, their meanings are essentially the same. For example, John D. McDonald writes:

The strategical situation in game theory lies in the interaction between two or more persons, each of whose actions is based on an expectation concerning the actions of others over whom he has no control. The outcome is dependent upon the personal moves of the participants. The policy followed in making these moves is the strategy.[8]

W. J. Baumol places considerable emphasis on the rules involved:

The strategy really becomes an extensive book of rules indicating what the player intends to do, in every contingency, from the beginning of the game to the end. Thus the strategy commits the player to an entire sequence of moves which is contingent in a fully specified manner upon what is done by the other player.[9]

For the purpose of our definition here, strategy includes the element of sophisticated conflict behavior. It includes a set of interrelated decisions. It includes a temporal dimension which is not included in game theory. Strategy, while long range, is flexible in that it is continually reviewed in terms of new information so it represents sequential decision-making. Thus strategy may be considered a long-range plan or pattern of action by means of which the planner seeks to optimize achievement of his goals within a field of mutually conflicting and cooperating participants and varying unknown states of nature. It is a particular type of plan.

Programs

The word "program" is often used in connection with the concept of plan. In engineering development work, the term PERT, or Program Evaluation Review Technique, appears. According to a description of programming by a spokesman in the POLARIS project, "The POLARIS Management Sequence consists of three principal phases; definition of

[7] Thomas C. Schelling, *The Strategy of Conflict* (Cambridge, Mass.: Harvard University Press, 1960) p. 3.

[8] John D. McDonald, *Strategy in Poker, Business and War* (New York: W. W. Norton & Co. Inc., 1955), p. 16.

[9] William J. Baumol, *Economic Theory and Operations Analysis* (Englewood Cliffs, N.J.: Prentice-Hall, Inc., 1961), p. 359.

program objectives, program planning and implementation, and program evaluation."[10] The *POLARIS Management* publication goes on to say:

They (program management plans) present specific tasks, responsibilities, and key milestones within a logical structure deriving from the total program objectives; establish a uniform basis for performance reporting in the Special Projects Management Center; provide a common frame of reference for presenting effects (of performance facts on planned effort) in major areas of effort; and provide a basis for decision making. They are an official expression of top level and branch level planning.[11]

PERT was developed to minimize and control the time for large projects. One of its basic attributes is the statistical estimates of time for completion of each event and for the entire project.

It appears from a study of the literature of planning for research, development, and engineering projects that a program in this context may be a plan which is quite detailed, is characterized by defining the interrelationships of goals in terms of sequence and timing, and involves concurrent networks of actions which define times at which major decisions must be made. Yet, this is not always the case. For example, R. K. Stolz writes: "*Programming* develops specific research objectives and guidelines that make possible sound decisions on project selection. It defines the fields that should be studied and the emphasis that should be placed on the different kinds of research within each field."[12] If the output of programming is assumed to be a program, then a program consists of objectives and outlines for achieving these objectives.

Another form of "program" is the output of a linear programming model. Linear programming is used to help solve problems where limited resources are specified in order to obtain a particular objective such as least cost, least time, or highest profit. While linear programming is problem-solving rather than planning, the question might be raised as to whether the outcome, a proposed course of action, is a plan. In general, the answer is that it is *not* a plan. While a course of action is specified, the timing of action is not. Even when a minimum-time problem is solved, the result is not a plan, since no starting and ending date or interval of time for accomplishment of the action appears in the representation of the result.

In administrative fields, "program" may designate a large-scale course of action or set of integrated projects for achieving a major objective.

[10] Special Projects Office, Dept. of the Navy, *POLARIS Management* (Washington, D.C.: U.S. Government Printing Office), Rev. Feb., 1961, p. 4.

[11] *Ibid.*, p. 10.

[12] Robert K. Stolz, "Planning—Key to Research Success," *Harvard Business Review*, May-June, 1957.

For example, in the Report of the President's Commission on National Goals (1960) the Commission refers in its letter of transmittal to the Report as an outline of coordinated national policies and *programs*. However, in the Report itself, no time schedules are given and no deadlines for completion of action are mentioned. The sub-title of the popular publication of the Report does generalize the time aspect—"Programs for Action in the Sixties." This is so vague that we could not deduce that a program as used in this context must include a schedule.

A less technical but common use of the word program occurs in the arts, entertainment, and sports worlds. The program is a description of events which will take place at a given time. Often additional information is included in the program such as the characters involved, location, and starting time. Usually, the termination time is not specified.

In attempting to develop the theory of management, it is important that terms be clearly defined. We find that the word "program" is used with quite variable meanings by people engaged in executive planning. The problem is to determine whether "program" should be identified as synonymous with "plan" or it should have a different meaning. In the final analysis, this can only be an arbitrary choice. We believe that a commonly used term is desirable to describe courses of action which are interrelated but which have not been scheduled. We will therefore, assign this meaning to "program." A plan may then be considered to be a (time) scheduled program.

Types of Plans

Plans may be categorized as single use, repeat, standing, standby, or rejected. The single-use plan is one that serves a particular purpose and is never used again. In a rapidly changing environment, there will be many single-use plans designed to achieve objectives arising from new problems. A repeat plan is used under more stable conditions or under parallel conditions. For example, a company may develop a recruiting plan. Whenever it is necessary to recruit a number of professional people as the firm expands, it puts its recruiting plan into effect. Suppose that a company's sales force is geographically decentralized. A new sales plan may be developed which is to be put into effect in each territory. Thus the plan is repeated in a parallel rather than series time sequence.

The standing plan is a repeat plan but one that automatically goes into effect. Standing plans are best exemplified by the procedures spelled out in a business firm's operating manual. Thus the operating manual may specify a plan for processing grievances. Each step of the process and the maximum time allowed for each step would be given. Whenever a grievance is initiated by an employee, the plan becomes effective automatically. In the case of the repeat plan, a decision must be made each time as to whether to put the plan into effect. The repeat plan must be triggered off by someone in authority; it is not put into operation each time automatically.

As for the standby plan, we could argue that all standby plans are part of the total plan. Yet, since the standby plan is a parallel plan to accomplish the same objective as the chosen plan, and since it may be a general plan itself, it appears advisable to distinguish it for analytical reasons. The standby plan may become the operative plan if (1) conditions change so that the standby plan is more appropriate or (2) if the operative plan appears inadequate during testing or beginning of operations.

Actually, the standby plan may be identical to the operative plan up to a certain point. Therefore, we may substitute the standby plan for the operative plan with no difficulty at any time before the two diverge.

Characteristics of a Plan

A plan may be described in terms of a number of characteristics. These characteristics describe both the plan itself and considerations involved in its formulation. The characteristics of a plan are listed below.[13]

1. Scope
2. Complexity
3. Depth
4. Organizational level or preparation
5. Organizational level at which plan is to apply
6. Environment in which plan is made
7. Environment in which plan will be operative
8. Resources (men, money, materials, time) involved in the plan
9. Forward time or projection into the future
10. Timing of the plan (when it will start)
11. Decision points
12. Certainty, risk, and uncertainty involved in the premises
13. Balance
14. Integration
15. Value of the plan
16. Cost of the planning process
17. Authorship
18. Acceptance
19. Ease of implementation
20. Ease of control
21. Measurement—features.

[13] See also Ralph C. Davis, *The Fundamentals of Top Management* (New York: Harper, 1951), pp. 46–51, and Preston P. LeBreton and Dale A. Henning, *Planning Theory* (Englewood Cliffs, N.J.: Prentice-Hall, Inc., 1951), p. 23.

The development of a set of characteristics of a plan is essential to the development of a science of planning. First of all, such characteristics allow us to define a plan to a far greater extent than is possible on the basis of popular usage in business publications. Secondly, such characteristics are valuable not only for theoretical reasons, but for practical reasons in the process of planning. For example, in the planning process, the characteristics provide a checklist to insure that the plan is as complete as is desired. We may check the completed plan to make sure that each quantitative characteristic is present in the desired amount or to the desired degree. Clear definition of the elements which make up a plan cannot help but lead to better planning by the serious manager.

CONCLUSION

A basic characteristic of scientific method is the initial definition of terms to be used and classification of knowledge concerning these terms. In the area of planning, there is a voluminous body of literature, but little attempt has been made to establish a foundation of understanding for the purpose of inquiry and communication. The above discussion is intended to stimulate thinking about basic concepts of planning and plans rather than offer the ultimate answer.

10. Programming: Its Role in Organization Theory*
Edward A. Lehan

The term "program" has developed as a descriptive symbol and as a unit of policy analysis. The word has a protean or rubbery quality. It is applied without much discrimination to both complex and simple activities—to the trivial as well as the sublime. The Space Program illustrates one end of the scale; at the other, systematic efforts to wash walls or replace light bulbs in a city hall is another illustration.

Programs are ubiquitous. Interest groups demand them; politicians put them forward; administrators push them along. Almost any form of public administration can be called a "program" without violating anyone's sense of semantic fitness. The word seems now completely interchangeable with the concepts of "function," "service," and "activity." It is increasingly preferred in place of organizational concepts such as department, division, bureau, and section, which seem to convey unfashionable nuances of bureaucratic power and rigidity. It has an anti-institutional flavor about it, and suggests openness, dynamism, purpose, and progress. Best of all, it seems to imply results. Such a powerful abstraction deserves careful study—and, one might add, much more discriminating use.

The techniques of PERT, simulation, linear programming, etc., came into vogue as programming aids. The promise of these specialized procedures called forth the broader processes of PPBS and systems analysis, which provide more generalized approaches to program identification and analysis. Yet despite this proliferation of techniques, one senses that the lack of a specific or technical meaning for the term "program" hinders attempts to put the use of public power on a more solid base of evidence and logic. This paper explores this taxonomic problem, then turns to procedural aspects of programming.

DUBIOUS VALUE OF PROGRAM STRUCTURE

As experience has accumulated in the PPBS movement, we are learning that the idea of a rather universally valid identification scheme, or program structure, is a relatively unproductive technique, drawing away energy from the crucial work of policy analysis and stirring unnecessary antagonism among affected interests. At the same time, pressure for comprehensiveness in program identification leads to the formulation of "end product summaries" which must be abstract enough to cover logically the diversity of subsumed activities.

* From *Connecticut Government*, Vol. 25, No. 3 (Spring, 1972), 6–8. Reprinted by permission.

Many questions ensue, such as: Shall we subsume street lighting under the safety or transportation symbol? Is a police effort to improve its community relations a "program," or merely another specialized police service? Does vice squad activity belong under crime prevention or crime investigation? Comprehensive formal assignment of all activities to program summaries is of dubious value to an analyst who is working on a specific problem and needs flexibility to draw program boundries to fit the contours of his analysis.

Furthermore, recognizing that "the medium may be the message," a program structure, by its neat hierarchical arrangement of mono-value categories, unwittingly suggests program autonomy, integrity, and productivity. Experienced analysts know that this façade of logic serves to hide rather than highlight the interdependence, contradictions, and ineffectiveness normally rife in any vigorous government of general jurisdiction.

Finally, the development of a comprehensive program structure, especially if it is employed for budget control, and thus has many categories which include inputs from disparate agencies, will probably cause more accounting maintenance trouble than it's worth. Policing budget codes is a significant problem everywhere, particularly in jurisdictions having program titles concocted by central staff units of which line agency coding clerks and their superiors have little true understanding (or sympathy).

A flexible, rather ad hoc, approach to program identification is preferable. It reduces the amount of time going into classification for its own sake—precious time which would be better spent on program analysis. Moreover, it has the additional value of associating program identification with management problem-solving rather than accounting and financial administration.

PROGRAM CRITERIA

Two criteria may be used to give the program concept a restricted or technical meaning. First, it is clear that we need a term which permits us to handle a dimension of policy, a goal, a concern, or a problem which cuts across organizational lines. Under this division of semantic labor, terms such as "function," "service," "activity," etc., can then be employed exclusively for intra-organization operations.

One need only scan the list of current day problems, drugs, alcohol, crime, high medical costs, pollution, social disorganization, etc., to know that no single agency can effectively cope with any truly important problem. Yet agency behavior belies this. Each is vested in the scheme of things; each tries to suboptimize in its corner of the market. All of us must agree that reducing the power of vested interests over the alloca-

95

tion of resources is a master problem for government at all levels. We must also agree that the presumed power of the program concept to liberate policy and procedure from existing political and bureaucratic perspectives is the main source of its appeal.

Secondly, a group of activities, to win designation as a program, should have operations based on critical relationships. For example, a municipal rodent control campaign, if in involves, as it normally would, a multiagency approach, the first criteria, may qualify as a program if its components are also justified by an assumed causal relationship between the size of the food supply and the size of the rodent population. (Beyond this principle lies the master concept of natural balance, a rat infestation being a symptom of an imbalance of natural forces.) On the other hand, the campaign would not qualify as a "program" if it were a mere extermination service as there would be no change in a casual variable.

TECHNIQUE OF CROSS-CLASSIFICATION

PPBS and system analysis have focused our attention on the technique of "cross-classification." Cross-classification is used to bring together data on a single program which may be scattered among several jurisdictions or organizational units. This technique is also useful in dealing with a most intractable problem, the problem that almost all programs serve more than one value or goal. This circumtsance is, of course, a major stumbling block for implementation of the PPB system if its theoreticians insist on mono-value or single-goal program structures.

It seems much more profitable to recognize the multidimensions of programs and use cross-classification as a method of facilitating insight and understanding. For example, a city's budget, normally divided into the functional classes of general government, public safety, community development, health, education, welfare, and recreation, could be cross-classified by geography within functions, and aggregated for all functions by district. Would not such a cross-classified budget produce different patterns of expenditure than one based on functions alone?

Cross-classification permits policy makers and recommenders to explore several dimensions of the expenditure pattern, highlighting and emphasizing the relationships which are always potentially and actually present in public programs. For example, a park budget could be classified as serving recreation, education, and crime prevention. Recreation can be recognized as play, social work, and preventor of juvenile delinquency. Day care, a new emerging public function, can be classed as education, social service, and recreation. Cross-classifications, by attaching different verbal symbols to the same expenditure pattern, cannot fail to develop wider and deeper understanding of the nature and linkage of public policies.

It is also well to bear in mind that each program has its own unique presentation requirements which will likely change from year to year. In this connection, standardization of cost centers and their stability over the years for the sake of comparability is certainly important, but should not be an overriding consideration. It is much more important to be able to focus policymaking attention on what are thought to be the significant problems in each program. In some years, this may mean a more or less extensive breakdown of program titles, depending upon the level of abstraction needed to do justice to the issues.

DETERMINING CAUSAL RELATIONSHIPS

As suggested previously, operations should be justified by causal relationship in order to qualify as a program; otherwise it should be called a service or activity. It could be said that services such as snow removal, street cleaning, and waste collection attack some condition in order to abolish it. In a sense this is true, but in a larger sense, each of these efforts abates a condition almost on its own terms. The goals of these operations are narrowly defined: bare pavements and waste removal.

It is, of course, proper to attempt to rationalize methods of achieving these ends in the manner of classic management analysis. However, it is the virtue of the systems approach to seek not only better means, but a restatement of the ends themselves. A search for critical relationships can radically reorder the ends and means of an operation. In the waste collection example, the critical principle might well be the "conservation of energy" with "resource recycling" the key program identification.

The well known Coleman Report on the inequality of educational opportunity provided insight into a number of important correlations in the troubled field of education. There were some negative findings. Certain sacred cows, such as quality of facilities and the teacher-pupil ratio, were not found to be significantly related to pupil achievement. In addition, schools on the whole were found to be dependent rather than independent variables in the face of neighborhood, class, and family background factors. On the positive side, the verbal facility score of teachers related positively to pupil achievement. Correlations such as these are the raw material of programming. Correlations and principles help establish boundary lines, validate means, and set goals. Best of all, we can study effects if the underlying principles of a program are well developed analytically.

Turning to the field of public safety for a last example of the power of critical relationships to illuminate the nature of operations, we note that large sums are spent on apprehension of suspected criminals in every city and state. There is no significant causal principle justifying this great effort. However, let us introduce into the situation, as a principle, the apparent tautology that most crimes are committed by criminals, i.e., by persons who have been apprehended before. Does not the principle of recidivism thus neatly nullify the apprehension effort, robbing it of any practical significance? Beyond recidivism lies the profound relationship which exists between family disorganization and criminal tendencies. What does the exploration of these principles mean for the distribution of funds between police and penal operations—or social welfare planning?

PROCEDURAL ASPECTS OF PROGRAMMING

While the key problems in programming will always be on the conceptual side because of the policy implications of program definition, the procedural side must not be overlooked. The country is inundated with public services which are weak in conception, but even weaker in practice. Procedural breakdowns and wasteful delivery systems are plentiful in many cities, particularly in the crucial health, education, and welfare functions. Program implementation is sure the Achilles heel of programming, particularly if a true program defines a concern, a goal, or a policy dimension which rides over organizational lines. Can program coordination be achieved without consolidating the organizational units which are the means of achievement?

The answer is a qualified yes, provided (1) the program is carefully documented and updated, (2) the document evolves in close consultation with those agency leaders who are expected to furnish the means of achievement, and (3) a coordinator is specifically assigned to monitor the program for the chief executive.

Once this writer sought to expand Hartford's effort to enforce codes concerning backyard conditions, then exclusively the province of health inspectors. Without observance of these three rules, the leader of Hartford's waste collection unit was asked to devise a checklist-type form to identify backyard conditions needing correction, the form to be used by the men who carry out barrels from yards to the curb for collection. As the men visited every yard weekly, it seemed a "natural" to give them a simple form to gather information on rats, dilapidated sheds, litter, abandoned cars, broken windows, etc. The men were enthusiastic and flooded us with data. Within a few days the referral system collapsed, however, because the health department would not accept the information at face value, but insisted on a de novo inspection, which could not be supplied without more manpower. Professional status and legal issues befogged this inter-agency experiment.

Trying again for a multi-agency approach at a later date, the writer asked for assignment of eight men from the waste collection unit, to be trained by health department inspectors to work with them to deliver waste collection services to code inspectors. This failed also because the men dropped their waste collection identification as soon as they could and were rejected by their fellows as "high-hat" inspectors.

Our next attempt at backyard sanitation involved a true program approach with a proper document, extensive consultation between "agency leaders," and a central staff program analyst and coordinator. This program, which had an educational rather than service goal, designed to alter tenant behavior, was judged a success—at least conditions changed while the pressure was on. Planned withdrawal of the pressure has been achieved and we are now watching to see if code violations, particularly in regard to rats, will build up to the pre-existing level. This effort also furnished a number of suggestive leads for further programming, illustrating the linkage between practice and new policy.

CONCLUSION

Programming has been stressed as a way of liberating policy and procedure from the weight of tradition, ignorance, and routine, a way of redirecting settled, and often resisting, organizational energies toward novel ends. The technique of cross-classification also has been emphasized—that is, the showing of the same expenditure under more than one title. Cross-classification multiplies angles of vision, yet permits us to maintain the clarity and familiarity of functions and organizational units. With this technique we can cut across traditional and legally prescribed perspectives to group and focus resources flexibly, without radically ordering administrative relationships or purchasing and accounting procedures. This is no small advantage.

This view pictures the program approach as a compensatory strategy, providing ways of overcoming the rigidities and partial viewpoints of men organized in normal bureaucratic patterns. Programming thus does not replace hierarchy or functional specialization as an organizing principle. However, it is also clear that programming, if applied, introduces more, not less, complexity into organizational forms. Neat lines of authority and responsibility will inevitably blur as information and decisions are based on viewpoints wider than those normally comprehended by any particular agency.

Yet despite the fact that programming and its supporting techniques are supposed to put the use of public power on a more solid base of evidence and logic, and thus may tend to strengthen established power in the end, there is a pronounced anti-institutional flavor hovering over the program approach. On the whole, this anti-institutional flavor should be nurtured. Facts and the product of scientific study are important, but the real measure and the future of the program approach lies in its capacity to develop value judgment. The advance of decision aids such as those associated with the planning/programming/budgeting system can greatly improve aesthetic processes merely because precision in describing policy choices sharpens up the values upon which decisions, in the last analysis, really turn.

11. Planning and the Management Information System*

Jonathan A. Cunitz and Ronald B. Lee

Science fiction readers have no doubt read the tale of the Earth space ship launched on a journey to a planet two light years away. The crew, with its biological processes suspended, expected the ship to reach the planet in 200 years, at which time they and their descendents would start a new civilization. But when the ship finally reached its destination, its crew discovered a city already 100 years old, founded by another group of Earth colonists who reached the planet in six months through later-discovered "time warp" space travel.

A little farfetched? Not at all. Similar events occur daily in present-day industry. Countless times an organizational group will embark upon a new venture while new technology will make their work obsolete before its completion. The solution to this predicament, as well as that of our space travelers, is coordinated planning based on mature, finely honed information.

WHY PLAN?

Planning is an essential factor leading to success in any competitive environment whether that environment be businesses competing against each other, or Government agencies competing for funding. Without necessarily limiting other benefits accruable from planning, it can contribute to more effective management in the following ways:

1. Planning can lend credibility in the future to decisions that have to be made today. By considering uncertainties during the decision-making process, managers attach greater reliability to the determined action.

2. Planning helps prevent premature technological obsolescence. The lead time required to accomplish tasks is often longer than phase changes in technology, not only for space exploration, but also in such fields as data processing, communications, and medicine.

3. Planning highlights obstacles to growth and prepares management to overcome them. It facilitates raising key issues before events close out alternatives and assures that such alternatives are properly considered.

4. Proper planning assures coordination of organizational elements toward consistent objectives. It helps an organization take advantage of the synergistic effect of people, elements, and systems working together. It is obviously more effective to work on one straight line toward

* From *The Federal Accountant*, September, 1970, pp. 55–64. Reprinted by permission.

one goal than on two divergent paths toward possibly incompatible objectives.

5. Planning encourages developers to design in adaptability to prevent irrevocable obsolescence. For example, third generation computer systems should be adaptable for future compatibility with fourth and fifth generation equipment.

6. Planning allows management to take advantage of the firm's long-range strengths. By planning the fullest exploitation of profitable products or services, top management can utilize its competitive advantage to the fullest.

Unfortunately, many of these planning potentials are overlooked through a natural but harmful desire for speedy, visible results from the planning process.

THE CHANGING PLANNING ENVIRONMENT

Planning, more than practically any other management activity, must be conducted in the flux of modern environment. Management cannot assume that the types of pressures both external and internal to the firm will remain the same, nor that present assumptions will be valid in five, ten or twenty years.

In projecting a firm's future products, its management must consider possible technological developments which might impinge upon any sector of its operation. In the space of only the last twenty years, significant strides have occurred in electronics, transportation, space exploration, construction, and manufacturing automation, just to name some of the more prominent fields. And all indications are that almost unlimited potential still exists for further development in these and other areas.

In addition to hardware developments, new management tools are now available for planning. Systems analysis, operations research, communications and information theory, decision theory, and heuristic computer programming provide new and imaginative approaches to solving dilemmas faced continuously by decision-makers.

The human resources available to the firm are also improving. Better education, better health, greater flexibility, and more diversified backgrounds all upgrade the quality of the human input into the black box of production.

Because of progress made in the past, planning must consider new goals from year to year. In athletics, a four-minute mile is no longer a realistic objective for an olympic champion. NASA scientists are no longer content to put an astronaut in orbit; they want him on the moon. At one point, the Post Office Department was fortunate for Boston mail to reach California at all; now that agency is focusing on overnight delivery for coast-to-coast mail.

Not only are these changes significant, but also is can be shown that the rate of environmental change is increasing. In the 2,500 years between King Solomon and George Washington, few changes in the manner of living and working could be observed. They both used the same means for communication, transportation, construction, and printing books. Yet, since the Industrial Revolution, dramatic changes have occurred in every phase of our lives and have placed paramount importance on the time element in the change process. Thus, the informed planner will ask not only what he can do to stimulate markets and influence the environment of the future, but how other markets and environmental factors will influence him.

ELEMENTS OF INTEGRATED PLANNING

An attack on the problems of the future environment can be made with three phalanxes (or elements) of integrated planning, that is, a managerial framework for analysis, systems and procedures, and methodologies and techniques. While in actual practice it is difficult to separate the activities of each of these areas, they probably can be defined exclusively. The information needs of one should not be confused with the information needs of another element, or of the integrated planning system as a whole.

Taking each element in turn, let's focus first on the framework for analysis. This is the set of forecasts, objectives, strategic plans, programs and budgets. These sub-elements, in varying degrees of sophistication and with varying emphasis, are necessary for all viable organizations.

Forecasts are eclectic assessments of the environment in which the organization must be successful and should cover the entire spectrum of activities in which the organization is engaged. For example, the Post Office Department is currently attempting to derive such exogenous forecasts as educational levels, degree of urbanization, and cost of available mail substitutes. Simultaneously, they are concentrating on future estimates of endogenous factors such as relevant skill composition, work-hour trends, productivity, and equipment technology.

The stated aims of any organization are reflected in its objectives. Recent experience in developing such goals for the $7 billion Postal Service showed that objectives should indicate priorities through a stated hierarchy, be as precise as possible, be succinct, be translatable into management programs and actions, and be clearly understood by management. Since the ultimate utility of objectives lies in their use by managers in guiding their decisions, it is important to eliminate any shortcomings in meeting these standards.

At the core of the integrated planning system are the strategic plans comprised of the milestones necessary to accomplish objectives. Plans

103

should be mutually compatible and all-inclusive of major programs, projects, studies, and activities to be undertaken by the organization. Individually, each plan should spell out functional responsibilities, tasks to be accomplished, methods to be employed, and deadlines to be met. These strategic plans are not only the extension of current operations, but are the embodiment of new ventures which alter the course of current practices.

An organization's programs quantify the resources required over a given time period to achieve planning goals. They should generally be organized around specific outputs and be relatable to specific plans. Experience in large organizations has shown that programs should encompass at least a five-year period; a shorter period limits the lead time available for obtaining funds, while too long a period generates too much uncertainty about resource availability.

The final component of planning's analytical framework is the budget. Without spending time on this well-exposed device, it should suffice to say that budgets serve the planning system as expressions of fiscal priority and as controls for resource allocations.

The second element of integrated planning is composed of systems and procedures. It is in this category that one finds the managerial structure, the program structure, functional planning processes, processes for budget justification, and review and analysis procedures. The results of neglect in this area are organizations whose approaches to management degenerate to handling sequential crises and whose executives rarely anticipate decision opportunities. In the Post Office Department, for example, processes are being designed at this very moment in four main areas of managerial consideration: productivity, products, investments, and logistics. These procedures must be designed and then redesigned. The manager of a large activity who can design the perfect organization or perfect procedure the first time probably has not been born. All managers must develop the "masculinity" to change. Good procedures will not spring Topsy-like from an organizational form one *assumes* incorporates all of the necessary lines of communications. The simplest method of determining procedural needs is to divide the organization into its major decision areas and flow-chart the process for identification and resolution of issues in those areas.

The third element of integrated planning is based on methodologies and techniques. There is no paucity of literature and expertise in these areas. Systems analysis, operations research, decision analysis, statistical sampling, and so forth have been written about almost to excess. They provide the means for injecting analytical adrenalin into the decision-making system.

DEPENDENCY ON THE MANAGEMENT INFORMATION SYSTEM

The not-so-remarkable fact underlying the potential success of integrated planning (and actually the point of this article) is its total dependency upon the organization's management information system. Not only does the information network support each separate element of planning, but it is vital to adhering the three elements together to form the core from which organizational progress can grow.

As a start, let's consider the derivation and interrelationships of the analytical planning framework. Again, this framework is composed of forecasts, objectives, strategic plans, programs and budgets. The supporting M.I.S. is designed around management needs in this framework, in contrast to the common situation of the framework being designed around existing information patterns.

It was mentioned earlier that a comprehensive forecasting system was being developed in the Post Office Department. For this sub-element of the framework, the Department relies on a diversity of information channels, many external to the agency. Population forecasts are based upon *Current Population Reports*; population density projections are derived from the *Statistical Abstract of the United States*; and levels of educational attainment are determined from the *U.S. Census of Population*.[1]

The hierarchy of departmental objectives is doubly dependent upon the M.I.S. Accurate information is needed first to establish realistic objectives. Then a reliable M.I.S. is required to convey those objectives to managers and assure their consistent and continuing consideration in the decision-making process. For example, an objective to reduce the average cost per mail delivery impinges upon decisions regarding mail vehicles, carrier productivity, wage rates, route scheduling, and other associated costs. An objective to reduce the average transaction cost at a post office lobby window influences decisions on clerk hours, window design, stamp manufacturing costs, and the types of services offered to the public. The M.I.S. is a necessity if managers intend to maximize the accomplishment of objectives through their decisions.

Strategic plans are likewise dependent upon the M.I.S. for their existence and usefulness. In particular, corporate planners need detailed information to develop their plans, to assure their compatibility, to assist their coordination, and to aid in their completion. If we again view the Postal Service, we see plans to expand the use of containerization. These plans were only formulated after significant data were ob-

---

1 Each of these documents is published by the U.S. Bureau of the Census, Washington, D.C.

tained on the cost and applicability of containers to postal operations. Likewise, the M.I.S. provides data on transportation developments, such as high-speed trains and jumbo aircraft, which affect the applicability of containers. At the same time, long-range plans for the use of mail bags must be considered in relation to changing demands. The M.I.S. therefore plays a vital role in the effective *application* of strategic plans.

Programs and budgets similarly look to the M.I.S. for their very existence. Exact information on manpower and dollar resources is a necessity for the allocation and control of funds according to programs. The Post Office Department now assembles a five-year Program and Financial Plan, detailing resource requirements for each of its major programs. These requirements are translated into budget accounts (through a computer program) to which Congress ultimately appropriates funds. Spending, in turn, is controlled through adherence to specified budget levels. Each stage of this process relies upon a detailed cost M.I.S.

To illustrate the interrelationships among these preceding five factors of the planning framework, a specific example will be cited. As the reader may be aware, the Post Office Department has embarked upon the erection of Self-Service Postal Units (SSPU's) in shopping center parking areas throughout the country. These facilities offer an extensive line of postal services and are each accessible 24 hours a day.

A present objective therefore might be "to expand the economical use of SSPU's to supplement post office window services." Forecasts of shopping center growth over the next twenty years indicate the number of sites meeting the Department's criteria for SSPU installation. Plans are therefore drawn up to construct and operate an equivalent number of units during the time period indicated. The program for the immediately succeeding five years is then prepared showing the required manhours and dollars required for the SSPU's, and the budget is adjusted accordingly. Additionally, the impact of SSPU's on other post office window hours will be considered so that service adjustments can be applied. As can be observed, the M.I.S. flows smoothly from one end of the framework to the other.

Just as the analytical framework is dependent upon the M.I.S., so are the organization's systems and procedures. In most cases, systems and procedures are defined in terms of the information they employ or are designed to deliver. Therefore, the quality of those devices is critically dependent upon the quality of the M.I.S. supporting them. Integrated planning would obviously be unable to lift from its launching pad without data to measure the utility of the management structure, strength of the program structure, practicality of plans, and compliance with budgets. Even if such data were available, the planning vehicle would not venture very far without further feedback information monitoring performance schedules, network reliability, and quality of service.

Likewise, the M.I.S. is integral to the continued support of methodologies and techniques. In this case, the M.I.S. takes the form of special, one-shot information rather than continuing data flows. Systems analysis studies, for example, can rely on data adapted from existing information systems. Estimates, samples, approximation, and assumptions are typical devices for obtaining the necessary data at a minimal cost. Again, the results of these studies are only as useful as the quality of the material supporting them.

CONCLUSION

From trial and error experience in introducing integrated planning to the Postal Service, a number of observations can be made. It is hoped that similar pitfalls can be prevented by others in their pursuit of planning.

1. Top management must be made acutely aware of the need for planning. Their eventual support of the planning process is critical to its success.

2. Planners must thoroughly assess both the current and expected planning environment. A basic knowledge of planning resources is fundamental before planning can effectively commence.

3. A total framework for integrated planning must exist for planning to be successful. Forecasts, objectives, strategic plans, programs, and budgets must be generated in compatible formats.

4. Systems and procedures permit the periodic re-evaluation of the usefulness of each section of the planning framework. Too often, the framework itself deteriorates in the haste of fire-fighting and is overlooked because of system and procedural inadequacies.

5. Methodologies and techniques must be based upon information systems in existence for other purposes. Efforts to establish continuing data generation for the support of special studies is both costly and confusing to the organization.

6. A well-grounded M.I.S. is critical to the integrated planning system and provides a medium for linking the framework from forecasts through budgets. The M.I.S. must therefore be compatible with the entire framework and should be designed around the needs of the framework.

Planning, although gaining recognition as a vital corporate strength in the competitive environment, is still far from maturity in most organizations. An integrated, rather than a piecemeal, planning approach is highly beneficial but rarely achieved. The development of an integrated

M.I.S. in support of planning, as "planning" has been used here, faces the same strong obstacles planning once faced. Regardless of their managerial knowledge and belief in the value of M.I.S., decision-makers are still people given to all human resistances.

12. Use of Management Tools in Health Planning*

Mary F. Arnold

Health professionals are taught to be objective, plan rationally, set objectives, evaluate, and assess all elements of a problem. But we have found that problems are never neatly arranged for rational analysis, and time for planning disappears under the pressure of numerous emergencies. Nevertheless, we in public health have challenged ourselves, through the Commission on Community Health Services, to cope rationally with an array of health-related activities so diverse that the Commission's recommendations themselves are internally inconsistent. We have challenged ourselves to plan rationally in a milieu of political jurisdictions developed for an agrarian economy, and to compound our dilemmas, we have been challenged by Congress with the passage of Public Laws 89–749 and 89–239 simultaneously to organize, develop, and implement effective plans for dealing with current and future health problems at every level of an expanding society.

These challenges are formidable, and we will not be able to meet them by merely reshuffling old activities. We will have to change organizational structures, learn new tools and technologies, and develop new ways of thinking about the value of health. All these changes will be traumatic, for they will add new uncertainties to a world that already has too many for comfort and security.

THE MEANING OF PLANNING

To some people planning means specifying a plan of action; to others, determining the most efficient allocation of resources; to still others, identifying the means by which we determine the kind of future we want.[1, 2] Sometimes the term "planning" infers managerial planning within a circumscribed system such as an agency; at other times, planning for an open system such as a State or nation.

There is one factor common to all these approaches—the application of scientific reasoning to problem solving. This reasoned problem solving involves analysis of causality, prediction of outcomes with some order of preference, and a conscious rational choice from among alternative actions.

To have meaning, these general ideas about scientific reasoning must be considered in terms of the specific kinds of planning we expect to do.

* From *Public Health Reports*, Vol. 83, No. 10 (October, 1968), 820–25.

1 Bolan, R. S.: Emerging views of planning. Amer Inst Planners J 33: 233–245, July 1967.
2 Petersen, W.: On some meanings of "planning." Amer Inst Planners J 32: 130–142, May 1966.

Thus, much of the confusion in the meaning of the term "planning" is related to the situation in which we expect to operate.

Another aspect to this confusion is in the changing modes of scientific thought permeating all fields. Just as in the health field we are beginning to take an ecological approach to the study of man in his environment, we are changing our ways of thinking about phenomena ranging from the atom to social organization.[3] These changes in ways of thinking, coupled with our expanding knowledge from science and technology, have increased our uncertainties about planning at the very time we wish to plan rationally to solve the problems of the health system.

One result of these changes has been the development of a new array of technical management planning tools that are often seen as panaceas for all the problems of planning.[4] To begin to understand the issues of planning, it is useful to look at what has happened to organizational planning and how these tools fit into the scheme of things.

CHANGES IN ORGANIZATIONAL CONCEPTS

The field of administrative management has recently entered a new phase of conceptualization in an attempt "to graft modern scientific thought onto the empiricism which has largely served it in the past."[5] These new approaches to management have affected how we think about planning. The first movement toward developing a science of management came in the early part of this century and emphasized structure on the assumption that all tasks could be divided into separable and discrete units. A rational organization was a logical one in which there was a clear-cut division of labor, with a hierarchial authority structure. Through such works as those of Mary Parker Follett and the Hawthorne studies, we soon learned that the social process within an organization must be considered, and on the basis of broad generalizations from a few studies, we fixed on motivation and began to emphasize process rather than structure.

Reconciliation of process and structure orientation, however, was very difficult, and it was not until some new scientific concepts from mathematics and engineering were set forth in the late 1940's that new ways of thinking about organizations advanced to the point at which we could begin to combine our knowledge about both process and structure.

With developments in cybernetics, information, and systems theories, two new approaches to the real world of management evolved—the dynamic model and an output orientation. The idea of system, of feed-

---

[3] Toulmin, S., and Goodfield, J.: The architecture of matter. Harper & Row, Publishers, New York, 1962.

[4] Boguslaw, R.: The new Utopians. Prentice-Hall, Inc., Englewood Cliffs, N.J., 1965.

[5] Hanika, F. deP.: New thinking in management. Hutchinson & Co. (Publishers) Ltd., London, 1965, p. xv.

back, evaluation, and control is a dynamic concept and assumes change, forcing us to think in terms of a dynamic rather than static equilibrium. This shift to dynamic constructs starts with the new assumption that the whole is made of interacting rather than discrete parts and that the output of the system is the important variable. Thus, within the past 50 years administrative thinking has shifted from a focus on a rationality of structure, through an emphasis on social process and interpersonal relationships, to an orientation to mission or task.

We can see evidence of these shifts in the American Public Health Association's standards for local health departments. From the Emerson report in 1945, which set the structural pattern for local health departments with the "basic six," we moved in 1951 to a focus on process— "supervision and regulation, recording and analysis of data, operation, coordination."[6] In 1964 we began to shift toward an output orientation with the functions listed as "promotion of personal and community health, maintenance of environment, and an aggressive attack on disease and disability."[7] The current emphasis on comprehensive health planning is a continuation of this change. However, most of the public health agencies of this country have been caught up in the rigidities of legislated structures and are still bound into a rigid, bureaucratic organizational pattern that was logical under the old structural orientation.

Burns and Stalker suggest that such a bureaucratic organization, called mechanistic, is characterized by specialized differentiation of tasks, precise definition of rights, duties, and obligations regarding responsibilities of position, and hierarchical control, authority, and communication.[8] This mechanistic type of structure leads to an emphasis on means rather than ends or objectives, and is therefore appropriate for a stable, repetitive situation. But Burns and Stalker suggest that under conditions of change and uncertainty, an organic form of organization is more appropriate.

Their organic form emphasizes planning and contributions of special skills and knowledge, rather than explicit rights and duties. It requires continual redefinition of individual tasks through interaction with others and involves a wide commitment to the organization as a whole rather than to subunits. Its organizational structure is a network, rather than a hierarchical pattern of authority, control, and communication. Today, organizational planning is expected to take into account the dynamics of changing internal and external environments. At the same

6 Local health departments—services and responsibilities. Amer J Public Health 41: 304, March 1951.

7 The local health department—services and responsibilities. Amer J. Public Health 54: 135, January 1964.

8 Burns, T., and Stalker, G. M.: The management of innovation. Tavistock Publications, Ltd., Social Science Paperbacks, London, 1961, pp. 119–125.

time a new management science technology has emerged that emphasizes decision making under conditions of uncertainty.[9]

PROBLEMS WITH THE NEW PLANNING TOOLS

Some of the new techniques depend upon mathematical models, probability theory, and the use of quantitative methods. We have statistical tools to estimate probabilities for the future, mathematical models such as linear programming to aid in optimizing our decisions about resource allocation, network analysis techniques such as program evaluation review technique (PERT) to aid in controlling complex operations, and program-planning-budgeting to aid in integrating all aspects of a program.

But all these tools require quantification and specificity of activity that are difficult to achieve, and this rigor often creates resistance to their use. Although the logic of the management sciences is now taught in most classes in administrative management, there still remains a nagging, almost intuitive feeling that the resistance to this rigor of specificity is reasonable and should be looked at carefully.

These management planning tools are based on an assumption that activities are involved in a complex system and attention should be placed on output rather than on structure or process. But this assumption may be overly simplistic, for we are not yet equipped with the strategies we need to apply these tools easily. In fact, we do not yet know enough about human systems to apply indiscriminately the highly valued engineering and mathematical models that have been so effective technologically.

These reservations make it imperative that we learn these new tools and techniques well so that we can apply them in appropriate situations. If we believe that man can have some mastery over his fate, then we have some exciting new tools to aid in making our decisions more rational. But to use these tools effectively, we must know their limitations.

Difficulties in Specifying Objectives

One difficulty usually found in the use of the new management technology is the clear specification of goals or objectives. There are many reasons for this difficulty, probably the least of which is the change in our patterns of thinking. There are other compelling reasons, such as possible loss of means for reducing the strain of value conflicts and an increased risk of loss of influence and social power.[10]

Health has developed into an industry, important to the economy, during a period when its goals were widely accepted. Until technology

9 Shuchman, A.: Scientific decision-making in business. Holt, Rinehart and Winston, Inc., New York, 1963.

10 Moore, W. E., and Tumin, M. M.: Some social functions of ignorance. Amer Sociol Rev 14: 787–795, December 1949.

made realizing health goals possible, as in disease eradication, public health has not been required to justify its goals of decreased deaths and disability. Despite the fact that these goals are vague and ever receding, there has been an assumption that the mere addition of more resources can reduce disease, prevent death, and so forth. Additionally, because of success in communicable disease control and in the use of new scientific knowledge, the lifespan of individuals has been increased.

However, we have not faced well the uncomfortable idea that while we have reduced deaths, we have increased chronic disability and other attendant problems of old age. Perhaps the strong, almost psychic resistance to explicit goal setting is an unconscious mechanism for protecting us from the continual stress and trauma of the value conflicts inherent in our work.[11]

A second problem in specifying objectives is political. Everyone would like to believe in a fairy-tale world—a world of consensus—that willing cooperation is just around the corner. But, no matter what the extent of good will, since the world is increasingly specialized and demanding of services, there is the reality of conflicts of subunit interests, differences in personal ambitions and perceived obstacles to be surmounted, and a scarcity of resources necessitating differential control and allocation of the resources or skills of influence. This is the political reality within and between organizations. This political reality is a major barrier to the explicit specification of measurable benefits and goals. Once goals are specific, trade-offs are easy and the question is whose program will be the one to be devalued.

Thirdly, Blau has suggested that under conditions of uncertainty there is a high potential of loss of power if a planned outcome is unsuccessful.[12] Although high achievement results from successful risk-taking, people often prefer not to risk loss of status or power by spelling out in advance what they expect to achieve. It is easier to rationalize outcome if it has not been specified originally. In a program-planning-budgeting system and other such mechanisms, an even greater premium is placed on successful risk-taking, with strong emphasis on evaluation. It is conceivable that in the future administrators may set program objectives or goals that do not entail risk-taking or innovation. In our organizations we usually want to be known as number one, not as the one that just tried harder but didn't succeed.

Difficulties in Detailing Program Activity

In program budgeting and in cost-effectiveness and cost-benefit analyses, it is necessary to detail program activities. In our teaching ex-

11 Rogers, E. S.: Public health asks of sociology . . . . Science 159: 506–508, February 1968.
12 Blau, P.: Exchange and power in social life. John Wiley & Sons, Inc., New York, 1964.

perience we find great resistance to this kind of detailed analysis. "It takes more time than doing the job," or "everybody knows that" are the kinds of complaints we hear, yet time and time again specification of details reveals differences in perception and understanding that could have been detrimental to the planned program.

Any careful analysis of the system for planning purposes requires detailed information about activities performed. But we are all familiar with the resistance that occurs whenever a time study is undertaken, even when great effort is taken to depersonalize the data. One reason for this resistance may be that specification of activities reduces the freedom of the individual. He becomes committed to a particular pattern of activity, and such commitment can be used as a strong controlling mechanism. It seems quite possible, therefore, that another resistance to specific detailing may be an unconscious or unexpressed resistance to rigid controls.

In addition, the client-oriented professional in his one-to-one relationship with his client learns to deal with uncertainty in a very special way. The physician treating a patient with certain symptoms learns first as much as he can through a history, observation of the patient, and tests, and then makes a diagnosis based on his knowledge of probabilities that certain characteristic symptoms occur with specific disease processes. But the professional's diagnosis is always subject to change, depending upon response to treatment, progress of symptoms, and so on.

Thus, the professional uses a heuristic learning process in serving each client that enables him to apply his special knowledge to this unique and dynamic situation—he tests out a series of hypotheses over time. To reveal in advance exactly what will be done and to make contingency decisions before the contingency occurs and before information is available seems to be a major shift from the usual professional behavior. (In actuality, the physician does know the potential contingencies and watches for them.) It is essential that there be continuous feedback of adequate information to make wise decisions about detailed activities under conditions of uncertainty, but the organizational situation differs from the unique client situation in that the specification of what information will be needed must be planned for and made explicit for organizational use in decision making.

In addition to these reasons for possible resistance to specifying details, there is a great deal of tedious, time-consuming, hard work involved. It is boring and does not give the satisfaction of action, and it is much easier to shortcut specification than to go through the process. And there is a good reason for this. Bruner and co-authors suggest that a person in the process of categorizing objects is likely to reduce the strain of paying attention to myriads of details since he is usually under time pressure.[13] There are two principal ways in which the strain may be reduced—reduction in the number of attributes considered, and combining or recoding attributes into configurations. They also suggest that persons develop a taste for methods of grouping and that these are probably learned and reflect subcultural biases. Thus, the identification of activity categories as required by these new tools of the management sciences is quite a strain because of the unusual method of categorizing and the requirements for detail.

Many people have difficulty thinking in terms of specific activity output. They do maternal and child health or disease control or health education or, even more ambiguously, they integrate or coordinate. But, if asked for specific examples of such activity, only the rare person can find a way to describe it in terms of output or benefit.

Resistance to detailed specification of activity is perhaps a natural response of people who have learned a certain method of perceptual conservation that was highly satisfactory under a different set of conditions. For example, under the usual expenditure accounting methods, attention is placed on activities rather than on results of activities. Doing what is now required for cost-utility or cost-benefit analysis is a waste of time when only simplistic efficiency criteria are used in auditing governmental activities and when dealing with innumerable uncertainties.

POLITICS OF PROGRAM IMPLEMENTATION

The new tools of management are challenging, exciting, and powerful, but not for the reasons usually given by their advocates. If used wisely, there is an opportunity for the first time to promote the kind of communitywide planning dialogue that will enable societal decisions to be made more rationally. To achieve this there must be familiarity and facility in the use of these tools, which can provide the stimulation of new perceptions and new ways of thinking. For example, Shaefer and Hilleboe have applied output thinking to the manpower problem.[14]

It is important not only that these tools be mastered as techniques, but also that it be known whether they are being used well or poorly by the technical expert. The systems engineers and operations research specialists have these tools and models at their fingertips for analyzing the operational problems of hospitals, governmental agencies, and industrial concerns, but these specialists may not be experts in the system to which they are applying the tools. Nothing is more important than adequate information about the operational details of the system being analyzed.

Some simplistic assumptions about health matters can be made by

---

[13] Bruner, J., Goodnow, J. J., and Austin, G. A.: A study of thinking. John Wiley & Sons, Inc., New York, 1956, pp. 45–49.

[14] Shaefer, M., and Hilleboe, H. E.: The health manpower crisis—cause or symptom? Amer J Public Health 57: 6–14, January 1967.

intelligent people. Without guidance, the uninformed systems specialist can make decisions that may reflect popular beliefs about disease processes and about activities in the health field. Today there are many systems experts now applying their knowledge to the health field. For example, the aerospace industry has recently turned its attention to governmental and health problems, and there is a major effort to apply the space-age techniques to governmental administration as well as to health services administration in the private sector. To the uninitiated, mathematical symbols and formulas have a mystery and an aura of infallibility that, coupled with the computer's fantastic extension of man's cognitive capacity, create a barrier to learning. And, as a result, all decision responsibilities may be granted the technician by default.

PLANNING AT THE COMMUNITY LEVEL

A broad definition of planning may help to clarify the difference between planning within an organization and planning at the community level. If we define planning as those activities required to organize and implement an intervention in current patterns of activities with the purpose of achieving a different outcome (or set of outcomes) than would have occurred if there had been no intervention, we can identify four underlying assumptions within this definition. There is an assumption of an ongoing process that will result in a less desired outcome than one which might be planned, another that activity is organized and can be consciously controlled and rational, a third of purpose or a consciously desired outcome, and a fourth of deliberate choice from among alternatives.

Given these assumptions, there are two fundamentally different kinds of decisions involved in planning. The first is related to desire—it is value-laden and ethical rather than rational, inspirational rather than computational. To make these choices, it is necessary to know what the alternatives might be and the expected probability of consequences from these alternatives. These things help in making a choice, but the desired outcome must be based on the values we wish to enhance.

Once we have decided what might be preferred for the future, more rational decisions can be made, and these new decision-tools and models from cost-benefit analysis to game theory can be applied. The management tools depend upon a strong assumption that utility or benefit is a measurable commodity and that all aspects of the system can be transformed into the same measure.

This is the point at which many of us unfamiliar with the logic become disturbed. "You can't measure pain in dollars," but it is now being done, if not from an economically rational point of view. Every time a budget is set based on last year's estimates, something is measured in dollars. When priority is given to an immunization program over screening for chronic diseases, a utility decision has been made, even though it may have been made intuitively rather than on the basis of a consciously rational decision model.

In California, and elsewhere, I presume, the technicians have been called in to solve the problems of criminal justice, welfare, transportation, waste management, and information processing under an assumption that these are analytical rather than political value problems.[15] Under such circumstances, the politically wise move of the administrator is to ask for help before the legislature or governor does. This allows him to maintain control of the recommendations that result.

For the company contracting to provide the service, the logical and rational recommendation is for further study since adequate data is almost never immediately available. Further study is also to the advantage of the administrator who does not want to have the balance of influence shifted. Thus, it is to the mutual disadvantage of both the contractor and the administrator to implement suggested change. On the basis of this logic, we can expect in the near future a rash of studies without much actual change resulting.

This lack of change may be advantageous because it is questionable whether a group of systems technicians should be the only persons whose values set what government shall or shall not do. Until the program administrators understand these new techniques and learn to use them wisely in the pursuit of social values developed in a dialogue with the polity about alternatives, it may be better than some major changes are not implemented.

Perhaps the most important function of the health professional in community planning is that of finding better ways to measure benefits and delineate health values. If he does not meet this challenge the measures of the technicians will be used, and they may represent a quite narrow value system about health. For many programs in the health field, the utilities sought are closely related to what might be defined as the "good life." Health, illness, and disease are intimately intertwined with socioeconomic status, education, geographic location, occupation, family patterns, and so forth. But what constitutes the good life for some is not even in the realm of conjecture of others, and even our personal definition changes as age, economics, or other circumstances change.

Therefore, the really troublesome problem is resolving conflicting values and clarifying and identifying shifting value premises. Rogers and Messinger are attempting to develop some new methodologies for deal-

15 Hoos, I. R.: A critique on the application of systems analysis to social problems. Working paper no. 61, Space Sciences Laboratory, University of California, Berkeley, May 1967.

ing holistically with this problem of system purpose.[16] But until these methods provide a more rational base for determining utility, the problem will have to be resolved on a political rather than analytical basis.

The knotty problem to be solved in planning, whether at the organizational or the societal level, is to find a tool that will aid in defining the utilities to be maximized and the timespan that is to be considered. Management tools can help us plan how to get somewhere and learn where we are going, but they cannot help us decide where it is we want to go.

[16] Rogers, E. S., and Messinger, H. B.: Human ecology: toward a holistic method. Milbank Mem Fund Quart 45: 25–42, January 1967.

13. The Planning-Programming-Budgeting System: Rationale, Language, and Idea-Relationships*

Samuel M. Greenhouse

An understanding of what the Planning-Programming-Budgeting System (PPBS) purports to be and to do for the U.S. Government rests, I believe, upon recognizing the primacy and interplay of two PPBS ingredients. These two "molecules"—as they stand individually, contribute proportionately, interact, and interdepend—compose the vital core of PPBS.

Let me begin by identifying the two ingredients, as a prelude to defining and discussing them.

A single concept, dealing with the accountability of the Federal agency apparatus, forms the philosophic base of the PPBS structure.

The main structural members of PPBS are eight terms with definitions so special that, in effect, PPBS has a "language all its own." True, none of the words and phrases in the language is really new. But each is used so very differently in the PPBS context that earlier-entrenched images (which our minds seem to conjure up whenever the terms are heard) may in some cases prevent comprehension. The eight terms are: objectives, programs, program alternatives, outputs, progress measurements, inputs, alternative ways to do a given job, and systems analysis. A true understanding of PPBS cannot derive from reliance upon the traditional definitions of these terms. Each has a particular meaning and significance in the rearrangement of established ideas which PPBS represents.

The fresh design which emerges from this rearrangement, rather than the individual ideas themselves, is what is new about PPBS.[1] But in rearranging, in linking and relating the ideas, a trimming and fitting had to take place. Through this tailoring process, the terms remained unchanged while the ideas (which the terms had so long and effectively stood for) took on subtle differences of flavor and shade. Given these new meanings, the terms have become coordinates with distinct functions, hierarchical placements, and highly significant relationships within the flow and overall framework of PPBS.

THE BASIC CONCEPT: ACCOUNTABILITY

PPBS is a multi-purpose system. If it is implemented and instrumented soundly, it should have a variety of uses. Only one of these—and per-

---

* From *Public Administration Review Symposium* (n.p., n.d.)

[1] In this regard, PPBS is not surprisingly like many conceptual "innovations." It is often said that there is "nothing new under the sun." That many discoveries consist in rearranging and regrouping ideas which are, individually, already known, does not diminish the usefulness of the results. The important question is whether and in what directions PPBS may prove useful.

haps not the most important one, although it is receiving predominant attention at this stage—is the improvement of individual Federal agency operations. Whether the regulation of Federal agency activities is a key purpose or not, the careful installation of PPBS in the individual agencies is of surpassing importance, because the agencies are indispensable building blocks in the overall system. That is to say, PPBS could not exist disembodied from the individual agencies, even if the main purpose of PPBS were, say, to accelerate the economic growth of the United States rather than to introduce a new technique of agency management. This may help to explain why the bedrock concept of PPBS concerns the matter of Federal agency accountability.

Now, what is the PPBS concept, and how is it different?

The PPBS concept is that each Federal agency is accountable to the President and to Congress for the production of goods and services, and more particularly, for the distribution of these goods and services to the American people.

This is a considerable departure indeed, for, until PPBS, the Federal agency apparatus, was considered to be held accountable by, and to, the President[2] for providing the Presidency with "administrative support." Application of this vague concept has become more difficult as the Federal apparatus has grown and diversified. Our Presidents have become too busy to locate, identify in specifics, and hold direct reins of responsibility.

The PPBS accountability concept focuses the attention of each agency on the question: What is our business? The PPBS concept provides a basis for particularizing the answers to the question: Accountable for specifically what products (goods or services), delivered to whom?

The PPBS concept matches the reality of today's Federal agency operations, demonstrating once again that "theory interprets established fact." The agencies are producing goods and services, and distributing them to the American people.[3] What PPBS adds to this reality is the assumption that product delivery to the American public is the central purpose of agency operation rather than merely a happenstance or a by-product of other, more characteristic purposes.

Of course, all Federal agencies perform other functions besides distributing goods and services to the public. For example, each agency generates goods and services for purely internal uses; for the use of other agencies; or for the President and Congress. However, an understanding of PPBS depends upon recognizing that all "inside-the-government"

[2] And to the Congress.

[3] In some cases, the agencies contract for goods and services, and perform the distribution themselves. So long as the production is government financed, and performed under government auspices, it can be regarded the same way, for PPBS purposes, as in-government production.

efforts and interchanges are considered subordinate to the central purpose. Inside-government activities are not pertinent for PPBS accountability. Unless this is recognized, the ideas which underlie the terms "objective," "program," "output," and "input" cannot be clearly discerned nor can the interplay of these terms be comprehended. The discussions of output and input allude in greater detail to this crucial matter.

If the agencies are to be held accountable for discharging the central purpose of distributing agency-produced goods and services to the American public, the public becomes, conceptually speaking, the market for the agencies' products and services. Thus, the explicit business of each Federal agency is to satisfy the public's actual and potential market demands for the agency's particular product/service lines. Accountability discharge becomes subject to evaluation in terms of each agency's success in (1) gauging the nature and proportions of the market demands, and (2) fulfilling these demands.

OBJECTIVES

With this background, it becomes clear that the apex-term of the PPBS idea-structure is "objectives." As the preceding discussion indicates, a more precise way to visualize the idea here denoted is to expand the term to "market objectives." Each agency is supposed to generate explicit market objectives, to make possible a genuine agency-wide understanding and a common agency approach toward their achievement. Satisfactory market objectives would, one supposes, provide specific grounds upon which to base the answers to three questions[4] about each main class of items produced by a given agency:

What class of goods or services is contemplated for production? (Each agency has at least one main class of items, or product line; most agencies have more than one.)

What market group is each product line (good or service) intended to satisfy? (Some agencies have readily identifiable groups of customers, e.g., veterans; other agencies serve fluid and only temporarily associated groups, such as air travelers.)

What specific needs, of the market group served, is the product designed to satisfy? (For example, if the American Indian, say, were assumed to need help in achieving economic well-being comparable to the "national average," what indications of this need might be cited in support of programmatic intentions?)

If this theme correctly interprets PPBS, customer-oriented market objectives are destined to become key standards for agency self-appraisal and accountability. Such standards are quite common for

[4] These questions appear useful to the author to illustrate the concept of market demand which PPBS implies. They are not to be found in the available PPBS literature.

private industry, except the total sales volume is a more readily obtainable index of market needs and satisfactions than will be available in government.

Allowing for the absence of various profit mechanisms in government, the effect of PPBS will be to bring governmental practice to a somewhat closer approximation of common industrial practice than has been possible before.

PROGRAMS

What idea underlies the term "program"? In PPBS language, a program is a package which encompasses each and every one of the agency's efforts to achieve a particular objective or set of allied objectives.[5] If the objective were to provide economic assistance to the American Indian, the program would be composed of all agency activities and expenditures put to that purpose.

Bear in mind that this idea of program is very different from the traditional governmental usage. Prior to PPBS, all agencies used the term to characterize functions and professional disciplines. Hence, "procurement," "data management," "engineering," and many other activities were called programs. The habit persists even now, because PPBS has not yet succeeded in making its point.

Those agencies which did not understand the new meaning of the term in advance of generating their initial PPBS "program structures," will certainly need to redo program structures if PPBS is ever to gain solid ground. Individual activities, functions, and professional disciplines are the very anti-theses of programs in the PPBS sense. The whole PPBS idea is to facilitate the drawing together, the summation of all agency efforts to meet particular objectives, so that the validity of each program may be assessed in terms of overall approach, dimension, and costs and may be compared with other competing programs, potential or existing. It should be recognized, then, that in the future, a program which mirrors (corresponds with) a given agency's established organization structure will be a rarity, unless the agency happens to have only one program. An agency with a functional-type organization must break down functional efforts and apportion them among programs, in order to successfully sum each program.[6]

As the foregoing discussion may have indicated, there is a strong conceptual relationship between objective(s) and program. In "PPBS language," there are no objectives recognized except those which suggest a program designed specifically to fulfill them; and there can be no

[5] Whenever the term "objectives" is used hereafter, it should be read as "customer-oriented market objectives."

[6] However, it is not required that there be change in the established organization structure; merely a change in the accounting will do.

recognized entity describable as a program unless it is designed to accomplish explicit objectives (customer-oriented market objectives).

PROGRAM ALTERNATIVES

The term "program alternatives" is next in the PPBS hierarchy.[7] Within any one agency, this term means other possible programs besides those already decided upon. Consequently, it suggests a comparison of two or more programs (i.e., two or more possible approaches) toward fulfilling the same market objective(s). For example, as in the hypothetical case mentioned earlier, suppose that an agency wanted to accomplish the objective of raising the economic well-being of the American Indian to some mythical level such as the national average. Presumably, any one of several programs, existing or new, might succeed in bringing this about. The agency would wish to choose the "best" program for the purpose, and to disregard other program alternatives.[8] Or, it might simply wish to evaluate a number of program alternatives so that, having selected one, it could demonstrate the wisdom of the selection by revealing the inadequacies (in the discarded programs) which the comparative evaluation had uncovered.[9]

OUTPUT

In PPBS language, an output must have, conceptually speaking, all of the following properties:

It is a product (either a good or a service).

It is produced by a Federal agency, or is produced under the agency's auspices.

It is a tangible outgrowth of a particular program (i.e., it is the result of a calculated program effort).

It is the sort of product which can be appropriately singled-out as an indicator of program results. (Logically, therefore, it must be a program end-product, and an important one, at that.)

It is considered by the agency as satisfying an explicit market objective (or related set of objectives).

The foregoing list of properties should serve to illustrate the connective tissue which runs all the way through PPBS. That is, the idea of output is inseparably linked to the earlier discussed ideas of market

7 Of course, these PPBS terms may be considered in any order, but the author finds the order of presentation given here easiest to work with for definition purposes.

8 The term "systems analysis" will be defined later, at which point the mechanics for selecting a "best" program from among the possible program alternatives will be suggested.

9 There are two other types of alternatives in PPBS language. One is "alternative ways to do a given job," to be defined later. At that time, the distinction between "program alternatives" and "alternative ways to do a given job" should become manifest. The other, which could be termed "comparison of all agencies' programs" is not discussed in this paper because it is not a prominent part of PPBS as applied in the individual agencies. It is applied, however, by the President and his executive staff.

objectives and program(s). And this idea-connection is highly significant for interpreting the PPBS notion of output. It means that many types of products which the agencies have been accustomed to regard as outputs can no longer be so regarded. PPBS has preempted the word, so to speak, for a much narrower, sharper-focused usage than the traditional one. In order to be considered an output in PPBS language, the good or service produced must satisfy an explicit market objective and must be an indicator of program results.

Let us appraise a few items traditionally considered outputs, in light of these definitional criteria. Suppose that an agency decides upon a program to build schools. The agency's procurement division places a series of contracts with construction firms. One month later, the agency's statistical division prepares and forwards to the agency director a "construction progress report." Are the contractual documents properly countable as outputs? No! Is the statistical report an output? No! Why? Neither the documents nor the report satisfies a customer-oriented market objective, and neither represents an indicator of program achievement (although both of them do represent divisional, that is, internal, achievements).

They are intermediate, or contributory products, rather than outputs in the PPBS sense.

What would constitute program achievement, and thus be an output in the PPBS sense of the word, could in the example cited above be the number of schools built, number of new classrooms available, or number of new classroom seats set into place.

The distinction between intermediate or contributory products and output is a very critical matter, insofar as understanding PPBS is concerned. If we would follow the logic-structure of PPBS, we must reconstitute our thinking. We must consider many of the things we are accustomed to producing (and claiming output-credit for) as mere intermediates. This is not so illogical as it may at first appear to be. Coal is the output of a miner, but is only a contributing factor for the completion of industrial processes, rather than an output of any of those processes. In turn, the processes' outputs are, or may be, salable commodities. One man's output is, to another man, merely a contribution to his output. The logic of how to classify an item, such as coal, depends entirely upon the intent and purpose of the classification, rather than upon some immutable principle. For purposes of PPBS output, the government's many agencies may be regarded as analogous to the separate divisions of any large corporation. The corporate outputs, in any such enterprise, are only those items produced to reach the public. Neither those items consumed by and for the production processes themselves, nor those exchanged between the corporate divisions, are regarded by the corporation as outputs.

Given the realization that this is the output focus of PPBS, we can now get a clearer fix on the PPBS idea of progress measurement.

PROGRESS MEASUREMENT

The notion that progress should be measured in some fashion is not likely to trouble many people. The question that may be vexing some students of PPBS is: What does PPBS want us to measure? Or, put in another way: What does PPBS regard as progress in a given program?

If output means only those programmatic end-products which satisfy explicit market objectives, then program fulfillment must imply that both of two conditions have occurred:

The output which had been planned has materialized, and
The output distribution which had been intended has been completed.[10]

If that is fulfillment, then progress must imply one of two questions, depending upon what stage the program happens to be in at the time when progress is measured:

Either, how closely does the product progress match planned progress?
Or, how well is the output distribution proceeding, as compared with the distribution plan?[11]

INPUT

Of all the words in the special language of PPBS, input is probably the easiest to grasp, because the PPBS definition is fairly close to the traditional usage of the term. If all of the inputs to a given program were expressed in dollars, the sum would comprise the total costs incurred by the program (during the time-period that the program had been in effect). In other words, the total quantity of manpower, facilities, equipment, and materials applied to the program, expressed in either units or dollars, is the program input. Note, however, that the facilities, equipment, and materials applied may, in a given program, include some intermediate or contributory products.[12]

ALTERNATIVE WAYS TO DO A GIVEN JOB

The concept of "alternative ways to do a given job" is input-related,

10 At this early stage in the evolution of PPBS, with the distribution aspect not yet generally recognized, few agencies disregard distribution considerations altogether. If PPBS "makes it," this situation will change.

11 The question of how to measure what PPBS wants measured is touched upon later, when systems analysis is discussed.

12 In which case, we may be classifying as inputs, for PPBS purposes, some items which would have been classified, in pre-PPBS days, as outputs. But remember: don't duplicate inputs—that is, whether summarizing input units or input dollar costs, don't count both the intermediate/contributory products and the manpower, facilities, equipment, or materials that were used in their production. Count either one or the other as input, but not both.

insofar as PPBS is concerned. The "given job" notion means that the output to be produced and the distribution pattern for that output have already been decided upon. The question, at any phase of the program subsequent to that decision-point, becomes: Can we alter the production or distribution technique and by so doing improve either:

The timing of the production or delivery, or
The quantity or quality of the item(s) being produced, or
The unit or total cost of the production or delivery?

Every one of the three questions above is input-oriented. That is why defining the term program alternatives separately (as was done earlier) is advantageous. True, the word "alternatives" appears in both "program alternatives" and "alternative ways to do a given job." The first is output-related; it suggests substituting an entirely different program (and therefore a different output or outputs) for a program already planned or in progress. On the other hand, "alternative ways to do a given job" takes the program as given, and raises possibilities for changing the mix of inputs, and thereby redirecting the program.

Viewed in another way, the first involves policy questions, while the second involves operational matters. It is quite useful to distinguish between these two, as an aid in placing responsibility. That is to say, any single group of executives need not, sometimes should not, and often cannot answer both types of questions. However, the agency head, able in a given case to distinguish the PPBS situation as either policy or operations, is well on the way toward getting appropriate action taken, because he will know which group of his executives to contact.

SYSTEMS ANALYSIS

Of the eight terms characterized as important for understanding PPBS, only systems analysis remains to be discussed.

In the foregoing, the attempt has been to establish a distinct identity for PPBS. If this has succeeded, the reader already knows that systems analysis isn't PPBS, and that PPBS isn't systems analysis. The number of people who appear to regard these two things as one and the same is astounding.

Purely for purposes of differentiating the two, PPBS may be captioned as a bag of premises, concepts and relationships; whereas systems analysis may be captioned as a bag of techniques attached to a way of approaching problems. No disparagement of the latter is intended. To the contrary. The cause of technique is not advanced by confounding it with the very content to which it can be most profitably applied.

If systems analysis isn't synonymous with PPBS, what is it? More particularly, what is it insofar as PPBS is concerned?

A capsule definition would be: systems analysis is the application of "benefit-cost" analytical techniques to several areas of the PPBS anatomy.[13]

From the standpoint of the individual Federal agencies, two PPBS areas are especially amenable to benefit-cost techniques. One is the posing and evaluation of program alternatives, i.e., ascertaining the benefit-cost advantage (if any) of shifting to different outputs and/or distribution patterns so as to satisfy market objective(s) better. The other is the measurement of progress in a given program, i.e., ascertaining the benefit-cost advantage (if any) of changing the input mix so as to produce and/or distribute the output more efficiently.[14] In either case, the function of the systems analyst is to diagnose the benefit-cost situation as it exists, so that the agency head may have the opportunity to make his decision on a benefit-cost basis if the circumstances suggest to him that such is the appropriate basis. If other considerations suggest to the agency head that the decision should be predicated upon different or broader criteria than simply benefit and cost, that remains his prerogative. He should have the benefit-cost data in any case, so that he can know what sacrifice, if any, the exercise of the prerogative entails.

The preceding only skims the surface of systems analysis. A more complete treatment is beyond the scope of an essay on the nature of PPBS.

SUMMARY

What is PPBS? It is a structure with a base unusual for government, and with key structural members so interdependent that comprehension must extend to all, or true perception of the "building" is impeded. The base is accountability in the citizen market. Therefore, the objectives must be product supply and distribution. Accordingly, programs are conceived and executed as production/distribution entities.

Consequently, program alternatives are different production/distribution entities which might offer better benefit-cost ratios than existing ones. End-products become the only items construed as outputs. And, progress is viewed and measured in terms of output/distribution timing and effectiveness vs. planned timing and effectiveness. Hence, the inputs are "whatever resources it takes to get the production-distribution job done." As a result, alternative input-mixes become important comparison bases within any given program. Finally, systems analysis contributes diagnosis and appraisal to the whole.

Those familiar with PPBS will have noted the omission of many details. The workaday requirements in planning, programming, and

13 In the broader context represented by economic theory, benefit-cost techniques have been described for a century as "marginal utility" analysis.

14 A special and very useful application of systems analysis, which overlaps both foregoing cases, is the benefit-cost evaluation of program expansion/contraction.

budgeting; the preparation and time-phasing of "program memoranda" and "program and financial plans;" the problems and reasoning associated with below-the-first-tier program structuring; the many different ways in which the cost-benefit approach and techniques (marginal utility theory) may be applied—all of these have been omitted or touched lightly, in large part because they have been treated thoroughly and in depth by many. Hopefully, the details will take on greater meaning within the framework of the "larger architecture" which this essay has sought to delineate.

14. PPBS in Fairfax County: A Practical Experience*

Robert A. Luther

The budget system of Fairfax County [Virginia], prior to the attempt to develop PPB, was traditional line item–object budgeting with an increasing emphasis on the use of management studies and systems analyses. These two, though an important factor in PPB, were still on a line-object orientation rather than program orientation. Since 1950, however, radical changes have occurred in the county that have required considerable attention to the development of improved systems rather than a modification of the old concept.

Fairfax County has experienced a population growth of over 300 percent in the span of less than 20 years, going from a population of 98,000 in 1950 to over 400,000 in 1968. In addition, the character of the community, itself, has taken a radical change. Twenty years ago, the county was a rural, even somewhat agrarian, area disassociated from the developing metropolitan Washington area. It is now an almost self-contained sector of this same urban complex which it once skirted. As a necessary result, both the nature of the community and the types of services demanded changed drastically from those of a rural community to those of an urban area. Faced with this, the county organization and collection of services to meet these demands grew vastly.

In order to cope with the problems of multiplicity of programs, frequently duplicated, and the struggle for departmental autonomy, a continuous and effective program of management analysis was adopted. Again, the county was faced with the problem of having to treat the symptoms of the disease, and at the same time, trying to cure the disease itself. These studies, performed by the budget and research division, a staff arm of the office of the county executive, became and continue to be in-depth analyses of organization-wide problems and, in essence, have become a more systems-oriented approach to the old expenditure control techniques used in the traditional line item–object budgeting process. A good example of this was a problem of printing and printing facilities maintained by county departments. Each department controlled and maintained its own facility for all printing which was a massive duplication of effort—inefficient and uneconomical. Through a detailed analysis of the procedures, needs of individual departments, and demands on the total county organization, a central self-supporting county agency for printing was created.

* From *Municipal Finance*, Vol. XLI, No. 1 (August, 1968), 34–42. Reprinted by permission.

If the transitions were as simple and as smooth as this, one would say that management studies, in the final analysis, are the answer to the overall budget-management-systems syndrome that faces all local governments in the same situation. Two problems, however, can be pointed out that restrict their effectiveness. First, the semi-autonomous departments were, and are, reluctant to accept the solution. Department heads are reluctant to give up complete control. Consequently, there is a continuous effort on their part to return to the old system. Second, the management study was, in fact, a stopgap measure to correct an existing situation and not an attempt to return to the original need, i.e., develop a new system for the total organization and proceed accordingly. Management studies, therefore, as used in the context of a total system or, eventually in a PPB approach, have been but successful attempts to alleviate an immediate problem which was brought on by this onrush of growth and "changing community character."

Further illustration of this problem was brought out in a recent report prepared for the county government:

Not all problems can be studied by a staff unless that staff is of considerable size . . . Staff recommendations no matter how good do not carry the necessary weight to gain implementation of the recommendations, i.e., there is a tendency for difficult recommendations to be ignored . . . there are also recommendations difficult for staff people to make since the recommendations necessarily imply criticism of present and past practices, and objectivity is lost in some cases because of the internal relationship with the organization being studied.

Closely related to management analysis, and possibly more closely associated with PPB as an organization moves toward that end, is a program of systems analysis. In Fairfax County, however, systems analysis is specifically "machine problem" oriented. That is, individual departments are confronted with specific tasks which can be either improved or made more efficient through the use of data processing type equipment. The data processing division systems analyst develops a computer "system" to perform a specific task required by the department. There is, and will continue to be, an effort to develop an overall management information system. Again, however, as with management studies, in many cases the practical problem of finding successful remedies for immediate problems and demands is foremost. There is, presently, a continually increasing need to develop comprehensive systems utilizing data-processing equipment to cope with basically clerical-type workloads. Machine oriented systems developed to date include accounting and clerical processes for tax billing, payrolls, welfare payrolls, voter registration and budget preparation. A significant step toward any systems approach to budgeting requires improvement and purification of computer procedures for these clerical tasks before total organization programs and systems may be developed.

PERFORMANCE BUDGETING

An attempt was made several years ago to adopt some of the facets of performance budgeting. It was felt that the traditional budgeting process, because of its orientation to individual items, did not permit an adequate analysis and review of the effectiveness of services provided to county citizens. Work program forms were included with annual budget request forms requiring each agency to quantify, itemize, and estimate cost of work units related to each of the services performed. The ultimate goal was to be a county-wide costing of services that cover more than one department. This budget technique was used for several cycles but was eventually abandoned for several reasons.

First, there was considerable difficulty on the part of participating departments and agencies to quantify, or even categorize within their department, units of work. The problem was, indeed, legitimate for the difference between a process and a work unit is difficult to make. For example, does the buildings and grounds division quantify custodial supplies or custodial services; or, does the library administration quantify all procedures associated with the receipt and issue of a book or record or lump all procedures into one work unit? In the former case, the division chief did noting; in the latter, the chief lumped all procedures into one. Neither is acceptable.

Second, with only a few exceptions, the collection of these work units became nothing more than another budget procedure begun, collected, completed and submitted in the span of one month's time. Consequently, all data given were estimates and not particularly accurate ones. Only those departments that used this type of data in their day-to-day operation, e.g., police department, presented accurate current data. Third, and probably most important in the long run approach to PPB, the entire concept of this data collection and the need for it was questioned by department heads. Consequently, each work unit activity and service was viewed as an acceptable, unquestionable program with views only toward expansion rather than possible alteration of the activity or service. Without this vitally needed departmental cooperation, the program was destined to be only a budget exercise.

PROGRAM BUDGET

The use of the work program technique was replaced in 1967 with a program budget consisting of all known or determinable activities. Each was determined and identified without regard to conventional organizational or fiscal breakdown; this technique permitted closer scrutiny of services or programs with the aim of determining County performance

131

and reasons for this performance of any particular function. Following the general concept used by the Federal government each program included a general description of goals, possible quantitative measures and known trends.

Initial identification of programs was provided by the individual departments during the submission of budget requests. Staff instructions to the department heads asked them to: List programs to be performed; give particular consideration to all departmental operations; define and state the purpose and goal of each defined program.

As was the case previously with the work unit approach, the resulting information was inadequate and, in some cases, not even germane to the request. One department, for example, provided as its program information a detailed justification of personnel requests for the fiscal year and a detailed breakdown of a proposed reorganization in the department. This information was relatively useless in program analysis. Another department submitted detailed statistical data which would have been much more appropriate in the preceding year's work unit requests. The result was a somewhat one-sided determination by the staff of program definition, deliniation, and objective. From this, one hundred and four separate programs were defined with a cost estimate attached to each.

This program grouping and analysis which was included with the formal budget document, was well received in the community for several reasons. It provided a summary of the budget *in toto* in an easily understood format. Additionally, it served somewhat of a public relations function, for many interested citizens had seen and read about the PPB system in operation in the Federal government. Criticism too, was to be expected, e.g., 104 programs were far too many. This early acceptance and interest in the program budget led to the formulation of a plan of action to develop a PPB system in Fairfax County.

Many reasons have been given for this development; two, however, as stated below present all quite succinctly:

1. It has become increasingly difficult to evaluate and make decisions about requests for funds among competing programs within agencies—it has been especially difficult to determine longer range implications of budget decisions made on an annual basis.

2. As demonstrated by the approval of the 1967 program budget, the community needs and demands more each year a more understandable and sensible budget process. The various departments and accounting alignments have complicated the substantive program aspects of the budget to a point where it has made citizen participation in the budget and planning process difficult.

A major problem with which the county was confronted, however, was the general confusion and conflicting statements about what PPB was. Also, a total absence of a complete system in any local government put the county in a pioneering position.

The county's approach to PPB recognized four central characteristics of PPB which, together, make up a single cohesive system.

1. Identification of the fundamental objectives or goals of the government, and a determination of how government programs relate to the achievement of these objectives.

2. Projection of programs into the future on a planned and controlled basis, so that budgeting is a continuing process.

3. Consideration of all pertinent costs of programs including capital outlays.

4. Analysis of costs and effectiveness of alternative ways of reaching objectives.

Plans to develop and implement the system were in several phases:

The *first phase* was to involve identification of existing programs to determine what government objectives apparently were. Although some work had been done along these lines in the 1967 program budget, it was felt that more work should be done in close collaboration with department and agency heads to be accurate and to encompass capital improvement, debt service and trust funds. Specifically, forms would be designed to be used by department heads to determine in what meaningful programs their agency was participating. Emphasis was to be on discussions with department heads by staff people in order to provide an understanding of the concepts involved in PPB. Budget instructions would include the 1967 program summary to be used as a guide in identifying new programs or modifying those listed. It was to be pointed out that programs identified were to portray the direct services to the public or the support of a direct service provided by another agency or group of agencies. Dollar requirements were also to be determined.

The information obtained from the agencies would be used in describing objectives and grouping programs as they related to the achievement of objectives. It was to be implied in instructions that there should be a definite reason for a program to exist and that grouping of reasons into general objectives should give a framework for analysis. Work in this phase would be included in the 1968 budget document.

Phase two would involve projecting into the future all interrelated programs over a five-year period—and that it would be desirable to formalize the work into a carefully defined system capable of using data processing equipment. This would eliminate much detail work in the annual updating of the plan, and should also make it possible to test alternative program emphasis. It was planned that forms for this phase also be designed and distributed to all department heads and that the

133

budget staff personally contact them and work with them on the development of their program requests for the future five years. This phase was to also encourage agency heads to consider what mix of programs would be most effective in achieving desired goals over the time period.

Phase three would involve a compiling of agency projections into a summarized form showing programs grouped under related objectives and projected over the future five years. Results of the findings were to be discussed with the County Planning Commission staff and Board of Supervisors prior to proceeding to the next phase.

Phases four through seven were to involve testing the feasibility of projections by drawing schedules showing the projected revenues over the time period including bond sales and federal and state aid; conversion of completed work to data processing; preparation of a procedural manual; and preparation of a survey report on progress achieved and further work required.

The following questions were asked in order to obtain necessary information for the planned PPB program: Does each program correspond to any listed in the 1967 program summary, or is it a modification of one listed or it is a new program? What are the goals and purposes of the program? What are your agency's contribution to this program? Who is the coordinator of the various programs? What other agencies participate in the program and what are their contributions as you see them? What, if any, statistical data is available relative to performance? Other comments?

Realizing the problems that had occurred in the past with particular reference to cooperation of the individual department heads, the staff worked closely with each department. Each budget analyst normally in charge of the preparation and review of the agency's budget entered into discussion involving agency participation in specific programs and methods of assigning costs. Probably most important was the attempt over several months to orient department personnel to the concept of many departments contributing to the achievement of one program.

Though the results were not as successful as earlier anticipated, major improvement was made in: (1) refinement of the elements within the individual programs; (2) a better understanding of what the budget staff was attempting to do. Again, as before, several of the department heads were still unable to comprehend the concept of an interdepartmental program. Consequently, considerable information provided was but an explanation of the activities submitted in previous years under the work program concept.

Much of the information was presented in the form of "canned" answers which were indicative of either failure to understand the questions asked or, hopefully, inability to grapple with the needed information.

The latter case demonstrated, at least, an effort to cooperate. In summary, department heads, though not so much as in previous attempts, demonstrated a general apathy or possible fear of the approaching system. Conversely, some department heads cooperated fully but were faced with legitimate problems of the elements constituting the program. A common error was the inclusion of "administration" as an agency program, which was obviously a task or function not a program. Owing to the ingrained conventional system, there was a basic resistance to any change, justified or not. One further observation need be made with respect to the entire process: on returning to speak with department heads after the submission of the initial data, the staff attempted to clarify and logically extend some of the data. In some cases these department heads were reluctant to offer any additional assistance and, in others, they became almost vehement in their denunciation of the program, for the essence of the clarifications was the question of justification of departmental existence. This could be taken initially as a rejection of the entire concept; however, it would seem more logical that this attitude reflected an awareness rather of the eventual worth of the system and its possible ramifications in changing either the department thoroughly or, at least, seriously revamping existing programs and procedures.

In order to complete a significant portion of Phase I, programs were costed and grouped based on both the data provided from the submitted forms and from the various discussions with department heads. Because of a time lapse, it was impossible to include portions of this in the formal 1968 budget presentation; however, after completion of staff preparation, a status report on Phase I became available during the fiscal year. The purpose here was to stimulate interest among the department heads with particular regard again to education in the concept of PPB.

The process of preparation of the program listing and costs allocated to them created, if nothing more, considerable introspective thought on the budget process itself. It refined the staff's awareness of the problems facing the county and, possibly more important, it made the staff more sympathetic toward the problems facing the individual department heads.

The major program definition was, by and large, a four-stage process. It was necessary, initially, to prepare a list of all funds and agencies within those funds, including additionally the more difficult capital outlay, debt service and trust funds in order to determine departmental participation in the total program picture. The second list included all programs and functions as submitted by the individual departments. Function was included here because departments were, in many cases, unable to differentiate between a "function" and a "program." A third list was prepared in which the staff refined actual programs, excluding what were believed to be functions. Each program in this listing was, then, assigned to each individual performing department. Necessarily, in many cases there was multi-participation by several departments in one program. The fourth listing was a further refinement of the program definitions wherein the actual number of programs was reduced by collecting what was initially determined to be small programs in individual agencies into broader programs encompassing several agencies. Actually, it could be considered an extension and refinement of the third listing rather than a totally new listing. The complexities of these refinements of and limitations to the programs were formidable.

The tracing of the cost requirements was also complex, for in some funds which act as collecting accounts for miscellaneous expenditures the specific assignment to one program was either difficult to determine or, once determined, difficult to compute. "Unclassified Administrative Costs Account," for example, was of this type. Included are such items as county contribution to insurance programs, social security, et cetera. In that each determined program used personnel in some form or another, costing of that program would require, certainly, partial assignment of these unclassified personnel costs. The control of minutia that this entails is readily apparent. It was evident that the most practical approach to this was an additional governmental objective to be named "Supportive Services" with the stated objective of providing administrative support to enable the effective and efficient accomplishment of the other major objectives of the government. This definition had an uncomfortable similarity to many agency descriptions of their program goals. Any contribution or unclassified cost that could not be specifically assigned to a specific program was placed in this category.

The same was true with respect to the "Contributions Account," in which are included all contributions to outside organizations, supplementing the services and programs of individual operating departments in the county.

Eight objectives were determined into which all programs could be placed (see Figure 1). The relating of specific programs to the broad objectives was another complex and difficult procedure. It was difficult to determine, for example, whether welfare programs such as aid to dependent children, foster child care or old age assistance belong under health or welfare departments, for both departments seem intrinsically involved. Contributions to various private community agencies could be grouped with individual agencies or in a collecting objective. All programs involving youth could be grouped into one objective or placed with the other adult-oriented objectives. The library system in some respects is certainly oriented to the educational objective but it, too, is an

Figure 1.
Fairfax County Program Structure

I—PROTECTION OF PERSONS AND PROPERTY
Goal: To minimize injury to persons and loss of property from unexpected events or violent acts.
Police Protection
Fire Suppression
Fire Prevention
Rescue and First Aid
School Safety Program
Control of Dogs and Other Animals
Inspection of Building Construction
Inspection of Electrical Installations
Street Lighting
Civil Defense
Contribution to Fairfax County Safety Council

II—ADMINISTRATION OF JUSTICE
Goal: To settle disputes between individuals in the community and between the government and individuals and to assess and provide penalties or rehabilitative service to those found guilty of criminal acts.
Courts
Sheriff (including service of process and court bailiffs)
Prosecution of Criminal and Traffic offenders
Prisoner Confinement
Law Library
Contribution to Regional Detention Home
Contribution to District Probation and Parole Office
Contribution to Legal Aid Association

III—PROTECTION OF HEALTH AND WELFARE
Goal: To protect people in general from sickness and disease, both physical and mental; and specifically to provide for those who are unable to help themselves.
Hospital and Health Center Commission
Construction of Hospital Facilities
Construction of Health Centers
Home Nursing Services
School Health Nurse Program
Control of Environmental Health
General Health Clinics
Mentally Retarded Centers
Institutional and Other Care
Housing Advisor
Fairfax House
Juvenile and Domestic Relations Counseling
Public Assistance to Adults
Aid to Dependent Children
Foster Care of Children
Child Protective Services
Construction of Sanitary Sewers
Inspection of Plumbing and Sewer Systems
Collection and Treatment of Sanitary Sewage
Contribution to Cerebral Palsy Development Center

Contribution to Mental Health Center
Contribution to Alexandria Community Health Center
Contribution to District Home
Contribution to District Nursing Home
Contribution to Higher Horizons Day Care Center
Contribution to Coop. School for Handicapped

IV—EDUCATION
Goal: To give all people the opportunity to develop their intellectual resources to the maximum.
Construction of School Facilities
Operation and Maintenance of Schools
Support of Higher Education
Construction of Library Facilities
Operation of Library System

V—CONTROL OF ENVIRONMENT
Goal: To provide for pleasant, orderly and effective environment in the County by regulating and controlling its physical aspects.
Planning Commission
Comprehensive Planning
Rezoning Processing
Land Use Control
Zoning Administration
Sidewalk Construction
Other Public Works Construction
Public Works Engineering
Control of Streets and Subdivision Design
Drainage and Storm Sewer Maintenance
Soil Analysis and Conservation
Contribution to Northern Virginia Regional Planning Comm.
Contribution to Historical Landmark Commission
Contribution to Northern Virginia Transportation Commission
Contribution to Washington Metropolitan Transportation Authority

VI—LEISURE TIME OPPORTUNITIES
Goal: To provide opportunities and facilities for constructive and healthful use of recreational and leisure time.
Acquisition and Development of Park and Playground Areas
Operation and Maintenance of Parks
Community Playgrounds and Recreation
Organization of Sports
Recreation Activity Classes
Support of 4-H Clubs
Farm and Garden Advisory
Homemaking Demonstration Services
Contribution to Youth Council
Contribution to Teen Centers
Contribution to Fairfax County Cultural Association

137

VII—COMMUNITY SERVICES

Goal: *To accomplish those objectives desired by the citizens of the County which can best be accomplished by group action of the government as contrasted to individual action.*

Collection of Refuse from homes
Roadside Refuse Service
Operation of Sanitary Landfill
Promotion of Industrial Development
Recording of Deeds and Other Legal Documents
Condemnation of Alexandria Water Company
Public Utilities Commission

VIII—SUPPORTIVE SERVICES

Goal: *To provide administrative support to enable the effective and efficient accomplishment of the other major objectives of the government.*

Legislative Services (Board of Supervisors)
County Executive
County Attorney
Fiscal and Management Analysis
Central Data Processing Service
Personnel Administration
Purchasing and Warehousing
Real Property Assessment
Personal Property Assessment
Business Tax Assessment
State Income Tax Administration
Accounting and Treasury Management
Employee Benefits
Office Facilities
Miscellaneous Administrative Support
Voter Registration
Elections

important part of the leisure time objective. The final decisions are indicated in Figure 1.

At the staff level, some attempt was also made to determine measurable criteria for the eight objectives. The major problem in this process involved quantification. The not-so-readily-quantifiable were, for example, in the objective of "Administration of Justice": length of time between filing and final disposition of cases: length of time to appellate review; the relationship between caseload and workload capacity of judges and court rooms available; the availability of court-appointed attorneys; public attitudes including creating confidence in the judicial system; and recidivism. The objective of "Control of Environment" created assignment problems with respect to such matters as making miles of sidewalk, storm sewers, and rapid transit the measurement of "improving the environment."

Some interesting observations were brought out in this process. A common assumption concerning health and welfare programs is that the poor segment of the community benefits from governmental activities. In fiscal 1968, eighty percent of the Health and Welfare Objective would finance programs not benefiting just the poor, but all citizens regardless of level of income. Operations of the sanitary sewer system and construction of hospitals were two of the more obvious benefiting all citizens. In the "Administration of Justice" objective, over eighty percent of costs of achieving the goal was in the area of prosecution, court administration and prisoner confinement. Only twenty percent was rehabilitative costs. Also to be noted was that dollar amounts indicated in this PPB category did not include federal or state assistance.

FIVE-YEAR PROJECTION

With the completion of the Phase I status report, portions of Phase II were attempted, including the determination of program requirements over a five-year period. Forms again were designed and submitted to agencies and contained objectives and related programs peculiar to each agency. Additionally, private organizations supported in part by the county government were requested to estimate program requirements for the approaching five-year period. Each agency was instructed to review in detail programs with which it was concerned and determine financial requirements for both capital and operating for the future five-year period. To assist in this determination, the staff suggested that projections be based on historical growth, inflationary trends and anticipated demands. In order to provide the broad picture of development, the staff, itself, prepared all estimates of debt service and supportative programs.

As a whole, information received was somewhat better than that obtained in past inquiries; however, most projections were estimated on a purely mathematical historical basis. Again, as an observation, this was due largely to lack of knowledge or training on the part of county agencies, and, with regard to the outside private agencies, lack of ability or staff to provide such data. A partial reason for this, too, was the lack of major policy decisions which determine the general direction toward which long-run planning must direct itself.

Those projections which the staff determined as valid were included in the "Plan for Orderly Growth," an annual capital improvement plan compiled by the staff each year. Alternatives were not determined by the individual departments, which limited in many respects the accuracy of the report. However, the most recent 1969 edition pointed out that the purpose was to provide a basis for considering the achievement of county goals within resource limitations over the next five years.

Criticism of this plan indicated some of the broad problems involved in developing an effective PPB system. Though certainly some of the criticisms were unwarranted, some, indeed, showed merit and demonstrated an understanding of the problems facing the staff as it proceeds toward a more effective system. There was and continues to be a lack of broad political policy-making decisions which seriously affects any attempt at an effective PPB system. This was particularly noted with respect to overall total county land use planning. As stated, a statement of alternatives was not proposed. This is, of course, the core of the system, and closely associated with this, alternatives should be viewed in the light of cost-benefit analyses, minimizing cost and maximizing service performance to the citizens of the county.

CONCLUSIONS

The development of the PPB system in Fairfax County has been an evolutionary one; possibly this is the one "universally applicable" observation that may be made. It was a process of trial and error in which the input from departments caused the staff to reevaluate the techniques of the system and return again to the operating agencies. In this sense the county has moved forward from the original work unit technique first envisioned.

It has been demonstrated that a necessary reciprocal cooperation is imperative between the implementing staff and the line departments. Without this cooperation, the system will be destined for failure. In many cases there was frustration on the part of the budget staff as it tried to build up interest for the system in department heads. However, this forced the staff to refine and clarify its techniques which, in the end, was a step forward.

Difficulty in communcation of the worth of the system itself, and the specific techniques, were created by a lack of technical knowledge on the part of both staff and department heads. Consequently, an essential factor in the development of PPB is a trained technical staff to deal with the problems of establishing accurate criteria and quantification of inputs and the actual use of this data once collected.

Another very important result of the process was the effect on the budgeting system as a whole. It forced the staff to be more rigorous in its analysis of the entire budgeting process; and, possibly more important, it forced the department heads, some for the first time, to take an objective, critical view of their own operations and goals, with particular emphasis not on expansion alone but on study of their programs as they relate to benefits to be derived by citizens of the county.

15. PPBS Reexamined: PPB and State Budgeting*

William M. Capron

Should state governments follow the federal government's lead and attempt a basic restructuring of their budgetary systems by introducing planning-programming-budgeting? Professor Mosher and I have been asked to present two views of PPB as a candidate for introduction into state government and the significance and impact its introduction might have. I address this topic diffidently because of my meager knowledge of state government generally and state budgeting specifically. However, I have been a close observer of, and sometime participant in, the introduction of PPBS into the federal budget process.

IS PPBS DIRECTLY RELEVANT FOR, AND APPLICABLE TO, STATE GOVERNMENT?

If one takes a narrow and strict view which confines the meaning of the initials PPBS to *the* "system" as it is evolving in Washington, then the answer is certainly no. Significant modifications would be required to adapt and modify this system as defined by the Bureau of the Budget in an attempt to move in the PPB direction at the state government level. Such adaptation would take account of the particular structure of the individual state government, of the state's existing budgetary process and procedures, of the role of the governor, and of the role of the state legislature. Certainly as a *system*, PPB will look very different from one state to another and in the states from the way it is evolving in Washington.

Even if a state government decides *not* to move in this direction, its key officials should understand *something* of the system because of the growing importance of federal-state fiscal relations. The grant-in-aid system, even with revenue sharing and block grants, is here to stay and will grow. It is imperative that state governments be able to translate from the federal budget approach, format, lexicon, and ideology, into its own budgetary process, procedures, format, etc., and more and more systematic analysis *and* evaluation will be required of the states—much more "planning," which is a synonym for analysis as I use the terms. At the simplest and most obvious level, there will be real advantages in many program areas to adopting something close to the program structure development in Washington. At a minimum, state governments may find it useful to translate their own program structure into that used by the federal government. Much more important than these "mechanical"

* From *Public Administration Review*, March–April, 1969, pp. 155–59. Reprinted by permission.

elements is the impact on the states of the increasing demand for analysis and evaluation which the federal government is making in administering grant-in-aid programs. State plans are now required in many such programs, and we can expect these plans will have to meet standards which are increasingly rigorous.

An additional reason for urging states to move in the PPB direction is provided by the importance of better integration of federal programs which are administered by local government but funded through the states. A common program structure, to say nothing of the use of analysis and evaluation, will reduce the present confusion at all three levels of government in grant-in-aid programs operated in this fashion. Moreover, in most states a large fraction of state revenues are passed back to the localities (to support such activities as elementary and secondary education) and a PPB-type approach may offer significant improvement in developing and implementing such programs. It is important that state budget officers moving in this direction work closely with local officials so that they will accept and understand PPB.

Quite apart from the requirements laid on the states by the federal government, analysis, or, if you prefer, "planning," and I would add (since I think the two go hand in hand) evaluation, is certainly one important piece of the total PPBS pie which every government should wish to put on its menu. Systematic analysis can improve the operation of state government in a number of ways. For example, analysis can help:

In the specification of objectives ("what are we really trying to do with Program X?")—can we identify useful indices of performance in Program X? Even though complete *measurement* is rarely possible, are there indirect measures which can be used as indicators of performance?

We are now running Program X in a given fashion; are there alternative techniques which would more effectively achieve the same purposes ("more effectively" can be read either as "larger output for a given budget" or as "the same output using fewer resources")?

Are the returns (benefits) per unit of input devoted to Program Y increasing, decreasing, or stable? Are we enjoying all possible scale economies or is the program not at a sufficient level to be worthwhile at all? How does the ratio of benefits to costs in this program compare with alternative programs?

Should we undertake a new program designed to reach different objectives in a given field?

What are the implications for future year budgets of this decision we are taking now?

WHO BENEFITS FROM PPBS?

There are a number of potential gainers, and perhaps some losers, from a move in the PPBS direction at the state government level. In Washington, it is the chief executive who was not only the prime mover, but initially viewed as the chief beneficiary of PPBS. Even though in many states the governor has limited official power over large numbers of state programs, he does have influence, and PPB can help him exercise that influence more effectively. Certainly it will help in those parts of the state budget over which he does have official cognizance. Those governors who really wish to govern can gain in their ability to do so by improving the kind and quality of information which informs the decisions that they must make. PPBS can be viewed as an *information system* designed particularly to improve the quality and organization of information for executive decisions.

Quite apart from the role of the governor, another potential set of prime beneficiaries are department and agency heads. Particularly where department and agency heads are elected or are appointed officials, they can very easily become the captives of the bureaucracies over which they have nominal control and responsibility. PPBS provides a set of "handles" which can be used to allow top officials to exercise much more effective and less arbitrary control over their programs. This suggests by implication who the potential "losers" are to the extent that state governments move in the PPB direction: the bureaucracy, or at least those members of the bureaucracy who perform their tasks by rote. Information *is* power and ignorance *is* weakness. To the extent that budget and program preparation are surrounded by lots of "lore," to the extent that specific and systematic statements of program purpose, program operation, program "success" are absent, the appointed or elected official who is a "short-timer" will inevitably be in a very weak position to assert his nominal leadership over the permanent bureaucracy. When well applied, PPB forces the asking and the answering of hard specific questions. Even where our ignorance is great and the answers cannot be very specific or complete, just asking the hard questions, putting the hard issues, can illuminate the dialogue that produces governmental decisions. Those civil servants who are content to go on year after year with the same old program administered in the same old way may find this question-asking process very uncomfortable. They may be forced to examine premises long since accepted but no longer applicable, and they may have to do better than say: "We do it this way because we've always done it this way."

Bargaining will continue among the various players in the decision process, and will characterize that process. The effect of an innovation like PPB on the process of government is not nearly as dramatic as the kind of basic organizational restructuring such as, for example, has been proposed in several constitutional revisions in several of our states in recent years—including my own home state of Maryland where, unhappily, a new constitution which would have increased the power of the governor, reduced the number of separately and independently elected officials, etc., was defeated. But PPB will, if at all effective, have an effect on the *relative* position of certain of the key players at the bargaining table. And it will, as suggested above, tend to change somewhat the form and content in which the dialogue is conducted among the various participants—the chief executive, the department head, the bureaucracy, members of the legislature, private interest groups—or at least it *may* do so.

It is certainly true that the injection of systems analysis throughout the decision system in the Defense Department has "infected" almost all parts of that large and complex organization so that today the form and style in which proposals are developed at the working level and transmitted first of all to the Joint Chiefs and second to the Office of the Secretary is very different from the style of the 1950's and before. I hasten to add that it is very different to suggest that the particular decisions that have been reached are different because of the use of analysis, and certainly I know of no objective basis for asserting that the decisions have been better than they otherwise would have been. (It is my personal judgment that a number of key Defense procurement decisions have been better because they were grounded in analysis.) This is an important point to emphasize: one must not confuse an assertion that analysis is valuable to decision makers in better informing them, with a statement that the decision maker can, in part or in whole, be relieved of his responsibility for exercising judgment.

The proposal to inject systematic analysis into state governments is not a proposal to substitute a computer for bureaucrats, department heads, or governors. I say this for two very different reasons. On the one hand, in most fields of government activity, we are a very long way from being able to perform the kind of really satisfactory and rigorous analysis which someday we may hope to achieve. We have too little understanding of such complex activities as, for example, public education, and we are certainly years away from having the necessary data to make possible rigorous, comprehensive, and complete analysis. On the other hand, many of us question whether we will ever develop analytic techniques and data which will permit us within a single comprehensive and rigorous analysis to make comparisons between widely diverse programs. In the jargon of systems analysis, we will have to be content for the foreseeable future with relatively low-level suboptimization studies (because we cannot specify unambiguously an acceptable "social welfare function," among other reasons).

I was asked to emphasize the affirmative side in this "debate" and confess to having cheated and anticipated limitations of PPB. Having done so, let me reiterate that, at a minimum, an attempt to develop a capability in various parts of our state governments to perform such analysis and to use such analysis—in the governor's office, in the offices of the major department and agency heads, and in the operating units— will, over time, produce significant improvements in the manner in which public services are performed. As far into the future as I can see, the resources which the various units of government can persuade the populace to give up, in the form of tax revenues, will be less than the same public's demand for increased, improved, and new public services of all kinds. In short, we face a permanent "budget squeeze" situation, not only in Washington, but certainly at the state and local level. This suggests to me a powerful incentive for key political players to adopt every management innovation and tool which promises to improve the effectiveness with which public resources are employed. Planning-programming-budgeting by itself is not the total answer, or the only answer, but I am persuaded that it is an important part of the answer.

THE ORGANIZATION OF PPBS, THE BUDGET PROCESS, AND ALL THAT

As I have suggested, analytic strength needs to be developed on at least three levels in any governmental structure: the chief executive, the department head, and the operating unit. On balance, I also believe the legislature needs an independent analytic capability. It seems to me further that if the analytic efforts are to have any impact on improving the performance of state government, it is imperative that in some way the fruits of analysis be injected into the decision process so that they will have real bite and real impact. This in turn suggests—however the organizational structure is worked out in detail—that the programming and analytic elements at each level need to be closely related to the budget process: there must be a *system*, and analytic output must be a part of that system since it is primarily through the development and implementation of the budget that executive decisions are reflected and, indeed, are forced. The notion of using analysis in many areas of government and of developing systematic evaluations is by no means new. But up until the present, it is my impression that too many of these analyses and evaluations are conducted completely outside and disconnected from the mainstream of the decision process, and that, therefore, no matter how good they may have (occasionally?) been, such studies rarely have had a direct impact in leading to improved government resource use and program operation. While recognizing, as I have already, that the specific PPBS organizational structure and *modus operandi* in each state may be different, it does seem to me imperative that crucial linkages be made between the various parts and elements included under the general term "PPBS."

145

REORGANIZATION AND PPBS

The logic of PPBS will, over time, dictate certain restructuring of state governments, bringing together organizational units (which may today be completely separate) where they are performing functions which, from a programmatic point of view, are closely related. I am well aware of all the resistances to such restructuring, but PPBS can help a governor or a legislature overcome the strong inertia which inhibits attempts at sensible and effective reorganization. Looking ahead, one can hope that a really effective PPBS system will permit decentralization or, as I prefer to put it, will permit a rationalization of authority so that appropriate delegations can be made to operating unit heads down the line, reserving only the kinds of decisions which should be made by the governor and department head at that level. As things stand now, there is almost inevitably a tendency to excessive centralization of certain types of decisions in the executive office of the presidency—or at least periodic attempts to get such centralization—since without such improper "centralization" the President has had very little way of controlling the activities of the various agencies for which he has some responsibility. To the extent that governors really wish to control state government, this same tendency must exist, but it is my impression that few governors have gone this route in a sustained fashion.

The reason I suggest that the present tools of budgeting may lead to excessive centralization deserves a further word. If a chief executive wants genuine control over activities, he will need information and the levers which permit him to use that information. Today, given the input-oriented information base, the governor or other chief executive inevitably becomes involved in detailed review of what should be operating managers' decisions. If one has no useful index of output, then judgment on a given agency's budget request will turn on such questions as, "Does that office really need three more clerk typists?" With more information on program objectives and some basis for assessing past performance, those at the higher levels in the hierarchy would not need to become involved in such detailed issues, on which, in any case, they are ordinarily ill-informed to make sensible decisions.

While I have focused here on overcentralization—a tendency for detailed operating decisions to be made at too high a level—the other side of this problem is the reaction which one sees too often (especially in state government, I suspect), namely, the lack of any substantive review of program plans and budget requests by the chief executive. When this is the pattern, budgets are set by arbitrary ceilings having little or no relation to program effectiveness. (Or they represent nothing more than bundling agency requests together for transmittal to the legislature.)

This, in turn, encourages legislative usurpation of executive and administrative prerogatives.

It is my view that an effectively operating PPB system can contribute to reducing these twin weaknesses in most budget systems operating today: de facto abdication by the chief executive of his proper functions, or improper centralization of detailed decisions at the chief executive level. (The governor's budget office will, of course, need to continue to monitor the detailed input decision of the operating agencies, at least on a sampling basis, and occasionally become directly involved in these decisions. But the chief executive should make his budget decisions in PPB terms.)

It should be clear that the so-called "old" approach to budgeting, with its emphasis on inputs and its close association with the existing organizational structure, cannot be thrown out. After the governor and the administration of a state have made their recommendations to the legislature, and after the legislature has made its appropriation decisions, then in the implementation of the budget, inputs do become important, and the particular inputs which each administrator of an operating organizational unit has been authorized to use must be made known to him so that he can be properly accountable for his activity. Moreover, the "old" budget format is relevant as an aspect of budget formulation, although top-level executives—the governor and his principal aides and department heads—will focus on the decision-oriented program budget.

A STIMULUS TO INNOVATION

Finally, let me call attention to what I consider to be one of the most important virtues of an effort by state government to adapt a PPB system to its own situation: this effort can unleash inventive and innovative potential which I am persuaded lies dormant in many of our state governments and in many of our state bureaucracies. It is not only that there is some virtue in large organizations of change for change's sake; it is also my view that PPBS, if its implementation is anything more than formal and on paper, forces key officials at all levels to think once more and sometimes very hard about what they are really up to, and this, it seems to me, can be of great value. The development within state government of the capacity to engage in systematic analysis and evaluation of public programs promises to contribute to a revitalization of the states and to a significant strengthening of our federal system.

16. PPB: The View from the States*

Allen Schick

In these speeded-up times, an administrative reform usually has only a few years to make it. If a newly minted innovation fails to win quick acceptance, it is shunted aside in favor of some other "most important innovation." Yesterday's greater expectations are today's forgotten and untried ideas, waiting to be rediscovered under some new label that excites a future generation of reformers.

This hurried pace accords each innovation its own brief period of attention and adulation. The innovation is trumpeted at professional conferences and in journal articles, and the word spreads like wildfire across the continent. But this truncated life cycle does not allow time for needed maturation and experimentation, for the seeping in of under-standing and experience, for working out conceptual loose ends and practical difficulties, and for contouring the general reform to the special circumstances and opportunities of each government. Given months instead of years, few innovations have been able to ripen into productive reality.

This has been the fate of Planning-Programming-Budgeting (PPB), not only in most of the States but in the Nation's capital and in American counties and cities as well. As late as the mid-1960's, PPB was little more than a concept and a set of initials. Then came President Johnson's 1965 order to emplace PPB in all major federal agencies, and PPB soon was being discovered by state governments. By the close of the decade, this complex and difficult reform appeared on its way to application in fully half of the States. In March, 1969, the Council of State Governments surveyed the States to ascertain the progress of PPB.[1] Twenty-four of the responding States replied affirmatively to the question, "Are you developing an integrated planning and budgeting (or PPB) system?" Sixteen additional States indicated that they were planning to undertake PPB-type innovations in the future, and only two States reported no PPB intentions whatsoever.

Yet this mercurial rise in PPB's fortunes was virtually negated by an equally steep fall from grace. With none of the fanfare that had attended PPB's arrival, many States quietly abandoned their PPB aspirations or settled for some minor tinkering with forms and technique. At the present time, only a handful of States have advanced from thinking about

* From *State Government*, Vol. XLV, No. 1 (Winter, 1972), 12–18. Reprinted by permission.

[1] See Council of State Governments, *State Progress in Planning and Budgeting Systems* (Lexington, Kentucky, 1969).

PPB to doing it, and few budgeters hold the high expectations that were commonplace just a couple of years ago. In many States there remains scant evidence of PPB's application while in others PPB survives only as a set of special procedures loosely tied to the budget process. But there also are a few States in which PPB flourishes and where progress far outstrips federal developments.

This post mortem tries to interpret the events of the recent past in the light of many disappointments and some notable successes. Although there are many legitimate explanations for PPB's unhappy career, the one pursued here is that PPB failed because it was not incorporated into the central budget and program-making processes of state governments. Where PPB was a vital part of the State's decisional process, its prospects were improved.

THE FEDERAL INFLUENCE

For most States, interest in PPB was not an indigenous response to contemporary opportunities for improved decision-making, but a direct product of the federal initiative. Before 1965, only a few lead States (notably California, New York, and Wisconsin) had shown much interest in this type of reform. As a consequence, the States generally did not make PPB their own or vest it with adequate support and relevance. No matter what backing was forthcoming from Washington, it could not compensate for the lack of strong state support. The federal government could give PPB its initial impetus, but the rest was up to the States themselves. Federal publicity was backed by concrete moves aimed at spreading PPB to other levels of government. The State-Local Finances Project assisted the pilot installation of PPB in five States and in equal numbers of cities and counties. The project prepared and distributed a series of instructional pamphlets and it liberally offered high-quality advisory services to many state officials who inquired about the new system. HUD's "701" planning grants were allocated to several States for PPB development and several States successfully tapped other federal funds for this purpose. The Civil Service Commission opened its various PPB training courses to state personnel and also contracted to provide special courses for interested States. Perhaps the most direct federal involvement was the Federal Technical Assistance Program which sent squads of "flying feds" on week-long visits to selected States. These teams (which still are functioning) furnish on-site guidance concerning PPB and related management problems.[2]

Even more influential than these specific actions was the role of the federal government in shaping the character of PPB and its overall development. Because they lack a firm understanding of the purpose of

2 During 1971, the Federal Technical Assistance Team visited two States—Connecticut and South Dakota.

PPB and how to apply it, many States eagerly followed the federal approach, even adopting federal nomenclature and procedures as their own. Ironically, though they emulated federal practice, state officials generally were unaware of the difficulties PPB was experiencing in its birthplace. In fact, by the time most States joined the bandwagon, federal interest in PPB already was on the wane.

Had the States carefully evaluated the federal experience, they might have perceived that a PPB system which is segregated from the on-going budget process stands little chance of implementation or endurance. In setting PPB into motion, the U.S. Bureau of the Budget (now the Office of Management and Budget) left the existing budget arrangements intact and established a small PPB apparatus with its own instructions, data base, timetable, and organizational relationships. This divorcement of PPB from the regular decisional channels inevitably meant that the new PPB system would not be used when critical program and financial choices were being made.

ATTEMPTS TO INSTITUTIONALIZE PPB IN THE STATES

In looking to Washington for guidance, most States also walled off their nascent PPB operations from the entrenched budget process with the result that the potential for significant innovation was destroyed at the start. Paradoxically, the very strategy used to institutionalize PPB— to give it independent strength and standing—served to isolate it from state decision-making.

The attempt to institutionalize PPB proceeded in a number of ways. One of the first steps was an expression of interest and support from the Governor, especially in those States where the impetus for PPB emanated from the Governor's policy staff. Often this backing was nominal rather than active—a pronouncement issued in the Governor's name, a few remarks at a PPB conference or at a meeting of department heads, a memorandum reporting the Governor's interest in the new system. None of these moves committed the Governor to act according to the dictates of PPB, but the Governor's name was helpful in launching PPB, attracting publicity, and getting recalcitrant or uninterested agencies to go along with the new system.

Second, many PPB States established new analytic staffs, either within the central budget agency or in close relationship to it. In some PPB States, staffs (or liaison positions) were set up in the departments as well. These staffs gave PPB an institutional base from which to campaign for the support of budgeters and other policy officials. PPB did not have to depend on the regular budget staff in order to survive and gain a foothold in state decision-making. The staffs also provided spokesmen for

PPB, who had vested interests in the success and advancement of the new system and who were not bound to the old ways of budgeting.

Third, in many States, PPB came with its distinctive package of techniques and procedures; program structures for classifying information according to function and purpose; multiyear plans and projections for showing the long-term spending implications of current programs; and analytic studies for comparing the cost effectiveness of alternative programs. These special techniques enabled practitioners to relate PPB to the routines of budgeting and to identify it with concrete actions and requirements. As a result, PPB could be presented as a set of specific procedures leading to budget decisions, not merely as an amorphous attempt to improve decision-making.

Fourth, many States invested in training programs to orient their officials to the purposes of PPB and to the methods of economic analysis. Thousands of high- and middle-level personnel attended PPB courses varying in duration from a single day to a month or longer. These courses brought the message and techniques of PPB to program managers who otherwise would have known little about it.

Finally, most PPB States tried to develop new sources of information to serve their planning and analytic efforts. In some, this took the form of program structures which supplemented the traditional budget classifications; in others a substantial investment was made in comprehensive informational systems.

Each aspect of institutionalization imposed some costs and constraints. Gubernatorial pronouncements in support of PPB backfire when they are not followed by specific actions which demonstrate a genuine interest in PPB. It does not take a bureaucrat long to distinguish between publicity and reality and to discover that a superficial promise of change has not penetrated the government. If a Governor and his aides preach PPB but practice the old budgeting, they will create a credibility gap that cannot be overcome. Of course, the fact of the matter is that no Governor or budget director can afford to use PPB unless it is reliable, but it is questionable whether PPB can become productive if it is not buoyed by gubernatorial action.

The analytic staffs gave PPB a home base but denied it direct entry into the heartland of budgeting—the examination staffs in budget agencies. Separate does not mean equal as long as budgeters command the decisional apparatus and analysts are outsiders engaged in specialized irrelevancies. From the standpoint of PPB institutionalization, staff separation seemed to be necessary because it protected the embryonic analytic enterprise against bureaucratic subversion and inertia. But this strategy isolated PPB from the budget process and protected budget traditions against innovative challenge. It also diverted the inevitable (and not so inevitable) complaints about PPB from the budget office to the analytic staff. The analysts were blamed for the problems of PPB, including those provoked by the non-cooperation of the budgeters. Moreover, because of staffing limitations, the separate analytic units were cast in the role of monitoring agency compliance with PPB instructions and had little opportunity for policy analysis. Central monitors rarely are popular, especially when they have the task of prodding reluctant agencies to change their ways and to abandon the favored budget traditions of the past.

Another form of separation, the association of PPB with special techniques, also was costly. For many, PPB was perceived as the routine business of classifying expenditures according to a program structure, filling in the columns of multiyear financial projections, and drafting program memoranda. Techniques that were intended to serve analysis became its master, with the results that very little useful planning and analysis were produced via PPB. Perhaps the triumph of technique was foreordained; it is a regular occurrence in bureaucratic life. Yet the segregation of PPB from the main—and still decisive—budget process gave additional prominence to the form and turned PPB into a procedural exercise.

Many States tried to overcome these disabilities by launching training programs for agency and central staff. While the length of the courses and the number of participants varied widely, most courses were one- or two-day orientations for small numbers of managerial and policy officials. Somehow it was expected that training would compensate for the difficulties and limitations of PPB, that it would succeed where PPB itself could not. As a consequence, much of the training was not *for* PPB, but a *substitute* for PPB. For many trainees, the final day of the course was the last time they heard about PPB. Those who had been turned on by the course quickly were turned off by the lack of visible progress. When that happened, selling became overselling and public officials became disenchanted with the gap between publicity and performance.

In sum, the attempt to institutionalize PPB was engineered in ways that greatly compromised its chances for success. Except in a few States the effort was premised on a separation between PPB and budgeting. This course minimized the risks of innovation but at the cost of also diminishing the possibility of change. In its quarantined institutions, PPB was allowed to do its thing, provided it remained cut off from decision and action.

PPB VERSUS BUDGETING

If the strategies pursued by the States were self-defeating, why didn't they press for fuller integration of planning and budgeting? After all, this integration was one of the central aims of PPB. A cynical answer might be that state budgeters were not genuinely committed to PPB innovation, that they wanted the appearance of being innovative while preserving their comfortable budget traditions. To be sure, not all budget people were equally committed to reform, but this interpretation of the failure of PPB is wide of the mark. The fact is that PPB was successful in raising the level of budgetary expectations far above what it had been a few years earlier. The prevailing standard of "good budgeting" was redefined and upgraded as budget makers were exposed to PPB's criticism of the prevailing methods of public choice. One of the reasons why so many States rushed to PPB was that budget and policy leaders were seeking better ways of making policy and financial decisions.

But in turning to PPB, state officials confronted the problem of reconciling the several diverse functions that had to be served by the budget process. Traditionally, the budget has been used as an instrument for securing financial control over expenditures and improving administrative performance. To these established purposes, PPB brought a third mission, that of determining public objectives and programs. Although every budget process includes aspects of control, management, and planning, one function tends to predominate. As a practical matter these functions are competitive; emphasis on one diminishes the possibility for achieving the others. If they use the central budget process to maintain close surveillance over agency spending, it is unlikely that budgeters will have the opportunity for program planning. The several budget functions require different skills and perspectives and also have divergent informational bases.

The problem of PPB thus stemmed from the coexistence of budgeting's several functions: how to provide the necessities of financial control without driving out planning and analysis. The solution adopted in most States was to separate PPB from the mainstream of budget activity, in the hope that planning and analysis would be able to flourish without being constrained by the traditional budget functions. This "crosswalk" relationship between PPB and budgeting was regarded as the easiest, least disruptive course of action, and one that would allow a fighting chance for innovation. The entrenched budget machine was left alone, and no major analytic organization rivaling the budget staff was established. All that was necessary was to link a small-scale analytic process to the budget cycle. This was accomplished by means of the program categories, multiyear plans, and program memoranda—the constituent routines of PPB. There would not have to be major upheavals or departures to accommodate the new system. The press releases would announce a major innovation, but insiders would know that the core had remained intact and that changes at the periphery would not challenge the established way. Nothing old would have to be traded away to get the new, and the figures in the budget would continue to have their old meaning and reliability.

In terms of minimizing the difficulties of budget innovation, the cross-walk approach was clear and necessary. But in terms of the quality of public choice and the capacity for innovation, the crosswalk relationship of planning and budgeting was defective. By making PPB heavily dependent on a tradition-bound budget process, the innovator sealed PPB's fate as a minor adjustment in budgetary procedure.

WHERE PPB SUCCEEDED

However, this bleak diagnosis does not apply to the small number of States in which PPB was successfully implemented. The successful States differed from one another in their conception of PPB and their implementation strategies. Alaska concentrated on policy analysis for the Governor and his chief aides. Wisconsin invested in an overall accounting system and the installation of new program classifications. Pennsylvania opted for a comprehensive planning and analytic system covering all phases of the budget cycle. Hawaii adopted new legislation which delineated the kinds of information to be included in the Governor's budget and in various supporting documents. Despite their different approaches, these States shared two essential characteristics: they took PPB seriously and furnished PPB with resources and support commensurate with the difficulties that had to be surmounted, and they made PPB a central component of their budget and decisional process, not merely a peripheral aspect. Rather than the standard separation between budgeting and PPB practiced elsewhere, these States—and a few others which enjoyed some measure of success—were determined to revamp their preexisting budget processes in order to accommodate meaningful planning and analysis.

Considering the great difficulty inherent in any effort to dislodge budget traditions, it is remarkable how little most States did in behalf of PPB. A common pattern was to assign a single staff man with PPB responsibility or to load PPB atop the regular chores of the examiners. PPB could not possibly survive or become relevant with such meager support. The story was quite different in the successful States. In Pennsylvania, the Legislature responded to the drive for PPB by appropriating roughly half a million dollars for it. In Hawaii, the Legislature rewrote the basic budget law and the staff of the legislative auditor gave strong and continuing support to the PPB effort. In Wisconsin, the Department of Administration worked with legislative leaders to make the new program structure the cornerstone of the State's accounting, budgeting, and appropriations systems.

Success also was due to the integration of the PPB apparatus with the established budget routines. In Alaska, the Governor used PPB analysis to issue program and financial guidelines to the agencies prior to their preparation of detailed budget estimates. In Wisconsin, the program structure is the classification scheme used for budgeting and appropriations; no crosswalk is necessary. When PPB is fully operational in Hawaii, the Governor's budget submissions will include multiyear projections, statistical measures of program size and effectiveness, and a variance report that compares actual and expected performance. The PPB system in Pennsylvania, if its operation proceeds according to design, will be the budget system itself; there will be no PPB system apart from the budget apparatus.

It should be noted that a number of factors often associated with the prospects for PPB success or failure appear to have little bearing on the actual results. One such factor is reliance on in-house capability rather than outside consultants. Both Pennsylvania and Alaska retained consultants to design their PPB systems and to participate during the installation phase. But Hawaii and Wisconsin drew primarily on their own staffs though they used outsiders for specialized tasks such as PPB training. When outsiders are used, it is important that they be in close contact with state administrative leaders at all stages of their work; when regular staff is used, it is important that the key PPB personnel possess the leverage to diffuse PPB throughout the budget process.

It also makes little difference whether PPB initiative comes from the Legislature or from the Governor's office. In most cases, the Governor's staff is likely to have the lead role, but where the Legislature starts the process and maintains a continuing watch, the outlook for PPB also is favorable. This happened in Hawaii where unusually active and skilled legislative leadership took place. What PPB always needs is a strong and persistent patron, not a forgotten niche in the organization chart.

The experiences in all of these successful States attest to the error made by early PPB promoters who insisted that PPB be given its own separate staff. While there may be some temporary advantage to staff independence, the long-run costs—in the form of isolation and irrelevance—are ruinous. Hawaii started with a special PPB staff attached to the Planning Department, but it was only after this staff was abolished and PPB was welcomed into the mainstreams of budgeting that substantial progress was made. Neither Alaska nor Wisconsin operated with a separate staff and Pennsylvania made do with a single PPB coordinator whose job was to maintain liaison throughout the system. Again the lesson is clear: separation in any form dooms PPB to failure.

It does not appear to matter much whether the design and installation of PPB are compressed into a brief period or stretched over many years. A tight schedule does have the advantage of sustaining high interest during the critical early years and forces key personnel to use PPB outputs quickly rather than wait until the full system is nailed down. But as the sad events in many States show, an unreasonable timetable often is accompanied by fuzzy and unrealistic expectations about PPB. Pennsylvania stuck to a 30-month schedule because it wanted PPB to be operative before the Governor completed his term of office. Wisconsin's PPB development stretched through most of the 1960's because state leaders wanted to iron out all problems in one stage before proceeding to the next. Hawaii's PPB legislation specifies a timetable that will bring PPB to complete fruition only in the mid-1970's. But Alaska's Governor wanted to show immediate PPB results and his State's PPB system was engineered to provide a flow of analytic information in time for the next annual budget cycle.

Finally, States can be successful either with a comprehensive, systematic approach or with a partial implementation. Clearly, comprehensiveness demands more in terms of state support, resources, and administrative competence. All of these were amply present in Pennsylvania and Hawaii. But if these prerequisites are lacking, it would be far wiser for a State to proceed in piecemeal fashion. It would be folly, however, to use caution as a smokescreen for irrelevance. In many States a piecemeal strategy meant selecting some unimportant issue for analysis. By the time the analysis was done, nobody cared about it any more.

PPB systems which achieve a measure of success inevitably face a gubernatorial transition problem that has not plagued any of the less fortunate PPB efforts. Inasmuch as a PPB system must be styled to the political and administrative patterns of each Governor, the changeover from one Governor to another means that PPB, too, has to adapt. The next Governor might not want to be enchained by the successes of his predecessor and he might want to claim credit for launching his State on a proper budgetary course. Furthermore, when the next Governor takes office, a successful PPB system usually is moving beyond the flashy installation stage, to the routine and business-as-usual condition. PPB as routine may not be very exciting, but it is absolutely essential to the long-term survival and usefulness of PPB.

In the States where PPB has gone through a gubernatorial transition, it appears that major elements of the system have survived, though with less sustained high-level support than was enjoyed previously. This has been the case in Pennsylvania and Wisconsin, where incoming Governors were confronted with policy-making systems tailored by, and closely identified with, Governors from different political parties. That PPB has been able to survive a political transition does not assure its long-term durability, but it does offer some promise that significant changes in policy-making machinery can be institutionalized in state governments.

FAILURE IS NOT INEVITABLE

Although failure has been the predominant outcome, it was due to the divorcement of PPB and budgeting, not to any innate PPB deficiencies. Part of the problem of PPB implementation was the failure to recognize that what might have been necessary at the start was not appropriate several years later. Without concrete steps to create a permanent structure for PPB, it might have withered for lack of support, even if some useful analyses had been produced under it. In the long run, therefore, the survival of PPB can be enhanced by institutionalization, provided that the institution created for PPB is within the ambit of budget making. However, this was not often the case.

In appraising the PPB story, at least one thing is certain. The business of budget improvement was not concluded with the recent cycle of innovation. PPB has left in its wake many unfulfilled expectations, much as earlier budget reforms (such as performance budgeting in the 1950s) departed the scene only partly realized. A future round of reform will take the unrealized potential of PPB, cast it into a somewhat different and more contemporary form, and provide new impetus for budgetary improvement. If they carefully build on the successes of PPB and avoid the pitfalls, the next generation of innovators will have a far more favorable record because they will know that the path to success requires a reorientation of the budget process which unites it with coequal planning and analytic procedures.

17. Planning for Manpower Utilization*

Burckhardt Wenzel

Even though there is no uniformity in defining manpower planning today, there is general unanimity existing on the problems manpower planning is concerned with. These objectives can be classified:

Step 1. Planning future manpower needs as a whole. How many people in terms of quality as well as quantity will the company need altogether in order to operate its business in future periods?

Step 2. Planning the future manpower balance. How many of those presently employed by the company will stay with the company in future periods? In this phase we are concerned with, as in step 1, both the qualitative and the quantitative manpower balance. The difference between manpower needs and manpower balance is the basis for further actions that will be taken. The surplus manpower needs become evident to the degree that manpower needs exceed manpower balance. Consequently the next task of manpower planning will be

Step 3. Planning of those activities aimed to provide the company with the required personnel. In case manpower needs are smaller than manpower balance the next step would be

Step 4. Planning for laying off the manpower surplus. It is important to follow the right succession. Without having given consideration to steps 1 and 2 it would not be at all useful to start planning activities concerning steps 3 or 4, because they would not have any secure basis to build upon. This basis can only be provided by steps 1 and 2.

MANPOWER PLANNING—NOT FORECASTING

Referring to steps 1 and 2 the term manpower forecasting instead of planning is used rather often. It seems, however, that the term planning is the more appropriate one. Forecasting refers to those factors which cannot always be governed by the individual company as, for example, the business cycle. Thus, forecasting implies a more passive process, aimed at anticipating the "inevitable" events which the company will have to adapt to, since there is no way of influencing them.

The determination of future manpower needs, quantitative as well as qualitative, is not of this passive type. On the contrary, the decisions concerning the company's future targets, and the activities necessary to reach these targets, determine the future overall manpower requirements.

These targets, as well as the activities directed toward reaching them,

* From *Personnel Administrator*, Vol. 15, No. 3 (May–June, 1970), 36–40. Reprinted by permission.

are subject to very distinct decisions which have to be made by management itself. No manager would accept the statement that his job is only good for anticipating future changes and developing a passive strategy of adapting to them. As he sees it, his task lies in making active decisions, the results of which are plans containing alternate courses of action.

Various courses of action imply different consequences concerning manpower requirements.

One outstanding characteristic of these decisions is that they are made using the background of as much information as is available. One important part of this information is the manpower situation. As things are, for example, in Germany today, the lack of manpower is in many cases the factor limiting production and sales facilities. This is true not only with managerial and professional manpower, but especially on the level of skilled workers and secretarial employees.

Selecting one course of action out of various ones implies the decision for one unique set of manpower needs. This special manpower mix has not been imposed on the company by somebody else, it results from the company's own decisions. It has been planned. And it can be altered by later correcting decisions.

For example, the degree of introducing both organizational change and automation to the company are the result of clearly made, active decisions. These decisions involve e.g. substitution of manpower by the use of labor-saving machines and technical devices.

They are under control and planned. Here is where manpower planning starts. Consequently it is proper to apply the term manpower planning, which embraces all the four steps mentioned above, not only steps 3 and 4. There is no need to refer to steps 1 and 2 as manpower "forecasting."

This is not—as it might appear at first—only an issue of terminology, but a question of the scope of manpower planning.

MANPOWER PLANNING—ITS DETERMINANTS

A company's manpower needs are not an arbitrary figure, but a variable determined and influenced by various factors. Therefore it is to be highly recommended that these factors be explicitly investigated and stated. Whether or not the company has an influence on these factors, the internal and external determinants of manpower should be differentiated.

EXTERNAL DETERMINANTS OF MANPOWER NEEDS

External determinants of manpower needs are those which cannot be planned or decisively influenced by the company itself. The company is forced to predict probable developments, and to adapt its own planning to these predictions. Generally they are identical with those factors

159

which, among others, are influencing the overall business plan. Consequently their influence on manpower needs is more an indirect one. A great deal of these factors become part of other business plans and thus determine, among other factors, future manpower needs. Especially, the following external determinants of future manpower requirements are to be emphasized:

1. The general political situation during the planning period establishes the background in which the over-all business plan is developed. Foreign policy as well as internal economic, financial, and social policy deliver the framework in which the company must act.

2. The importance of the Gross National Product's status becomes obvious when the business cycle expected for the future is predicted. Both business cycle and GNP are—within certain boundaries—determined by actions taken by the government (compare 1).

3. The over-all technological development is not determined by any one company. Invention and application of new products and production methods influence manpower needs.

4. The company has only little influence over the development of competing companies. The competitors' plans and actions, however they are anticipated, have to be taken into account when establishing plans and actions of their own company.

5. The same applies to the development of substitution-products. Even though the company is not able to establish a control, it has to take into account possible situational changes. This is of course difficult, as the company normally doesn't have any knowledge of what the substitution-products will be, which implies that it doesn't know how that will influence its own position.

In making predictions of the described type it is found that for each of these determinants different developments might be probable. In each case, however, those developments which are taken as a final basis for further planning operations have to be mentioned expressively. In case the real development differs from the predicted one, it is possible to take measures to correct the original plan for manpower needs. The starting point for such a kind of correction is easily to be found by naming the wrong planning assumption.

INTERNAL DETERMINANTS OF MANPOWER NEEDS

1. As stated above, since personnel is needed to meet the goals set up by management, the company's manpower needs cannot be determined without regard to its own objectives. The most important targets that planning manpower needs are dependent on are those listed in sales and production plans.

From this it follows that sales and production plans are a basis of planning manpower needs. For long-range manpower planning the plan of investments, which in turn is based on long-range sales and production plans, has to be considered.

Plans concerning other areas, as, e.g., stocks of materials, purchases and administration have a certain importance, too.

In case there is a bottleneck in areas other than sales or production, each will be affected in the course of further planning. For example, if the bottleneck is financial, then there is not much use in trying to derive the plan of manpower needs out of the financial plan only. Following the financial bottleneck the results for the plan of manpower needs can only be computed when a provisional plan of manpower needs has been set up on the basis of sales and production plans.

The proposed financial outlay has to be compared with the financial resources. In case the financial resources are not sufficient to meet the planned manpower needs, the whole planning process has to be adjusted.

Obviously sales and production targets have to be reduced. This implies also a reduction in manpower needs. This method of planning is best described as a feedback process. From this it follows, that the financial plan cannot be the starting point for manpower planning operations.

It is, however, the yardstick that the manpower plan, once established, has to be measured against. This way the financial plan imposes restrictions on the manpower plan. This shows again, that manpower planning is more than a passive adaption to forecasted situations, and that it takes a very active part in the whole planning process.

2. The second internal factor influencing manpower needs is labor productivity. A specified amount of work can be done by different numbers of people. Decisive for the manpower needs to be realized is the productivity units per day, and one worker produces 100 units per hour. There will be a manpower need of 10 workers, assuming the normal working time is 8 hours per day. (100 units per hour $\times$ 8 hours = 800 units per worker per day $\times$ 10 workers = 8,000 units per day).

If a new target of 9,600 units per day is set in the production plan, then the manpower needs might change. Different variations are possible:[1]

Case 1: The output per hour for each worker remains stable; two additional workers are employed (100 units per hour $\times$ 8 hours = 800 units per worker per day $\times$ 12 workers = 9,600 units per day).

Case 2: The productivity of the already-employed 10 workers raises from 100 units per hour to 120 units per hour. (120 units per hour $\times$ 8

---

[1] The assumption is that the working speed is independent of other processes in the plant, i.e., it is an unlimited variable.

hours = 960 units per worker per day × 10 workers = 9,600 units per day). The rise in productivity of the already-employed workers eliminates the employing of additional workers.

Case 3: The productivity of the already-employed workers raises from 100 units per hour to 110 units per hour (110 units per hour × 8 hours = 880 units per worker per day × 10 workers = 8,800 units per day). In order to meet the target of 9,600 units per day, another 800 units have to be produced. If there is an additional worker employed, whose productivity is 100 units per hour,[2] which means 800 units per day, then the planned production is equaled (8,800 + 800 = 9,600 units per day).

If the productivity of the new worker is on the same level as the productivity of the experienced ones, then the result will be: 8,800 + (110 × 8) = 9,680 units per day. That means, the new worker could be employed with other tasks for about 43 minutes per day [(60 minutes ÷ 110 units) × 80 units].

The following figure shows the determinants of manpower needs altogether:

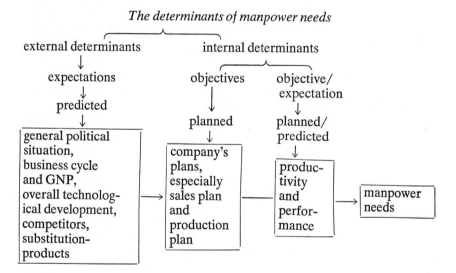

The determinants of manpower needs

MANPOWER PLANNING—THE UNDERLYING PRINCIPLE

It follows from outlining the internal determinants that no determination of manpower needs is possible unless other basic plans have been set up. These other basic plans determine the manpower planning process. The manpower planning process in step 1 is the process of investi-

2 This assumption seems to be more realistic than the second one; for the newly employed needs a certain lead time in order to do his job with the same rate of productivity as the experienced worker (learning-curve effect).

gating the various single plans of the whole planning system with their effects on manpower needs.

Therefore planning manpower needs can be referred to as derived planning. It is derived out of other plans. Because manpower needs are not planned before other plans have been established, an original process of planning manpower needs is impossible.

In this lies a characteristic of planning manpower needs. The underlying principle of planning manpower needs is based on its derived character. Because manpower needs are not autonomous, planning manpower needs has to start with those factors determining them. Relationships have to be looked for between the present situation as well as the forecasted and planned development of the determinants on one hand and manpower needs on the other hand. These relationships, which of course should be as stable as possible, become the foundation of the manpower planning process. In this way the underlying principle shows where investigations must be started concerning methods to be applied in planning manpower needs.

18. Issues in Measuring Results of Action Programs*

Clarence C. Sherwood

It must be admitted that to date very limited results have been produced by controlled, scientific evaluations of action programs. It seems, therefore, that any productive discussion of issues in the measurement of results of planning and action programs must start with, or at least include, a direct confrontation with that rather well established fact. This state of affairs appears to be the product of a set of forces which range all the way from very technical methodological problems of measurement and experimental design to some deeply rooted thought and attitudinal patterns of our culture which deny the logic and methods of scientific research. It is the writer's impression that the latter are much more important factors in the current situation than the former and that the purely technical problems of evaluation design are probably the most easily solved of all the obstacles and resistances presently impeding the development of a broader and more effective program of evaluation research within the field of social action.

A basic question that has to be raised is: Why isn't there greater demand from various segments of our society—public officials, the public itself, program administrators—for hard evaluations of action programs that attack one or more of the social ills of our social system? This general absence of a demand for a hard accounting of the effects of social interventions is all the more astounding when some of the central themes of our culture are considered: getting one's money's worth; the profit motive and realizing a return on investtment; and the general focus placed on those entrusted with the handling and spending of public and private funds.

The basic assumption of this paper is that more and better evaluation studies of social action programs are needed if our society is going to be able to make increasingly more rational allocations of resources to the solution of social problems. Rational is defined here as that dimension of the social decision-making process which utilizes scientifically gathered evidence rather than depending on fad, fancy, whimsy, or faith.

If a growing and more successful evaluation research program is to become part of our social action culture, evaluation research must be recognized as consisting of a broad set of strategies and skills which transcend the narrowly defined technical skills of social research—

* From *Welfare in Review*, Vol. 5, No. 7 (August–September, 1967), 13–18. Reprinted by permission.

research design, measurement, statistical inference, and the like. These strategies and skills, which can be called social action research engineering, include elements of sociopolitics and all the related educational, persuasive, and technical strategies for gaining access to the required information, getting and maintaining support for the evaluation effort, and, perhaps most important of all, creating a climate both for patience for the sometimes slow-to-arrive findings and for the incorporation of those findings in the decision-making process.

The social action evaluator or researcher generally raises the vital but difficult to answer question: "What difference does this particular program make in the lives of its target population?" What he must also ask himself is "What difference will the evaluation of this program make in the decision-making, resource-allocating, action world of which it is presumably a part?" If this latter question is taken seriously—as supposedly it must—then careful, long-range strategies must be worked out as part of the whole action-research package. Such strategies would have as their aim the building of a system which will increasingly want, support, and then actually use evaluation research procedures and their findings. The repertoire of the action-researcher must ultimately include an action philosophy and the skills required to overcome obstacles to the inclusion and use of that action philosophy in the over-all intervention efforts for society.

For any intervention, the final overall distribution of expenditures of time and money is the net result of an extremely complex decision-making process, whether it be rational or irrational, conscious or unconscious. Each intervention has, explicitly or implicitly, a set of goals, a target population, and a set of procedures by which it hopes to reach and change members of its target population. Therefore, decisions must be made concerning three basic dimensions of social action: (1) the problems to be attacked; (2) the scale on which each problem will be attacked; and (3) the method or methods by which each problem will be attacked. Within an evaluation research action philosophy, this basic question should be continuously asked: "Is the current or planned allocation of resources to problems the most efficient possible, and have provisions been made for continuous feedback of research information?"

There are obstacles to adequate evaluation, one of the most serious being prevailing attitudes which press for the utilization of all available funds for action or program purposes and resist the use of funds for research, particularly evaluation research. The attack upon this source of resistance must be launched from two directions simultaneously: (1) ways must be devised to make increasingly efficient use of available evaluation dollars and to derive solid results from them, and (2) society must be shown the benefits of such expenditures.

One way of improving the efficiency of evaluation research is to establish procedures whereby multiple evaluations of a number of similar interventions are conducted simultaneously by the same centralized evaluation unit. There are at least two very important reasons for proceeding in this fashion—one is theoretical, the other practical. The theoretical reason is the basic need for comparative data. Our knowledge will be greatly augmented if similar information can be obtained about a number of programs which use different methods (casework, groupwork) but have the same general objective (employment). If different programs in similar kinds of communities can be compared with similar programs in different kinds of communities our knowledge will be even further advanced. The practical reason relates to available resources—financial and human. Allocations for evaluation research are likely to remain in critically short supply for some time to come, even by the most optimistic estimates. And the shortage of skilled personnel to carry out the evaluation effort is likely to turn out to be much more difficult to overcome than the financial problem. To the extent that pooled systems of program evaluations can be adopted, a great amount of duplication of effort can be eliminated and scarce resources much more efficiently utilized. Also, the potential return on the same investment will be enhanced manifold.

The second line of attack involves the gradual persuasion of the general public as well as the guardians of public and private funds that, in the long run, evaluation research can pay for itself many times over by eliminating the most wasteful uses of social action funds and substituting new ways of inducing the social changes desired by society. Wasteful is defined in this context as either not producing any impact— i.e., a desired change in the program's target population—or producing a relatively small or disappointing amount of impact per dollar of program investment. This point of view also involves a redefinition of per capita cost of service as it has been traditionally viewed. (Per capita cost of service is defined as the quotient obtained by dividing the total dollar cost of a program by the total number of individuals exposed to it.)

Convincing any significant segment of the American population to think about social action in this way will undoubtedly require long and time-consuming efforts by at least a few pioneers, but it will be worth it. If, for example, a particular training program involves a thousand individuals and costs a half million dollars, traditional calculations would indicate that the per capita cost of service is $500. But if, as well might be the case, only 100 of these individuals were placed in steady jobs as a result of their training the per capita unit cost per impact would be $5,000—a vastly different amount. The per capita cost view has resulted in a distinct preference for those programs which "serve" the largest numbers for the least amount of money. However, if programs were to compete on the basis of how much it costs to achieve one unit (however defined) of desired outcome, it is the writer's contention that the ultimate selection of programs would be very different.

A method of evaluation, cost-benefit analysis, is gaining recognition among program planners. It is a distinct improvement over per capita cost of service, but as it is usually applied it does not go far enough in either defining or providing the kind of information that is needed in making decisions about social action programs. Whereas the former measures service in terms of per capita cost, it does not attempt to measure either outcome (desired program goals) or impact (program-related success). Cost-benefit analysis attempts to measure outcome but it often does not distinguish between outcome and impact.

There are those who are opposed to evaluation research on what can be called the "philosophical" level. Proponents of this position appear to admit the need for evaluation, that is, the need for some basis to judge the worth and effectiveness of action efforts. Their resistance seems to be based primarily upon assumptions about the inapplicability of the scientific method to the study of human behavior. According to this point of view, every human being is unique and therefore cannot be studied in the aggregate. Proponents of a more modified version of this position say that the important aspects of behavior and behavorial change cannot be measured by the ordinary existing procedures of evaluation research.

The extreme version of this position—that human beings and their behavior are simply not studiable scientifically—may be impervious to ordinary attack. All of the trends in the fields relating to the study of human behavior are in the direction of quantification, rigor and the application of the canons of scientific research and experimental design. A basic issue for a strategy of evaluation research would seem to include a recognition of those instances where this philosophical position is assumed (but not truly believed) as merely a camouflage for other types of resistance to evaluation research.

The more modified version of this position, that social scientists are not able to measure the important variables, seems to represent an important challenge to the innovative quality and ingenuity of social science research. It is quite clear that considerably greater effort, and many more resources, must be thrown into the battle of developing valid, reliable measures of what are deemed to be the really important categories of behavior—character, problem solving ability, curiosity, and the like. Concomitantly, program designers and researchers must not only make greater efforts to collaborate in spelling out in theoretical detail what variables are crucial to the solution of social problems but

167

also must develop experimental procedures to measure those variables. Ultimately, these instruments must be capable of measuring change in characteristics, or variables, since it is change that interventions (social action programs) are aimed at.

A related "philosophical" type of resistance to evaluation research is on what can be called the intuitional plane. Proponents of this position also appear to agree that a basis for separating good programs from bad ones is needed. The difference between this position and the evaluation research position advocated in this paper is in the method or procedures by which the decision about the worthwhileness of a program is made. The intuitionist relies on so-called personal and professional experience; he "knows" when a program is good. He can tell just by observing a program and its participants in action. This widespread, well-known and easily recognized position is perhaps most clearly exemplified by the practitioner who simply knows that what he is doing is good, although he cannot say why. "I've been doing this for 30 years," says he, "and I wouldn't have continued at it if I didn't know that it was good." To a considerable degree, this type of resistance can be reduced to an age-old epistemological problem of how we know that we know something. Although such an issue cannot be explored in any detail in this paper, its importance to the whole area of the measurement of results of social action programs cannot and should not be minimized. A total strategy for a rational attack on the social problems of our society must include all of the known weapons, an important one being a proper kind of co-operation between practitioner and evaluation researcher.

The reflections presented pertain primarily to prevailing concerns in our society about the costs of evaluation research as well as to some basic prevailing misunderstandings concerning the necessary logical and procedural ingredients of adequate evaluation. There are a number of other related problems that deserve to be listed in this context.

Prominent among these is the time problem. The decision as to the length of the evaluation period should be based on a detailed consideration of the goals of the intervention to be evaluated and the general theoretical impact model by which it is hoped that the particular program will induce the desired changes. The two key timing issues that the impact model should deal with are (1) the length of time the participants need to be exposed to the program for its effects—as defined by the impact model—to take place and (2) the period of time that must transpire after termination of exposure to the program before the desired outcomes can be expected to manifest themselves. It is the writer's conviction that if one were to examine and spell out carefully all that is implicit in theoretical models underlying action programs, two-, three-, and even five-year demonstration periods would seldom be long enough to plan, launch, conduct, and evaluate the program in such a way that anything in the way of sensible, solid measurement of results could take place.

Closely related to the timing problem of the demonstration model is a much more mundane but nevertheless critical one, namely, the general pattern of short-term, what we might call serial, funding. The funding of a demonstration program should be logically related to its general overall theoretical model, particularly to the timing elements of that model. The result of the prevailing practice of short-term and renewal funding is a substantial waste of human energy devoted to interim report writing and refunding proposal writing which seriously reduces the proportion of time, skill and energy which could otherwise be directed to implementing the demonstration itself. High turnover among personnel (with great losses in personnel training investments), vacillating motivation and a number of related problems further serve to reduce the quality of the product.

There is another basic impediment to the development of a sound program of evaluation. It is what might be called the "success cult" or the "rose-colored glasses syndrome." In its simplest and most extreme form it admits that no evaluation is needed since the program is regarded as a success to begin with. The problem is not to find ways of evaluating the program or to obtain findings concerning its effectiveness but to find ways to convince others of its success. This type of resistance—perhaps more appropriately termed indifference—to evaluation research is most likely to come from persons with a heavy personal commitment to the success of a particular program: public officials, heads of action agencies, and occasionally, unfortunately, administrators of funding agencies. From their point of view, there can be no questioning of the value or success of a program—which is implicit in any evaluation. Funds have been committed to the program; its aim is to help people; it was designed by experts and is being run by professionals. Where is the need for evaluation, they ask. Whatever motivation there may be—fear of evaluation or sincere belief in the worth of the program—this point of view obviously represents a major obstacle to the development and implementation of an evaluation research action philosophy.

To change such attitudes, a new set of criteria must be adopted concerning the performance of public and private officials who have the responsibility for allocating society's resources. They must be judged and rewarded, not in terms of the claims of success which can be made but in terms of the extent to which they have provided for a feedback of information concerning the program's performance relative to its goals and the extent to which they make decisions concerning future allocations of resources on the basis of that information.

Under these criteria the valuable official—whether of a community, a foundation, or an agency—is the one who builds in procedures for gradually improving the level of efficiency with which he allocates resources. There are many large-scale social problems which must be dealt with and many different ways in which they can be attacked. At the same time resources are limited. In terms of the rational use of limited resources, it seems to be obvious that the decision-maker who supports an unsuccessful program but who admits that the program has not achieved its objective is far more valuable than the one who supports a program, claims its success, and then without proper evaluation pours more money into it.

For the encouragement of this change in social thinking we must look first to the foundations and public funding agencies. However, before such organizations can make refunding decisions in terms of what has been learned—whether favorable or unfavorable to the programs under consideration—a climate must be developed which would permit them this mode of operation. The issue should be decided on evidence not appearance. That certain programs have received the best press or have been publicized by other means should not influence decisions. What constitutes useful evidence as distinguished from appearance is perhaps the major challenge confronting the advocate of evaluation research.

If it is agreed that (1) there is a need for more and better evaluations of action programs; (2) adequate and effective evaluation research involves a battery of skills and strategies which are, at best, in an infant stage of development at the present time; and (3) there is a shortage of personnel who are both trained and interested in the field of evaluation research, it appears clear that a long-range concerted program will be necessary. This program should include:

1. Research on evaluation research itself which would involve surveys of community understanding of and attitudes toward evaluation research and studies of the relationships between evaluation research and the decision-making and action components of the community.

The purpose of this research program would be to provide information and insights to aid in the development of strategies aimed at a broadened and more effective evaluation program.

2. Research into the development of the technical tools of action research—instruments to measure socially significant variables—and the development of generalized impact models. Research should also include the development and application of new statistical devices, particularly variations on prediction instruments and related techniques.

The purpose of this research program would be to contribute toward the development of a repertoire of technical skills, procedures and devices which would, as much as possible, tailor action research efforts, and particularly their evaluation components, to the needs of the decision-making and action world they aim to affect.

3. Experiments in training personnel for better program evaluations —including the involvement of people at all levels who are associated with the program: political figures, agency board members and agency staff, citizens groups and potential evaluation research specialists. Ideally, this third component—designated somewhat inadequately above as training—should continuously incorporate into its program the findings derived from the first two components.

The general program suggested is intended to serve as an outline for more intensive and effective use of evaluation research in attacking the social problems besetting our society. More and better evaluation studies can aid immeasurably in finding solutions to these problems which call for urgent and immediate action.

SELECTED READINGS

Books

Burkhead, Jess. *Government Budgeting.* Cambridge, Harvard University Press, 1956.

Caro, Francis G., ed. *Readings in Evaluation Research.* New York, Russell Sage Foundation, 1971.

Churchman, C. West. *The Systems Approach.* New York, Dell Publishing Co., Inc., 1968.

Conant, James B. *Manual of Performance Standards and Evaluation.* Harrisburg, Commonwealth of Pennsylvania Office of Administration, 1968.

Grossbard, Stephen I. *PPBS For State and Local Officials.* Research Series No. 15. Kingston, R.I., University of Rhode Island, 1971.

Herzog, Elizabeth. *Some Guide Lines for Evaluative Research.* Children's Bureau Publication No. 375. Washington, D.C., Government Printing Office, 1968.

Hinrichs, Harley H., and Graeme M. Taylor. *Program Budgeting and Benefit-Cost Analysis.* Pacific Palisades, Calif., Goodyear Publishing Co., Inc., 1969.

An Introduction to Planning Programming Budgeting System. Harrisburg, Commonwealth of Pennsylvania Office of Administration, 1969.

Levin, Richard I., and Charles A. Kirkpatrick. *Planning and Control with PERT/CPM.* New York, McGraw-Hill Book Company, 1966.

Lyden, Fremont J., and Ernest G. Miller. *Planning Programming Budgeting.* Chicago, Markham Publishing Co., 1972.

Mowitz, Robert J. *The Design and Implementation of Pennsylvania's Planning, Programming, Budgeting System.* University Park, Pa., Pennsylvania State University.

O'Toole, Richard, ed. *The Organization, Management, and Tactics of Social Research.* Cambridge, Mass., Schenkman Publishing Co., Inc., 1971.

Schick, Allen. *Budget Innovation in the States.* Washington, D.C., The Brookings Institution, 1971.

Suchman, Edward A. *Evaluative Research.* New York, Russell Sage Foundation, 1967.

State-Local Finances Project of George Washington University. *Implementing PPB in State, City and County.* Washington, D.C., George Washington University, 1969.

U.S. General Accounting Office. *Glossary for Systems Analysis and Planning-Programming-Budgeting*. Washington, D.C., Government Printing Office, 1969.

Wildavsky, Aaron. *The Politics of the Budgetary Process*. Boston, Little, Brown and Company, 1964.

Articles

Alloway, James A. "PPB: The How and Why of It," *New Jersey Municipalities*, June, 1970, 11, 30–32.

Balls, Herbert R. "New Techniques in Government Budgeting: Planning, Programming and Budgeting in Canada," *Public Administration*, Vol. 48 (autumn, 1970), 289–305.

Blick, Larry N. "An Approach to Implementing PPB," *Municipal Finance*, Vol. 41, No. 4 (May, 1969), 148–54.

Botner, Stanley B. "PPBS: A Tool for Smaller Cities?" *Municipal Finance*, Vol. 43, No. 4 (May, 1971), 173–78.

Branch, Melville C. "A Missing Link in Planning," *California Management Review*, Vol. 6, No. 1 (fall, 1963), 75–80.

Brown, Paul L. "An Operational Model for a Planning-Programming-Budgeting System," report presented to the Post Audit Seminar, Lexington, Ky., June 17, 1970. Condensed in Fremont J. Lyden and Ernest G. Miller, *Planning-Programming-Budgeting: A Systems Approach to Management*, Chicago, Markham Publishing Company, 1972, 183–95.

Burke, Edmund M. "The Road to Planning: An Organizational Analysis," *Social Service Review*, Vol. 39, No. 3 (September, 1965), 261–70.

————. "The Search for Authority in Planning," *Social Service Review*, Vol. 41, No. 3 (September, 1967), 250–60.

Cotton, John F. "Planning-Programming-Budgeting Systems for Local Government," *Municipal Finance*, Vol. 41, No. 1 (August, 1968), 26–33.

Deeks, D. J., and A. J. Reynolds. "Critical Path Method—A Technique for Project Planning," *Management Controls*, February, 1966, 24–32.

deNeufville, Richard. "Systems Analysis: A Decision Process," *Industrial Management Review*, Vol. 2, No. 3 (June, 1970), 49–58.

Denhardt, Robert B. "Organizing the Budget Function," *Municipal Finance*, Vol. 63, No. 4 (May, 1971), 167–72.

Donaho, John A. "Planning-Programming-Budgeting Systems," *Municipal Finance*, Vol. 40, No. 1 (August, 1967), 17–25.

Drew, Elizabeth B. "HEW Grapples with PPBS," *The Public Interest*, No. 8 (summer, 1967), 9–29.

Durham, Edgar J. "Desirable Features of Line Item Budgeting," *Municipal Finance*, Vol. 34, No. 2 (November, 1961), 93–95.

Elkin, Robert. "Framework for Decision-Making—Applying PPBS to Public Welfare Program Structure," *Public Welfare*, April, 1969, 157–66.

Enthoven, Alain. "What Systems Analysis Is and Is Not," hearing before the Senate Subcommittee on National Security, September 27 and October 18, 1967.

Feingold, Eugene. "The Changing Political Character of Health Planning," *American Journal of Public Health*, Vol. 59, No. 5 (May, 1969), 803–808.

Fifer, Ellen Z. "Hang-ups in Health Planning," *American Journal of Public Health*, Vol. 59, No. 5 (May, 1969), 765–69.

Gibbs, Wesley F. "Program Budgeting Filters Down to Education," *Nation's Schools*, Vol. 82, No. 5 (November, 1968), 51–59.

Gordon, Jay H. "Accounting Problems of Planning-Programming-Budgeting Systems," *Municipal Finance*, Vol. 41, No. 3 (February, 1969), 122–26.

Gorham, William. "Sharpening the Knife that Cuts the Public Pie," *Public Administration Review*, May–June, 1968, 236–41.

Graham, D. Robert. "The Florida Budget—The Old Myth and New Reality," *Florida Planning and Development*, Vol. 20, Nos. 3, 4 (March–April, 1969), 1–7.

Gross, B. M. "What Are Your Organization's Objectives? A General Systems Approach to Planning," *Human Relations*, Vol. 18, No. 3 (August, 1965), 195–216.

Harnish, Thomas I. "Regional Medical Program Planning," *American Journal of Public Health*, Vol. 59, No. 5 (May, 1969), 770–72.

Higgins, Harry F. "PPBS and the Reform of the Budgetary Process," *Public Affairs Bulletin*, Vol. 8, No. 5 (1969).

Hitch, Charles J. "Program Budgeting: An Appraisal," *Management Forum*, Vol. 18, No. 3 (September, 1968), section IV.

Holder, Lee, and Lynn Denison. "A Decision-Making Approach to Comprehensive Health Planning," *Public Health Reports*, Vol. 83, No. 7 (July, 1968), 559–68.

Johnson, A. W. "PPB and Decision-Making in the Government of Canada," *Cost and Management*, March–April, 1971, 12–19.

Kaufman, Herbert. "The Politics of Health Planning," *American Journal of Public Health*, Vol. 59, No. 5 (May, 1969), 795–97.

Lewis, Verne B. "Toward a Theory of Budgeting," *Public Administration Review*, Vol. 12, No. 1, 42–54.

Lish, Monty C. "Organizing for a New Approach to Budgeting," *Municipal Finance*, Vol. 41, No. 4 (May, 1969), 155–62.

Morris, Robert, and Robert H. Binstock. "Decisions Confronting a Planning Specialist," *Social Service Review*, Vol. 40, No. 1 (March, 1966), 8–14.

Mott, Basil J. F. "The Myth of Planning Without Politics," *American Journal of Public Health*, Vol. 59, No. 5 (May, 1969), 797–803.

Murphy, Joseph S. "The Quiet Revolution in Government Planning Techniques," *Management Review*, Vol. 57 (April, 1968), 4–11.

O'Donnell, Cyril. "Planning Objectives," *California Management Review*, Vol. 6, No. 2 (winter, 1963), 3–10.

Person, H. S. "Research and Planning as Functions of Administration and Management," *Public Administration Review*, Vol. 1, No. 1 (autumn, 1940).

Reynolds, John W., and Walter G. Hollander. "Program Budgeting in Wisconsin," *State Government*, autumn, 1963.

Sage, William G. and James J. Holodnak. "PPBS and Accounting in San Diego," *Municipal Finance*, Vol. 41, No. 3 (February, 1969), 134–37.

Schick, Allen. "The Road to PPB: The Stages of Budget Reform," *Public Administration Review*, Vol. 26, No. 4 (December, 1966), 243–58.

Spindler, Arthur. "PPBS and Social and Rehabilitation Services," *Welfare in Review*, Vol. 7, No. 5 (April, 1969), 22–28.

Wachs, Melvin W. "Planning-Programming-Budgeting and Management Information Systems in Mental Health," *American Journal of Public Health*, Vol. 59, No. 2 (February, 1969), 262–66.

Wallace, David A., and William C. McDonnell. "Diary of a Plan," *Journal of the American Institute of Planners*, Vol. 37, No. 1 (January, 1971), 11–25.

Weinrich, John E. "Budget Analysis and Fiscal Efficiency," *Administrative Sciences*, Vol. 33 (1967), 305–13.

Wildavsky, Aaron. "Political Implications of Budgetary Reform," *Public Administration Review*, Vol. 21, (autumn, 1961), 183–90.

Wilsey, Carl E. "Program Budgeting: An Easy Guide with the Confusion Removed," *American School Board Journal*, Vol. 156, No. 11 (May, 1969), 16–19.

Organization is the process by which major program responsibilities are systematically divided into homogeneous segments of manageable size. It includes the assignment of personnel and facilities to accomplish the objectives of the organization; it provides for direction, supervision, control, and coordination of the activities of individuals and units by specifying to whom each is responsible; it defines the extent of authority delegated to individuals and units to enable them to carry out assigned responsibilities; and it also provides for the planning of organizational change, or reorganization, as indicated by performance results. Thus, the structure of the organization becomes the framework for its management, while the lines on the organizational chart represent the interpersonal relationships of its personnel.

Limitation of an executive's capacity to adequately perform all required managerial functions necessitates hierarchical organization. The need for hierarchy is also aggravated by organizational growth. Delegation of work to a lower level tends to reduce the manager's workload, hopefully to a degree greater than the attendant increase in supervisory duties.

The term *span of control* frequently used in management literature refers to the number of subordinates a manager can effectively supervise. Koontz and O'Donnell point out that much more than mere control is involved, and they prefer the term *span of management*.[1] There is considerable difference of opinion among managers about the number of subordinates a manager can effectively supervise. This number doubtless will vary with organizations and managers. When the number of subordinates exceeds the number the manager can effectively supervise, another organizational level may be added to relieve the situation. Thus, the span of management is directly related to the number of levels in the hierarchy. The smaller the span, the greater the number of organizational levels; conversely, the larger the span, the fewer the organizational levels. The biblical account of Moses leading the Israelites out of Egypt recorded in the Book of Exodus is one of the earliest recorded cases of organization. Moses was kept so busy dealing with the problems of the people he had little time left for other responsibilities, while the people were forced to wait in long lines for the one man who could help them. Jethro, Moses' father-in-law, observing the confusion, counseled Moses

[1] Harold Koontz and Cyril O'Donnell, *Principles of Management*, 3rd ed. (New York, McGraw-Hill Book Company, 1964), 216.

177

to appoint rulers of thousands, rulers of hundreds, rulers of fifties, and rulers of tens to share the burdens with him.

Historically and traditionally, managers of both industrial and governmental organizations have tended to stress organizational structure, at times almost to the exclusion of human considerations. There is a tendency on the part of managers to forget that there is an informal organization with which they must deal and which, in some respects, may be as important to the accomplishment of goals and objectives as the formal organization. The paternalistic and individualistic theory of management, with its authoritarian overtones of the past, has largely given way in practice to management by groups ranging in size from a few persons to thousands of individuals. The groups operate through a hierarchical arrangement which may be the result of either formal planning or informal processes.

The article "The Theory of Organization: A Note," by George Graham, provides an excellent overview of previous concepts and schools of thought expressed in management literature. The author appropriately distinguishes between the approach of the "classical theorists" and that of the "behaviorists" and discusses the effect of organization on the motivation and morale of the organization's personnel.

Moving from the theory of organization to organization in practice, we present Henri Fayol's concepts of hierarchy, some problems inherent in it, and how these problems can be minimized in practice. Following in Fayol's footsteps, other "principles" of organization and management are examined in "Division of Labor," by Luther Gulick, and "Unity of Command," by Roy F. Hendrickson. "Span of Control," or span of management, is discussed by the United States Civil Service Commission Bureau of Training in a one-page statement. The conclusion is that there are no absolutes, that the span depends upon conditions, and that it is a matter of judgment. The statement presents certain guidelines for supervisors. "Staff and Line Organization," by Marshall Dimock, highlights the confusion that can arise from the improper use of staff and the importance of clearly defining who has what authority and responsibility for work requirements.

At this point we move from formal organization, represented by an organization chart, to informal organization. In "Examining the *Other* Organization," Jacob Jacoby discusses some of the differences that exist between formal and informal organizations. Formal and informal are not opposites; neither are they separable. Both are essential. Formal concepts came first; informal theories came when it became clear that the formal did not tell the entire story.

John M. Pfiffner and Frank P. Sherwood, in their book *Administrative Organization* (pages 20–27), present "Informal Organization and the Concepts of Overlays" to illustrate how the informal organization tends to alter and modify the organization as formally established. Four illustrations are presented for sociometric overlay, functional overlay, power overlay, and communications overlay. These illustrations are designed to show some of the interaction that takes place between members of the organization that is informal in nature and which is in the interest of effective organizational performance.

Any publication dealing with management and organization, of necessity, must be concerned with reorganization to meet changing environmental, economic, political, or other conditions. The short statement attributed to Petronius Arbiter in 210 B.C. presents the negative view, which may too often describe situations that exist. This statement is followed by an article by B. Douglas Stone, Jr., "Reorganizing—More Than Drawing a New Chart." Stone enumerates some of the factors that must be taken into account in reorganization. His article is appropriately followed by "Organizational Analysis: Some Notes on Methods and Criteria," by C. Dwight Waldo. Waldo's article includes a practical checklist for reorganization in the form of specific questions that serve as a means of solving problems of organization and reorganization.

Organization development is a subject to which many present-day management writers are giving increased attention. Various ideas are expressed by different authors about the meaning of organization development. In the article "Is Organization Development Possible in Government?" Frederick F. Fisher presents the definitions of three well-known writers: Warren Bennis, Richard Beckhard, and Warner Burke. Fisher emphasizes the need for the change in certain values to make organizational development effective in a public agency.

For a change of pace, Peter Cossette offers some positive approaches to the problems growing out of hierarchical pressure and the need for motivation in his article "How to Beat the Peter Principle." For the manager to whom the concepts of organizational development are new, Lyman K. Randall gives a practical, down-to-earth review in "Common Questions and Tentative Answers Regarding Organizational Development." The last article, by John W. Gardner, "How to Prevent Organizational Dry Rot," lists nine rules and requirements for organizations interested in self-renewal. It is particularly applicable to government agencies at all levels.

19. The Theory of Organization: A Note*

George Graham

The literature on organization has very largely been focused on the subject of management or administration. Management itself cannot be fully understood without a knowledge of the conceptual framework within which it works, namely, organization. Thus writers on management have frequently made essays into the theory of organization. This was the approach adopted by Henri Fayol, whose monograph on *General and Industrial Management*, first published in book form in 1925, stimulated wide academic interest in management.[1] His approach has been adopted by many subsequent writers.

However, there appears to be little agreement among writers on the concept of organization. J. G. March and H. A. Simon in their exhaustive survey of the literature on the subject came to this conclusion: "The literature leaves one with the impression that after all not a great deal has been said about organizations, but it has been said over and over in a variety of languages. Consequently, we require a serious effort toward the construction of a common language."[2] E. Wight Bakke acknowledged the same difficulty in his contribution to a symposium:

A survey of the current literature related to what is beginning to be called "organizational behavior" reveals a relatively small concern with the clear definition of the nature and structure of a social organization. The current literature is filled with generalizations relevant to the interaction of, interdependence of, mutual impact of, divergent interests of, power relations among, competition between, organizations. . . . But seldom does one find a careful and systematic description of the nature and structure of the "thing" with whose internally and externally directed activity the hypotheses are concerned.[3]

H. A. Simon's *Administrative Behavior*, which preceded these surveys, was written "partly as a result of the author's dissatisfaction with the so-called 'principles of administration' that are to be found in the current literature of administrative theory.[4] A whole chapter of the book is devoted to a demolition of what he considers to be wrong and ambiguous usages of terms.

A study of organization theory leaves one groping for clearer defi-

* From *Public Administration*, Vol. 46 (Summer, 1968), 191–201. Reprinted by permission.
1 H. Fayol, *General and Industrial Management*, translated from the French edition (Dunod) by Constance Storrs, London, 1949.
2 J. G. March and H. A. Simon, *Organizations*, London, 1959, p. 5.
3 M. Haire (ed.), *Modern Organization Theory: A Symposium*, 1959, pp. 16–17.
4 P. 18.

nitions of concepts, and one cannot help casting envious glances at other branches of knowledge with their more sharply defined concepts. The study soon becomes an exercise in the reconstruction of the elements of organization from a multiplicity of postulates, as the following examples show.

J. D. Mooney's definition of organization is as follows: "Organization is the form of every human association for the attainment of a common purpose." He considers it as "a pure process." He then indicates the delimitation of functions and concludes thus: "Organization therefore refers to more than the framework of the edifice. It refers to these functions as they appear in action, the very pulse and heartbeats, the circulation, the respiration, the vital movement so to speak, of the organized unit." His view of co-ordination is as follows: "Co-ordination is the orderly arrangement of group effort, to provide unity of action in the pursuit of a common purpose. When we call co-ordination the first principle, we mean that this term expresses the principles of organization in toto; nothing less.[5]

Mary Parker Follet's "four fundamental principles of organization are as follows: (1) Co-ordination as the reciprocal relating all the functions in a situation. (2) Co-ordination by direct contact of the responsible people concerned. (3) Co-ordination in the early stages. (4) Co-ordination as a continuing process. These four principles show the basis of control, show the process of control, show that control is a process."[6]

Chester Barnard's definition of "formal organization" is "a system of consciously co-ordinated activities or forces of two or more persons."[7]

These three different statements illustrate the lack of clarity and the disagreements in terminology. According to the definitions of Mooney and Barnard, co-ordination is fused with organization; while Mary Parker Follet's is a composite concept of organization, co-ordination, and control.

However, G. E. Milward maintains that co-ordination is "essentially a consequence of organization."[8] In other words, co-ordination as a concept can be differentiated from organization and has its own distinctive quality. The problem is how to illuminate the distinctive qualities of co-ordination and the other major concepts in organization theory.

What seems to be broadly agreed in the three definitions quoted above is that organization is concerned with creating a system or order in human activities. Non-organized activities relate to no order. A queue is

[5] J. D. Mooney, *The Principles of Organization*, rev. ed., New York, 1947, pp. 1–5.

[6] L. Gulick and L. Urwick (eds.), *Papers on the Science of Administration*, New York, 1937, pp. 161 and 166.

[7] C. Barnard, *The Functions of the Executive*, Cambridge, Mass., 1938, p. 73.

[8] G. E. Milward, *An Approach to Management*, London, 1946, p. 69.

an organization in contrast with a stampede. A queue does not require co-ordination either, which lends support to Milward's contention. The distinctive characteristic of organization seems to be the orderliness and the definitive nature of activities which are undertaken by human beings. This is brought out by the definitions of L. Urwick and G. E. Milward. Urwick's "strictly limited and technical meaning" of organization is as follows: "determining what activities are necessary to any purpose (or 'plan') and arranging them in groups which may be assigned to individuals."[9] Milward's definition is similar: "Organization is the process of dividing work into convenient tasks or duties, of grouping such duties in the form of posts, of delegating authority to each post, and of appointing qualified staff to be responsible that the work is carried out as planned."[10]

The remaining difficulty is that the term is regarded by all, except Barnard, as denoting a process. It is clear, however, that when the term is used it is meant to refer not to a process but to something in the nature of a framework, for, either at inception, or at any point in time while it is working, an organization can be reduced to a structure of posts or positions denoting definite activities. Thus organization as a concept is, we think, static rather than dynamic. Mooney refers to it as "the form of every human association" and this cannot be reconciled with his subsequent assertion that it is "a pure process." The performance of activities by the members of this human association may constitute "a pure process" but not "the form" *per se*. Barnard refers to organization as a system, and a system is static as a concept. Milward also contends that "organization by itself does nothing; it is the staff making up the organization who do the work, who achieve the objective, aided or impeded by the organization."[11] If we agree that organization is a "system," which "by itself does nothing," then it follows that organization cannot be a process because a process always produces something. The point then is that the working of an organization, which is a process, must be distinguished from organization, which is static.

Again, since Milward claims that organization may aid or impede the staff, it follows that the staff stand apart from the organization. Their relationship to the organization is through the posts which they fill to work the organization—a system. The staff cannot be said to be the organization. They belong to a "human association." They may be members of a department or a corporation, but a department or a corporation has an organization—a system—by which it works. Similarly, Barnard excludes machines and equipment from the concept of organi-

---

9 L. Urwick, *The Elements of Administration*, London, 1947, pp. 35 and 36.
10 Ibid., p. 34.
11 Ibid., p. 30.

zation.[12] We cannot talk of the organization of machines or buildings or land. These constitute the environment of activities. We can only talk of activities performed by the personnel with, in, or on, these. Of course, the planning or layout of these physical resources is very important as it may facilitate or impede the working of the organization.

From the foregoing analysis we can conclude that the distinctive feature of organization is that it is a system of human activities aimed at the achievement of a specific objective or objectives.

CO-ORDINATION

Since Milward is the only one of the writers referred to above who contends that co-ordination is a consequence of organization, his definition of the term is of particular interest. According to him, "Co-ordination is the assembly and harmonizing with policy or objective, of work, or interests, which have been separated or divided, in the process of planning and organization."[13] He also makes this point: "The suggestion is that co-ordination of policies or plans results in an integration which is not the same as the sum of the plans, but may be greater or less mathematically in that it merges details and develops the whole, or the combination of details, into a common policy or plan."[14] It can thus be said that co-ordination is concerned with adjustments to what flows from the working of an organization. If this result, actual or anticipated, indicates that the objective will be achieved as conceived or planned, then the organization can operate without much need for adjustments or co-ordination. If not, then there may be disproportions in the planned activities of different sectors of the organization. Co-ordination is thus directed towards adjusting the scale of activities, increasing or reducing the extent of activities in the different sectors in order to ensure the achievement of the overall objective.

Co-ordination may be conceived as the process of adjusting activities to achieve a harmony in the working of an organization. While co-ordination is of necessity dynamic, organization is static as a concept. Co-ordination is a very important element because, except in a relatively small-scale organization, it is generally difficult to determine or define activities precisely, and moreover circumstances may arise which will require changes in the plan of activities, if the overall objectives of the organization are to be achieved. The larger the scale of organization the greater the need for co-ordination. Co-ordination is thus an essential and continuous feature of large-scale organization.

PLANNING

Planning as a concept is the least riddled with disagreements. It is only its

12 Ibid., p. 67.
13 Ibid., p. 35.
14 Ibid., p. 66.

scope which may be re-stated. Milward's definition is as follows: "A plan of operations is a detailed statement of 'how' the given objective may be attained, and the process of 'planning' consists of their re-assembly in the form of efficient and related procedures . . . Policy planning is the extension of the same principles to another level of Administration or Management . . . the expression at a high level of an attitude of mind of the whole organization towards their work, an analytical attitude which demands to know how they are to do a job, before work on it is started."[15] Planning then is a process of selection from possible alternatives of what activities are to be performed and with what physical resources. Organization is itself the product of planning. Planning is also concerned with the securing or deployment of physical resources. It is a periodical exercise, its frequency depending on the nature of activities.

CONTROL

According to Fayol, "Control consists in verifying whether everything occurs in conformity with the plan adopted, the instructions issued and principles established."[16] Control is the outcome of a relationship between two or more persons or institutions where one has the authority to request specific action (or inaction) of another. Control is exercised on the basis of a certain established criterion.

It may be argued that the imposition of limitations in the form of definition of activities is itself control. We rather consider this to be an organizational action which seeks to establish a *ne plus ultra* for the exercise of legitimate authority. Action beyond this is by its nature *ultra vires* and a higher authority can act to impose restraint. This will clearly be control. Control then is mainly exercised at the margin of legitimate authority. It is at this margin that initiative is exercised by a subordinate. Control is essential here to ensure that initiative is exercised in terms of the overall objective of the organisation. The dynamism in the working of an organization depends on how control at the margin is exercised.

THE ESSENCE OF ORGANIZATION

One can agree with March, Simon and Bakke that there is still little coherence in organization theory. Indeed Fayol, in his pioneering work in this field, acknowledged this predicament.[17] So did Barnard.[18] Much of the literature deals almost exclusively with industrial organization, with case studies of particular techniques of management, but this leaves out of consideration other spheres in which organization operates. Yet organization is fundamental to various forms of human activities of

15 Ibid., pp. 34 and 35.
16 Ibid., p. 35.
17 Ibid., p. 15.
18 Ibid., pp. 1–7.

which industrial activity is only one. The scale of organization which attracts the attention of writers is also almost always large, and there is hardly any examination of small-scale organization, particularly the organization by the individual of his own affairs. Yet Fayol made the point that organization applies as much to the activities of the individual as it does to those of the group, and Barnard brought out the immense significance of the individual's organization of his own affairs and how this affected his role in group activities—what may be referred to as the "organization sole" as opposed to the "organization aggregate."[19]

Barnard outlined the nature of the problem in organization theory in his foreword to Simon's book, and this is worth quoting at some length. He saw three levels of knowledge of organization. The first was the level of "concrete behaviour in specific situations." The second was that of "specific organization practice." These two levels he thought were generally adequately treated. He went on to say that

the third level of knowledge is, of course, the one exemplified in this book. I shall say no more of it. But what justifies the belief that general knowledge of administrative behaviour or organization is attainable? Professor Simon has not demonstrated this, nor have others who have been working in this field. We merely assert or assume it. I can only give the grounds for my belief briefly. Professor Simon's abstractions seemed sound to me because they express aspects of my experience under a wide variety of conditions. A university president tells me that his principal organization difficulty is the "following which, of course, is peculiar to universities." He then describes a problem I have encountered a hundred times but never in a university. I listen to the Commanding General of the Air Transport Corps lecturing on organization problems of that Corps. I have never had military experience, I have read little of military organization, yet I think I understand him almost perfectly. I give a lecture mistitled "The Principles of Organization" at the Air War College. The questions and discussion in the hour following indicate that I have made myself fairly well understood. Such experience forms the ground for the belief that abstract principles of structure may be discerned in organizations of great variety, and that ultimately it may be possible to state principles of general organization.[20]

If organization relates to the activities of individuals as well as to the activities of groups, and its scope is so varied as to touch on practically all types of human activities, then for a general theory to be tenable it should bring out the common factor in the concept of organization which seems to be eluding definition. There is no doubt that a number of hypotheses about the essence of organization might be explored to discover the silver thread which weaves all types of pre-planned activities into a single conceptual fabric, whether these activities are undertaken by

[19] Cf. The idea of the "corporation sole" and the "corporation aggregate."
[20] H. A. Simon, *Administrative Behavior*, Glencoe, Ill., 1947, pp. xi–xii.

individuals or by groups. The approach to this problem which is suggested here is that we can discern a factor common to all organized activities if we try to define the primary purpose of organization per se. Effectiveness or efficiency in the performance of activities is the purpose mentioned by many writers. A hypothesis worth considering is that the primary purpose of any organization is the maximization of the performance of activities in relation to a given time-scale. The idea of a time-scale is crucial, for it is the scarcity of time in relation to a set of activities to be performed which makes organization essential. The corollary of this hypothesis may well be stated as the maximization of time-value in relation to the performance of activities. This more neutral idea of maximization avoids the suggestion that effectiveness and efficiency are automatic attributes of organization, for an organization may prove ineffective or inefficient for attaining the specific objective for which it was created. The contention is that while effectiveness and efficiency are desiderata, maximization is fundamental, indicating the primary purpose or function of organization per se.

We believe that this hypothesis may stand up to some tests, although a more exhaustive demonstration of its validity is beyond the scope of this paper. As far as economic organization is concerned it is clear that the primary concern of any industrialist is to maximize performance— in economic jargon, to raise productivity to the highest level possible. The same purpose of maximizing performance can be discerned in military organization. As far as the organization of social and political life is concerned the establishment of rights and obligations leads to a fuller life for all; without such organization, to use Hobbes's immortal phrase, life would be "poor, nasty, brutish and short."

This primary purpose of organization is not to be confused with the objectives of organized activities which are varied and depend on the motives of the individuals or groups involved. An illustration will clarify the distinction. The overriding objective of an industrial concern is to make profits: this derives from motive. Organization is an aid for achieving this objective and its primary purpose is the maximization of the performance of activities in which the concern is engaged during limited working hours. Effectiveness will depend on the capacity of the organization to cover the performnace of all necessary activities, while efficiency will depend on proper co-ordination and control to ensure that the level of operations is at a requisite optimum: that targets are achieved within reasonable approximations. Over-activity is as much a bane as under-activity. Provided that the organization operates effectively and efficiently a high level of productivity will normally have the effect of delivering the profits. Whether the profits are actually made or not will depend on endogenous as well as exogenous factors. The endogenous factors relate to such matters as the capacities of the personnel and their relationships, equipment employed and its lay-out, and the effective and efficient working of the organization to achieve planned targets. Exogenous factors relate to such things as unforeseen changes in market conditions or a change in government policy which affects the operations of the industry. Thus deficits may be incurred though the organization is efficient, while profits may be made though the organization is inefficient, but in either event the circumstances will be exceptional. Under normal conditions an efficient organization will ensure the realization of profits.

COMPARISON OF THE CLASSICAL AND BEHAVIOURAL SCHOOLS

We have already stated that the essential characteristic of organization is that it is a system. A system naturally implies definite relationships between its parts and procedures or regulations by which it works. One thing which creates complications in the understanding of organization is that apart from the relationships between the parts or posts of the organization which can be defined in exact terms—in a constitution and directives—there is also the factor of human relationships between the personnel filling these posts, which are difficult to define in any exact terms. These indefinable human relationships can, however, have an important extraneous influence on the way the whole system works. It is an endeavour to understand the effects of this human factor on the working of an organization which underlies the writings of the "behavioural" school of H. A. Simon and others. They mainly adopt a psychological approach to an understanding of the working of an organization. It appears that they conceive the interactions between these two types of relationships as constituting co-ordination, as is evident from the following statement by March and Simon: "Organizations are assemblages of inter-acting human beings and they are the largest assemblages in our society that have anything resembling a central coordinative system."[21] They go on to speak of "the 'stimuli' that impinge on the individual, of the psychological 'set' or 'frame' of reference that is evoked by these stimuli and of the 'response' or 'action' that results." They indicate that they are interested "particularly in how these unanticipated consequences restrict the adaptiveness of the organization to the goals of the top administrative hierarchy."[22] Further on they assert

Our analysis suggests that influence over the motivation to produce is a function of influence over (a) the evoking of action alternatives for the individual, (b) the consequences of evoked alternatives anticipated by the

21 Ibid., p. 4.
22 Ibid., pp. 35 and 36.

individual, and (c) the values attached to consequences by the individual. Each of these aspects is partly under the control of the organization but partly also determined by extra-organization factors.[23]

The other school of thought is referred to by March and Simon as the "classical theorists." Writers of this school, like Henri Fayol, F. W. Taylor, L. Urwick and others are more concerned with the mechanism of organization itself rather than the extraneous influence, though they give this some attention. This school has two main streams. F. W. Taylor and others, in their "scientific management" approach, are more concerned with efficient planning of physical resources, with the most thorough definition and timing of every activity in the organization, and with efficient control of the performance of each group of activities. They deal with the human situation through elaborate regulations and cash inducements, believing the cash nexus to be an enduring bond in group effort.[24] Others like Fayol, Urwick and Milward, while acknowledging the importance of the human factor, emphasize the importance of a clear organizational pattern and the mechanisms of control.

Half-way between these two schools of thought stands Chester Barnard. Although he may be mainly considered as a classical theorist he also reached out into the behavioural school. The first part of his book, already referred to, is an exposition in depth of the pure theory of organizations. As he sees it, man, individualistic by nature, with his own private affairs to organize, is pitchforked into organized group activities which in essence require conformity. A large part of the executive process, as he sees it, consists in conditioning individuals by training, inculcation of attitudes and the creation of incentives to make them play their required roles in group activities.[25] He examines the biological and physical limitations in organization and also deals with the psychological and social factors in organization. Operating on these psychological and social factors, he says,

is in a sense internal and involves the direct invention of effective methods of human relationships. This process as a special technical field has hardly been recognized until recently; and though in fact in innumerable fields of practical endeavour it has been the object of intense detailed effort, it has received little scientific study except, perhaps, in the stage of last refinements, in what was once called "scientific management," or in such systematic technical processes as accounting.[26]

It is this field which has been receiving the attention of the behavioural theorists.

23 Ibid., p. 82.
24 *Vide*, F. W. Taylor, *Scientific Management*, 1911.
25 Ibid., p. 15.
26 Ibid., p. 55.

Human conduct is difficult to reduce into a comprehensive code of norms applicable in any human situation. The same type of situation may often be modified by other factors, personal and circumstantial. Thus unless we take a certain minimum set of norms as what might be expected to be acted upon in a situation, we are in danger of launching on a much wider study of what man is. This is largely what March and Simon set out to achieve, as is implied in their "focus on a different set of qualities of the organization member—his characteristics as a rational man."[27] On the other hand, the problem can be limited to what man, as a rational being, would normally do in a particular situation that might arise in the working of an organization. What concerns the behavioural theorists is not confined to organization but applies to any situation relating to organized or nonorganized human activities. Every organization, however, has a code of conduct (or regulations) which helps to minimize the unpredictability of the human factor. Thus *ceteris paribus*, human relationships are determinable to a very high degree according to an organizational code of conduct. This makes possible the construction of a more limited conceptual framework within which one can study the working of an organization, which is what the classical theorists elect to do. Significantly, March and Simon admit that "knowledge of the program of an organization permits one to predict in considerable detail the behaviour of members of the organization."[28] What they consider as "programming" is what the classical theorists conceive as "organization."

The writings of the behavioural theorists differ from those of the classical theorists mainly in methodology. While the former examine the dimensions of organization, the latter postulate the structure which embraces these dimensions. The definitions of the former are generally in very wide terms (what one might consider as "macro-organization" theory). For example, E. Wight Bakke's definition of organization is in these terms: "A social organization is a continuing system of differentiated and co-ordinated human activities utilizing, transforming, and welding together a specific set of human, material, capital, ideational and natural resources into a unique problem-solving whole engaged in satisfying the particular human needs in interaction with other systems of human activities and resources in its environment."[29] H. A. Simon's view of co-ordination is as follows

By the exercise of authority or other forms of influence it is possible to centralize the function of deciding so that a general plan of operations will govern the activities of all member of the organization. This co-ordination may be either procedural or substantive in nature: by procedural co-ordina-

27 Ibid., p. 136.
28 Ibid., p. 143.
29 M. Haire (ed.), op. cit., p. 37.

tion is meant the specification of the organization itself—that is the generalized description of the behaviours and relationships of the members of the organization. Procedural co-ordination establishes the lines of authority and outlines the sphere of activity of each organization member, while substantive co-ordination specifies the content of his work.[30]

The classical theorists, on the other hand, are interested in defining every single important factor in organization (what one might consider as "micro-organization" theory). Their definitions are in more limited terms. Their writings analyse static models and have illuminated the basic elements of organization. They, however, do not examine the factors which come into play when an organization is activated.

The dynamics of an organization is mainly concerned with the relationships and interactions of the personnel. It is this dynamic situation which attracts the interest of the behavioural theorists. Much of their writings throws light on the complexities of human relations or industrial relations. Their writings may thus be considered as a valuable complement to, rather than a departure from, the writings of the classical theorists.

[30] Ibid., p. 10.

20. The Hierarchy*

Henri Fayol

The hierarchy is the series of officials which runs in order of rank from the supreme authority to the lowest employee. The hierarchic channel is the road which all communications leaving or addressed to the supreme authority follow in passing through all the ranks of the hierarchy. The need for this channel arises both from the need for safe transmission and from unity of command but it is not always the quickest channel, and in very big enterprises, the State in particular, it is sometimes disastrously long. As, however, there are many operations whose success depends on rapid execution, we must find a means of reconciling respect for the hierarchic channel with the need for quick action. This can be done in the following way:

Let us suppose that it is necessary to put function F in communication with function P, in an undertaking whose hierarchy is represented by the double ladder G-A-Q. In order to follow the hierarchic channel, we should have to climb the ladder from F to A and then go down from A to P, stopping at each rung, and then repeat this journey in the opposite direction in order to get back to our starting point

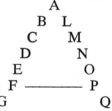

It is clearly much simpler and quicker to go straight from F to P by using the "bridge" F-P, and this is what is most frequently done. The hierarchic principle will be safeguarded if E and O have authorized their respective subordinates, F and P, to enter into direct relations, and the situation will, finally, be perfectly in order if F and P immediately tell their respective chiefs what they have agreed to do. So long as F and P remain in agreement and their actions are approved by their immediate supervisors, direct relations can be continued, but as soon as either of these conditions ceases to exist, direct relations must stop and the hierarchic channel be resumed.

The use of the "bridge" is simple, swift, and sure; it allows the two

* From *Industrial and General Administration*, 28–29. Translated from the French by J. A. Courbrough for the International Management Institute (London, Pitman Publishing Company). Reprinted by permission.

employees F and P, in one meeting of a few hours, to deal with a question which by the hierarchic channel would go through twenty transmissions, inconvenience many people, entail an enormous amount of writing, and waste weeks or months in arriving at a solution. It seems impossible that such practices, which are as absurd as they are disastrous, should be in common use, but, unfortunately, there is no doubt that they are used in matters connected with State services. It is generally agreed that the chief cause of this is the fear of responsibility, but I personally believe that it is due rather to lack of administrative ability among the men who are in charge. If the supreme authority A made his assistants B and L use the "bridge" and saw that they made their subordinates C and M use it too, the habit of taking responsibility would be established and the courage to accept it developed at the same time as the use of the shortest route.

It is a mistake to leave the hierarchic channel without good reason, but it is a much greater one to follow it when doing so will harm the undertaking; in certain circumstances, this can be a very serious mistake indeed. When an employee has to choose between the two methods of procedure and cannot get the advice of his immediate superior, he must have sufficient courage and feel himself free to adopt the one which the common good demands. In order that he may be in a suitable state of mind to do this, he must have been prepared beforehand for such a situation by the example of his superiors, for example must always come from above.

21. Division of Labor*

Luther Gulick

Why divide work? Because men differ in nature, capacity and skill, and gain greatly in dexterity by specialization; because the same man cannot be at two places at the same time; because one man cannot do two things at the same time; because the range of knowledge and skill is so great that a man cannot within his life-span know more than a small fraction of it. In other words, it is a question of human nature, time, and space.

If subdivision of work is inescapable, co-ordination becomes mandatory. There is, however, no one way to co-ordination. Experience shows that it may be achieved in two primary ways. These are:

1. By organization, that is, by interrelating the subdivisions of work by allotting them to men who are placed in a structure of authority, so that the work may be co-ordinated by orders of superiors to subordinates, reaching from the top to the bottom of the entire enterprise.

2. By the dominance of an idea, that is, the development of intelligent singleness of purpose in the minds and wills of those who are working together as a group, so that each worker will of his own accord fit his task into the whole with skill and enthusiasm.

* Originally published as "Notes on the Theory of Organization" in L. Gulick and L. Urwick, eds., *Papers on the Science of Administration*, 3–6. Copyright 1937, Institute of Public Administration. Reprinted by permission.

22. Unity of Command*

Roy F. Hendrickson

Everyone in an organization should know who's who. Everyone should know where he fits into the organizational pattern. He should know his superiors and his proper relation to them—not so he will know when and where to kotow, but so he will know to whom he may go for advice and counsel, to whom he must look for supervision, and to whom he may turn if necessary to find access to still higher authority. Sometimes an organization in which lines of authority are hopelessly confused rationalizes by explaining that clear-cut lines are unnecessary because everyone is so cooperative: it is just "one big, happy family." But men cannot do their best, floating aimlessly about in a sea of ill-defined "cooperation." Good intentions or mere cooperation is not enough. To be effective, cooperation must be directed. It must follow some pattern or plan.

* Originally published as "Organization" in U.S. Department of Agriculture, Office of Personnel, *Personnel Bulletin*, Vol. 1 (July, 1940), 3.

23. Span of Control*

There are a number of considerations which affect the difference between wide and narrow span of control. Planning for effectiveness is essential. Supervisory responsibility varies with the number of employees and the kind of work that is involved. For example, a supervisor with a group of card punch operators can manage more personnel than a supervisor in a unit having responsibility for employees engaged in actuarial computations. The number depends upon: (1) the amount of instruction and guidance employees require, (2) extent to which work must be reviewed, (3) how often questions arise that must be resolved by the supervisor, and (4) the amount of the supervisor's time that must be spent in resolving questions of differing degrees of complexity. The following factors affect managerial decisions in this regard:

Narrow span	*Wide span*
Nonroutine work	Routine and repetitive work
Application of judgment required	Relatively small number of techni-
Need for specialized knowledge	cal questions that call for the
Great amount of review of work products required	supervisor to answer
	Minimum supervisory review required

OTHER SUPERVISORY PROBLEMS

When subordinates are widely separated in locations apart from the supervisor, lack of proximity also becomes a factor that may present problems. Day-to-day supervision may be more difficult due to this wide physical dispersion. Some operations require employees to work in separate buildings and in different areas away from (and on) an installation; for example, messengers, security guards, and special delivery mail personnel. Such dispersion of significant numbers of persons from the work group imposes special considerations regarding span of control.

There is no firm rule. Judgment enters into the equation. A supervisor must have personal contact to supervise. The number of employees reporting directly to one person should be based on the complexity, variety, and proximity of the jobs involved.

* From U.S. Civil Service Commission, Interagency Training Program, *Introduction to Supervision* (Washington, D.C., U.S. Civil Service Commission, Bureau of Training, General Management Training Center, 1970), 6P1.

24. Staff and Line Organization*

Marshall Dimock

The staff officer must be kept in his place. But this does not mean that he must be kept down, that he must be discouraged, that his initiative and imagination must be checked. On the contrary, all these character-istics should be encouraged. The important question is, through what channel are they to be directed? They should, of course, flow through the responsible operating executive, not around him.

This process may be described in terms of the following sequence: the staff official makes a recommendation; it is approved by the responsi-ble executive who, in his authoritative capacity, announces to those below him in the hierarchy that the recommendation is going to be adopted. Thereafter there are many details in connection with putting it into effect that can be carried out more effectively by the staff official than by the line official and with a saving of time to the latter. So long as the subordinates in the hierarchy are aware that this delegation is authorized and that the staff officer is not acting independently, unifica-tion of managerial responsibility is not impaired and there is no loss of influence and responsibility on the part of the executive.

Just as the chief executive is aided by staff officials in the carrying out of his program, so also do subordinate line executives establish normal and continuous relationships with staff officials in the development of their work. If the line official cannot satisfy the staff assistant as to the necessity of his proposal, then the door of the executive's office must be open to him and he should be free to state his recommendation, explain any points of difference he has with the staff assistant, and leave the decision to his superior. As a general proposition also, if the decision is close, the chief executive should decide in favor of the line official, since presumably he knows his own needs better than any staff assistant be-cause he is closer to them and is responsible for results. If the chief executive fails to back him up then he is bound to feel that his judgment is in question. This injures his initiative and self-confidence—as well as his confidence in his superior—and is to be avoided if possible. Ordi-narily, however, if both line and staff men are competent, they will be able to reach an agreement and make a unified recommendation. Close decisions are rare when all the facts are known.

In some organizations where staff assistance is overemphasized, from the standpoint of both the influence and the number of staff officials, the

* Originally published as "The Meshing of Line and Staff," in *The Executive in Action* (New York, Harper & Brothers, 1945), 102–104. Reprinted by permission.

chief executive is likely to be cut off from his department heads. An executive should never lose sight of the fact that his closest contacts must be with the heads of the operating departments, and that it is upon them more than any others that the success of the program depends. If he permits himself to become cloistered because of the more favored position of the staff officials, the morale and driving force of the program will be impaired.

25. Examining the __Other__ Organization*

Jacob Jacoby

As most students of organizational phenomena will readily admit, there are two overlapping and interacting structures existing within any complex industrial organization.

One is usually referred to as the "formal organization" and the other as the "informal organization."

Typically, the structure of the formal organization is defined by a blueprint known as the organization chart. Such charts describe the role relationships (involving such factors as patterns of authority, responsibility, and flow of communications) deemed desirable by the organization's upper echelon for optimum, efficient performance.

The structure of the informal organization, however, is defined not by upper echelon fiat, but by the patterns and interconnections of social relationships which do in fact exist within the organization.

Simply stated, the formal structure is usually designed to serve the goals of the organization while the informal structure develops to satisfy the needs of individuals. Thus, the formal organization may be considered the blueprint for the ways in which individuals within the organization should behave, while the informal organization describes ways in which they actually do behave.

EFFECTS ON PRODUCTIVITY

It is generally accepted that the informal organization can have both inhibiting and facilitating effects upon worker productivity. The classic Western Electric Hawthorne study in the Bank Wiring Room,[1] in which group pressure served to restrict output, was the first to clearly demonstrate these negative effects. Perhaps because of early results from this and similar studies, the negative effects were unduly emphasized and managers sought ways to control and reduce the effects of the informal organization.

More recently it has been empirically demonstrated that the informal organization can actually operate as a positive force, thereby serving to increase productivity.[2] In fact, the recent Tavistock Institute studies of

* From *Personnel Administration*, November–December, 1968, 36–42. Reprinted by permission.

1 F. J. Roethlisberger and W. J. Dickson, *Management and the Worker*, Cambridge, Mass., Harvard University Press, 1939.

2 D. G. Bowers and S. E. Seashore, "Predicting Organizational Effectiveness with a Four Factor Theory of Leadership," *Administrative Science Quarterly*, Vol. 11, No. 2, 238–63; R. Likert, *New Patterns of Management*, New York, McGraw-Hill, 1961; and M. Patchen, *Supervisory Methods, Group Standards, and Performance at the Dobeckmun Company*, Ann Arbor, Mich., Institute for Social Research, 1960.

British coal miners illustrate that significant increases in productivity can actually result from allowing formal organizations to be structured according to patterns formed in the development of the informal organizations.[3] Van Zelst's earlier study involving work teams of bricklayers and carpenters obtained similar results.[4]

Consequently, it has become more important than ever for both management theorists and administrators to understand the structure and dynamics of the informal organization.

SOCIOMETRIC MEASURES

Methods for measuring the structure of certain classes of informal organizations have already been developed. Typically, these have been based upon sociometric principles. Preferences or rankings of colleagues on certain variables are collected from employees, or their patterns of behavioral interaction are observed and recorded. This latter technique, called the "contactual survey," was first proposed by Seiniger[5] and later successfully employed by others.[6] Though such techniques are valuable and their application has yielded a considerable amount of understanding of small group phenomena, there are certain limitations inherent in such techniques which become obvious when trying to measure the informal structure of large, complex organizations.

For example, consider applying these techniques to study the informal organization of an enterprise with as many as 10,000 or 20,000, or even as few as 1,000 employees. Sociometric questionnaires become impractical and direct observation and tallying of behavior virtually unfeasible. In developing the "contactual survey" Seiniger himself commented as follows: "It is recognized that any attempt to undertake a contactual survey of the entire organization at one time would be so complex as to be unwieldy."[7]

The problem thus becomes one of devising an efficient technique for studying the informal structure of large organizations.

COMMUNICATIONS LINKS

From a conceptual standpoint, the most significant aspect of the informal organization is that the various elements in the structure are tied together through lines of communication. Informal organizations often spring up to implement the formal in order to serve as a communication

[3] E. Trist, G. Higgin, H. Murray and A. Pollock, *Organizational Choice*, London, Travistock, 1963.

[4] R. H. Van Zelst, "Sociometrically Selected Work Teams Increase Production," *Personnel Psychology*, 1952.

[5] W. B. Seiniger, "Charting the Informal Organization," *Advanced Management*, Vol. 16, No. 11, 24–27.

[6] E. Dale, *Planning and Developing the Company Organization Structure*, New York, American Management Association, 1952; and K. Davis, *Human Relations in Business*, New York, McGraw-Hill, 1957, 105.

[7] Seiniger, *op. cit.*, 25.

system. Seiniger wrote: "Through this system flashes a myriad assortment of intangible facts, suggestions, opinions (and even suspicions) that cannot pass through formal channels without raising issues calling for decisions, taxing available executive time, or threatening executive prestige. The usual charts and manuals do not show these informal channels of communication."[8]

Thus, the prime function of the informal organizational system is to disseminate information of interest to employees and relevant to their needs. Such information may be organizationally relevant (e.g., news of new promotion policies) or organizationally irrelevant (e.g., news of the death of a former employee).

UNOFFICIAL WORD RAPID

Although some amount of distortion usually occurs, it is not unusual for the informal organization to operate more rapidly and effectively than the formal organization in disseminating organizationally relevant information. For example, disclosure of a new promotion policy in a large organization is usually handled via "official" communications passed downward through the various levels of the hierarchy. However, the information is frequently transmitted through the networks of the informal organization to many employees long before any "official" (i.e., formal) communication reaches them.

CIRCUMVENTING THE FORMAL STRUCTURE

Another function of the informal organization is to transmit the mores and values of the work group to new employees (as was done in the Bank Wiring Room). Not infrequently, the informal communication structure is used to deliberately circumvent the formal structure. Usually this is done because informal communication is easier (e.g., no need for the message to be typed in quadruplicate and filed accordingly) and faster. In fact, it appears reasonable to hypothesize that the more the communication channels of the formal organization become clogged with "formalities" (such as a requirement for excessive formal coordination, or excessive file copies of written memoranda), the greater is the tendency to engage in informal communication.

It is important to note that friendship associations, although normally a part of the informal organization, are not a necessary pre-condition for its existence.[9] As conceptualized here, the sole prerequisite for the

---

8 *Ibid.*, 24.

9 Those citing data which indicate that there are many workers who do not belong to social groupings on the job or have social contacts with coworkers off the job, and who seem to imply from this that the informal organization is of minor importance in industrial organizations (cf. R. Dubin, "Industrial Workers' Worlds: A Study of 'Central Life Interests' of Industrial Workers," *Social Problems*, 1956, 136, 140; and H. M. Vollmer, *Employer Rights and the Employment Relationship*, Berkeley and Los Angeles, University of California Press, 1960, 75), appear to have overlooked the most essential and primary characteristic of the

existence of an informal organization within the boundaries of a formal organization is that there be a flow of communications along channels not specified in the organizational chart.

A SMALL WORLD

Given that the informal organization may be conceived of as a communications system, it then becomes possible to study its structure through examining and mapping its pathways. The methodology for doing this in large organizations has recently been developed and utilized in another context by the Harvard University social psychologist Stanley Milgram. Working in a system of 200 million people, the United States, Milgram was able to effectively chart pathways which are in many respects analogous to the paths taken by informal communications in large industrial organizations. With minor modifications, this technique can easily be adapted to empirically study the informal communication structure of complex organizations.

Briefly, Milgram was interested in a phenomenon personally experienced by almost all of us at one time or another, that of "encountering someone far from home, who, to our surprise, turns out to share a mutual acquaintance with us. This kind of experience occurs with sufficient frequency that our language even provides a cliche to be uttered at the appropriate moment . . . We say, 'My, it's a small world.' "

Aside from its very obvious entertaining aspects, solution of the small world problem has important ramifications for conceptualizing the structure of societies.

Milgram began to attack the problem with the following assumption:

The actual process of establishing the linkages between two persons runs only one way: from person A to person Z. Let us call person A the *starting* person, since he will initiate the process, and person Z the *target* person, since he is the person to be reached.[10]

It follows that what is necessary is to first select a source person to initiate a message and a target person to whom the message is directed, and then

---

informal organization, viz., its communication function. Furthermore, in a system such as the informal organization, where the participants are free to initiate, maintain, and sever interactions almost at will, considerable evidence exists (G. C. Homans, *The Human Group.* New York, Harcourt, Brace, 1950, 112, and *Social Behavior: Its Elementary Form*, New York, Harcourt, Brace, 1961, 181–87; T. M. Newcomb, "The Prediction of Interpersonal Attraction," *American Psychologist*, Vol. 11, 575–86; and C. Flament and Erika Apfelbaum, "Elementary Processes of Communication and Structurization in a Small Group," *Journal of Experimental Social Psychology*, Vol. 2, 376–86) to indicate that interpersonal attraction and group structurization can be predicted from frequency of interactions (where interactions are defined in terms of exchange of information and are therefore communicative). Though interpersonal attraction can later feed back to affect the frequency of interactions (qua communication), it is the latter which must be logically considered as being temporally prior to the former.

[10] S. Milgram, "The Small-World Problem," *Psychology Today*, Vol. 1, No. 1, 63.

to map the path taken by the message in going from the source to the target. In Milgram's study, two individuals living in the Boston area were selected as targets. Sources were selected from geographically distant Wichita, Kansas, and Omaha, Nebraska, and were obtained through letters sent to residents in these cities requesting their participation in a study of social contact in American life. Milgram wrote as follows:

Each person who volunteered to serve as a starting person was sent a folder containing a document which served as the main tool of the investigation. Briefly, the document contained:

1. The name of the target person as well as certain information about him. This oriented the participants toward a specific individual.

2. A set of rules for reaching the target person. Perhaps the most important rule is: "If you do not know the target person on a personal basis, do not try to contact him directly. Instead, mail this folder . . . to a personal acquaintance who is more likely than you to know the target person . . . it must be someone you know on a first-name basis." This rule sets the document into motion, moving it from one participant to the next, until it is sent to someone who knows the target person.

3. A roster on which each person in the chain writes his name. This tells the person who received the folder exactly who sent it to him. The roster also had another practical effect: it prevents endless looping of the folder through participants who had already served as links in the chain, because each participant could see exactly what sequence of persons had led up to his own participation.[11]

In addition to the document, the folder contained a stack of 15 business reply or "tracer" cards. Each person receiving the folder took out a card, filled it in, returned it to Milgram and sent the remaining cards along with the document to the next link.

IMPORTANT FEATURES OF THE STUDY

Milgram continues:

Several other features of the procedure need to be emphasized. First, each participant is supposed to send the folder on to one other person only. Thus the efficiency with which the chain is completed depends in part on the wisdom of his choice in this matter. Second, by means of the tracer card, we have continuous feedback on the progress of each chain. The cards are coded so we know which chain it comes from and which link in the chain has been completed. The card also provides relevant sociological characteristics of the senders of the cards. Thus, we know the characteristics of completed, as well as incomplete, chains. Third, the procedure permits experimental variation at many points.

In short, the device possesses some of the features of a chain letter, though it does not pyramid in any way; moreover, it is oriented toward a specific

11 *Ibid.*, 64.

target, zeroes in on the target through the cooperation of a sequence of participants, and contains a tracer that allows us to keep track of its progress at all times.[12]

The results of Milgram's study are fascinating. Of the 160 chains started in Nebraska, 44 were completed. The other chains died out simply because a certain proportion of participants did not cooperate. For the 44 completed chains, the median number of intermediaries it took to get from the source person to the target person was only 5. Considering the distances traversed, a median of five intermediate persons is quite impressive.

POTENTIAL APPLICATIONS

Milgram reports that he is now applying the small world methodology to the study of communication between Negro and White subcultures within American society. However, as he indicates, the technique has tremendous potential for studying other sociological phenomena.

Upon reading Milgram's thought-provoking paper, it appeared to this writer that the informal communication structure of complex organizations would be legitimate and fertile ground for the application of these procedures. Minor adaptations would be necessary. Instead of having the intermediaries mail the folders to the next link, the instructions would require that they be handed directly to the link instead. The tracer cards would be dropped into the organization's internal mail system. Target and source individuals would be deliberately selected from various functional areas (e.g., sales, R&D, accounting, etc.) and at various hierarchical strata (e.g., workers, foremen, middle managers, executives) so as to provide an over-all description of the informal organization's pathways.

As Milgram has noted, "the procedures permit experimental variation at many points." For example, the transmission characteristics of organizationally relevant and organizationally irrelevant information through the informal organization could be studied independently. Or, both sources and targets could be selected from one stratum (or one functional area), and the manner in which links from outside that particular stratum (or functional area) are drawn into the network could be studied. In another variation, the "one-way" assumption could be dropped, the roster accompanying the packet omitted, and the instructions worded so that individual links would be able to receive the packet more than once. The presence of communication loops, as well as the frequency with which certain individual links receive the packet, could be studied in this manner.

12 *Ibid.*

WHICH TYPES OF INFORMATION
CAN SUCH STUDIES PROVIDE?

As a start, they can supply answers to such practical questions as the following: In any given organization, what are the pathways of such communications? How does it compare to the flow of formal communications? Do certain organizations (or individuals) handle a significantly greater amount of such traffic than do others, i.e., are there pivotal organizations (or individuals) which are more centrally tied into the informal communication structure? Are there organizations significantly isolated from the informal communication structure? Is participation in the communication structure a function of certain identifiable and controllable variables? If so, can relatively isolated organizational units be tied more closely into the informal communication structure?

What types of messages flow fastest? What types of messages flow most accurately? Is the informal structure an effective means for disseminating organizationally relevant information? Can complex formal organizations benefit from an examination of the informal organization, i.e., can it be modified so as to approach the reputed speed and effectiveness of the informal communication structure? What are the administrative control implications of the informal communications structures?

Melcher and Beller, in a recent theoretical treatment,[13] have specified conditions under which formal communication channels, informal communications channels, or a combination of the two would prove to be the most effective technique for administrators to use in transmitting information to subordinate levels. However, the authors nowhere indicate either how to tap into the informal communication network, or at what point in the structure such insertion would be most effective. The methodology suggested above could provide answers to these questions.

USES

In his presentation of the contactual survey, Seiniger[14] rhetorically asked what practical uses could be made of information regarding the informal organization. He cites seven uses:

1. As an aid in checking the accuracy of the formal organization chart;
2. As an aid in planning anticipated organizational changes;
3. As an aid in installing such managerial devices as budgetary controls;
4. As an aid in solving problems of communication;

---

13 A. J. Melcher and R. Beller, "Toward a Theory of Organization Communication: Consideration in Channel Selection," *Academy of Management Journal*, Vol. 10, No. 1, 39–52.
14 Seiniger, *op. cit.*, 25–27.

5. As an aid in locating people who can be counted upon to facilitate action, dissipate resentments or clear up misunderstandings;

6. As an aid in learning the "right" contacts to make in order to get action, approval or information;

7. As an aid in locating leadership material.

On a more theoretical level, such a technique could be useful in determining what the general properties of informal communications networks are and how these vary from organization to organization or, within the same complex organization, how the structure varies as a function of the type of information being handled. Given that informal communications are believed to undergo distortion during transmission, it would be interesting to determine the nature and extent (if any) of such distortion, and to see if it adopts forms similar to the assimilation, leveling, and sharpening described in the classic Allport and Postman study of rumor.[15]

Furthermore, what consequences result from the primary effect created when the employee's first exposure to an officially (i.e., formally) disseminated organizationally relevant message is through the informal communications structure? Finally, not only would utilization of such a technique provide greater understanding of the informal organization, but as Dimock, et al have noted, "until it has been corrected by what informal organizational theory has to offer, formal organizational theory is likely to be inaccurate and incomplete."[16]

CONCLUSION

The technique outlined is simple and inexpensive to employ. It does not require interruption of normal working activities, nor does it demand any excessive amount of time from the individual participants. The potential insights and practical benefits to be derived from using such a procedure appear to be manifold. All things considered, it is time for behavioral scientists to stop talking about the informal organization in the abstract and to empirically demonstrate its existence and modes of operation.

[15] G. W. Allport and L. Postman, *The Psychology of Rumor*, New York, Holt, 1947.

[16] M. E. Dimock, Gladys O. Dimock and L. W. Koenig, *Public Administration*, rev. ed., New York, Holt, Rinehart, and Winston, 1960, 132.

26. Informal Organization and the Concepts of Overlays*

John M. Pfiffner and Frank P. Sherwood

While *formal organization* is concerned with structure and mechanics of organization, *informal organization* gives recognition to the people and processes that tend to modify and change the organization as formally established. Many of these processes are concerned with the daily and hourly interaction between members of the organization and can conse-

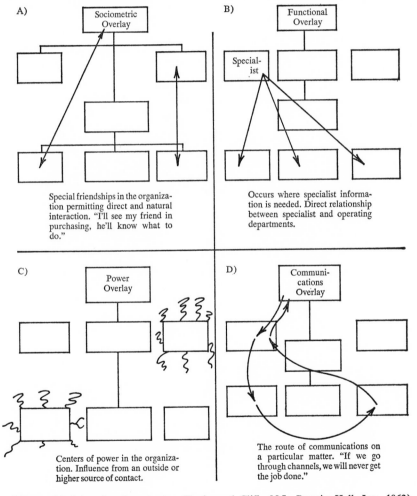

A) Sociometric Overlay

Special friendships in the organization permitting direct and natural interaction. "I'll see my friend in purchasing, he'll know what to do."

B) Functional Overlay

Special-ist

Occurs where specialist information is needed. Direct relationship between specialist and operating departments.

C) Power Overlay

Centers of power in the organization. Influence from an outside or higher source of contact.

D) Communications Overlay

The route of communications on a particular matter. "If we go through channels, we will never get the job done."

* From *Administrative Organization* (Englewood Cliffs, N.J., Prentice-Hall, Inc., 1962). Reprinted by permission.

quently be charted. Other forces that have their impact upon the organization such as culture, status, personality, etc., cannot readily be charted for graphic presentation. The concept of overlays presented below represents attempts to more fully analyze and understand organizations by isolating, for academic purposes, various processes—involving people—that make up the so-called informal organization. They should not be considered as being mutually exclusive.

27. Reorganization

Petronius Arbiter, 210 B.C.

We trained hard, . . . but it seemed that every time we were beginning to form up into teams we would be reorganized. . . . I was to learn later in life that we tend to meet any new situation by reorganizing, and a wonderful method it can be for creating the illusion of progress while producing confusion, inefficiency, and demoralization.

28. Reorganizing—More Than Drawing a New Chart*

B. Douglas Stone, Jr.

The writers of most articles on the subject of organizing seem to have assumed that a new firm or department is being set up. Reorganizing an existing operation is, however, the organizational problem that managers face far more frequently.

The manager must deal with at least three sets of restrictions that are more limiting when reorganizing than when he is organizing a new unit. The first set of restrictions exists because of the characteristics of the existing planning and control systems. Still other restrictions are economic and are seen primarily in the salary and wage costs of the proposed versus the existing organizational structure. When reorganizing, then, the manager must consider not only management problems, but people problems and economic problems as well.

MANAGERIAL FACTORS

An effective organizational structure is the responsibility of management, of course, but not that of top management alone. Every member of management shares the responsibility for insuring that his unit is most appropriately structured to accomplish his goals.

The starting point in every organization is a review of your goals. What results are you and your subordinates expected to accomplish? Not in the past, but now, and in the future. The goals and activities of each section must support and contribute to the goals of the department, just as each department must support each division, and each division, the company. Your activity will be ineffective and inefficient unless your goals are kept clearly in focus.

Besides knowing your goals, you must know your resources and the time available to reach your goals. Time is just as much a resource as your men, material and machines. Your goal determines what you are to do, your resources determine how you are to do it and time determines when. If little time is available, then more men, material and machines are required *and* a different organizational arrangement, also.

No section, department or division operates in isolation. The seemingly endless coordination efforts by formal and informal committees and meetings amply show this. Each unit must cooperate in many ways with other units to accomplish its goals. One particularly important way in which units are tied together is through the communication and paperwork systems. Such systems grow up in response to needs for informa-

* From *Personnel Administrator*, July–August, 1965. Reprinted by permission.

tion. Unfortunately, however, the systems are not always changed when the needs change. Paper-work systems seem to have a vitality all their own due to vested interests and inertia. Thus, systems may represent a limitation to what is possible in reorganizing and are an important factor to be evaluated.

PLANNING THE ORGANIZATION STRUCTURE

Your goals represent the work that must be done. Considering all available resources, what is the best way to divide the total work into manageable parts? There are a number of bases for organizing including:

1. The function to be performed.
2. The product or project.
3. The skill or education required.
4. The kind of equipment or facilities used.
5. The process.
6. The customer.
7. The location of the work.
8. The number of people.

Every aspect of the organizational structure should be fully scrutinized with as little carry-on of previous thinking as you can manage. Do you need more or fewer levels of supervision? Can the work of several supervisors be rearranged to require fewer men at that level? Should work now done in the field be brought into the home office? If you are organized on the basis of your "customer," would "product" or "process" be a more efficient basis?

Managers often overlook an important resource in reorganizing. Who knows more about the details of the work than those who actually perform it? Who knows the inconsistencies, the uneven work-loads, the uneconomical layout, the duplication better than those who live intimately with the details from day to day? Experience shows not only that you will get good suggestions from your subordinates, but that they will strive to make the new structure succeed when they have contributed to it.

The tasks or work elements that are combined to form a job should be grouped logically and should be mutually compatible. They should not require rare or bizarre combinations of education, experience and interests. (How many people do you know who are competent to head the technical design, budgeting and sales functions simultaneously?)

Another cardinal rule underlying efficient organization is that of avoiding overlapping authority. Are there clearcut differences among the proposed jobs? Will the men who hold these jobs have to hold frequent, long meetings to determine who is to do what? Have you left undefined areas of responsibility for the empire builder to move into? Will you or higher management have to spend much time clearing up misunderstandings about who is responsible for what?

Of course, the other classic principles of organization (e.g. unity of command, scalar chain, flexibility) should be observed. The ones discussed above are usually more crucial in the reorganizing situation.

DELEGATION: IMPLEMENTING YOUR PLANS

Delegation is the managerial process by which you (1) activate the organizational structure you have planned, and (2) share your authority with subordinates.

Communication is a key factor in delegation. Each subordinate must understand precisely what he is expected to do as well as not do. You should specify the controls you plan to exercise to evaluate his responsibility or accountability to you for achieving the goals you have established. Indicate to him the ways you will measure his performance and progress toward his goals.

One way of ensuring mutual understanding and agreement between you and your subordinate is a "Manager's Letter." Periodically require each of your people to write you a letter stating his current and future goals, authority, and obstacles as he sees them. The use of this technique provides you with the material for a review of the soundness of your organization. Reviewing these letters should help you identify problems that may have developed, such as overlapping authority, poor communication among units or changed emphasis.

PERSONNEL FACTORS

The occasion of a reorganization is the time to evaluate critically your people resources. Taking a fresh look at your people is just as important, if not more so, than a reexamination of the work to be done.

Look for employees whose talents have been hidden under the previous organizational arrangement. A common source of waste is the failure to identify people with talent and to encourage them to develop and use that talent. It is easy to associate an employee with the particular type of work he is currently performing and overlook his potential for greater contributions in other areas. For example, do you have a man who is highly imaginative and creative but who is holding a job that is purely routine?

Look for employees who have stopped developing. This is more a matter of attitude than age (some should retire at 30, others not until 80). Among those who have reached their peak, some will be effective in their present position; others will have started to slip. Do you have an employee at his peak who is blocking the progress of other employees with promotion potential? Is he enforcing a "make-no-waves" policy on his subordinates to protect himself? This situation often encourages the departure of your able people while the less able stay and conform; thus, the firm's talent gradually grows weaker and weaker.

Look for technically-oriented employees who are in supervisory positions. You rarely get a good bargain when you try to make a supervisor of a technically-oriented man without consideration and development of his supervisory talents. By judicious coaching you may help interested subordinates prepare for supervisory responsibilities. A man is not a supervisor simply because he has people reporting to him.

Look for subordinates who avoid crises by good planning and follow-up. While the "fire-fighter" may be more visible, how many of his fires does he cause by his own poor managing? Don't fall prey to the "squeaking-wheel-gets-the-grease" tactic!

INFORMAL ORGANIZATION

The informal organization is a social phenomenon. People who continuously work together for a length of time will (1) develop certain standards for the behavior of members of the group, (2) develop expectations about the purposes of the group, and (3) "select" one or more leaders for the activities of the group. Associated with this will be the development by the group of sanctions or penalties that are imposed on members who do not conform to the group's standards.

The solidarity or cohesiveness of the group depends upon such factors as the importance of the group's goals to the members, the importance of membership in the group to each individual, and the opposition by some outside agency to the group's progress toward its goals. The members of a top management group develop an informal organization as do the workers in, say, a factory department or office.

Generally, informed organizations among employees make some substantial degree of commitment to the goals of top management. But the sentiments of an employee group are rarely 100 percent for or against the employer.

Extensive research in the work-place and elsewhere indicates that an informally organized group that accepts management's goals as its own will get the work out regardless of, even in spite of, the formal organization structure. If, on the other hand, the group's goals are incompatible —whether opposed or neutral—with management's, the best imaginable formal structure will be ineffective. Work is accomplished by people, not organization charts.

STATUS

Employees are more or less conscious of status symbols. Such symbols are a convenient shorthand system for determining an individual's standing in a group, that is, where he stands in the "pecking order."

This sensitivity to status may work for you or against you. Perhaps you have learned the hard way how upset people can get at what you may regard as a perfectly logical organizational change that they believe will affect their status. On the other hand, you may grant status symbols as a reward. A better office, desk, parking place, etc. is much appreciated and noticed by those who do and do not enjoy such privileges. Proposals to promote an individual so that he may get a better parking place are not unheard of.

The inevitable development and existence of informal organizations and status has important implications for the manager who contemplates reorganization. First of all, the organizer must be aware of the existing informal structure, to know how his people are actually accomplishing the work and to seek clues as to why the existing structure is less than satisfactory.

Second, an organizational change that is viewed as threatening by the group will cause it to take defensive action and will strengthen the group's solidarity. This will probably result in poorer output as the group members spend more time and energy in "defending" than in "producing."

A third implication for reorganizing is that it takes quite a while for informal organizations to become stable and efficient. Therefore, a massive reorganization will lead to a period of readjustment and re-development which may last several months. During this period the output will probably be lower than formerly. Therefore, any serious evaluation of the effectiveness of a new structure should not be attempted for as much as a six to twelve months period. Any considerable changes made in the interim will simply prolong the adjustment period. The more frequent and/or more drastic the changes, the less efficient the employees will be permitted to be.

ECONOMIC FACTORS

Since the organizational pattern adopted affects salary and wage costs, the "before and after" costs of every change should be studied. The truth of this is not as obvious to some members of management as you might think. Even in the face of the clear and present need to reduce overhead costs, managers have been known to attempt various strate-gems to evade their responsibility; for example, they may transfer people "on paper" from line to staff job titles to avoid reducing the actual num-ber of supervisors and, therefore, the total salary cost.

A man's value to the organization is measured by the value of the work he is now performing, not by his longevity or education or poten-tial. If you have an Einstein performing routine calculations, the value of the calculations to the firm is the measure of the man's value to the firm.

214

As compared to the old organizational arrangement, will the changes you propose:

1. Require higher job classifications and salaries?

2. Require higher classification secretarial assistance and higher wages?

3. Mean that some of your subordinates will be in higher salary classifications than the proposed jobs require? Are you prepared to adjust their pay and status downward?

4. Mean that salaried personnel will be forced to perform secretarial and clerical work? Is it economical to pay a $10 per hour man to perform $3 per hour work?

Because every change involves a period of confusion while the people work out new formal and informal relationships, there is a hidden cost due to the reduced efficiency following the change. This factor alone suggests the value of a conservative approach to reorganizing. The organization should be changed only if the expected savings and improved output justify the measured and unmeasured costs.

CONCLUSION

Effective reorganization decisions require the thorough and complete analysis of the managerial factors, personnel factors, and economic factors as they exist in the enterprise. A major determinant of the success or failure of the new structure is appropriate recognition by the manager of the interactions among the factors. This is especially true of the reaction of the personnel to the expected effects on their status and informal working arrangements of the proposed changes.

29. Organizational Analysis: Some Notes on Methods and Criteria*

C. Dwight Waldo

1. IS THE PROBLEM "ORGANIZATIONAL" OR "PROCEDURAL"?

The relationship between organization and procedure is an intimate and puzzling one, and to the extent that they may be only different aspects of the same thing the distinction between them is false. Nevertheless, the distinction serves a useful pragmatic purpose. Organizational analysts should be acquainted with the techniques and criteria of procedural analysis, and vice versa; but specialization in one or the other is justified as an operational matter.

Organizational studies are undertaken as a result of some sort of irritation in the body politic. It may be, however, that the irritation is procedural rather than organizational in origin and nature. Usually a decision whether a problem is primarily organizational or primarily procedural can be made prima facie. Sometimes, however, considerable investigation is necessary to get to the root of the matter. In general the organizational component is greater in the "higher" aspects of administration, the procedural component greater in the "lower" aspects of administration. If the problem that is posed is one of executive manageability or functional unity, therefore, it is unlikely that procedural remedies will be adequate. But if the problem involves such a matter as cooperative use of personnel or equipment, an eye should be kept cocked for the procedural remedy which, being less drastic than the organizational, is nearly always to be prescribed. It is a safe generalization that measurable economies can be shown much more easily and frequently through procedural than through organizational changes.

2. WILL EXECUTIVE CONTROL, POLICY COORDINATION, AND FUNCTIONAL COHERENCE BE FACILITATED?

These three factors are logically and analytically distinct. Yet they are overlapping and interlocked (like Ballantine's purity, body, and flavor), and to draw them apart even for purposes of discussion tends to destroy an organic unity. The analyst must be constantly alert to the problem whether a proposed change will or will not facilitate executive control. Not merely the control of the chief executive must be considered, but the effect on controls and cross controls at every level of the chain of command. Is it necessary that an executive personally "make

* From *Public Administration Review*, Vol. 7, No. 4 (1947), 240–43. Reprinted by permission.

policy" for a given agency? Or is it sufficient if he exercises only general surveillance over its making? Is it desirable that the executive manage "housekeeping" functions in the area in question as well as control policy formulation? In any case, what are the proper tools and organs, and will organizational change help or hinder?

With regard to functional coherence, it is sufficient to re-emphasize that it is not the simple matter once supposed. The naive idea that there is some single pattern of departmental organization which will fulfill all demands of logic and aesthetics has long since gone by the board, of course; but the analyst, no matter how enlightened from his preparatory study, will soon acquire a sad sense of the temporary nature of his most pleasing combinations of functions. In truth no organizational unit, no matter how small and rudimentary, is single purpose.

3. IS THERE NEED FOR AUTONOMY OR "INDEPENDENCE" AND WILL THIS NEED BE SERVED?

Different organization units operate according to different standards of administrative morality and at various levels of efficiency. In the case of a merger of two units with varying standards, what is likely to be the resulting set of standards? Is there an administrative Gresham's law which will dictate the adoption of the lower standards? If there will be a tendency in this direction how can it be arrested?

4. WILL MANPOWER OR MATERIALS BE SAVED?

The problem here is primarily the familiar one of eliminating un-necessary "duplication and overlapping." There is no more persistent motif in the study of public administration than the attainment of "economy," and all students unite in its praise though conceptions of its dictates vary tremendously.

Nobody wants unnecessary duplication; but how is one to know when duplication *is* unnecessary? "Unnecessary" can only be judged in rela-tion to ends served, and the administrative ends, even if one looks no further than the statutes, will often be found to be vague or disparate.

Will consolidation of two organizational units permit a reduction in the total number of typists, or accountants, or entomologists? Will a transfer of Bureau X to Department Y release a set of expensive scien-tific instruments for use of Department Z? These are the types of ques-tions the analyst must seek to answer—in terms of dollars and cents, if possible; otherwise, in general terms that will bear close scrutiny. And having demonstrated an economy, he must then weigh it in the balance against any tangible or intangible losses.

5. WILL COOPERATION BE FACILITATED?

Irrespective of whether two organizational units have a "common purpose" is there an advantage in bringing their personnel together for consultation or a joint effort? If so, do the advantages outweigh the disadvantages? Irrespective of the existence of "common purpose" are there advantages in sharing or pooling equipment and supplies? If one organizational unit "services" another will any demonstrable purpose be served by bringing the two into closer organizational relationship? Or conversely, by terminating the service and arranging for another source of supply?

A distinction that must constantly be borne in mind is that between organizational proximity and geographical proximity. A change in either of these may be quite independent of the other. A physical move to bring two organization units into contiguous quarters may produce the optimum degree of cooperation. Conversely, bringing the same two units into the closest organizational contiguity will avail little if they remain physically far apart.

6. WILL CLIENTELE, BENEFICIARY, WARD, OR EMPLOYEE CONVENIENCE, WELFARE, OR SATISFACTION BE SERVED?

The direct convenience, welfare, or satisfaction of the persons with whom the government deals may in some cases be easily measured, but more often it is not. The organizational unity of certain related services may demonstrably save travel, time, and money on the part of users of the services. On the other hand, in the more common case in which intangibles are important the conscientious analyst will spend some sleepless early morning hours trying to decide whether the welfare of a certain group will be advanced by an organizational change.

Should employee convenience and satisfaction be weighed? I feel the answer is an indisputable "Yes."

7. ARE PERSONAL FACTORS INVOLVED THAT MUST BE CONSIDERED?

I am aware that there is a school of thought which holds that personal factors should be disregarded in favor of "sound principles" of organization—that tailoring an organization to the capacities of its component individuals is (to use one writer's exact metaphor) like designing an engine according to the whims of one's maiden aunt instead of the laws of mechanics. Nevertheless, I hold it to be a self-evident truth that personal factors cannot be (or, what comes to the same thing, will not be) ignored in dealing with organization.

8. SHOULD THE FACTOR OF TRADITION OR *ESPRIT DE CORPS* BE CONSIDERED?

In three types of organization the factors of tradition and *esprit de corps* may be especially important—scientific research organizations, military and semimilitary organizations, and organizations in which the element of professionalism is strong. The destruction of a tradition or the breaking up of a group with a strong corporate spirit should not be done for "light and transient reasons." On the other hand, tradition and corporate spirit may by virtue of their very strength impede the accomplishment of large objectives, and organizational change may be desirable to reduce their effect.

30. Is Organization Development Possible in Government?*

Frederick F. Fisher

That is one of those questions that can only be answered with a "Yes, but, however, only if."

It looks like a simple question, thus requiring a simple answer—but in reality, it is a very complex question, and one which cannot be dealt with effectively in just a few minutes.

First of all, it will be useful to define "organization development." While everyone seems to define it a bit differently, here are three descriptions by practitioners of the art that seem to be reliable:

Warren Bennis—"Organization Development is a response to change, a complex educational strategy intended to change the beliefs, attitudes, values, and structure of organizations so that they can better adapt to new knowledges, markets and challenges, and the dizzying rate of change itself."

Richard Beckhard—"Organization Development is an effort (1) planned, (2) organization-wide, and (3) managed from the top, to (4) increase organization effectiveness and health through (5) planned interventions in the organizations' 'processes' using behavioral-science knowledge."

Warner Burke—"OD is a process which attempts to increase organizational effectiveness by integrating individual desires for growth and development with organizational goals. Typically this process is a planned change effort which involves a total system over a period of time, and these change efforts are related to the organization's mission."

Note some of the buzz words that characterize OD—*process, planned change, total systems, values, increased effectiveness, organization mission, planned intervention.* Let us take a look at a few of these terms from the viewpoint of OD in a public agency.

CHANGES IN THE VALUE SYSTEM

Organization development implies a value system about individuals within an institutional context. Unfortunately, many of the values held by most state and local governments are not in tune with the values typically associated with OD efforts. This would suggest that OD will only work if some basic changes can be made in the values held by these organizations. Here are a few value changes that I see necessary if organization development is to stand a chance of success in state and local government.

* From *Minnesota Municipalities*, May, 1972, pp. 134–37. Reprinted by permission.

220

First, these levels of government do not have a history of investing in the development of their human resources. Training and development is a low priority item if, in fact, it has priority at all. An ICMA survey in 1970 of 787 cities turned up a total of 38 full-time training directors who have over-all responsibility for training and development activities within their cities—26 of these were in cities of over 100,000 population.

Even in these cities, the resources earmarked for training and development could not effectively match the task at hand. Most city managers will tell you that training is the first item to get the axe at budget time. Granted, money is scarce and hard to come by in state and local governments, but little thought is given to expanding the potential of the human resources, although the bulk of tax money ultimately goes into salaries. Doesn't it make sense to consider programs and efforts that would increase the effectiveness of the organization's biggest resource—its employees? A recent survey by the Industrial Relations Center, University of Chicago, indicated that municipal management and supervisory personnel in the Chicago suburbs appear to be operated only at about 50% efficiency in utilizing the human resource in their organizations. What is the level of efficiency in your agency?

Another aspect of the value system that must ultimately change, if OD is to work, is the view of the public employee as a dull, lazy, unmotivated self-serving bureaucrat. Too often the image is justly earned. State and local governments have not been the glamour employees of the twentieth century. Unfortunately, this tarnished image of state and local governments often pervades the total community and is, therefore, tough to change by purely internal actions. And, of course, it tends to influence decisions that are directly tied to the subject under discussion —human resource development within the public agency. I am convinced that the image problem directly affects the willingness to allocate funds for developmental programs. Many elected officials come into office with a jaundiced view of the organization they will be directing and the people who will be carrying out their policies.

There is another aspect of the image problem that is even more serious and that is the perception that public employees hold about themselves as individuals. Too many public employees have a battered and bruised self-esteem because they work for the city, county or state. Public servants! That's what we call them. Well, when are we going to shed the belief that employment in the public service is some kind of servitude? It is not only demeaning, it's downright ineffective.

Another value system dilemma we face in making organization development a reality in state and local government is the somewhat sordid love affair many agencies have with bureaucracy. While industry is just

221

as vulnerable to the trappings of bureaucracy as an organizational life-style, they are at least in the habit of denying it. As a result, they have bought a little more flexibility in the way they organize tasks and re-sources. Most state and local governments are organized around func-tions defined two or more centuries ago. Furthermore, these functions have become locked into place by legal requirements and categorical aid programs that make alterations virtually impossible. OD, as a man-agement strategy, will not work effectively unless there are opportunities to free up the bureaucratic system, to reorder the way of doing things in line with the fluid change that characterizes this era. It is a piece of the value system that will be hard to crack. It spans the organizational malaise from dysfunctional authorities, boards and commissions, to the rigid militaristic public safety delivery system.

Finally, there is a value at play in state and local government that is difficult to identify and will be the hardest to penetrate in any serious organization development effort. It is the value that works against openness, trust, and candor. The behavioral scientist tells us that dys-functional defensive behavior must be minimized if individual or organ-izational development is to succeed. And yet, the public administrator, thrashing around in shark-infested waters, is very reluctant to drop his defenses when his superiors may have no time for such values as open-ness and trust. This is particularly true of the city manager who finds his employment contract being renegotiated at each council meeting. And yet, any OD effort to be effective must start with him.

Many of the personal attributes, required for OD to work success-fully, are not revered in public agencies. Marksmanship, game playing, out-maneuvering, creating the image, being what one is not—these are all accepted survival procedures in the jungles of state and local em-ployment, where politics is close to the people. Undertaking an OD effort in Texas Instruments or TRW, Incorporated, out of public eye-sight, is quite different from pursuing the same in the fishbowl existence of state or local government. Among other things, OD takes time and continuity. Both are in relatively short supply where the leaders are apt to be here today, gone tomorrow.

The question has been posed, Is organization development possible in a public agency? The answer is, of course, yes—but, some values will have to change if the effort is to succeed. There must be a willingness to devote major resources—time and money—to the process; the attitude about the public employee must be enhanced; there must be commit-ment to change the bureaucratic structure within which most govern-ments ply their trade; and we must find a way to infuse the system with openness, trust and candor without raising the individual risk of such behavior to untenable heights. These are big obstacles to overcome if organization development is to work in your agency—or any public agency. But, I believe they can be overcome. Furthermore, I believe the potential rewards of OD far outstrip the monetary and psychological costs involved. There are many other issues at stake in public agency OD efforts, but time doesn't permit their exploration at this time. A recent article in ASPA's *Public Administrative Review* by Bill Eddy and Bob Saunders goes into considerable depth about these and other problems. It is good reading and I recommend it to you.

OD OBJECTIVES AND THEIR ACHIEVEMENT

Let me now go back to the fundamentals of any OD effort. What can you hope to achieve for your organization by engaging in an elaborate education strategy called OD? OD specialists generally agree that the process aims at achieving the following objectives:

To create an open, problem-solving climate throughout the organization;

To supplement authority associated with role or status with authority of knowledge and competence;

To locate decision-making and problem-solving responsibilities as close to the information sources as possible;

To build trust among individuals and groups throughout the organization;

To make competition more relevant to work goals and to maximize collaborative efforts;

To develop a reward system which recognizes both the achievement of the organization's mission as well as individual efforts toward personal development and achievement;

To increase the sense of "ownership" of organization objectives throughout the workforce;

To help managers to manage according to relevant objectives rather than according to "past practices" or according to objectives which do not make sense for one's area of responsibility;

To increase self-control and self-direction for people within the organization.[1]

Given these worthy objectives, how do you go about installing an Organization Development effort in your agency?

First, there must be a general dissatisfaction at the top of the organization about the way things are being accomplished within the organization. Someone at the top or near the top must recognize that the potential for achieving organizational success is not being tapped effectively and, furthermore, he must want to do something about it.

Secondly, there must be a general awareness about the processes of OD. After all, it is difficult to become committed to something you don't understand or even know exists. Often gaining awareness is akin to getting religion. Someone stumbles into a management development

1 Taken from "What is OD?" in NTL Institute *News and Reports*, 1968. Number 3 (June).

program and zap! he comes out all aglow, wondering where he's been all these years. Other times, it happens more slowly as the manager develops an understanding of the social technologies available to make organizations more adaptable and effective in today's world of rapid change. No matter how the awareness develops, it remains essential to the ultimate installation of an OD program.

I suppose the third stage depends upon the willingness of those "bit with the development bug" to follow through and get something going in their own organization. There are many organizations and individuals who specialize in OD efforts, and they are found in a wide variety of settings—universities, research bureaus, private firms, non-profit organizations. All stand ready to be of assistance, if the price and commitment is right. It may be helpful to mention just a few of these resources to give you a notion of the depth of the OD movement. Many OD programs or management development approaches are built upon a common learning experience. Such is the case with the Managerial Grid, developed by Drs. Blake and Mouton and offered through their firm, Scientific Methods, Inc. This program, adopted by Hennepin County, builds its whole rationale around a common learning experience for all management and supervisory personnel. Initial involvement in the one-week Managerial Grid Seminar by all key management personnel constitutes phase I of a Grid OD effort.

Educational Systems and Design, a consulting firm on the East Coast, uses a similar learning approach to the Grid (what is known as an instrumental design). They do vary the content of their five-day seminar at higher levels of management in the organization, but most of it remains the same.

The National Training Laboratories, a non-profit educational institution long involved in development efforts, establishes its OD programs around laboratory training—some type of personal growth experience that puts a premium on communications, openness, and trust among members of the learning and working group.

Rensis Likert and his colleagues at the Institute for Social Research, University of Michigan, rely heavily upon the collection of data about the organization with a feeding back of that information to the work teams in a systematic manner, using quantitative diagnostic surveys and performance criteria.

Richard Beckhard, a one-man consulting team out of New York City and MIT, puts his emphasis on team development, intergroup relationships, planning and goal setting processes, and educational activities for upgrading the knowledges, skills, and abilities of key personnel at all levels of the organization.

The Industrial Relations Center at the University of Chicago ideally likes to embark on an elaborate three-phase training program spread over 18–24 months which engages all the key managerial and supervisory personnel in 120 hours of formal training. These seminars cover leadership and human behavior in phase I; communication, coaching and developing subordinates in phase II; and decision making, and management by objectives in the final phase of the program. In addition to the formal education, the Center uses data gathering and third-party consultation as integral parts of its OD efforts.

Other organizations build their OD efforts on Management by Objectives or similar approaches that could be characterized as more traditional. The distance from one end of the OD spectrum to the other is great, with disciples clinging to a wide variety of approaches scattered along that spectrum. It is impossible to expose you, in a short time, to any more than a smattering of ideas about OD. The quick vignettes of different OD approaches mentioned above are dangerously simplistic. OD is complicated and each of the above-mentioned programs are much more complex than my brief accounts would suggest. I have tried to impress upon you the variety of organizations currently engaged in organization development and to show the common thread of basic objectives that runs through each of them.

Much of the ideology surrounding OD can be traced back to Kurt Lewin, an early-day social psychologist who believed that research and learning are practical management strategies for everyday application. To Lewin, there was "nothing so practical as a good theory." He is often identified with the initiation of such commonplace tools of psychology as group dynamics, sensitivity training, life space, and other concepts frequently used in individual and organization development programs.

DIAGNOSIS AND PLANNED INTERVENTION

Organization development is often broken down into two broad categories of process—*diagnosis* and *planned intervention*. Diagnosis includes data gathering about critical social processes within the organization. Common diagnosis techniques are surveys, interviews and first-hand observation. Some of the critical social processes diagnosed include communication patterns and styles, functional roles of group members, organizational climate, group problem-solving and decision-making, group norms and group growth, leadership and authority, and intergroup processes.

Intervention strategies are numerous in organization development. Team building is one of the most common OD interventions and many well-known OD efforts, including the Managerial Grid, place heavy emphasis on team development. After all, groups are the basic building blocks of organizations and intra-group and inter-group processes can ultimately make or break the system. Team building concentrates not only upon the task to be performed but on the interpersonal relationships and other processes that are taking place in task accomplishment. A natural extension of team building in today's complex organization is intergroup problem solving. Much has been written about the use of intergroup OD activities. A careful look at the diffusion of most municipal operations readily reveals the importance of developing better strategies for intergroup action.

Data feedback is another important intervention method. As indicated earlier, many OD practitioners have developed intricate ways of gathering information and feeding it back into the system for processing. Much of the work that Likert and his associates at the University of Michigan have been involved in over the past two decades has centered around institutional survey research.

Training, of course, is central to all OD efforts, although not always explicit. Many of the previously mentioned organizations, engaged in OD efforts, build their programs around a common educational experience for the key management and supervisory people in the organization. Training covers such activities as interpersonal competence; problem-solving knowledge and skills; skills in goal-setting, planning and systems diagnosis; understanding the processes of change, and changing; and communications.

Another intervention strategy for organization development involves techno-structural changes and is less often identified with OD, perhaps because the strategy is less behavioral based. Techno-structural interventions would include effective use or alteration of such factors as patterns of work flow, hierarchical relationships, personnel systems, the division of labor; job-enrichment programs; and financial systems.

As you can see, the technology available for organization development is significant. Much of it is as old as organization itself, while other aspects are new and considered innovative. What makes OD new, as an approach to management, is the comprehensive attitude it ultimately must adopt about individual and institutional improvement and its fanatic concentration on planned organization change in a world that is constantly in a state of unplanned and chaotic alteration.

CONTINUING EDUCATION SERVICE

Organization development is an exciting strategy to be applied to your organization. You will be hearing more about it in years to come. In fact, the major public interest groups representing state and local governments in Washington, have just created a new nonprofit institution that will have as its major focus, the development of human resources in public agencies. The *Continuing Education Service* will concentrate its efforts on the internalization of training and development as a major management strategy in state and local agencies. Hopefully, the best organization development theories and practices will be brought to bear on state and local governments through the efforts of CES.

The CES will pursue a course of action that makes much of what I've said earlier familiar territory. CES will seek from the top elected and appointed officials, an understanding and commitment to action training and research principles and practices through engaging them in the process. In other words, CES will go about "turning top officials on" to the potential of training and development. That is where it must begin.

Secondly, the Continuing Education Service will be prepared to train people within state and local agencies to carry out the development process. Where the agency is too small for such staff support, it will work through state leagues, universities and regional programs.

Finally, the CES will back these people up with onsite consultation, materials, and program development so that they are less likely to fail in their efforts. Out of this comprehensive program should grow a network of state and local agencies committed to the use of training and development as a major management strategy for bringing about change and improvement within their agencies. Through the CES, they will be linked together, able to draw upon the programs and experiences of each other.

Is organization development possible in a governmental agency? The answer is still a qualified yes, but the establishment of the Continuing Education Service should make it easier to install an OD effort in your agency. Organization development is an important major strategy for maximizing your resources and response.

31. How to Beat the Peter Principle*

Peter Cossette

When Prof. Laurence Peter wrote his best-seller, *The Peter Principle*, he obviously intended it to be a tongue-in-cheek satire on the business scene. But what if you don't find it funny—you think Peter has a point and want to prove him wrong?

Remember what Peter said: "In a hierarchy, every employee tends to rise to his level of incompetence."

The key word is "hierarchy."

Peter said business people eventually tend to slow down. But he did not explain why.

The conditions for this failure are present in hierarchies because they nurture pressure—"people pressure."

Failure because of pure physical pressure in business is infrequent. You only have to lift a 100-pound sack to know if you should take a job loading trucks in a flour mill. But "people pressures" are subtler and more damaging. They take their toll of the body and spirit. Situations causing unrelieved frustration finally bring on an ulcer. The race to satisfy impossible demands results in a near-fatal heart attack.

Does failure under these conditions mean the man has risen to his level of incompetence? I think not. He may have risen to the level of someone else's incompetence—the manager who brought the intolerable pressure to bear, or who deprived him of the chance to exercise initiative and imagination.

That manager might be you.

Few people can accurately judge their true competence. Some may be able to tell within rough limits how well they are doing, but there are facets of their performance that can only be assessed adequately by somebody else, usually their bosses.

Unless you are on the first rung of your career, you will probably be responsible for deciding on the competence of others. You may think you cannot beat the Peter Principle yourself, but you can help somebody else do so. In doing so, you may actually beat it yourself and avoid becoming one of the "Peter Proletariat."

We may define competence as ability to do the work. Have you looked recently at some of the position descriptions for the people who work for you? Can the job you describe be done by one man, or should it be shared between three men and a boy? Is it relevant?

As the world changes, so will the volume, relationships and kind of

* From *Toronto Financial Post*, June 27, 1970, 33. Reprinted by permission.

work in your business. The changes often bring internal stresses that can no longer be met by the old organization and the old position descriptions. If you think some of your people are approaching the level of their incompetence, look at the work you expect them to do and the conditions under which it has to be done. You may be in for a shock.

Consider "job enrichment." Could you add interest to the position by giving more authority and an expanded scope of action that will pull the job out of the hum-drum and make it worthwhile? It is often the needed stimulus for the man who seems about to prove Peter right.

What about shaping position descriptions to challenge the skills of the people who are in them? Sometimes people fail to produce their best work because their role is poorly defined.

What about trying job rotation? This can broaden the executive's horizons, give him new ideas and a better understanding of how the organization works.

If job rotation is impractical, or too expensive, you can achieve a similar effect by a coaching program that breaks him out of his own mold and makes him look around.

At the same time, you are showing him that you take an interest in him and his performance. A better job attitude and a rise in competence will probably result.

A word of warning: fight off the temptation to put your inimitable trade mark on the work of your subordinates. They may be doing things much better than you could do them yourself.

In addition to the "competents" who keep things running in the organization, there are those who think themselves "super competent" and some who believe they might be "super incompetent." One is always letting you know how good he is. The other is self-effacing and doesn't recognize his real value. Both may really be "competents." Both could probably do a much better job if their self-images were put into proper perspective.

One of the best ways of doing this is to send them to a first-class university seminar on management development. Pick a university noted for student participation in its programs.

In the rough-and-tumble discussions, the supposed "super competent" will find he is not as smart as he thought. The "super incompetent" finds that his ability to hold his own with the rest has given his ego the boost it needed. Both of them will probably come back to the job better for having their egos realigned. They may also have picked up some new business ideas.

What happens if none of these measures succeeds? Your man may need the services of a good psychologist. Don't raise your eyebrows— hundreds of executives are in need of psychological help.

If you have one of these men, you may be doing him and your company a great favor by arranging a series of interviews with a psychologist. Many companies are now doing so, not only for humanitarian reasons, but because it makes hard economic sense. The cost of replacing the man is only part of the price you pay if you let him go. With him he takes years of background knowledge—and some of the morale of those he leaves behind. A firm cannot let an executive go without raising a small doubt in the minds of those who remain.

These are a few suggested courses of action. If you are not a "Peter Principle person," you can probably think of others. If you cannot, you may be running the risk, as Professor Peter foresaw, of proving the Peter Principle.

32. Common Questions and Tentative Answers Regarding Organization Development*

Lyman K. Randall

More people in business and government are searching for more meaningful, more effective, ways to get work done. As a result of their search, they are becoming optimistic about initiating creative and purposeful change in work organizations. They label their activities and concepts *Organization Development*. The search for new answers, however, also leads to more questions. Listed are many of the questions commonly asked about Organization Development. The answers which follow are tentative simply because the field is still emerging and the conclusions are not final.

BRIEFLY, WHAT IS ORGANIZATION DEVELOPMENT?

Organization Development is a reorientation of man's thinking and behavior toward his work organizations. It applies the scientific method and its underlying values of open investigation and experimentation to individual and work group behaviors as they are directed toward the solution of work problems. It views both man and change optimistically. It applies a humanistic value system to work behaviors. It assumes people have the capability and motivation to grow through learning how to improve their own work climate, work processes and their resulting products. It accepts as inevitable the conflicts among the needs of individuals, work groups, and the organization, but advocates openly confronting these conflicts using problem-solving strategies. Its goal is to maximize the use of organization resources in solving work problems through the optimal use of human potential.

IS ORGANIZATION DEVELOPMENT SIMPLY THE HUMAN RELATIONS MOVEMENT IN A NEW FORMAT?

Although related to earlier human relations work, OD differs from it in several ways. Many managers interpreted the message of human relations to be: "If morale is high, productivity will increase; and morale can be increased by 'being nice to people.' " For these managers "being nice to people" eventually meant emphasizing what Frederick Herzberg later categorized as work hygiene factors: employee benefits, working conditions, facilities, administrative policies, and social relationships.[1]

Organization Development, on the other hand, concentrates on the

---

* © 1971 by The Regents of the University of California. Reprinted from *California Management Review*, Vol. XIII, No. 3, pp. 45–51, by permission of The Regents.
1 For a fuller discussion of Herzberg's theory regarding hygiene factors vs. motivating factors, see "One More Time: How Do You Motivate Employees," *Harvard Business Review*, (Jan.-Feb. 1968).

accomplishment of work and the solving of work problems by people. The improvement of relationships between people and work groups is not an end in itself, as it often turned out to be in human relations. Instead, interpersonal and intergroup behaviors are the focus as they are relevant to the successful problem-solving efforts of the work unit.

IS ORGANIZATIONAL DEVELOPMENT PRIMARILY CONCERNED WITH RESTRUCTURING ORGANIZATIONS?

No. Many people assume that the term, *organization development*, is closely related to the organization planning process with its emphasis on organization charts, and the like. Although the restructuring of an organizational unit could be one of the results of an OD effort, this activity might be only one consequence of OD.

ON WHAT CONCEPTS IS ORGANIZATION DEVELOPMENT BASED?

The concepts fundamental to OD can be placed in two general categories: those that apply more often to work groups and large organizations and those that apply to the individual. Naturally, these concepts are interrelated.

OD Concepts Regarding Work Groups and Organizations

SYSTEMS. Organizations are laced together by systems and subsystems such as budgeting, purchasing, inventory and stores, and so on. All subunits or parts of a system are interrelated to the whole. When one part of a system is changed, the total system is affected. In OD, thinking in systems terms is necessary when planning the tactics and strategies of change.

PROBLEM-SOLVING INTERDEPENDENCE. This concept is closely related to *systems*. When individuals and groups are working toward the solution of problems which affect other persons and groups, the problem is said to be interdependent rather than independent. In this situation people and groups have a common stake in the outcome and therefore need to have a voice in the solution. Treating interdependent problems as if they are independent usually leads to resistance to change and win/lose conflict between those who had a chance to have their say and those who did not.

WORK CLIMATE. Research indicates that work climate affects the kinds of results that individuals, groups, and total organizations produce as atmospheric climate affects the quality of crops that a farm produces. Work climate is comprised of the values, attitudes, and underlying assumptions which determine how work gets done. Work climate is closely related to *OD Values* and *Theory Y* discussed later.[2]

[2] See George Litwin and Robert Stringer, *Motivation and Organization Climate* (Boston: Harvard University, 1968).

FORCE FIELD. This theory states that any given behavior of a work group is held at a given level by two opposing sets of forces: driving forces which push the level of performance up to a certain point; restraining forces which prevent the behavior from rising beyond this same point. Using this concept we can see there are two basic options open to us if we wish to increase any behavior or set of behaviors such as, for example, work group productivity. We can add more driving forces to increase productivity or we can identify and remove some of the restraining forces which keep productivity from going any higher. The first option is more often used, but the second option often holds more promise for results since it removes a force that most individuals see as negative. Although OD focuses on both driving and restraining forces as determinants of job behavior, it often emphasizes the latter since restraining forces are more often overlooked in the analysis of work problems.

PROCESS AND TASKS. Work groups and individual jobs exist to accomplish tasks needed for the organization to survive, remain healthy, and grow. Specific tasks are determined by goals of the group or corporation. Process, on the other hand, is what happens between individuals and groups as they work on their tasks. In the Broadway musical, "Zorba," *life* is described as "what happens to you as you are waiting to die." Similarly, process is what happens among people as they are working on tasks. Typically managers focus on tasks much more frequently than they do on process although process problems usually cause below-standard task achievement. Perhaps the most difficult aspect of OD for many managers is learning to deal with process issues. Several specific factors distinguish *tasks* from *process*.

Task (the job to do)		*Process* (the "happenings" of getting tasks done)
Usually concrete and based on objectives	*vs.*	More nebulous and difficult to identify
More static and often repetitive	*vs.*	Very dynamic and fluid
Outside of ourselves	*vs.*	Involves "tuning-in" to what's going on inside ourselves
Much "There and Then" time orientation	*vs.*	"Here and Now" time orientation
Usually dealt with intellectually	*vs.*	Involves much feeling and subjective perception

DATA COLLECTION AND DIAGNOSIS. For years businessmen have been collecting data about such factors as markets, new product performance, and capital expenditures in order to diagnose problems that need to be resolved. These same men have only recently begun to learn to collect data about the human interaction process in their organizations. Problems involving individual and group perceptions, feelings, assumptions, and attitudes often provide the key for improving the accomplishment of work group tasks. Usually data are collected either by using anonymous questionnaires or by an outside resource person who interviews selected individuals. A summary of the data is then fed back to the group for discussion and problem-solving.

OD Concepts Regarding Individuals

OD VALUES. These are values which people must regard highly before an OD effort can succeed in an organization. They are important ingredients in the work climate of an organization involved in OD. Many of these values have a concomitant skill or behavior which can be learned and practiced by individuals. These values and related skills include the following:

Trust and openness: This is perhaps the cornerstone of all OD work. Trust in interpersonal and intergroup relationships is essential if full and open communication is to occur. An open and nonmanipulative sharing of data is required for the effective solving of work problems. In most organizations or work groups, trust does not exist automatically. Traditional work orientations based on the manipulation of people have generated widespread distrust at all levels. This widespread distrust of supervisors, other work groups, and other employees is one of the initial problems often encountered in an OD effort. Building trust and openness throughout an organization is therefore one of the continuing goals of OD.

Leveling: "Tell it like it is!" OD work is usually called leveling. An individual with the skill and courage to share candidly with others meaningful information about how he thinks, reacts, and feels about work issues and co-workers is unfortunately the exception in today's organization. However, leveling skills are essential if OD is to succeed.

Feedback: People tend to make many assumptions about other people—how they feel, what they think, why they behave as they do—without ever checking out the accuracy of what they have assumed. Feedback is simply a communications skill for verifying or correcting these assumptions and thereby providing more accurate data on others as well as on ourselves. To be useful, however, feedback must be shared in a helpful, nonaccusatory manner. Feedback that begins, "The trouble with you is . . ." is generally destructive rather than helpful. Feedback can be given and received successfully only when relationships are based on trust and mutual respect. The result is a deeper and more accurate comprehension of what is going on in the process of accomplishing work.

Confronting conflict: OD values hold that conflict is a natural occurence between people and work groups. Conflict issues should therefore be dealt with openly and problem-solved. Unfortunately traditional work orientations, perhaps influenced by the military, hold that conflict

234

is negative and should be avoided, denied, or smoothed-over whenever possible. The result of this approach is the perpetuation of unresolved problems. Conflict confrontation skills include such factors as trust, leveling, and the ability to give and receive feedback.

Risk-taking: This refers to the ability of individuals to "stick their necks out" in meaningful ways. Examples include taking an unpopular stand in an important issue, conflicting with a superior on preferred solutions to a problem, trying to initiate action on a problem seemingly avoided by others, and sharing with co-workers personal feelings such as commitment, concern, anxiety, or caring.

Owning of personal experience: In today's organizations it is very easy to point the finger of blame or responsibility at others. In fact many, many people have spent years learning how to defend themselves from real or imagined accusors by denying responsibiilty, concern, and feeling regarding their work experiences. Personal experience also underlies an individual's ability to level about himself, give feedback to others, build interpersonal trust, take risks, and to confront conflict—all of which are essential to OD activities.

SELF-ACTUALIZATION. This term is used by Maslow to describe man's highest order of motivational need. It includes his personal needs for learning, growth, achievement, competence, recognition, and the striving toward his fullest potential. These are the elements Herzberg has recently formulated as the Motivating Factors of people at work. Self-actualization is premised on an optimistic view of man. A self-actualizing man is an individual behaving at his most creative and productive level. An individual is most likely to behave in self-actualizing ways is the climate in which he works is characterized by openness, trust, confrontation, and so on, and he has challenging goals.

THEORY Y. In reviewing the findings of behavioral science research in industry several years ago, Douglas McGregor formulated a set of assumptions about man at work that seemed to be supported by the research. He called this formulation Theory Y.[3] It is built on the following premises:

Work is as natural to man as play and rest.

Man will use self-direction and control when he is committed to objectives.

Man learns, under proper conditions, to accept and even to seek responsibility.

Creative ability is widely dispersed among individuals.

In industry, man's potential is only partially utilized.

McGregor then contrasted Theory Y with another set of assumptions

3 Douglas McGregor, *The Human Side of Enterprise* (New York: McGraw-Hill, 1960).

about man at work. He labeled these Theory X, and observed that most organizations behaved as if they believed these assumptions rather than Theory Y. Theory X assumptions include:

The average man dislikes and will avoid work.
He must be forced, controlled, and directed to work.
He prefers to be directed in his work since he has little ambition.
He seeks only security.

Obviously, OD is based on Theory Y assumptions. Many of the work climate values and organizational practices which are change-targets for OD stem from Theory X assumptions.

T-GROUPS. T-Groups are specially designed learning experiences which focus on most of the OD concepts discussed above, i.e. trust, openness, process, leveling, feedback, risk-taking, owning experience, and so on. For many individuals, T-Groups provide unique opportunities to assess themselves regarding where they stand in relation to these values and skills. For this reason, some version of a T-Group is often used as a first step in launching an OD effort in an organization.[4]

HOW DO MANY ORGANIZATION DEVELOPMENT EFFORTS GET STARTED?

Many OD activities begin when a manager becomes uneasy about the effectiveness of his own work group. Often he is not aware of the causes of ineffectiveness although he can usually point to several symptoms. These might include frequently missed deadlines, conflicts between employees that are never dealt with directly, low-level innovation in problem-solving, distrust between individuals or groups, the disowning of personal responsibility, et cetera. In other words, OD begins with a manager looking for more effective ways of accomplishing the goals of his group and the organization. He is usually a man who sees himself as reasonably competent but with more to learn.

IS IT TRUE THAT ORGANIZATION DEVELOPMENT MUST ALWAYS BEGIN AT THE TOP OF THE ORGANIZATION?

A recent survey by the National Industrial Conference Board found that approximately half of the OD efforts studied had been initiated by corporate presidents or board chairmen. In the other organizations the early OD experimenting and risk-taking was done by managers further down the hierarchy.

"OD must begin at the top!" is sometimes used by a person who wants to deny any personal need or responsibility for change. In this case he is actually saying, "My work group is in fine shape, but it's those S.O.B.'s

[4] Chris Argyris, "T-Groups for Organizational Effectiveness," *Harvard Business Review* (March-April 1964).

who always foul-up things!" Pointing to the top of the organization gets him off the hook nicely since there is little he can do personally to make top management aware of *their* need to change.

Eventually OD must include top management. Organizational climate is formed at the top. Similarly the rewards for and restraints against risk-taking, leveling, and confronting conflict issues are established here. The overall quality of teamwork characteristic of the organization is heavily influenced by the behaviors of the top team.

WHERE CAN AN INDIVIDUAL FIND AN ORGANIZATION DEVELOPMENT PROGRAM TO FIT HIS NEEDS?

Many managers are accustomed to thinking about their activities in terms of concrete programs that begin at a specific time and end by a preset date. It is therefore natural for them to expect OD to fit this same pattern. Unfortunately, it does not. By definition OD must begin where individuals and the work group are. This requires an initial collection of data from members of the work group followed by a basic diagnosis of restraints that seem to be interfering with the work group's problem-solving efforts and the achievement of its goals. Planning specific OD activities must evolve from this initial diagnosis.

DOES OD HAVE A BEGINNING, MIDDLE, AND END LIKE MOST PROGRAMS?

This question is closely related to the question above. As mentioned above, many managers are accustomed to thinking in terms of programs which have clearly defined start-up and conclusion phases. If, however, an OD effort is successful, it will become "a way of organization life" and therefore will have no identifiable conclusion. This is often a difficult and frustrating point to understand. Just as *managing* is a means to an end, OD is also a process rather than an end product. One of its goals is to build into an organization the human dynamics essential for continuous self-renewing change. OD should lead a work group toward continuing purposeful adaptation and away from reactive change.

Several reasonably distinct phases of the OD process can be identified.[5] Initially a key manager must feel some heightened discomfort from internal or external pressures before an awareness of serious problems can occur. If none of his usual options for handling the problem prove effective, he may then look for new ways of attacking it. This is often the point where a behavioral science consultant is included in the work. The organization then goes through what is often called "an unfreezing process." Common psychological and communication restraints are purposely diminished. Because people and groups are now freer to

5 Larry Greiner, "Patterns of Organization Change." *Harvard Business Review* (May-June 1967).

237

communicate, considerably more relevant data and ideas become available for diagnosing and resolving the critical problems. As increasing degrees of trust and openness are built into the climate, more people become involved with and committed to creating the changes necessary to resolve the problem of the group. This greatly reduces the commonly encountered resistances to change. The next stage of change is characterized by increased experimentation and testing of new ways for working together and solving problems. If moderate to considerable success is experienced, the new work values and approaches to problems become the new work norms. This improved level of reintegrating work resources represents the final phase which makes possible a natural recycling of the whole process. At this point, managers in the group have learned to become OD managers.

MUST A MANAGER ATTEND A T-GROUP OR MANAGEMENT TRAINING LABORATORY BEFORE HE CAN UNDERTAKE OD IN HIS GROUP?

Although attending a T-Group is not a prerequisite for a manager interested in initiating an OD effort, it usually helps to prepare him for the experience in several ways. It enables him to experience what it is like to learn purposefully from his own experience. T-Group experience also helps him to learn more about OD concepts and related skills such as: process, "owning-up," trust, openness, leveling, giving helpful feedback, risk-taking, and confronting conflict. These cannot be learned except through experience, and T-Groups provide a shortcut to this kind of experience.

WHAT IF A MANAGER CANNOT AFFORD THE TIME OR EXPENSE DEMANDED BY AN OD EFFORT?

This question is also based on the already-examined assumption that OD is some kind of new program that an organization carries on in addition to everything else. As we saw earlier, this assumption is false. Instead OD is a process through which work is accomplished more efficiently and effectively and without the human fallout and contamination often resulting from more traditional orientations toward work. Its payoffs are to be found in the saving of time and resources.

IF OD IS SO PROMISING, WHY AREN'T MORE GROUPS OR ORGANIZATIONS PRACTICING IT?

OD is not more widely practiced at the present time for at least three reasons. First, individuals have only started to learn within the last twenty years how to create the process of change and growth within their own organizations. Before this, change was something that happened to them. OD is an attempt to integrate what we have learned in this area, and is a very recent idea. Another reason is that OD is a complex process and requires considerable time to spread throughout a total organization. Finally, OD has not always been an irrefutable success. People and organizations are still learning about OD.

WHY IS IT OFTEN DIFFICULT TO GET THE TOP EXECUTIVES OF AN ORGANIZATION INVOLVED IN OD?

There are many reasons. Many top executives have been successful in their careers, in part, because they have learned to live by the traditional values of the organization. It is difficult for them to contemplate modifying or discarding that for which they have been so well rewarded.

In some cases top executives are among the last to know about some of the serious problems which drain an inordinate amount of time and energy from the organization. As John Gardner recently noted "We have still not discovered how to counteract the process by which every organization filters the feedback on performance in order to screen out the things it doesn't want to face up to."[6]

Other executives may fail to see any interdependence between their own behavior and the problems they identify at lower levels. Some executives believe that they cannot afford the time to engage in OD efforts.

Finally, most executives are also human beings. They have the same anxieties, or perhaps even stronger ones, about more openly exposing themselves as vulnerable individuals. They have valid reasons to distrust others in the organization who often try to influence them by using distorted information and manipulation. They perhaps even sense some of the seething anger and frustration at lower levels of the organization and hesitate to put themselves in a position to have these feelings dumped on them.

IF OD ENCOURAGES PEOPLE TO EXPRESS THEIR FEELINGS, DOESN'T IT LEAD TOWARD SUBJECTIVE ANARCHY AND AWAY FROM A RATIONAL AND SCIENTIFIC APPROACH TO MANAGING?

Feelings and subjective experiences are as relevant to the successes and failures of organizations as are budgets and statistical reports. However, until recently they were largely ignored since they were considered nonrational and therefore inappropriate. It is paradoxical that the more we learn about our own feelings, the more rational we become.

WHAT ARE THE MOST COMMON OBSTACLES TO OD?

OD efforts must overcome obstacles that commonly block any other

6 John W. Gardner, "We, the People," Millikan Award Address, California Institute of Technology, November 21, 1968.

management activity: misusing authority to bring about change; denying or avoiding conflict of central importance; disowning personal responsibility for initiating action or taking a stand on an issue; waiting for someone else to make the first move; resting on early or easy successes instead of pushing on for higher levels of effectiveness; involving only a few people at the top in the planning of change rather than working toward widespread involvement; reacting to failure experiences by finding a scapegoat rather than searching for the real causes of failure; expecting to accomplish new levels of effectiveness without learning essential new concepts and skills from qualified experts; taking action without having clear goals in mind due to an initial lack of data. Fortunately, however, these are all specific problems to which OD efforts are particularly sensitive.

HOW CAN YOU EVALUATE THE PAY-OFF OF AN OD EFFORT?

OD results are extremely difficult to evaluate in a strict, scientifically controlled design for several reasons. OD is a slowly evolving process involving numerous people over an extended period of time. Many variables, such as key personnel promotions and transfers, occur during the OD experimentation period and also have an impact on the results accomplished by an organization. Who is to say whether improvements are attributable to the OD effort or to the change in leadership? Both are likely influences toward change.

Robert Blake and Jane Mouton conducted an OD experiment several years ago at a Humble Oil Refinery which Louis Barnes and Larry Greiner from the Harvard Business School were asked to evaluate. Although Barnes and Greiner argued logically and persuasively that the experiment resulted in several millions of dollars of profit, they were unable to prove the direct cause and effect relationships.[7]

There are two different ways in which the results of experiments can be judged. One approach is called *quantitative validation*. It attempts to demonstrate statistically quantified relationships between experimental activities and the results achieved. To a limited extent OD efforts can be measured by this method. For example, an initial diagnosis might be made of a work group's perception of itself using a written questionnaire. The OD activities which follow can then focus on the problems identified by the diagnosis. Later a similar written survey can again be conducted to determine if the earlier problems have been resolved. The results of the two surveys can be statistically compared.

A second approach is called *experiential validation*. It places importance on judgments individuals make about their own experiences.

[7] Robert Blake and Jane Mouton; Louis Barnes and Larry Greiner, "Break Through in Organization Development," *Harvard Business Review* (Nov.-Dec. 1964).

As an example, research shows that subordinates are reasonably accurate in discriminating between an effective and ineffective boss. They base their judgments on their own private experiences with the world of bosses. OD results can more readily be judged through this same kind of experiential validation than by quantitative means. Most individuals in a work group that is involved in an OD effort can point to several critical incidents which would probably not have happened if OD had not been underway.

AREN'T THE VALUES ON WHICH OD IS BASED SOMEWHAT AT ODDS WITH PRACTICAL ORGANIZATIONAL REALITIES?

Yes, they are. One of the basic goals of OD is to change the traditional climate of organizations in order to utilize their resources more fully. Often the phrase, *practical realities*, is used by persons who feel the need to defend the status quo against the need for change. Being practical and realistic are two norms frequently advocated in the management-world of organizations. But who is to define what is practical and what is real? OD is built on the assumption that it is more scientifically valid to engage a large number of people at all levels of the organization in the investigation and discovery of what is both real and practical.

IS ORGANIZATION DEVELOPMENT AN ATTEMPT TO BUILD AN INDUSTRIAL UTOPIA?

In many ways, yes. The goal of OD is to maximize organizational productivity through actualizing the potential of individuals and the work groups in which they are members. Certainly this is an idealistic objective, but does this make it an unreasonable one to strive toward?

The focus of OD is on the difference between what we are and what we are capable of becoming. Individual and organizational change are directed toward narrowing this gap. An executive involved in OD recently described the paradox involved in this type of goal: "We will continuously have to be dealing with resistance to change, including resistances within ourselves. People are not standing in line outside our doors asking to be freed up, liberated, and upended. Cultures are not saying: 'Change us; we can no longer cope; we are unstable.' Commitment to trying as hard and as well as we can to implement these [OD] values is not commitment to an easy, soft existence. On the other hand, the rewards we experience can be precious, real, and profound. They can have important meanings for us individually, for those with whom we work, and for our organizations. Ultimately, what we stand for can make for a better world—and we deeply know that this is what keeps us going."[8]

[8] Robert Tannenbaum and Sheldon Davis, "Values, Man, and Organizations," *MIT Research Report* (Oct. 1967).

241

CONCLUSION

In his recent book, *The Revolution of Hope Toward a Humanized Technology*,[9] Erich Fromm asks: "Are we confronted with a tragic, insolvable dilemma? Must we produce sick people in order to have a healthy economy, or can we use our material resources, our inventions, our computers to serve the ends of man? Must individuals be passive and dependent in order to have strong and well-functioning organizations?"

Organization Development is an attempt to provide humanly affirmative answers to these difficult questions.

[9] Erich Fromm, *The Revolution of Hope Toward a Humanized Technology* (New York: Harper & Row, 1968).

33. How to Prevent Organizational Dry Rot*

John W. Gardner

Like people and plants, organizations have a life cycle. They have a green and supple youth, a time of flourishing strength, and a gnarled old age. We have all seen organizations that are still going through the diseases of childhood, and others so far gone in the rigidities of age that they ought to be pensioned off and sent to Florida to live out their days.

But organizations differ from people and plants in that their cycle isn't even approximately predictable. An organization may go from youth to old age in two or three decades, or it may last for centuries. More important, it may go through a period of stagnation and then revive. In short, decline is not inevitable. Organizations need not stagnate. They often do, to be sure, but that is because the arts of organizational renewal are not yet widely understood. Organizations can renew themselves continuously. That fact has far-reaching implications for our future.

We know at least some of the rules for organizational renewal. And those rules are relevant for all kinds of organizations—U.S. Steel, Yale University, the U.S. Navy, a government agency, or your local bank.

The first rule is that the organization must have an effective program for the recruitment and development of talent. People are the ultimate source of renewal. The shortage of able, highly trained, highly motivated men will be a permanent feature of our kind of society; and every organization that wants its share of the short supply is going to have to get out and fight for it. The organization must have the kind of recruitment policy that will bring in a steady flow of able and highly motivated individuals. And it cannot afford to let those men go to seed, or get sidetracked or boxed in. There must be positive, constructive programs of career development. In this respect, local, state, and federal government agencies are particularly deficient, and have been so for many years. Their provisions for the recruitment and development of talent are seriously behind the times.

The second rule for the organization capable of continuous renewal is that it must be a hospitable environment for the individual. Organizations that have killed the spark of individuality in their members will have greatly diminished their capacity for change. Individuals who have been made to feel like cogs in the machine will behave like cogs in the machine. They will not produce ideas for change. On the contrary, they will resist such ideas when produced by others.

The third rule is that the organization must have built-in provisions for self-criticism. It must have an atmosphere in which uncomfortable questions can be asked. I would lay it down as a basic principle of human organization that the individuals who hold the reins of power in any enterprise cannot trust themselves to be adequately self-critical. For those in power the danger of self-deception is very great, the danger of failing to see the problems or refusing to see them is ever-present. And the only protection is to create an atmosphere in which anyone can speak up. The most enlightened top executives are well aware of this. Of course, I don't need to tell those readers who are below the loftiest level of management that even with enlightened executives a certain amount of prudence is useful. The Turks have a proverb that says, "The man who tells the truth should have one foot in the stirrup."

But it depends on the individual executive. Some welcome criticism, others don't. Louis Armstrong once said, "There are some people that if they don't know, you can't tell 'em."

The fourth requirement for the organization that seeks continuous renewal is fluidity of internal structure. Obviously, no complex modern organization can exist without the structural arrangements of divisions, branches, departments, and so forth. I'm not one of those who imagine that the modern world can get away from specialization. Specialization and division of labor are at the heart of modern organization. In this connection I always recall a Marx Brothers movie in which Groucho played a shyster lawyer. When a client commented on the dozens of flies buzzing around his broken-down office, Groucho said, "We have a working agreement with them. They don't practice law and we don't climb the walls."

But jurisdictional boundaries tend to get set in concrete. Pretty soon, no solution to a problem is seriously considered if there is any danger that it will threaten jurisdictional lines. But those lines aren't sacred. They were established in some past time to achieve certain objectives. Perhaps the objectives are still valid, perhaps not. *Most organizations have a structure that was designed to solve problems that no longer exist.*

The fifth rule is that the organization must have an adequate system of internal communication. If I may make a rather reckless generalization, I'd say that renewal is a little like creativity in this respect—that it depends on the existence of a large number of diverse elements in a situation that permits an infinite variety of combinations and recombinations. The enormous potentialities of the human brain are in part explainable in terms of such possibilities for combination and recombination. And such recombination is facilitated by easy communication, impeded by poor communication.

The sixth rule: The organization must have some means of combating the process by which men become prisoners of their procedures. The rule book grows fatter as the ideas grow fewer. Thus almost every well-established organization is a coral reef of procedures that were laid down to achieve some long-forgotten objective.

It is in our nature to develop an affection for customary ways of doing things. Some years ago a wholesale firm noted that some of its small shopkeeper customers were losing money because of antiquated merchandising methods. The firm decided that it would be good business to assist the shopkeepers in bringing their methods up-to-date, but soon discovered that many had no desire to modernize. They loved the old, money-losing ways.

Sometimes the organization procedures men devise to advance their purposes serve in the long run to block those purposes. This was apparent in an experience a friend of mine had in Germany in the last days of World War II. He was in Aachen, which had only recently been occupied by the American forces, when he received a message instructing him to proceed to London immediately. He went directly to U.S. Army headquarters, and showed the message to a sergeant in the Adjutant's office.

The sergeant said that the only plane for London within the next few days was leaving from the nearest airfield in thirty minutes. He added that the airfield was twenty-five minutes away.

It was discouraging news. My friend knew that he could not proceed to London without written orders, and that was a process that took from an hour to a couple of days in a well-established and smoothly functioning headquarters. The present headquarters had been opened the day before, and was in a totally unorganized state.

My friend explained his dilemma to the sergeant and handed over his papers. The sergeant scratched his head and left the room. Four minutes later he returned and said, "Here are your orders, sir."

My friend said he had never been in such an efficient headquarters. The sergeant looked at him with a twinkle in his eye and said, "Sir, it's just lucky for you we weren't organized!"

The seventh rule: The organization capable of continuous renewal will have found some means of combating the vested interests that grow up in every human institution. We commonly associate the term "vested interests" with people of wealth and power, but in an organization vested interests exist at every level. The lowest employees have their vested interests, every foreman has his, and every department head has his.

245

Every change threatens someone's privileges, someone's authority, someone's status. What wise managers try to do, of course, is to sell the idea that in the long run everyone's overriding vested interest is in the continuing vitality of the organization itself. If that fails, everyone loses. But it's a hard message to get across.

Nowhere can the operation of vested interests be more clearly seen than in the functioning of university departments. There are exceptions, of course: some departments rise above their vested interests. But the average department holds like grim death to its piece of intellectual terrain. It teaches its neophytes a jealous devotion to the boundaries of the field. It assesses the significance of intellectual questions by the extent to which they can be answered without going outside the sacred territory. Such vested interests effectively block most efforts to reform undergraduate instruction.

The eighth rule is that the organization capable of continuous renewal is interested in what it is going to become and not what it has been. When I moved to New London, Connecticut, in 1938 I was astonished at the attitude of New Londoners toward their city's future. Having grown up in California, I was accustomed to cities and towns that looked ahead habitually (often with an almost absurd optimism). I was not prepared for a city that, so far as I could discover, had no view of its future, though it had a clear view of its past.

The need to look to the future is the reason so many corporations today have research and development programs. But an organization cannot guarantee its future by ritualistic spending on research. Its research-and-development program must be an outgrowth of a philosophy of innovation that guides the company in everything it does. The research program, which is a way of looking forward, cannot thrive if the rest of the organization has the habit of looking backward.

The ninth rule is obvious but difficult. An organization runs on motivation, on conviction, on morale. Men have to believe that it really makes a difference whether they do well or badly. They have to care. They have to believe that their efforts as individuals will mean something for the whole organization, and will be recognized by the whole organization.

Change is always risky, usually uncomfortable, often painful. It isn't accomplished by apathetic men and women. It requires high motivation to break through the rigidities of the aging organization.

So much for the rules.

One of the ominous facts about growth and decay is that the present success of an organization does not necessarily constitute grounds for optimism. In 1909 it would have been unwise to judge the future of the

Central Leather Company by the fact that it ranked seventh in the nation in total assets. It would have been a disastrous long-term investment. A better bet would have been the relatively small Ford Motor Company which had been founded only six years earlier and was about to launch its Model T. As a company it wasn't huge or powerful, but to borrow a phrase from C. P. Snow, it had the future in its bones. (Not many of 1909's top twenty companies did—only four of them are in the top twenty today.)

Businessmen are fond of saying that, unlike other executives, they have a clear measure of present performance—the profit-and-loss statement. But the profits of today *may* be traceable to wise decisions made a good many years earlier. And current company officers may be making bad decisions that will spell disaster ten years from now.

I have collected many examples of organizations that experienced crises as a result of their failure to renew themselves. In the great majority, certainly nine out of ten, the trouble was not difficult to diagnose and there was ample warning of the coming catastrophe. In the case of a manufacturing concern that narrowly averted bankruptcy recently, the conditions that led to trouble were diagnosed by an outside consultant two years before the crisis came. In the case of another well-known organization, a published article outlined every essential difficulty that later led to disaster.

But if warning signals are plentiful, why doesn't the ailing organization take heed? The answer is clear: most ailing organizations have developed a functional blindness to their own defects. They are not suffering because they can't *solve* their problems but because they won't *see* their problems. They can look straight at their faults and rationalize them as virtues or necessities.

I was discussing these matters with a corporation president recently, and he said, "How do I know that *I* am not one of the blind ones? What do I do to find out? And if I am, what do I do about it?"

There are several ways to proceed. One way is to bring in an outside consultant who is not subject to the conditions that create functional blindness inside the organization.

A more direct approach, but one that is surrounded by subtle difficulties, is for the organization to encourage its internal critics. Every organization, no matter how far deteriorated, has a few stubbornly honest individuals who are not blinded by their own self-interest and have never quite accepted the rationalizations and self-deceptions shared by others in the organization. If they are encouraged to speak up they probably will. The head of a government agency said to me recently,

"The shrewdest critics of this organization are right under this roof. But it would take a major change of atmosphere to get them to talk."

A somewhat more complicated solution is to bring new blood into at least a few of the key positions in the organization. If the top level of the organization is salted with vigorous individuals too new to be familiar with all the established ways of doing and thinking, they can be a source of fresh insights for the whole organization.

Still another means of getting fresh insights is rotation of personnel between parts of the organization. Not only is the individual broadened by the experience, but he brings a fresh point of view to his new post. After a few years of working together, men are likely to get so used to one another that the stimulus of intellectual conflict drops almost to zero. A fresh combination of individuals enlivens the atmosphere.

In the last analysis, however, everything depends on the wisdom of those who shape the organization's policy. Most policy makers today understand that they must sponsor creative research. But not many of them understand that the spirit of creativity and innovation so necessary in the research program is just as essential to the rest of the organization.

The future of this nation depends on its capacity for self-renewal. And that in turn depends on the vitality of the organizations and individuals that make it up. Americans have always been exceptionally gifted at organizational innovation. In fact, some observers say that this is the true American inventiveness. Thanks to that inventiveness we now stand on the threshold of new solutions to some of the problems that have destroyed the vitality of human institutions since the beginning of time. We have already made progress in discovering how we may keep our institutions vital and creative. We could do even better if we put our minds to it.

SELECTED READINGS

Books

Beckhard, Richard. *Organization Development: Strategies and Models.* Reading, Mass., Addison-Wesley Publishing Co., Inc., 1969.

Bennis, Warren G. *Organization Development: Its Nature, Origins, and Prospects.* Reading, Mass., Addison-Wesley Publishing Co., Inc., 1969.

Blau, Peter and Richard Scott. *Formal Organizations: A Comparative Approach.* San Francisco, Chandler Publishing Co., 1962.

Etzioni, Amitai. *Modern Organizations.* Foundations of Modern Sociology Series. Englewood Cliffs, N. J., Prentice-Hall, Inc., 1964.

Hutchinson, John G. *Organizations: Theory and Classical Concepts.* New York, Holt, Rinehart & Winston, Inc., 1967.

Lawrence, Paul R. and Jay W. Lorsch. *Developing Organizations: Diagnosis and Action.* Reading, Mass., Addison-Wesley Publishing Co., Inc., 1969.

Mailick, Sidney and Van Ness, Edward H., ed. *Concepts and Issues in Administrative Behavior.* Englewood Cliffs, N.J., Prentice-Hall, Inc., 1962.

Pfiffner, John M. and Frank P. Sherwood. *Administrative Organization.* Englewood Cliffs, N.J., Prentice-Hall, Inc., 1960.

Schein, Edgar H. *Organizational Psychology.* Foundations of Modern Psychology Series. Englewood Cliffs, N.J., Prentice-Hall, Inc., 1970.

Schmidt, Warren H. *Organizational Frontiers and Human Values.* Belmont, Calif., Wadsworth Publishing Co., Inc., 1970.

Thompson, James D. *Organizations in Action.* New York, McGraw-Hill Book Company, 1967.

———, ed. *Approaches to Organizational Design.* Pittsburgh, University of Pittsburgh Press, 1966.

Thompson, Victor A. *Modern Organization.* New York, Alfred A. Knopf, Inc., 1961.

Articles

Argyris, Chris. "We Must Make Work Worthwhile," *Life*, Vol. 62, No. 18 (May, 1967), 56–68.

Bell, George A. "States Make Progress with Reorganization Plans," *National Civic Review*, March, 1972, 115–19.

Blake, Robert R., L. B. Barnes, L. E. Greiner and Jane S. Mouton.

"Breakthrough in Organization Development," *Harvard Business Review*, Vol. 42, No. 6 (November–December, 1964), 133–55.

Boynton, Robert E. "Attitude Change From Management Development," *Public Personnel Review*, Vol. 32, No. 1 (January, 1971), 20–25.

Burke, W. Warner. "A Comparison of Management Development and Organization Development," *The Journal of Applied Behavioral Science*, Vol. 7, No. 5 (September–October, 1971), 569–79.

————, and Warren H. Schmidt. "Management and Organization Development," *Personnel Administration*, Vol. 34, No. 2 (March–April, 1971), 44–56.

Conference Board. "Behavioral Science—What's In It for Management?" *Business Management Record*, June, 1963, 32–45.

Culbert, Samuel A., and Jerome Reisel. "Organization Development: An Applied Philosophy for Managers of Public Enterprise," *Public Administration Review*, Vol. 31, No. 2 (March–April, 1971), 159–69.

Dale, Ernest. "Some Foundations of Organization Theory," *California Management Review*, Vol. 2, No. 1 (fall, 1959), 71–84.

Dixit, L. M. "Management of Organizational Change," *The Indian Journal of Social Work*, Vol. 30, No. 4 (January, 1970), 311–14.

Eddy, William B. "From Training to Organization Change," *Personnel Administration*, Vol. 34, No. 1 (January–February, 1971), 37–43.

Hodgson, Richard C. "Viewpoint Toward More Effective Management: A Behavioral Science Viewpoint," *The Business Quarterly*, fall, 1966, 10–24.

Kegan, Daniel L. "Organizational Development: Description, Issues, and Some Research Results," *Academy of Management Journal*, Vol. 14, No. 4 (December, 1971), 453–64.

Martinez, Antonio Carro. "Principles of Organization in Public Administration," *International Review of Administrative Sciences*, Vol. 27, No. 2 (1961), vii–x.

Mathis, Robert L. "Organizational Development: Key to the Future Role of Personnel," *The Personnel Administrator*, Vol. 15, No. 5 (September–October, 1970), 25–28.

Reddin, W. J. "Managing Organizational Change," *Personnel Journal*, Vol. 48, No. 7 (July, 1969), 500–504.

Reeves, Elton T. "Management Development—A Conceptual Continuum," *Training and Development Journal*, Vol. 22, (September, 1968), 29–35.

Ross, Robert. "OD for Whom?" *The Journal of Applied Behavioral Science*, Vol. 7, No. 5 (September–October, 1971), 580–85.

Shepps, Ronald R. "Some Implications of Behavioral Science for the

Middle Manager," *Personnel Journal*, Vol. 50, No. 12 (December, 1971), 944–47.

Scott, William C. "Organization Theory: An Overview and Appraisal," *Academy of Management Journal*, Vol. 4, No. 1 (April, 1961), 7–26.

Weiss, Robert S. "A Structure-Function Approach to Organization," *The Journal of Social Issues*, Vol. 12, No. 2 (1956), 61–67.

In keeping with the concept expressed and emphasized in previous sections of this book that the most important resource in management is people, it is appropriate that this section deal with the development and utilization of the individual from a total organizational perspective. Individual growth and organization development and change can only come about and be continuously self-renewing when approached on this basis.

Management is responsible for performing the functions by which the established goals of the organization are effectively and efficiently carried out. The effectiveness and efficiency of any organization depend in large measure upon the ability of its management to properly select, develop, and utilize its human resources. The management of people is inherent in all organizations, and primary responsibility for personnel management rests with top management levels. However, except in the smallest organizations, certain responsibilities for personnel duties must be assumed and carried out at all levels of the organization. Since management is becoming increasingly complex, the manager at each level must have greater technical competence in the management of people.

Personnel management is the function which encompasses, among other things, the orientation, development, and utilization of all individuals who are engaged in the activities of the organization regardless of their role and function. Much has been written concerning the management of an organization's material and physical resources. This emphasis is understandable, since these factors are tangible and amenable to general rules and principles of management and control. On the other hand, there is a lack of good published material pertaining to the management of the manpower resources of an organization. This, too, is understandable, since human behavior is not easily subject to general rules or pat solutions. There are, however, certain principles and basic practices in the management of personnel which may serve as general guidelines in the development and employment of the human resources of an organization.

In standard texts of public personnel administration, subtopics such as recruitment, selection, examining techniques, classification, pay incentives, ethical conduct, security, loyalty, personnel development, and performance appraisal and counseling are treated in detail. The purpose of this section is neither to give the reader a detailed description of personnel management nor to cover all aspects of the personnel management process. Rather than focusing on techniques and procedures of personnel administration, the readings concentrate on the human problems involved in the development and use of the organization's personnel.

The effective use of human resources is without doubt the most challenging and difficult aspect of the management process. The future of any organization is dependent upon the success with which management is able to tap and release the energy, abilities, skills, and enthusiasm of its employees. No one is willing to admit that he doesn't understand people, yet this lack of understanding is everywhere apparent and leads to the wrong choice of employees, poor employee relations, inadequate production, and general employee discontent and separation.

The management of human resources in the seventies will tend to become more complicated and difficult than ever before. Revolutionary forces are challenging the traditional concepts and practices of management and expressing growing discontent and turmoil. Employees are becoming highly vocal, insisting on more purposeful work and demanding a greater voice in the affairs of the organization. As a means of protest against undemanding jobs and traditional practices, the employee is expressing his disenchantment in increasing absenteeism, poor work habits, and lack of productivity.

The readings in this part are addressed to the manager who desires to better equip himself to effectively deal with the human problems of his organization. It is not practical to think that a manager may rely entirely on either his present knowledge and skills or the organization's in-service training programs to keep him equal to the demands of his job in a rapidly changing world—he must rely on his own initiative for self-development. Career development and continuing education are continuous processes, and their challenge lies in the self-realization that one is preparing himself for more effective service now and in the future.

The article "Human Resources in Public Organizations," by H. George Frederickson, outlines and contrasts the traditional and modern approaches to the management of human resources. It emphasizes the importance of specific goals and the need to correlate the goals of the organization with those of its employees. Frederickson examines the extent to which the study of public personnel administration is culture bound and the possible and probable effects of automation on public employment.

Myron E. Weiner, in "Human Waste in Governmental Organizations," emphasizes the lag in the development of effective techniques to deal with people as workers in an organized grouping. He points out that many techniques that have been developed are, in effect, causing waste in the use of human resources. He goes on to show how this waste leads to conflict and inadequate production. In "Let's Revamp Merit Systems for Today's Needs," Mortimer M. Caplin reports on a study of merit systems throughout the United States and the need for changes—not so much in law as in the "archaic practices" that prevent full utilization of human resources. Ollie A. Jensen, in his article "Cultural Bias in Selection," deals with bias in selection that is "indirect," or the "nonselection" of individuals from minority ethnic groups. He points to the increasing need and urgency to develop a positive approach to this question.

The concept of staff training and development is not new. Government employees have for many years participated in such learning experiences as institutes, workshops, and seminars. Most public-supported organizations have organized programs of staff development. Learning, however, takes place on the job and during each workday. There is not much that can be done to stop learning from taking place. There is, however, much that can be done to see that staff development serves the goals of the organization in a postive way. This is the view expressed in "Training as a Management Strategy." Charles A. Willis, in "City Training Nears Point of No Return," provides many ideas and suggestions as guidelines for the manager who is interested in developing an effective program of staff development.

The basic philosophy of performance appraisal is to let the appraised employee know in advance what the job is and how well he is expected to perform it. Robert L. Noland's article, "Theoretical Foundations of the Appraisal Interview," provides some suggestions for the interviewer with reference to attitudes, objectives, and techniques. Along with the above article is that by Robert Hoppock, "Ground Rules for Appraisal Interviewers," which may be regarded as a guide dealing with the "how to" for the benefit of the manager inexperienced in performance appraisal. "Staff Evaluations: A Key to More Effective Performance," by Earl W. Wolfe, deals with staff evaluation from the standpoint of the supervisor. The ideas and suggestions are positive and constructive in nature and reveal a deep understanding of people on the part of the author.

Irving Paster, in "The Indispensable Man," deals with a problem that is seldom mentioned but is more prevalent than is usually realized. The article also has application to supervision and the disciplining of employees. The last article is that of John E. Horejsi—"Solving the Problem of Staff Turnover." The author deals with many of the human problems involved in modern management and uses a public welfare agency as his setting.

34. Human Resources in Public Organization*

H. George Frederickson

The modern complex organization has been described as "a planned system of cooperative effort in which each participant has a recognized role to play and duties or tasks to perform. These duties are assigned in order to achieve the organization purpose rather than to satisfy individual preferences, although the two often coincide."[1] Thus the basic components of an organization are: first, people; and second, their systematic cooperative effort to achieve some end. Any of a wide range of human objectives or needs may be subjected to organized pursual.

The chief component of any organization is people; therefore, almost by definition, the chief organizational problem is people. (The common law *cliché* "a government of law and not a government of men" is a piece of semantic footwork. All governments are governments of men. Most men agree on certain basic notions about law and government, but the government as an organization is a collection of men.) The manner in which this problem—people—is treated in both the practice of administration and the study of organization is based on *history, tradition,* and *current needs.* This essay will consider in detail the relationships between the contemporary teaching of public personnel administration in the university and the actual administrating practices in public organizations, as influenced by history, tradition, and current needs.

THE TRADITIONAL APPROACH

In the government sphere and in the American context, history, tradition, and current needs blend to comprise what we study in our universities under the rubric "public personnel administration." Generally speaking, the class in public personnel administration will deal with the obviously critical need in this large and complex society for highly-competent employees and will then proceed to deal with the historical and traditional factors which have shaped the development of public personnel systems. By way of example the early, informal "merit system" utilized by the first few Presidents of the United States will be described. Following this will be an extensive treatment of the "spoils era," which flourished under the Jacksonian democratic philosophy, outlasted the Civil War and Reconstruction, and then, at the assassination of Garfield, gradually succumbed to the civil service. The truly

* From *International Review of Administrative Sciences*, Vol. XXXIII, No. 4, 336–44. Reprinted by permission.
1 Herbert A. Simon, Donald W. Smithburg, and Victor A. Thompson, *Public Administration* (New York: Alfred A. Knopf, 1950), p. 5.

grass-roots character of the anti-spoils fight, led at least in part by no less distinguished persons than Woodrow Wilson and Theodore Roosevelt, will be discussed. After this foundation is laid, it will be observed that patronage and nepotism are still widespread, particularly at state, county and city levels. The remainder of the course will deal with the various traditional "best ways" for both securing and utilizing adequate personnel and for lessening or preventing further spoils. Subtopics such as the following will usually be treated at this point: organization for personnel administration; merit and politics; recruiting; selecting; examining techniques; position classification; pay rates and plans; training in the public service; employee relations; ethical conduct in the public service; security and loyalty.

In the standard texts in public personnel administration these subtopics are treated in detail.[2] As a result, personnel courses usually consist of detailed discussions or descriptions of these areas. Although this undoubtedly gives a comprehensive exposure to the subject, it is, in the opinion of many students, excessively detailed and insufficiently theoretical or conceptual in content. Therefore, many of these students gain from personnel courses a rather strong distaste for public personnel administration. These students contend that a comprehensive knowledge of various position-classification schemes is rapidly forgotten and not nearly as interesting as would be a broader approach relating, say, the concept of position classification to the ideas of organization, bureaucracy, government, and social science in general. Conversely, the teacher often holds that public personnel administration is an *applied* science, and that the more detailed information the prospective public personnel analyst can acquire while in school, the better equipped he will be when he goes to work.[3] Clearly the most desirable course would be one which skillfully mixes the details of personnel technique with conceptual content. If this were accomplished the student should leave the course knowing not only how things are done, but also why they are done that way and what plausible alternative ways there are of doing them.

THE MODERN APPROACH

The purpose of this essay is to attempt to develop an approach whereby details of technique might be related to larger concepts. To accomplish this it is first necessary to reiterate that the organization is de-

[2] The three standard texts are O. Glenn Stahl, *Public Personnel Administration* (New York: Harper, 1956); Felix Nigro, *Public Personnel Administration* (New York: Henry Holt, 1959); and Norman J. Powell, *Personnel Administration in Government* (Englewood Cliffs: Prentice-Hall, 1956).

[3] This difference of opinion is, of course, merely a reflection of the classic dilemma as to which is best, the liberal arts or applied undergraduate curriculum. The current trend is clearly in the direction of the liberal arts approach.

scribed as people, plus systematic cooperative effort toward some goal or goals. It is thus imperative that these people be seen as a part of a system for achieving some desired ends. People are as much a resource to the organization as are the finances, the supplies, the plant, etc. So, just as the evaluation of the financial resource needs of an organization is conducted in a systematic and goal-oriented way, so, too, should human resource needs be evaluated.

To effectuate this systematic approach to the utilization of human resources, the concepts and issues approach seems to be useful. By considering in this paper a series of current issues relevant to the utilization of human resources, it will be possible to combine discussion of the standard techniques and practices of personnel administration with application of what we now know of an empirical character. In this way, the empirical and the technique information can be blended, with emphasis on organizational goals, government, and the social sciences. It is hoped that what is learned and taught by this approach will be both useful and valid but, above all, interesting.

The following list of issues will be used as the vehicle for demonstrating this systematic approach to the utilization of human resources:

Is personnel administration too narrowly defined?

Do current organizational patterns in public administration reflect a lag between the organization and the environment?

Is complete goal agreement or attainment ever possible?

What have we learned about recruiting and selecting personnel?

Is it possible to make any valid generalization about career patterns?

To what extent is the study of public administration culture-bound?

What is likely to be the impact of automation on public personnel affairs?

IS PERSONNEL ADMINISTRATION
TOO NARROWLY DEFINED?

When personnel are seen as a resource in organizational goal achievement, it becomes clear that the degree of goal achievement can be directly correlated with the quantity and quality of personnel, and the extent of their commitment. People are, in the vernacular of the social scientist, an input to the system. There are certain "criterion outputs" from the system—such as what must be done, with what, and under what range of circumstances—which influence the character of human resource utilization. Further there are certain environmental factors—such as an imposed, civil-service-type merit system, or a given range of wage offerings, or a generally unfavorable societal attitude toward bureaucrats—which affect human resource utilization.[4] Since these en-

4 Robert B. Miller, *The Systems Approach to Personnel Problems* (American Institute for Research, Memorandum No. 7, February 1957).

vironmental and system factors are interrelated, it becomes logically possible to find alternative procedures of utilization that, within any given set of conditions, are the optimal route between what is available in manpower and what is wanted in manpower capability and output. When these environmental and system factors are not all considered in decision-making, it is unlikely that optimal decisions will ensue.

Traditionally, public personnel decisions are made in a strongly bifurcated way. The legislative body sets general policy guidelines and wage levels. The civil service agency or board handles recruiting, examination, determination of level of merit and assists in selection. The operating agency then selects from the top few on the eligible list. On the other hand, the agency then must do its best to mold from these selections a team to accomplish its objectives. Both the recruiting, selection activities and the team molding activities must be seen as personnel administration. Yet, in both the practice and teaching of personnel administration they are seen as separate packages.

Clearly the single most significant step in this process is the molding of the team to accomplish its mission. Yet, in the traditional personnel administration course or system, it is this step which is given the least attention. Thus personnel administration is defined to include recruitment, selection, promotion, dismissal, and certain tangential matters such as security and loyalty, position classification, and ethics. Certainly this has too severely narrowed the definition of personnel administration. Although recruiting techniques, examination techniques, various schemes of personnel classification, and the like are a legitimate concern, particularly for personnel technicians, they are only a portion of the whole subject of manpower utilization. Unfortunately, it is this strict approach which characterizes the standard academic treatment of public personnel administration.

So, there is usually a bifurcated approach to human resources in organizational practice, resulting in a narrow definition of personnel administration in the literature and in the classroom. In recent years there have been several developments in actual governmental operations which have tended to modify the bifurcated approach. The role of civil service boards and commissions has in some instances been diverted from detailed decision-making to broad policy concerns and review of practices or of appeals from dismissal decisions. There have been corresponding instances of greater latitude being given to agencies in selecting, transferring, and promoting, all of which has resulted in reduced control from the central personnel office. At the American Federal level, some of the newer agencies have been allowed their own separate civil service systems, on the assumption that they are best able to assess their human resource needs in relation to their perception of agency goals. These developments indicate a clear recognition that modern government needs to be less concerned with fighting spoils and more concerned with positive human resource allocation. This is a healthy trend.

In the past decade there have also been significant developments on the academic side of human resource allocation. Empirical studies such as those conducted under the direction of Rensis Likert at the University of Michigan's Institute for Social Research have provided sorely-needed data for really significant conclusions regarding organizational behavior.[5] The function of the *group* in the organizational setting has been explored and yielded valuable results.[6] Much has been learned about the "role" of the individual in the organizational environment.[7] Through research, there is now general empirical support for certain patterns of "supportive" supervision.[8] The psychological impact of organizational involvement has been treated in detail.[9] And a great many more breakthroughs are being made yearly.

What is now needed is a comprehensive synthesis of these research findings and an application of them to public personnel administration, defined broadly. Once a synthesis of this sort is available in the literature, it should be the central focus of the courses in public personnel administration.

DO CURRENT ORGANIZATIONAL PATTERNS IN PERSONNEL ADMINISTRATION REFLECT A LAG BETWEEN THE ORGANIZATION AND THE ENVIRONMENT?

Most organizations for public personnel administration are set up on the "fight the spoilsmen" model. Most personnel powers are located in the central personnel agency, although that agency has little responsibility for the degree to which the generic goals of the larger organization are achieved. Further, the philosophy and orientation of employees in the central personnel office often tends toward the technical application of rules and the rigid following of procedures. It is this approach which is widely criticized in the public personnel literature as being negative, more concerned with satisfying formal desiderata than with contributing

5 Rensis Likert, *New Patterns of Management* (New York: McGraw-Hill, 1961). See also, Peter Blau and Richard Scott, *Formal Organization* (San Francisco: Chandler, 1962).

6 George Homans, *The Human Group* (New York: Harcourt Brace, 1950); Dorwin Cartwright and Alvin Zander, *Group Dynamics: Research and Theory* (Evanston, Ill.: Row Peterson, 1953); Joseph McGrath and Erwin Altmon, *Small Group Research* (Holt, Rinehart and Winston, 1966).

7 Neal Gross, Ward Mason, and Alexander McEachern, *Explorations in Role Analysis* (New York: Wiley, 1958).

8 Likert, *op. cit.*

9 Mason Haire, *Psychology in Management* (New York: McGraw-Hill, 1956); and Harold J. Leavitt, *Managerial Psychology* (University of Chicago Press, 1958); Edgar Schein, *Organizational Psychology* (Prentice-Hall, 1965); and see the journal, *Personnel Psychology*.

to increased goal achievement. Wallace S. Sayre correctly identified this approach as "the triumph of technique over purpose."[10]

If the "fight the spoilsmen" model does not adequately meet the needs of the contemporary governmental environment, what sort of model would? Before describing this model, it is necessary to discuss those factors in the environment which seems relevant.

First, modern society expects an ever-increasing number of services from government, plus an improved performance of present services. Governing bodies seem to uncover annually some service or some form of regulation which in their judgment the public wants. Further, governing bodies are greatly concerned with the level of taxes and, therefore, continually make demands for efficiency and economy.

Second, modern society holds the civil service responsible for results. If the garbage is not collected or the airport safety system is not operating properly, it is the line or functional agency which must come up with an adequate explanation. To accomplish this mission in an adequate way, these agencies must have skilled people and must use them properly. This is very difficult, however, when the responsibility for securing the needed skilled people rests with another agency. This is particularly true when the responsibilities of the central personnel agency end as soon as they supply the line agency with what they feel is an adequate list of qualified applicants. How well these applicants perform on the job is not the basic responsibility of the central personnel agency.

Third, modern society is highly technical. To respond to this fact governmental activities have become increasingly technical. In this environment there is a premium on persons with either technical skills or broad management skills. Competition for these persons is extremely keen.

Fourth, modern society is characterized by rapid change and innovation. To be effective in this setting, government must be flexible, particularly in how it finds and develops its human resources. What might have been an adequate recruiting or selecting technique two years ago may now be sadly out of date, with the result that the inflexible government will be unable to effectively compete for scarce skilled human resources.

When there is a clear recognition of these four societal "givens" it is apparent that the old central personnel agencies and many of the other trappings of the "fight the spoilsmen" model are ineffective in the modern environment and are, today, little more than "social and administrative impediments."[11]

[10] Wallace Sayre, "The Triumph of Techniques over Purpose," *Public Administration Review*, Vol. 8 (1948), p. 107.

[11] Norman J. Powell, *Personnel Administration in Government* (Englewood Cliffs: Prentice-Hall, 1956), p. 175.

To reduce the incompatibility between the changing environment and the extant organization scheme for personnel administration, it is necessary to alter the scheme by: (1) reducing the powers of the central personnel agency to broad policy-setting, general classification and record keeping, and the review of appealed hiring and dismissal decisions; (2) significantly broadening line personnel functions to intertwine them with existing administrative activities; (3) acknowledging that the administrator and the supervisor are the primary personnel men, and that the model should therefore be built around them; (4) focusing on organizational goals and purposes in structuring the personnel scheme; (5) recruiting generalists for both line agencies and central personnel offices; (6) designing the scheme so that it can be easily adapted to meet changing needs.

A broad consideration of the nature of contemporary society and how it relates to manpower should be an important focus in a public personnel course. Students of public manpower should wrestle with the problem of how to reduce the lag between social needs and government personnel practices. This can be done by attempts to design a general personnel model such as that just described. A consideration of literature which has treated the general subject of social needs and characteristics coupled with government personnel practices should be central. Michel Crozier's detailed and thoughtful consideration of the nature of contemporary French bureaucracy is an example of the sort of reading material which is both technically and conceptually useful.[12]

IS COMPLETE GOAL AGREEMENT
OR ATTAINMENT EVER POSSIBLE?

The extent to which an organization can achieve its goals is related to the degree of goal specificity. A basic, relatively simple goal such as the pick-up and removal of garbage by a city can be easily identified and agreed upon. The various alternative means of achieving this goal may be evaluated in a scientific fashion and the optimal course of action may be selected. The human resources necessary to effect the chosen means of collection and removal can be secured, and the program can be operated and in time evaluated to determine the degree of its effectiveness. On the basis of such evaluation this program may be altered to raise the level of goal achievement.

Unfortunately, many of the goals of government are not so well-specified. The nebulous and sometimes contradictory character of many of the goals of the government has caused certain administrative theorists to criticize sharply modern attempts to approach organiza-

---

12 Michel Crozier, *The Bureaucratic Phenomenon* (University of Chicago Press, 1964).

tional problems scientifically.[13] (This scientific approach is usually some variation of the systems idea being described here. It is characterized by the development of a specific, testable hypothesis, the gathering of data, the development of alternative courses of action, and the selection of the alternatives which will come closest to achieving the agreed-upon goal. Obviously without the agreed-upon goal the logic of this whole process is lost.)

To achieve an effective utilization of human resources, goals should be a chief consideration, regardless of their degree of specificity. For example, few organizations have less specific goals than do universities. Yet, for effective human resource utilization, it is essential that university officials be cognizant of goals in respect to research, teaching and services, and consistently attempt to match their personnel decisions with their goals. If this is done—and it is extremely difficult, because of the decentralized character of most universities—higher levels of goal achievement will result. If it is not done, the university or department will fall into the state of drift that characterizes many schools and departments today.[14]

Because there is a difference between actual organizational goals and individual goal perception, it is necessary for those responsible for the utilization of human resources to determine what the employees and prospective employees perceive as the organizational goals and as their individual roles in achieving these goals. With this information it is possible to procure and align personnel so as to capitalize on their capabilities and goal and role perceptions, thereby improving the organization's goal achievement capacity.

The goal approach to human resource utilization has been rather fully developed in recent years by two prominent administrative theorists, Douglas McGregor and Chris Argyris.[15] Both feel that the theoretical assumptions which management holds about controlling its human resources determine the whole character of the organization. If management holds the notion that wages are the primary goal of all individuals in all organized settings, it will likely bet at least partially in error. Similarly, preoccupations with authority and hierarchy as key devices in securing management control may entirely miss the common finding that *real* authority is lodged in the natural leaders of informal work groups, and, therefor, they are the keys to control. These often-

13 Charles E. Lindblom, "The Science of Muddling Through," *Public Administration Review*, Vol. 19 (Spring 1959), pp. 79–88; John M. Pfiffner, "Administrative Rationality," *Public Administration Review*, Vol. 20 (Summer 1960), pp. 125–132.

14 James D. Thompson and William J. McEwan, "Organizational Goals and Environment," *American Sociological Review*, Vol. 23 (1958), pp. 23–31.

15 Douglas McGregor, *The Human Side of Enterprise* (New York: McGraw-Hill, 1960); Chris Argyris, *Personality and Organization* (New York: Harper, 1957).

incorrect managerial assumptions are based on what management feels it knows about human goals and motivations. What is needed is an accurate assessment of human goals and motivations and then a consistent attempt to correlate these human goals with organizational goals. This integration or fusion of personal and organizational goals is a reasonable approach to improving the utilization of human resources. It should also be a vital subject in the study of public manpower.

WHAT HAVE WE LEARNED EMPIRICALLY ABOUT RECRUITING AND SELECTING PERSONNEL?

The traditional public personnel approach to recruiting and selecting new employees has been widely criticized both for its basic assumptions and its usual procedures. A good, concise listing of these criticisms is provided by Norman Powell:

> The selection process has certain over-all characteristics: a) It is the civil service commission, not the operating department that has the basic authority to devise and effect the procedures to be used. b) The selection machinery is closely bound by legal requirements. c) The process is elaborate. d) Whether the employee works out well or badly is a matter of concern primarily to the operating agencies; when the procedure has been completed, the commission moves on to other problems. e) The procedures assume that the applicants are in ample supply and so fascinated by public service as to endure all the travail of a prolonged obstacle race.[16]

To this list can be added the observation that the examination process (both written and oral) is unable to assess intangible personality traits such as motivation, honesty and loyalty. Finally, eligible lists commonly have many names within a rather short range of scores, yet the operating agency must select from the top three or five.

Although all of these are true at least in some degree, anyone familiar with public organizational practices is aware that most operating agencies are inventive enough to hurry the procedure, wait out the eligible list to get the person desired, use the temporary slots for the person desired until the procedures can be satisfied and permanent positions secured; and utilize numerous other gimmicks to make the cumbersome system at least partially operative. When this inventive approach is understood and when it is recognized that operating agencies will always act thus, the above specific criticism of the traditional system becomes somewhat less significant. This is not to say, however, that reforms are not needed.

The more serious result of the traditional recruiting and selection system is its impact on societal attitudes. Because of the standard attitude of the mass media toward public service, and their dissemination

16 Powell, *op. cit.*, p. 211.

of stereotyped notions about low salaries, red tape, bumbling administrators, and intruding legislators, the public has a preconditioned
prejudice against civil service. This preconditioning causes many persons who are considering employment to dismiss even the possibility of
public service. This cannot help but have—as it actually has—serious,
long-range repercussions for the civil service. The talents and achievements of the people who work for government will not be superior to
the best of those who are originally attracted to the public service. Even
a good recruiting program will not automatically yield a body of highly-
qualified personnel, but a poor program, coupled with a strong anti-
public-service preconditioning, will guarantee that public employees
will be mediocre or worse.

Through the approach suggested here, governments will be able to
compete on a more equal footing with private organizations and institutions in the human resources marketplace. This will first require a basic
recognition that government employment is in many respects similar to
private employment. This understanding is gradually growing with
much of the impetus being provided by the space exploration and scientific activities of government and services such as excellent education,
recreation and health programs at the national and local level. Second,
of course, is the need for better pay and benefits, and this also is improving. Third, is the need for better recruiting and selection procedures
by governmental agencies, and evidence indicates improvement here,
also.

If recruiting and selecting for the public service were approached, in
the classroom, from this perspective, the student should know, at the
very least, that the subject can be approached empirically. Certainly,
this view of the subject is more challenging than the traditional treatment of alternative recruiting and selecting techniques.

HOW USEFUL ARE EMPIRICALLY BASED GENERALIZATIONS ABOUT CAREER PATTERNS?

Students of personnel administration have available the results of
several research projects which have attempted to discern the characteristics of different types of bureaucrats.[17] We now know about
"moralists" and "expedients" and "institutionalists," "hybrids," and
"specialists" not to mention the "upward-mobiles," "indifferents," and
"ambivalents." These studies are resplendent with details regarding
variations in age, religion, education, ethnicity, and the like, of the
persons placed in each category. These findings are solid support for the

[17] Neal Gross, Ward Mason and Alex McEachern, *Explorations In Role Analysis* (New
York: John Wiley, 1958); Dwaine Maverick, *Career Perspectives in a Bureaucratic Setting*
(Ann Arbor: University of Michigan Press, 1954); Robert Presthus, *The Organizational Society* (New York: Alfred A. Knopf, 1962); Victor Thompson, *Modern Organization: A General Theory* (New York: Alfred A. Knopf, 1961).

generally held notion that men do behave differently in an organized setting, and they provide some clues as to what kinds of persons are likely to behave in specified ways.

Those who teach public personnel administration should ask their students to explore the extent to which these findings are relevant to current manpower practices. Teacher and student should be asking if recruiting and selecting policies can or should be based on our "knowledge" of the behavior of different types in public organization. To what extent can or should personnel policy makers attempt to use this "knowledge" to modify the nature of the bureaucracy to include, say, fewer "expedients" and more "moralists"? Would such policy modifications be vastly different from changing personnel recruiting and selecting policies to broaden the socioeconomic background of the upper bureaucracy? If the upper level administration is primarily occupied by persons from high socioeconomic backgrounds, this might be regarded, normatively, as undesirable, and on the basis of this judgment policies can be altered to insure the recruitment and selection of more persons from middle and lower socioeconomic origins. Similarly, a normative judgment that here are too many "expedients" in bureaucracy (a common argument) and too few "moralists," might result in altered recruiting and selection policies. Is there enough known empirically about "expedients" and "moralists" to provide the basis for such policy making? Should this knowledge be the basis for policy making?

As more and more is learned about the characteristics of bureaucrats, the cogency of these questions will increase. Such questions should be central to any study of contemporary public personnel administration.

TO WHAT EXTENT IS THE STUDY OF PUBLIC PERSONNEL ADMINISTRATION CULTURE-BOUND?

As many other aspects of government, most students know woefully little of public personnel practices in other societies. Only recently have there been any systematic attempts to examine foreign bureaucracies and to relate them to their historical and societal setting. The body of literature known as comparative public administration—which is just now developing—will provide information of great utility to both the student and practitioner of human resource utilization.

Because literature of this sort has not been plentiful, most persons studying a foreign system, or having to work in one, are required to use the traditional American, British or French personnel models. Of course this results in very weak comparisons, because the traditional models are unique and complex and even after many years of operation are still being changed to meet the needs of a changing society.

267

In our rapidly shrinking world, it seems essential that students of the utilization of human resources be familiar with how and why things are done in other nations. With this knowledge our overseas missions in public administration might be more effective. To gain such familiarity, it could be useful to read an essay by Ferrel Heady entitled "Recent Literature in Comparative Public Administration."[18] Professor Heady lists a wide range of up-to-date sources on theoretical approaches to comparative study, studies of western administrative systems, and several single-country studies. Most of these references detail the manner in which human resources are utilized in given areas or nations. There are several other even more recent sources that are excellent, such as Fred Riggs' *The Ecology of Public Administration;*[19] Sybil Stokes and Ferrell Heady's *Papers in Comparative Public Administration;*[20] the University of Pittsburg's *The Comparative Study of Public Administration;*[21] and an essay by William Dill called "The Impact of Environment on Organizational Development" in Sidney Mailick and Edward Van Ness' *Concepts and Issues in Administrative Behavior.*[22]

Morroe Berger's study of the Egyptian bureaucracy coupled with Crozier's consideration of French administration would provide a unique means of comparing the impact of differing cultures on personnel practices.[23] On the basis of these kinds of studies, it is hoped that there will eventually develop a truly comparative study of public manpower utilization.

WHAT IS LIKELY TO BE THE IMPACT OF INCREASED AUTOMATION ON PUBLIC PERSONNEL AFFAIRS?

Because much that is generally regarded as the central part of personnel administration involves the keeping of great quantities of data, it appears certain that handling of this data will eventually be automated. To a central personnel office servicing a large organization, it would be exceedingly valuable to have an automated memory which could rapidly produce employee data forms, career histories, and work evaluations. Possession of such a memory could enhance the power of

[18] Ferrel Heady, "Recent Literature in Comparative Public Administration," *Administrative Science Quarterly*, Vol. 5 (June 1960), pp. 134–154. This entire issue of the ASQ is devoted to comparative administration.

[19] Fred Riggs, *The Ecology of Public Administration* (New Delhi: Indian Institute of Public Administration, 1961).

[20] Sybil Stokes and Ferrel Heady, *Papers in Comparative Administration* (Ann Arbor: University of Michigan Institute of Public Administration, 1962).

[21] James D. Thompson *et al., The Comparative Study of Public Administration* (University of Pittsburg Press, 1959).

[22] Sidney Mailick and Edward Van Ness, *Concepts and Issues in Administrative Behavior* (Englewood Cliffs: Prentice-Hall, 1962).

[23] Morroe Berger, *Bureaucracy and Society in Modern Egypt: A Study of the Higher Civil Service* (Princeton University Press, 1957); and Crozier, *op. cit.*

the central personnel agency through a greater command of information; however, this might be an unfortunate trend, in terms of earlier criticisms of central personnel agencies.

A far more probable impact of such automation would be to change the nature of the personnel required by the personnel office. Clerical positions of a strictly routine nature probably would gradually decrease in number, and there would likely be a corresponding increase in persons skilled in the operation of electronic data-processing machines. Thus, the education, motivation, needs, and interests of a substantial number of persons in the organization would change and this would alter the way in which organizational goals would be achieved. The organization and techniques for the utilization of human resources would have to respond to these changes; otherwise, a serious lag might develop which would inhibit goal achievement. So the personnel function must be flexible and adaptive, two attributes unfortunately rare in the traditional scheme. The move toward automation is likely, therefore, to place a great strain on monolithic personnel organizations and practices and, hence, constitutes a central concern in the contemporary study of public manpower.

Using this general human resources approach it would be possible to explore many other significant issues. Rather than make this exploration, perhaps it will suffice to list some other key questions:

Are there any abstract criteria for administrative responsibility?

Is there a logical line between career and non-career governmental employees?

Are industry and government moving closer together on employee relations problems?

Are blocks against lateral mobility hampering career development?

Are position classification and equal pay for equal work culture-bound concepts which have little validity in other cultures?

In a confusing metropolitan maze are residence requirements rational?

What should be the limits on the administrator in regard to discrimination in hiring and promotions?

Has personality testing been sufficiently developed so as to be useful in personnel decisions?

Is seniority a reasonable concept in our demanding society?

Would a strike by certain government employees, such as teachers or clerks, be any more disastrous than a strike by certain industrial unions, such as railroad workers?

Does a strict prohibition against political activity by civil servants foster an apathetic attitude toward political issues?

269

Does a "senior civil service" add prestige to the public services and thereby attract higher-quality personnel?

CONCLUSIONS

Personnel affairs are actually little bundles of the social sciences. They are in fact, case studies in sociology, social psychology, psychology, and political science. Although this is now clearly recognized, personnel affairs are still largely handled through techniques and procedures that were developed from an entirely different perspective. The technical, essentially negative approach to personnel affairs is based on assumptions that are rooted only shallowly in demonstrated hypotheses. What is needed today is a new perspective which will emphasize the social science character of personnel affairs and will facilitate the development and testing of meaningful hypotheses.

This new perspective should begin in the class-room. Rather than focusing on techniques and procedures, which are probably best learned on-the-job, the public personnel administration course would concentrate on the political, social and psychological implications of manpower policies. This will require a new and much broader definition of the subject. It will also require an altered pedagogy. The "issues" approach suggested here might be useful.

As scholars gradually synthesize social science literature and research, and apply it to problems of human resource utilization it is hoped that a wholly new perspective will result. This process is gradual, of course, because the student who will be tomorrow's civil servant is today just beginning to be exposed to these notions. And, it is hoped that tomorrow's civil servant will attempt to alter personnel affairs to better fit the world as he sees it, and as empirical research has shown it to be. Thus, in time, the social science approach should have a decided impact on the conduct of personnel affairs.

270

35. Human Waste in Governmental Organizations*

Myron E. Weiner

It is ironic that at a time in the history of man, when organized societies have developed such a high level of technological devices to enhance their stay on earth, there is a lag in the development of techniques to deal with human beings as they work in an organized grouping. The irony is intensified when we perceive that by and large the most important resource that we have in our society today is generally unrecognized as a resource at all. When observing the air conditioning of computer rooms, while employees swelter in unbearable heat, one could be led to the conclusion that today there is a tendency to take better care of machines than of the human beings in the same organization.

Could it be that the individual human is being used carelessly in organizational environments, with the result that most people in organizations—both management and workers—are not called upon for the fullest contribution that they can make to that organization? Is it the nature of the "wasted worker" in a bureaucracy that he has given his body to his organization but not his mind? Is it the paradox of the "wasted manager" that the one individual whose role is to serve as a motivator of workers generally is unmotivated himself?

An examination of the problem of human waste in governmental organization points to the impact of the population and technological explosions on society and our failure to tap the full measure of the human being for his work either for the benefit of his organization, or, even more important, for the psychic reward that the individual could receive from having made a meaningful contribution to society. The existence of this phenomenon has evolved over a long period of time and is a result of a network of complex, interrelated factors. This article summarizes some of these complex factors and analyzes the way in which they function.

DEVELOPMENT OF HUMAN WASTE PHENOMENON

The Merit System

The advent of the merit system to governmental organizations tended to be negative in its orientation, as its historic development in the late 19th century required for that period in our development of public administration. However, generally it has never reoriented its objectives

* From *Connecticut Government*, Vol. 21, No. 3 (May, 1968), 1–3, 8. Reprinted by permission.

in positive terms in government, and as such has played a major factor in developing the phenomenon of the human waste in governmental organizations. The present merit system, for the most part, encourages conformity rather than innovation and initiative. There is undue stress for protection of those who are in service with equal treatment to all regardless of their contribution. It is difficult to attract and keep people who have a high level of excellence in their field. There is generally no incentive for wanting to excel since each is treated the same in monetary awards, and non-economic awards are rare. The principle of "equal work—equal pay" often in reality becomes "unequal work—equal pay."

Unionization

The organization of employee groups was created, in part, as a result of dissatisfaction among the humans who did not find the psychic security of having made a contribution to their work situation. Unfortunately the advent of unionization did not eliminate this dissatisfaction among the workers;[1] in their anxiety to control their environmental situation, the person who could have most helped them—those in supervisory and middle-management positions—have been denuded, for the most part, of their power to motivate the working class.[2] Instead of overcoming the human waste that developed in organizations (the goal of most unions), the trend toward employee associations generally fostered the waste phenomenon.

The Staff Concept

The complexity of modern organization has created a shift in traditional organizational structures and developed staff positions of "technical specialists." The necessity for technical specialization in today's complex government and industry is generally accepted as warranted. It has, however, created a situation where, unless one is careful, staff agencies could undermine both management and workers and further enhance the phenomenon of the human waste in government.

According to one writer, Victor A. Thompson, there is a behavior pattern which contributes to human waste in organizations. Thompson terms this as *bureaupathic behavior* and describes it as follows:

... the growing imbalance between the rights of authority positions, on the one hand and the abilities and skills needed in a technological age, on the other, generates tensions and insecurities in the system of authority. Attempts to reduce such insecurity often take the form of behavior patterns which are dysfunctional from the point of view of the organization, although functional enough from that of the insecure official. From the standpoint of the organi-

---

[1] Chris Argyris, *Personality and Organization* (Harper & Bros., New York, 1967), p. 107.
[2] Argyris, *op. cit.*, pp. 167–169. See also Fritz Roethlisberger, "The Foreman: Master and Victim of Double Talk," *Harvard Business Review* 23 (1945), pp. 283–298.

zation such behavior is pathological, and in our analysis we shall refer to it as *bureaupathic behavior.*[3]

Thompson categorizes such behavior as the need to control, to "go by the book," quantitative compliance, resistance to change, exaggerated aloofness, and insistence on the rights of office.

Professionals and Politicians

Generally, there is a lack of understanding by politicians of the impact of their decisions, including matters dealing with "complaints" by employees. By the same token, there is generally a lack of appreciation by some "public servants" of the important role that politicians play in democracy. Where it exists, this lack of understanding between the two elements in government—the career employee and the politician—has left both elements feeling frustrated and unsatisfied. Such a situation only reinforces the phenomenon of the human waste in governmental organizations. All too often, one or the other is left with a feeling of "why fight city hall" or "why fight the system."

Level of Aspiration of Modern Society

The large stress placed on materialism and individualism in our society has left humans in work situations very unsatisfied, "lonely," and insecure. They look upon their job primarily as a source of income and receive very little satisfaction from the work itself, a satisfaction which can give them greater pay psychologically than any salary they can be making materially. For the most part, people are oriented with the feeling that "I'll take care of myself, buddy. You worry about yourself." Undoubtedly, this tendency in organizations results, in part, from the fact that most people feel insignificant in a population-exploding society under continual threat of nuclear obliteration.

The Game of Emperor's Clothes

You will recall the fairy tale of the emperor who thought he was wearing the finest clothes in the world since he was told it could only be seen by those who had intelligence; as no one wanted to admit that he did not have intelligence, all pretended to see clothes that actually were never there. This is quite true of our society today. To some degree, it is not what one knows nor is it what one is really worth that counts; rather, it is the exterior facade that people can judge that becomes important. Status symbols of all types become extremely important; people do not act nor treat each other in realistic terms. As a result, workers and management recognize and accept this as the standard for their contributions; the dignity of labor, held high during pioneering times, has gone.

[3] Victor A. Thompson, *Modern Organization* (New York; Alfred A. Knopf, 1963), pp. 23–24.

Security: 35–10–2

The emphasis on the need for security has brought about a lessening of the human being's willingness to participate fully in his work situation and an intensification of his concern for maintaining the status quo so that he can retire with security (i.e., a pension). In government, this results in the 35–10–2 club, which creates a feeling of being "trapped" by the system. In other words, if someone is 35 years old, has been in the governmental organization for over 10 years and has at least two children, he cannot or will not jeopardize his current position to risk the possibility of losing that position. As a result of an over-emphasized stress on an attractive pension, effectiveness in the organization can be diminished.

THE SCHOLARS' ANSWER: HOPE OR HOPELESSNESS?

Scholars have been studying this problem for a number of years and have come up with a large number of viewpoints on the subject. We can only attempt to review a few here.

Conflict and Fusion

Chris Argyris of Yale University has been concerned with the subject of people's behavior in an organization. He points out that the development of the human being and his personality goes through several stages: from childhood to a mature adult, from passiveness to self-determination, from dependency to being independent, from limited to multi-typed behavior, from casual to depth interest in things, etc.[4]

Argyris believes that it is almost impossible under our current principles of organization for any individual to have adult personality behavior in an organization. One must continually remain passive in a "chain of command" and has very little opportunity to determine his own destiny. "Specialization" in the distribution of work limits the average daily behavior of many workers, such as punch operators, calculating operators, typists, etc. For every factor in the development of an adult's personality, Argyris points out that it is impossible for such personality development to come about in an organizational structure. The demands of the organization, he concludes, are incongruent with the needs of an individual, and only conflict and frustration can develop.[5] The individuals react by attempting to leave or climb higher in the organization (trying to escape the results). Some undertake defense mechanisms, such as rationalizing, projecting, or becoming ambivalent in their approach toward their work; others seek to escape from their

---

[4] Chris Argyris, *Understanding Organizational Behavior* (Homewood, Ill.: Dorsey Press, Inc., 1960), pp. 8–9.

[5] Argyris, *op. cit.*, p. 14.

work situation by either not coping with reality or by daydreaming; still others develop psychosomatic illnesses.[6]

The requirements of formal organization act to inhibit the growth potentiality of the personality; thus they exemplify the dimensions of immaturity, not adulthood. The end result may be that *the employee is paid for his dissatisfaction while at work in order that he may gain satisfaction outside of work.*

Argyris suggests three approaches that can at best decrease the conflict that exists between the individual and the organization:

1. JOB ENLARGEMENT. Permit the individual to use more important abilities and perhaps reorganize work so that he increases the number of tasks that he is called upon to perform. In addition, permit the staff to have greater control over its work environment.

2. DEMOCRATIC EMPLOYEE-CENTERED LEADERSHIP. Increase the freedom and self-responsibility of workers by not giving them close supervision.

3. REALITY-CENTERED LEADERSHIP. Diagnose what is reality, then use the appropriate leadership pattern. This requires self-awareness on the part of others, awareness of the worth of the organization.

Argyris concludes that the organization needs the individual just as much as the individual needs the organization, that each is incomplete without the other. He calls the fusing of the individual's needs with the needs of the organization the *Fusion Theory* of humans working in an organization.[7]

New Patterns of Management

The style of leadership is the single most important influence in an organization.[8] Much research has been undertaken on the "patterns of leadership" as exercised by management in organization. The various approaches have been classified in a number of ways.

Supervision has been classified into two orientations: *job-centered* and *employee-centered*. *Job-centered supervision* places much pressure on workers to obtain high production output. For the most part, *job-centered supervision* is critical and punitive, and stresses economic rewards for the individual, over-estimating the economic motive in humans. This type of supervision assumes that by buying the individual's time, management has control over his behavior.

On the other hand, *employee-centered supervision* only gives general supervision to the workers; it defines their goals and gives them the

---

6 Argyris, *Personality and Organization* (New York: Harper & Bros., 1957), p. 36.

7 Argyris, *op. cit.*, p. 207.

8 Rensis Likert, *New Patterns of Management* (New York: McGraw Hill Book Co., Inc., 1961).

freedom to do their job by using their own ideas. It fosters unselfish, cooperative, sympathetic, and democratic treatment of human beings in the work situation. As a result, workers usually respond by giving a high level of production and showing enthusiasm toward the importance of their work. The *employee-centered* supervisor evidences genuine interest and unselfish concern in the success of the individual and his organization.

Researchers describe what they call *participative leadership*, which is neither over-directive nor under-directive, but permits the individual to use his initiative and avoids domination by providing group discussions where the individual can participate in management decision making. It has been found that the greater the group supervision, the greater is the productivity and job satisfaction in an organization.[9]

Research seems to indicate that the group approach of *participative leadership* not only develops high loyalty among members of the group, but increases production and creates a more favorable attitude toward work and less anxiety. In addition, there is more cooperation, sensitivity and self-responsibility, and a greater group identification. Not to be overlooked, there also is a reduction in absenteeism.

Likert's research has compared various leadership patterns and analyzed their impact on organization. Let us turn our attention to three areas: communications, performance, and supervisory behavior.

Communications

In *job-centered* authoritative leadership patterns, the supervisor-manager holds information and uses it to increase his own power and influence, creating as a result distrust and fear among his colleagues.[10] The implication is that communications upward in an organization are filtered and inaccurate; the subordinate gives his employer information which the latter wants. As could be expected, he shares successes with his boss, but not the failures.

On the other hand in *group* or *participative leadership* situations, the "group" shares the information, leading to the following results: special requests are discouraged because they must be presented before the group. Executives who may not be pulling their share in the organization are pulled up by other members of the group and there is no need to bypass them. In any one meeting, there is a wide contribution of know how, talents, and information, while top management is continually kept on the objective. In addition, there is motivation to communicate accurately all the important information. The group tells top management what no one individual would dare to tell. There is a

9 Likert, *op. cit.*, pp. 21–22.
10 Likert, *op. cit.*, pp. 107–111.

significant identification of the ego with goals of the organization, and there is a willingness to share jointly the overloads of work and little reluctance to broaden the responsibilities of each.

Performance

There is a problem in measuring different styles of leadership, research points out.[11] In the *job-centered* type of leadership pattern, the pressure of such leadership brings quick results that can be measured; these are called *end results*. In the process of this pressure, however, the quality of the human organization deteriorates, as can be illustrated by strikes, slow downs, etc. The tremendous loss of investment in human organizations is rarely indicated by an accountant on the balance sheet. The American management system seems to reward the fast, job-oriented manager by a series of fast promotions. As a result, the "producing" manager rarely has to account for negative results of his harsh treatment of subordinates. On the other hand, the long-term producer is not rewarded as much, even though he may have been building the human assets of an organization. Likert points out that *employee oriented*, cooperative motivation systems have no status in American management because results are too slow and difficult to measure.

Supervisory Behavior and Employee Response

Research has shown that there is a wide discrepancy between what supervisors say they will do and what they actually do.[12] For example, one survey points out a lack of consistent pattern between behavior reported by the supervisors themselves with that reported by their subordinates. In the survey, supervisors were asked, "Do you give your men privileges?" Fifty-two percent of the supervisors said "Yes," but only 14 percent of their subordinates agreed with them. To the question, "Do you give your men responsibility?" 48 percent answered "Yes" but only 10 percent of the subordinates reported they ever received responsibility. The supervisor was also asked, "Do you give your workers a pat on the back?" Eighty-two percent answered, "Yes, we do." The subordinates, however, said this was not true; only 13 percent of them felt the supervisor did so.

Likert calls for a pattern of mangament which he terms *supportive leadership*. The principles of *supportive relationship* recognize commonly-accepted principles: (1) All people want appreciation and a feeling of accomplishment and respect; (2) all want a place in this world; and (3) leadership must be certain that all relations of the organization with the individual will support and maintain the latter's sense of personal worth and importance.[13]

11 Likert, *op. cit.*, pp. 61–76.
12 Likert, *op. cit.*, pp. 90–92.
13 Likert, *op. cit.*, pp. 103–104.

THE FUTURE

It is difficult to say where management thinking in terms of human relations will go in the next twenty-five years. Rather than either extreme, *job-centered* versus *employee-centered* management, it appears that more emphasis will be focused on a midpoint where employees find satisfaction in work situations while still producing at a high level. The capability to hire, fire, suspend, and motivate on both an economic and non-economic level may be returned to first-line supervisors. Increasingly, the stress will be on participative management. There could and should be group consultation on many areas of decision-making with little regard for the chain of command. Unions also will probably participate in this type of leadership.

Yet it will be the role of management, more than anything else, to be the leader and motivator of employees, not only because management will make an impact on the lives of the latter and also on society, but it will serve the best interests of the organization in doing so. Several scholars have already begun to focus attention on this aspect as the major new pattern in management.

It is noteworthy that writers outside of the behavioral science field are beginning to be concerned with the "conflict" between the goals of employees and those of organizations. Some observers, such as Harvey Cox, imply that the behavioralists have been focusing too narrowly, that it is by means of organizations that humans reach fulfillment in life. As Cox notes, ". . . we must first realize that the organization is here to stay. There is simply no other way to run a world brimming with three billion people in the midst of an industrial epoch. . . . If we choose to live responsibly in the world, we must face the issue of how we can harness organizational power for authentic human purposes."[14]

[14] Harvey Cox, *The Secular City* (New York: The MacMillan Co., 1965), p. 173.

36. Let's Revamp Merit Systems for Today's Needs*

Mortimer M. Caplin

I am Mortimer M. Caplin, President of the National Civil Service League, and I appreciate the invitation for the National Civil Service League to appear before you. My fellow Officers and Board Members —all volunteers—are listed in our written statement. The League, as you know, is the initiator of civil service in the United States. For 90 years we have been the citizens' spokesman for modern, effective and efficient public manpower systems.

Today, I would like to speak for the League on how our nation's civil services—federal, state, local—can and should provide public employment opportunities for the disadvantaged under merit principles. We believe that government, as "employer of the *first* resort," can provide meaningful career opportunities for many who are unemployed or underemployed, and at the same time help meet severe staff shortages. And our society will have strengthened, improved, modernized merit systems of public employment as a result.

I would like now to tell you what the League has been working on in this area, a bit about what we have found in our work, and some of the policy implications that flow from our findings.

THE PUBLIC SERVICE JOB PROBLEM

Governments at all levels today employ 17% of the work force and spend $100 billion on direct payrolls. Demands for public services are such that one out of every four new jobs in the United States is in the public sector. Between October 1967 and October 1968, the number of civilian employees in state and local government grew from 8.9 to 9.4 million.

Few of these ½ million jobs went to the disadvantaged. Simultaneously, at least three million people in the country earned incomes below the poverty threshold, *even though they worked full-time*.

It is conservatively estimated that of the 500,000 new jobs to be created each year in state and local government, a minimum of 100,000 could go to the poor, *if existing barriers were removed*. Another 100,000 job vacancies could also be claimed for the disadvantaged, well-motivated worker through positive changes in existing systems.

Government turnover and job vacancy rates are estimated to provide 1,000,000 job openings at any given time.

* From a statement before the Subcommittee on Employment, Manpower and Poverty, Committee on Labor and Public Welfare, U.S. Senate (Hearings on the Manpower Training Act (S. 2838). Printed in *Good Government*, Vol. 87, No. 2, pp. 1–3. Reprinted by permission.

The National Civil Service League looked at these facts and decided that our public service faces a crisis of great magnitude—and one on which we should act.

Thus, the League has turned its attention to two areas of national concern: the growing shortage of personnel for government jobs, and the need of the disadvantaged for meaningful, "real" jobs. The League believes that each of these problems carries the other's solution. Yet civil service systems often seem to frustrate the hiring of would-be employees.

The League believes that rules and regulations designed to facilitate the merit system in the 1890's or the 1930's do not necessarily serve the 1970's. Further, the League knows that many jurisdictions around the country—state, county and city—want to revise their personnel structures to fit today. But how, and in what direction?

It is to provide leadership relevant to this age that the League developed a new project: Public Employment and the Disadvantaged. The League is working with public and private leaders in cities, counties and states to help bring the disadvantaged into public employ under merit principles.

Our method has been to assemble data; survey the field; examine the "state of the art" in public personnel management; develop a new edition of the League's famed Model Civil Service Law (earlier versions formed the basis of the federal civil service and nearly every other civil service in the nation); and publish a series of studies as part of a Model Program. Nearly two dozen pieces will be published, ranging from the economic, social and policy needs to such specifics as training, recruiting, job structuring, testing. We have conducted and spoken before local, regional, and national workshops and have offered policy guidance and technical assistance to some 30 jurisdictions.

During discussion Senator Gaylord Nelson (D-Wis) Committee Chairman, asked: "What techniques do you use to gain implementation of your recommendation, (1) on the code, for example, and (2) where you find, as you obviously have, instances of irrelevant job requirements? What do you do to get them to change?"

Mr. Caplin: "What we hope to do, Senator, is with this support we have had, the financial support, both from the public sector and private, and with the staff that we have been able to develop and the background we are developing, to have meaningful publications and put a searchlight on some of the problems. I don't believe a searchlight has been placed on the problems. I know your committee is doing this very thing. I think through the combined effects of publications, conferences, institutes, hopefully some newspaper-magazine attention, that all these things will help generate a reexamination of these requirements and standards which have outlived their usefulness, if they ever had any usefulness."

Senator Nelson: "I think the studies you are doing are tremendously significant and necessary. I am just wondering how you might further implement the usage of the studies you make."

These programs have been conducted under a joint grant from the Office of Economic Opportunity and the U.S. Department of Labor and a contract with the Department of Housing and Urban Development. We are continuing our work in this field; for example, we have just agreed to a further technical assistance program under the aegis of the Office of Economic Opportunity.

MEETINGS WITH MANY CITIZENS

In addition to the technical assistance and policy guidance given across the nation, we have met with, interviewed and developed data from literally thousands of public personnel officials, from representatives of the poor, and from both private and public agencies dealing with the employment problems of the disadvantaged. While our studies are not yet completed, we have published some materials and will shortly be publishing more, which our staff will be happy to provide as they are printed.

The League, in conceiving and promoting the merit principle has held to the two concepts that give it meaning:

1. equal treatment of all who would enter the credentialed civil service;
2. provision of some form of employee protection to prevent spoils practices.

We know there are five key elements to good personnel management systems: job definition, or structure; job specifications, or requirements; recruitment or outreach; selection, or examination; and training, or development. Our studies and technical assistance efforts have shown us that, if each of these are approached intelligently and with good will, jobs *will* be opened up for the "locked out" disadvantaged *and* merit systems will be stronger.

One significant part of our work deals with case studies of a great number of jurisdictions. These are studies of public services that have tried to meet the dual problems of jobs for the disadvantaged and improved staffing for government programs. It is very clear from these studies that a great deal can be done—and quickly.

In almost *no instances has there been a need to change an existing civil service law*. Rather, the need has been to change archaic practices that create rigidities and demean the merit principle. This usually requires little more than a willingness to examine past practices and change those that are irrelevant or in contradiction of true merit.

281

Sometimes it requires policy changes. Occasionally rules or regulations need to be changed. But that is about it. An important conclusion is that a systems approach to change and modernizing public personnel management is needed and will enhance the quality of the public service.

Here are some of our findings:

Restructuring jobs in a large jurisdiction (as they did in New Jersey) will create thousands of job openings.

Removing unrealistic education or experience requirements (as in one city that required a dog catcher to have two years experience—as a dog catcher) will not only open jobs for the poor, but will rid the jurisdiction of many "depression-born irrelevancies."

One state requires at least an eighth grade education and one year's experience in a commercial laundry for a beginning laundry worker ($3600 a year); the same jurisdiction requires a high school education and five years experience in a commercial laundry ($6500 a year) for a laundry section supervisor.

Recruiting via the ghetto shows that the educational level there is approaching the average of the nation, but that the people living there can't reach or aren't acceptable to private employers, and don't know about the availability of jobs in the public sector.

Performance examinations are more meaningful in many cases than written exams (most truck driver candidates, as well as Ph.D. candidates and the disadvantaged fear and resent exams which test little more than their ability to take tests).

One city gives a written exam for a washroom attendant, and the applicant must pay a fee of $3 to take the exam. In a recent examination, it took *six months* to grade the exam and notify those who passed. The job pays $3600 a year.

Training—pre and post employment—is crucial to job success in *any* case, and we have found many jurisdictions which see the reasonableness of giving a trainee who has satisfactorily completed his training a credentialed job.

These are some of the things we have been able to establish and which we will be publishing soon. One other thing we have found is that many jurisdictions really want to move into the last third of the 20th century with viable and effective manpower systems but they lack two needed stimuli:

One is the encouragement and stimulation brought about by specific mandates in federal programs and by programs of help and advice such as the League has been undertaking.

The second is the money and resources to implement change.

These latter are minimal, because they are essentially support services, but a small investment can have a tremendous payout. The former, handled well, will create more jobs in the next five years than can most non-government programs. This, only because it is *governments* that will provide the new jobs—and in the millions.

NATIONAL POLICY IMPLICATIONS

In response to your request for any insights we might have at this point on how federal law and programs might embody some of the principles we have learned, I am happy to submit the following for consideration:

1. In all federal grant-in-aid programs there ought to be specific, hard language *both* (a) barring discrimination at all job levels by any state or local recipient of grants-in-aid and (b) providing enforcement machinery at the federal level with requirements for reports.

These programs should carry the mandatory penalty of funds cut-off for violations and should establish a clear system of enforcement, with criteria.

One reason for so advising is that, though the civil services of our nation have, by and large, discriminated much less than has the private sector, they still do discriminate (see the U.S. Commission on Civil Rights 1969 report *For all the People . . . By all the People*). Such studies as we have seen (and our own observations) lead us to conclude that a mere "statistical reporting" is insufficient as is mere reliance on current grant-in-aid language. Analysis indicates that many "affirmative action" programs end up with minorities predominantly in the lower level, more menial jobs.

An important device springs from the federal contracts concept used in the Labor Department's equal employment opportunity program. This would stipulate that, before any examination be promulgated (written, oral, unassembled, performance, interview) it must be positively shown to be, and certified as, specifically relevant to the position for which the test is being given.

2. Specific funds should be made available for programs concerned with public employment of the disadvantaged. These would usually be within and occasionally outside the merit systems. Some examples follow:

A. Funds to recognize job-related social realities—for example:

(1) Day care for children of working mothers in the public sector; transportation assistance; supportive counseling; health needs.

(2) Short range subsidies to public employers who initiate compensatory preferential hiring (as in veterans preference, for example) for disadvantaged persons outside the regular merit system until

such time as the persons employed are fully qualified under standard criteria.

B. Specific training money for programs of public employment of the disadvantaged. We have found some of the most critical needs to be funds for:

(1) Training the disadvantaged individual, on a pre-employment and especially on a post-employment ("hire now, train later") basis;

(2) Upgrading incumbent staff, particularly at the lower levels among whom are many from disadvantaged backgrounds and who are frustrated in moving up and who see others coming as threats;

(3) Training supervisors to work with disadvantaged individuals, such training to be beyond "sensitivity training" and to get at how the supervisor and others can train, work with, supervise and develop those in need.

(4) Vocational education for the public service at high school and junior high levels.

C. Funds for special, sustained, outreach recruiting efforts. Traditional post office, city hall, regular newspaper and specialized (e.g., college) recruiting efforts are badly in need of modernization. Our studies show clearly that those in the "ghetto" are *not* being reached; that *employers tend to reserve marginal jobs for ghetto residents but that qualified persons are there*—usually underemployed rather than unemployed—who are not being reached by traditional methods.

D. Direct special technical assistance and policy guidance funds on pilot bases or broadly for national efforts and for state-local jurisdictions that are prepared to take a *systems* approach to *career* employment for the disadvantaged by updating and making employment systems fully relevant.

E. Funds to make studies on, and conduct experiments in, *validation* of employment practices (exams, job descriptions, etc.) on such a scale that true validation techniques can be applied, analyzed and evaluated. This envisages research in the literature, examination of what has been done, and establishing specific experiments (e.g., employing and following work of two groups of persons in sufficiently similar situations, but with one group taking the standard test while the other doesn't).

F. Funding broad national research, data gathering and information dissemination efforts on public personnel management changes and developments. This envisages reports, conferences, newsletters, etc.

In summary we are convinced that the whole area of job descriptions, specifications, recruitment, selection and training in the public sector needs a thorough revision for creating meaningful career opportunities for the disadvantaged within the merit systems generally. And, both money and incentive from the national government are needed.

We are convinced of two things: there is a need to create, communicate, and effect a civil service reform agenda that will be meaningful for the last third of the 20th century; and the pressures of intergovernmental relations development, the advent of collective bargaining in the public service, the problems of the needy disadvantaged to find careers in staff-starved governments, have generated a true "crisis of competence" in our public services.

Governments—federal, state and local—have an opportunity to meet part of this crisis by being the employer of the *first* resort to create real careers for the disadvantaged and meet desperate staffing needs.

37. Cultural Bias in Selection*

Ollie A. Jensen

Bias in selection can be deliberate and direct or indirect and incidental. This discussion deals with the second type of bias—the non-selection of individuals from minority ethnic groups, not because they lack potential, but because of the kind of education and experience they have had.

A conclusion which has been drawn repeatedly in the literature on ethnic group differences is that tests with high verbal skill loadings are not "fair" to all groups. This conclusion is indisputable for tests used to measure relative ability to learn (used as aptitude tests), but does not necessarily hold for tests used to measure developed abilities (used as job knowledge or achievement tests).

WHAT'S FAIR

Verbal skills are acquired through informal exposure and formal education. Use of a test of verbal skills to predict individual differences in ability to learn related skills is "fair" only if all test takers are approximately equally motivated and have had about the same exposure to verbal material. If there are widespread differences among the test takers in motivation or past exposure to books and good schooling, these differences, rather than differences in aptitude, will account for most of the obtained test score variance.

In contrast, the verbal skills test is "fair" to all competitors if the skills tested are required for success on a particular job and if the new employees are expected to be fully qualified after a fixed orientation or probationary period. Here, the only interest is current level of developed (immediately usable) ability.

The qualifications in the foregoing statement point up two widely differing current problems:

1. Often the level of verbal ability needed to pass a civil service test is far in excess of that required to be successful on the job. This needlessly discriminates against competitors with particular ethnic or socio-economic backgrounds.

2. While governmental agencies have routinely provided some form of orientation and skill training, they have not provided individualized remedial education. Organized minority groups are now requesting that governmental agencies do more selection on the basis of potential, and then provide whatever individualized remedial education is needed to bring achievement up to required levels.

*From *Public Personnel Review*, Vol. 27, No. 2 (April, 1966), 125–30. Reprinted by permission.

Whether the historical position of governmental agencies is "fair," and whether governmental agencies should go into the business of remedial education, are questions the voting public will have to resolve. The point that needs to be made here is that if individualized remedial education is to be given those hired, it is inappropriate to use a job knowledge test as a ranking device. In the remedial education situation, the ranking of eligibles should be on the basis of individual differences in potential or aptitude. If there are limits on the amount or kind of remedial education authorized, the job knowledge test can be used as a pass-fail screen. It also can be used for diagnostic purposes—to indicate the kind and amount of remedial education needed to bring a particular eligible to the full working level.

MYTH OR METHOD?

Efforts to construct culture-fair aptitude tests with useful predictive validity have not been particularly fruitful. This fact has led many psychologists to assume the following peculiar (though consistently negative) position stated by Howard C. Lockwood in his paper "The Testing of Minority Applicants for Employment": ". . . there is no such animal as a culture-fair test, but if there were it would be useless in personnel selection. . . ."

There are several reasons why such pessimism is unwarranted at this time:

1. The number of studies concerned with the utility of culture-fair tests in personnel selection is relatively small.

2. Studies which use as a criterion, supervisory rating of employees' performance during their first six months or year on the job, are by definition using a biased criterion—those who come to the job with the most fully developed, immediately useable skills receive the highest ratings regardless of their long-range potential. Studies which use as criteria measures of accomplishment during five, 10, or more years following initial testing (a) are scarce, and (b) indicate that culture-fair tests have higher predictive validity than their conventional counterpart.

3. Semler and Iscoe ("Comparative and Developmental Study of Learning Abilities of Negro and White Children Under Four Conditions," *Journal of Educational Psychology*, 1963) found that learning rate scores are not related to race. Testing the ability to learn material that is equally novel to all appears to be the most direct, fair approach to predicting ability to learn on the job. The *Raven Progressive Matrices* is probably the best culture-fair, miniature-learning-situation test in general use today. This test is 30 years old; it uses only one kind of test item and one kind of test material; it certainly can be improved upon.

4. Most of the major publishers of psychological tests have reported recently that they have major culture-fair test development projects under way.

287

IS A CHANGE NECESSARY?

One of the features of the ongoing "social revolution of the 60's" is the increasing pressure being exerted on governmental agencies to reduce cultural bias in selection. On the other hand, a selection system which is without bias is not a merit system. The only bias-free selection system is the perfectly conceived and operated lottery. What kind of bias is desirable? What kind is undesirable?

Deliberate and direct job-related bias, selection on the basis of merit, is the stated goal of all civil service selection programs. Deliberate and direct bias that is not job related (bias for or against individuals because of politics, race, religion, sex, etc.) is undesirable and prohibited by civil service law or rule. Indirect and incidental bias is both undesirable and unregulated.

It can be assumed that the combination of law and rule, general professionalization of personnel agency staffs, and alert vested interest groups (Fair Employment Practice Commissions, organized employee groups, etc.) provide adequate curbs on deliberate and direct bias that is not job related. The same assumption cannot be made about the more insidious indirect and incidental bias. Can this pest be controlled?

Professional application of known principles of good test construction, administration, and analysis, coupled with a sincere, knowledgeable, and pervasive "equal opportunity" recruitment and hiring effort can drastically reduce indirect and incidental bias in selection. In other words, the tools are available; the job can be done—for a price.

The value of any selection program is a function of acceptance, costs, and validity. Each personnel agency implicitly or explicitly determines the relative weight to be given each of these variables on a situation-by-situation basis. In one instance, the more costly performance test (job-sample test) is used because of doubts concerning public acceptance or validity of alternate approaches; in another instance, the device with the highest validity and acceptance is rejected in favor of one with only moderate validity and acceptance but which costs substantially less to develop or administer.

Should public personnel agencies change their formulae for evaluating cost, i.e., pay the price needed to more adequately control indirect and incidental cultural bias? If some of the well-intended but technically naive proposals of organized minority groups (e.g., elimination of the qualification appraisal interview and use of "rule of one") become law, this question will be academic.

STATUS QUO IS FOOL'S PARADISE

In any event, the *status quo* is a fool's paradise that can vanish in an instant:

Over the years, the slogan of civil service has been "equity and merit."

Over the years, the general public has come to believe that for the most part civil service personnelists are sincerely trying to do their "mediocre best" to live up to that slogan.

Over the years, the most consistent pressure on public personnel agencies has come from employees and management and has concerned classification and pay matters.

Over the years, limited budgets, increasing work loads, and the consistent pressure on classification and pay matters have forced a mechanical, superficial approach to much of the examining function.

Knowingly or unknowingly, evidence of uniformity in treatment of applicants, competitors, and eligibles has been substituted for truly equitable treatment, and face validity of selection devices and procedures has been substituted for selection on the basis of actual merit. The scattered exceptions to this rule are tributes to the effectiveness of particular local, occupational, vested interest groups.

IS THERE A DO-IT-YOURSELF KIT?

Before entering into an enumeration of specifics for reducing cultural bias in selection, there is one closely-related topic that should be touched upon. That is the importance of having a public image as an employer who is sincerely attempting to apply the principle of "equal opportunity" in day-to-day personnel practices.

A large private utility company discovered that the percentage of Negroes passing a certain written test was, with a single exception, quite low. In the exceptional case—one city in a statewide operation—the proportion of Negroes passing the test was equal to the proportion of whites passing. The only unusual feature of this case was the unstinting effort being made by the local personnel officer to convince the community that the company was an "equal opportunity" employer, and to help line supervisors put "equal opportunity" principles into practice. In this one spot, because a great many highly qualified Negroes applied for jobs, the company was able to hire a large number. As for the test, even in this exceptional situation, it probably underestimated the relative standing of those Negroes who passed; and probably an even higher percentage of Negro applicants should have received passing scores.

The point of this more-anecdotal-than-definitive study is, "Output can be no better than input, and input can be no better than the actual public image of an agency." If the input is at least an average sampling from a current labor market, what should be done to obtain an optimum output (list of eligibles)?

HOW TO REDUCE BIAS

The do's and don'ts for reducing incidental cultural bias listed below appear, for the most part, to be paraphrases or specific applications of well known principles of good test construction. This is as it should be. Technically speaking, incidental cultural bias is merely one kind of systematic error of measurement. The more professional the approach to examining, the smaller the error of measurement, regardless of source.

Rule 1. If the purpose is to measure developed ability, explore the feasibility of using a job-sample test battery. While job-sample tests generally are somewhat troublesome to administer and to score, costs need not always be substantially greater, and carefully conceived and executed job-sample tests are well received by competitors and keep cultural bias at a minimum.

Rule 2. If the purpose is to measure developed ability, and written tests are part of the selection battery, set up procedures for excluding verbiage, non-job-related jargon, and other terminology and phraseology which tend to favor individuals with particular educational or socio-economic backgrounds. Also, unless differences in speed of reading are important to job success, eliminate individual differences on this variable through the use of generous time limits.

Rule 3. Whether the purpose is to measure developed ability or ability to learn, make instructions understandable to the person who barely meets the requirements for admission to the examination. Also, in the administration of each test, make certain that the instructions are understood—even at the price of an extra proctor, possible boredom of the more test-wise, and increased total test administration time.

Offer Practice Material

Closely related to "Rule 3," if not actually part of it, is "Provide adequate practice material and feedback." The instructions and practice problems included in the "Directions Page" for civil service examinations generally are adequate for promotional situations in which the competitive group consists of employees familiar with the testing process. On the other hand, when those same "Directions" are used in open competitive examinations (a standard practice) they introduce, rather than control, cultural bias. They tend to rely on the fact that most natives of the U.S. white, middle class culture have taken many tests for many purposes. This is fine for most competitors, but devastating for those with backgrounds which do not fit the mold.

The unsophisticated test taker not only needs practice with item format and with recording answers on a separate answer sheet, he also needs practice in answering subject matter questions within the item format and an opportunity to compare his answers with the key answers. Ability to pick up clues as to the level of abstraction intended, fineness or grossness of distinctions to be made, etc., is acquired through ex-

290

posure. As this is a test-related (rather than job-related) ability, individual differences should be minimized. It is to be remembered that differences in test sophistication affect both power and speed.

Successive Hurdles Approach

Rule 4. Whether the purpose is to measure developed ability or ability to learn, remember that whenever the selection process consists of a series of hurdles, the total process is no better than the worst hurdle. The input for one hurdle is the output from the previous one. If the examination publicity reaches only WASPs, only WASPs will apply. If the publicity reaches all potential competitors in the recruitment area, but one segment of the potential competitive group finds the public image of the agency unsatisfactory, then few from the unsatisfied segment will apply. This is especially true of the better qualified people in that segment.

If the group of applicants is representative, but the first test hurdle is culturally biased, then the competitive group for the next hurdle will reflect that bias. No matter how "fair" the second or succeeding tests are, the selection process will yield a culturally biased list. If more than one hurdle is culturally biased, the error is, of course, compounded. Currently, public personnel agencies all too frequently set up a series of absolute selection hurdles. An "absolute hurdle" is one which must be cleared in one try—there is no second chance; there is no provision for achieving a compensatingly high score on other hurdles.

The reasons for choosing the "successive absolute hurdles" approach usually are expediency or increased economy, not increased validity. The least expensive selection devices (which also tend to be the most culturally biased and least valid) are used as the first hurdles:

1. Minimum qualification requirements for admission to the examination are inserted as a pretest hurdle. Often these qualifications more closely resemble "desirable qualifications" than they do minimum qualifications. In light of how difficult it has been for members of some minority groups to obtain " 'X' years of progressively responsible experience," this practice is biased in the extreme.

2. A group written test is frequently used to reduce the number of competitors who will be evaluated further by a costly individual test or interview. Here, all too frequently, the choice of test format and item content, style, or terminology inadvertently favors one discipline over another or favors formal course study over self development.

The gist of "Rule 4" is not "abandon the successive-hurdles approach to selection;" rather, it is, "don't use the successive-hurdles approach routinely, and in each instance of use, make a separate determination on how it is to be used:"

1. Set true minimum qualifications or admit all.

291

2. Selectively abandon absolute hurdles in favor of relative ones; hurdles which within situationally defined limits allow for compensating patterns of abilities.

3. Discover and then utilize other procedures and techniques for reducing the "compounding of error on error" so characteristic of today's successive-hurdles selection programs.

Key Test to Requirements

Rule 5. If a general aptitude test is to be used, make it appropriate in level and kind to the general aptitude requirements of the selection situation. This self-evident principle needs emphasis because it is ignored in day-to-day practice. Often the only general aptitude recognized is abstract intelligence, and the only recognition given to the differential requirements of jobs widely separated in level and kind of duties is a change in the level of abstraction, the number of questions, or the reconditeness and face validity of the vocabulary used.

The general aptitude needed for success in most low level classes is qualitatively different from abstract intelligence. It is an ability to carry out consistently a readily-learned routine with dispatch and accuracy. The key words here are "routine," "accuracy," and "consistency."

Routine. The distinguishing feature of low level jobs is the routine nature of their duties. The routine varies widely in content and, within narrow limits, in complexity, but in all cases the required ability is being capable of following implicit or explicit sets of directions.

Accuracy. Above a certain minimum level of speed, specific to each job, accuracy is more important than speed. The cost (time, money, manpower, public relations) for correcting one error generally offsets substantial differences in gross production.

Consistency. On routine jobs, inconsistency is characteristic of the over-qualified as well as the under-qualified.

Shortcomings of Current Devices

The main shortcomings of most devices for measuring the ability to follow directions are:

1. They are too short. Individual differences in accuracy due to fluctuating attention are not measured.

2. They are too highly speeded. While it is true that in a specific setting, speed and accuracy tend to be correlated, it is also true that short-burst speed is not related to sustained accuracy.

3. They are set up to yield a single speed-accuracy scale. Depending on whether the test is to be used as a pass-fail screen or a weighted part of the examination, (a) separate speed and accuracy cutoffs should be set; or (b) a speed cutoff should be set above which ranking is in terms of relative accuracy.

Rule 6. Don't use a low selection ratio as a substitute for careful test construction and administration. It is true that by selecting only one in 100, a test with low validity can produce an eligible list containing a high proportion of highly qualified individuals. The problem is that most of the factors contributing to the low validity of the test also contribute to its cultural bias. Consequently, the list is disproportionately loaded with white, middle-class Americans having an above average amount of formal education.

SUMMARY

The moral to be drawn from this illustrative rather than exhaustive discussion of cultural bias in selection is that expediency and tight-fisted economy in the operation of a selection program tend to produce the same result as corruption and incompetence—a downgrading of one segment of the competitive group and an upgrading of another segment for invalid reasons.

38. Training as a Management Strategy*

Hospital Research and Education Trust

. . . The degree to which training and continuing education can be used effectively in any organization is to a considerable extent dependent on the management perspective of the chief administrator, for he, more than anyone else, sets the tone and philosophy of the organization. In some instances, management is perceived as the controlling of human energies; in others, it is seen more as the development and releasing of human energies to accomplish the organization's goals. It seems likely that the use of training and continuing education as a management strategy will hold greater promise when the latter point of view is held.

THE CASE FOR TRAINING

It is somewhat of a paradox that many hospitals traditionally have supported an "inservice" training function in the nursing department while ignoring the need for similar efforts in other departments. Historically, of course, many more hospitals had nursing schools than is the case today, and the inservice activity may well have sprung up as a natural extension of the teaching activities of those schools. However, the question still arises as to why the training function was considered to be of value to the institution for one group of employees but was disregarded for other groups.

One need not look very far to uncover problems that strongly suggest the need for training. One obvious example is the problem of turnover. In 1968 the United Hospital Fund of New York[1] studied this problem and the costs associated with it, and concluded that the minimum direct costs for replacement at the lowest skill level were $300, while the cost of replacing a department head or an effective staff nurse could run anywhere from $500 to $1000. Inclusion of indirect costs produces still higher figures.

Analyses of turnover statistics indicate clearly that termination is most likely to occur during the first three months of employment. Termination interviews with employees leaving during this early period suggest that many of them feel that they have never been integrated into the institution's work force. They express their frustrations about unclear assignments and about inadequate instruction on how to perform the tasks and follow the procedures in use in their departments. In many

* From *Training and Continuing Education: A Handbook for Health Care Institutions* (Chicago, Hospital Research and Education Trust, 1970), 1–3. Reprinted by permission.

[1] *Analyzing and Reducing Employee Turnover in Hospitals.* New York: Training, Research and Special Studies Division of the United Hospital Fund of New York, 1968.

cases, they have been recruited, interviewed, hired, given the briefest orientation or none at all, and then put to work under the old philosophy of "sink or swim." As a result, there have been many drownings, each requiring that the cycle of recruiting, interviewing, and hiring begin all over again. It seems logical, if a sizable investment must be made in securing an employee in the first place, that management should take out some "insurance" on this investment by adding the necessary step of properly training the employee to do his job. For the employee, few satisfactions are greater than knowing what he is expected to do, being able to do it, and experiencing the sense of accomplishment that comes from knowing he is doing it correctly. As a rule, the satisfied employee is not the one who leaves.

There are a host of other problems that suggest a need for training. These are made evident by recurring patient complaints about employee performance, departmental labor costs that are excessive in comparison to costs of similar departments in other institutions, evidence of hazards to the safety of patients and employees, less than adequate productivity from some employees, chronic absenteeism and tardiness, waste of materials and supplies, errors in following procedures, and many other signs. All of these indicate the health care institution is not getting an adequate return for its investment in salaries, the largest single item in its budget.

This is not to suggest that training cures all problems. In fact, it cannot cure even all performance problems. However, training can and will, when properly organized and managed, make it certain that the employee *knows* what he has to know and *is able to perform* his assigned tasks with efficiency and with effectiveness.

RELATIONSHIPS OF TRAINING TO OTHER STRATEGIES

Training is not carried out in a vacuum. It functions in an environment of policies, procedures, standards, and institutional objectives and has intimate relationships to other strategies of management. For example, establishing performance standards is a prerequisite to any successful training effort. Without standards, toward what end are we training?

Industrial engineering, cost accounting, and other management strategies that have been mentioned have a common denominator. They all relate to problem solving, for all are logical responses to observed problems. Though the terminology may change from one strategy to another, the basic process does not change. It consists of these essential steps:

Becoming aware of, and defining a need for, improvement of some aspect of the institution's operation

Choosing among alternative solutions for overcoming the deficiency
Implementing a planned program to correct the deficiency
Following up to evaluate whether or not desired outcomes are achieved.

The private diaries of many managers are filled with sad stories of problem solutions that did not work. In many cases, even though needs were carefully defined and logical solutions chosen, failure occurred at the stages of implementation and evaluation.

If, for example, a new set of work standards for a maintenance procedure is arrived at through industrial engineering, the achievement of those standards will require a change in behavior on the part of the employees. If that behavior change is directed by memorandum or fiat, there is little likelihood that lasting change will occur. On the other hand, if a thorough analysis is made of the performance improvements needed, and a carefully planned instructional program is carried out, the chances for obtaining lasting improvement are considerably better.

It is a fallacy to assume that changes will take place simply because we want them to or because we dictate that they shall occur. Failure to give employees an opportunity to learn the meaning of changes, or to gain the skills needed to perform in the new procedure or system, is a frequent practice rather than an exception. All lasting behavior change takes place as a result of some learning experience. The purpose of training is to provide learning experiences that are functional, economical, and logical. Training, then, involves a systematic *process* by which the employee is permitted to learn the skills and acquire the knowledge and attitudes necessary for the performance of his assigned tasks. *Any other management strategy, if it produces a need for changes in employee performance, will be supported by the training strategy and will be more likely to succeed if training is integrated into the process of creating the desired change.* This will be true, however, only if the process for planning training sessions is systematic and thorough. The training process involves the same steps that were described for problem solving. First, learning needs must be accurately and specifically determined; second, appropriate learning objectives must be defined in terms that describe the expected changes in performance; third, a learning experience must be designed that takes into account the practical considerations of cost, scheduling, and achievement of the objectives; fourth, an honest evaluation must be made to determine whether or not the outcomes are as predicted in the objectives.

These are the steps that will be described and demonstrated in this handbook. For the trainer, it is a source book for the process and for methods. For the administrator, it provides the background that will make his management of the training function effective.

THE TRAINING SPECIALIST'S ROLE

Training is a *line function*. The supervisor is responsible for the performance and development of his employees. The department head is responsible for the performance and development of his supervisors and the departmental employees. The administrator is responsible for the effectiveness of the total work force.

The training specialist is in a *staff* assignment. He is a planner of learning experiences that will help the administrator, the department head, and the supervisors to achieve their goals. If he has designed a program to train employees, he should be accountable for whether or not they *are able to perform* a task or job. He cannot be, and should not be asked to be, accountable for the day-by-day performance on the job. *The maintenance of adequate performance levels is the responsibility of the supervisor.*

To think of the training specialist primarily as an instructor of line employees is to limit severely his value to the organization. To think of him as a resource, a consultant, a planner, an evaluator, and a trainer of those who should train line employees is to multiply his knowledge and skills many times over. Instructors and other specialized talent can often be recruited from members of the institution's staff, consultants, and personnel from local educational institutions.

THE ADMINISTRATOR'S ROLE: POLICY AND PRACTICE

Whether or not any health care institution maintains a climate and environment that is supportive of continuing development of employee capability is largely dependent on the expectations created by the administrator. If he believes that performance improvements can and should be made, and if he backs up this belief with action, a climate is set. If he uses his regular communication channels (such as department head meetings and monthly reports) to inquire of each department head what his plans and programs are for improving performance, he creates the expectations necessary to get action. If he follows up at regular intervals, he will reinforce the expectation and will convince his department heads that he really wants action. If he provides the staff resources and talent needed to plan and implement improvement, he will make the action possible.

39. City Training Nears Point of No Return*

Charles A. Willis

Today, employee training and development occupies an important position in local government activities. It is no longer up to an individual to improve himself on his own time. Local governments recognize that deliberate and systematic employee development does improve municipal services, reduce turnover, and replenish the reservoir of technical, administrative, and supervisory skills essential to the continuation of modern public services.

Training has not reached the point of acceptance or necessity as have other public services such as protection of life and property or waste collection and disposal, but it will.

The preparation and planning of a modern training program need not be a particularly difficult task. This article may serve as a set of general guidelines for planning, developing, and administering such programs.

The essential components of an employee development program are: a training policy, managerial and employee support, and, of course, training programs. The six basic steps in developing a training program are: identifying needs, stating objectives, collecting materials, selecting techniques, implementing training, and evaluating results.

SETTING THE POLICY

Training must be sold to employees, supervisors, managers, legislators, and the public. It must be defined, publicized, and supported. One way to enter into deliberate staff development is through an official written statement of policy.

A training policy statement serves many purposes: to clearly state intention of the governmental unit; to pinpoint responsibility for training; to spell out broad objectives; to set limitations; and to cite training hours, use of public facilities, and funds.

More important, however, a written policy gives direction and continuing support to employee training and development activities. It clarifies the fact that both the employee and employer have mutual responsibilities in providing better service to the public through an approach other than purchasing new equipment and hiring more people.

Although a training statement could be issued by anyone in authority, whether it be a departmental supervisor, a department head, a city

* Reprinted from the February, 1967, issue of *Public Management* by special permission. © 1967 The International City Management Association.

manager, a mayor, or a city council, the value of it is equal to the sum of the parts to which it applies and has meaning. Some statements, already on paper, could be modified and used by any governmental agency.

Appendices C and D of ICMA's *Post-Entry Training in the Local Public Service*[1] and the U.S. Government Employees Training Act of 1958[2] are excellent examples of comprehensive statements.

A policy statement is of little value unless it is carried out. It must be used to bring about specific training programs which meet the *needs* of the organization—the first step in the process of developing a training program.

IDENTIFYING THE NEEDS

What are your training needs? Where do you look for them? Do training needs remain static? Can they be predicted? Since employee training should be problem oriented and directed at improving some phase of your service, it is important to identify as specifically as possible, the skills, knowledge, and behavior that need to be improved. Furthermore, the identification process contributes to the development of understanding, formation of consensus, and creation of commitments to take corrective action.

Several devices and techniques can be used to identify training needs. Some are objective, others subjective in character. Your selection should reflect the degree of sophistication wanted, the extent to which employee training has been practiced, the number of persons employed, and, of course, the amount of public funds authorized for training activities.

Opinion and attitude surveys can be used to identify training needs. They can be purchased in ready-to-use form, or prepared to meet the requirements of a particular organization. As a rule, they are professionally prepared, comprehensive, and expensive.

Local industrial firms, universities, and management consultants would be helpful sources for more information on opinion surveys. Books and articles on the subject, written by educators and practitioners, may be found in most libraries. With such resources it would be possible to design an opinion survey for use in your organization. It is suggested that both open-ended and check-list type questions be used to encourage expression of views by many persons. The questionnaire should seek to determine the degree of interest in and need for training programs.

Employee performance records may be used to help identify the kinds of training needed. They also serve as a useful guide for coaching and counselling individuals toward self improvement.

1 The International City Managers' Association, *Post Entry Training in the Local Public Service*, Chicago, 1963.
2 Public Law 85–507, 85th Congress, S.–385, July 7, 1958.

Who knows the strengths and weaknesses of an employee? How much time can be set aside for systematic training? How critical the need is for training? It is the supervisor—the person who has the immediate responsibility for effective and efficient production.

While this approach to training needs identification produces subjective information, it is one of the more useful techniques. Supervisory participation in the first step of the process helps to stimulate an awareness for training, improve communication and cooperation, create support for training, and contribute to the development of the supervisors.

Observation as a method of determining training needs has limited value at best, and less value when done only occasionally or by someone unfamiliar with the skill and knowledge required at a given work site. It is a useful technique for the trainer because it acquaints him with the realities of a job.

Why do employees leave? A study of separation records may lead to a determination of the need to train some persons who remain on the payroll. A careful examination of other personnel records also helps to pinpoint training needs. Useful ones are: service complaints, accident records, absenteeism, grievances, and disciplinary records. Departmental performance records provide considerable insight into the kind of training that is needed.

Finally, needs may be revealed by an examination of the city's long-range development program, plan for fiscal action, projection of mechanical and service changes, retirement-replacement policies, and the city's estimate of strengths and potential of its personnel to fill vacancies or new positions in the future.

In short, training needs can be found in the gap between what is essential for effective performance and the present level of performance. Once that gap is clearly identified, other phases of training program development will follow with little confusion and few false starts. With a clear understanding of needs and priorities and the full backing of a training policy established at a high level, specific objectives of each training program can be established.

STATING OBJECTIVES

Objectives must be specific and attainable. It is not enough to say the ABC training program is designed to improve employee job performance. So stated, important questions are left unanswered, such as: At what point and on what topic is training to start? At what level of new performance will training cease? Can the new performance be measured?

Objectives must be within the reach of the employee and contribute to his ability to do a better job. Motivation can be built into the training process through clearly stated objectives that establish new levels of skill or knowledge that can be achieved by employees.

How many objectives should there be for one training program? There should be as many as necessary to indicate all of the new levels to be achieved as a result of training. Robert F. Mager's *Preparing Instructional Objectives*[3] is an excellent presentation of how to write objectives.

COLLECTING AND USING MATERIALS

The third step in developing a training program is collecting materials, information, and data to be used in the program. It might require research and writing original material from which the contents of the program can be developed. Material may be collected before or during a training program. The former is recommended since better training results can be achieved through pre-planning.

Where can materials be found? Sources often overlooked are libraries and educational institutions, including high schools, and professional organizations. The collection of materials within an agency is more efficient and effective when other supervisory personnel have participated in the identification of needs and preparation of objectives.

Collection is only part of this step; preparation of it for use is the other part. Based on earlier planning, it is now time to prepare the program content in a format most useful to the training class, such as, an outline, a syllabus, a training manual, an operations-training manual, or handout material. The choice should include consideration of needs, objectives, timetable, and student population.

SELECTING TECHNIQUES

The use of proper devices and vehicles in a training program is as important as getting on the Paris-bound jetliner when you want to go to Paris.

A lecture will not always move employees from one level of productivity to a higher level. A discussion may only leave questions unanswered, inject issues that can't be resolved in the training program or even fail to involve the students at all. Visual aids are essential to an effective program, but they can be too elaborate, or even redundant. Field trips, reading, or agency training assignments might not serve the objectives either. Role playing, case studies, incident processes, controlled-participation and simulated problem solving might consume too much time, or fail to reinforce the learning process.

Each technique and method must be carefully selected in order to reach the stated objectives. In the January, 1965, training issue of *National Safety News*, L. C. Smith presents an outstanding sum-

[3] Fearon Publishers, Palo Alto, California, 1962.

mary of the advantages and disadvantages of twelve common training techniques.[4]

Useful information on this and other training subjects is often presented in *Public Management, Personnel Journal* (PPA), *Training and Development Journal* (ASTD), *Supervisory Management* (AMA), and *Harvard Business Review*, to mention a few.

IMPLEMENTING TRAINING

Program implementation is that part of the training process concerned with the administration and conduct of a training program. Its placement as the fifth step in the process serves as a reminder that decisions and action on the following points must be taken by the time the first four steps are completed or training classes can not begin.

The points referred to are purchase of tools, equipment, and supplies; preparation of training aids including visuals, handouts, and quizzes; preparation of evaluation materials; selection of the date, time, and place of training classes; preparation of the classroom with tables, proper ventilation, and lighting, etc.

Further work includes announcement of the training opportunity; coordination of employee enrollment; development of an attendance recording system; announcement of standards for attendance, participation, and achievement; and selection and briefing of all resource persons.

Learning theories, especially regarding the adult population, should be understood before one begins to conduct formal training classes. In order to maintain a suitable learning environment for adults, we know class sessions should be short, frequent, and free of interruptions; salient material should be repeated and practiced by the students; errors need to be corrected promptly but privately; encouragement and recognition of achievement is essential; and finally, a variety of teaching methods should be used.

EVALUATING THE RESULTS

If the foregoing steps have been successfully completed, is it necessary to take time to evaluate the achievement of the training program and the level of employee performance? Certainly.

Without an evaluation, we might not know that the desired new level of performance could have been achieved sooner, at less cost, or with greater employee satisfaction through the use of different materials, techniques, speakers or scheduling. An evaluation might also reveal that despite good intentions, professional advice, and skillful preparation, the training program was substantially below or above the level of per-

---

4 L. C. Smith, "Twelve Ways to Train Employees," *National Safety News*, January, 1965, National Safety Council, Chicago.

sons participating in it. Accomplishment must be demonstrated or future proposals will meet resistance or rejection.

What evaluation techniques can be used? Where can they be found? It is important that the evaluation techniques be consistent with needs, objectives, and with the content of the training program. In fact, if those items are thoughtfully considered, a system of evaluation will become evident. The development of it, however, requires much work.

Many evaluation techniques are available, ranging from informal to elaborate, sophisticated systems. For further information, consult the publications mentioned earlier in this article as well as industrial relations and tests and measurement personnel.

BUDGETING FOR TRAINING

The process of determining a budget and financing for a single program or several training programs is identical to that used in most progressive municipalities.

Employee training is not a question of "how costly is it?" but, "how costly is it without employee training?"

On this point, O. G. Stahl said, "In most situations training of some kind necessarily takes place anyway; it is largely a question of its being systematic or haphazard, efficient or wasteful, effective or useless."[5]

He also observed: "It is more efficient to improve the skills of existing employees to a maximum than to rely solely on initial recruitment to provide a hypothetical supply of the highest-skills available."[6]

GETTING SUPPORT

Managerial and employee support are essential to any training effort. Like loyalty, support must be earned. First, there must be a written training policy, approved at the highest level of authority. Second, there must be programs that satisfy real needs, and improve individual abilities. Third, supervisors and employees must participate in planning and developing training programs.

On the last point, training committees and review boards have been successful. Informal groups of employees interested in self-development have also proved successful, as have task forces and problem solving teams. If none of these will work in your city, then other ways must be found to get both supervisors and employees actively involved in the training process.

The preparation of a training program is only part of the whole spectrum of employee training and development. Among the areas not covered in this presentation, but of equal importance, are: extension and

[5] O. Glenn Stahl, *Public Personnel Administration*, Harper & Row, New York City, 5th Edition, 1962.
[6] *Ibid.*

correspondence courses, tuition assistance, cooperation with other governmental units, internships, and self-improvement.

As local government officials, we can be certain that growing municipal needs will continue to place a strain on municipal revenues. New, untrained persons will be hired to fill vacancies, but, by increased employee performance made possible through training, we may be able to provide an expanding service program without unnecessarily increasing our budget for personal services.

40. Theoretical Foundations of the Appraisal Interview*
Robert L. Noland

If managers and supervisors wish to pay more attention to individual employee needs, to change poor behavior patterns of employees, and especially to develop the growth and leadership potential inherent in many workers, it appears that they must of necessity consider the use of the periodic appraisal of man's performance. The results of this appraisal, which includes the supervisor's day-to-day evaluation, is then made known to the employee in a scheduled post-appraisal interview.

But it becomes immediately apparent that the supervisor does not turn this matter over to trained personnel specialists and appraisal interviewers. Rather, he may be the technical-specialist-turned-leader who functions in a supervisory capacity without suitable or sufficient training. Thus it becomes his responsibility—trained or not, confident or not—to evaluate employee performance and to discuss the findings, in a developmental manner, with the employee. The following discussion focuses on such issues and procedures.

THREE BASIC PREMISES

This article is based upon recognition and acceptance of three basic premises:

1. As a result of the dramatic changes in our culture, technology, and management-labor relationships, management is faced with the necessity of satisfying many more needs and wants of the worker than ever before.

2. Management is being forced to rely more and more on the technical specialist as a source of future managerial talent. This requires that the specialist-turned-supervisor become quickly familiar with those leadership techniques which both realize management objectives and insure the continued satisfaction and development of employees.

3. Leadership attitudes and practices which embody good human relations principles and practices take into consideration both the satisfaction of worker needs and the achievement of organizational objectives.

The employee performance appraisal has had a bittersweet existence in its short tenure as a new management tool. Highly persuasive arguments have been published supporting and condemning both the concept of appraisal itself and the post-appraisal interview. The writer contends that employee appraisal is an essential fact of life in the work setting. The only question is that of how and on what basis it should be conducted.

* From *Public Personnel Review*, Vol. 28, No. 2 (April, 1967), 93–95. Reprinted by permission.

FOUNDATION OF THE INTERVIEW

Interviewing, no matter what its field of application, is based upon a foundation of facts organized into principles which in turn guide the actual interview. Before such principles find expression, they receive a color and a character consistent with the assumptions and attitudes which are basic to the personality of the interviewer. This can be better understood through the use of the following diagram:

General Principles of Interviewing

as interpreted by the

INTERVIEWER

Who am I?

What kind of person am I?

What type of leader am I?

leads to

INTERVIEW ATTITUDES

Regarding man in general?

Regarding this specific employee?

affect

INTERVIEW OBJECTIVES

What do I hope to accomplish in this interview?

What long-time efforts at change do I hope to set in motion in this interview?

SPECIFIC APPRAISAL TECHNIQUES

Note that the use of specific appraisal interviewing techniques does not occur by chance. Rather, it follows naturally and logically from attitudes which originate in and reflect the very structure of the interviewer's personality. These attitudes also affect the interviewer's perception, interpretation, and use of general interviewing principles.

Let us look at attitudes. We often speak of leadership types—autocratic, paternalistic, laissez-faire, etc. When we type a leader in this way we are really implying that as a person he acts in a relatively consistent and predictable way based on stable predispositions which we call attitudes.

The autocrat's attitudes toward men in general, and his employees in particular, obviously predispose him to interpret their behavior and to react in very specific ways. So too it is in interviewing. The autocratic interviewer acts on the basis of attitudes which he holds about man in general and about any specific employee whom he may be dealing with at the moment. The supervisor-interviewer may be aware of some of the attitudes which influence his behavior, but it is more than likely that there are other attitudes of which he is not aware. There are still other attitudes which the person does not possess but which perhaps he should possess if he really believes that a function of the management process is the development of subordinates as well as the attainment of organizational objectives.

Consider how an interviewer's acceptance or rejection of the following attitudes would influence his selection of principles, objectives, and techniques in an appraisal interview:

Attitudes of certain leaders—"Mr. Direct":

The typical worker will do only what he *has* to.

The typical worker is not interested in improvement of self or of the unit's capacity for mission attainment.

The typical person cannot be expected to get along without close supervision and must be helped in problem solving.

The typical worker thinks he is far better, more valuable, and more productive than he really is; because of this, he cannot be expected to be very objective in any self-appraisal.

On the other hand, note how differently he would react in an appraisal situation if he accepted the following attitudes:

Attitudes of certain leaders—"Mr. Develop":

The typical worker is generally interested in his job and in the attainment of unit objectives.

The typical worker has the capacity to develop into a more efficient, self-satisfied and productive worker if given proper incentives and opportunities.

The typical worker is a person of dignity and integrity—one who has a right to make decisions of major importance to him.

The typical worker is capable of positive steps toward self-development once interfering obstacles are removed.

Attitudes' Affect on Principles

Assuming that the attitudes of "Mr. Develop" are more acceptable to the interviewer, let us now see how principles are affected by attitudes and then translate these attitudes into techniques. As the supervisor becomes aware of these principles—more important, as he learns these principles well and they affect his attitudes—his behavior in the counseling situation will be immeasurably improved.

Principle A. Understanding which is developed primarily through one's own efforts is superior to understanding which comes primarily from information given to a person by someone else.

Probably the best example of what is meant here comes from the field of mathematics. Math problems may be solved correctly by almost anyone so long as each step is clearly outlined in a mechanical fashion. But, the person who understands why he takes each step, the person who sees the relationships between each step, is a far more capable person.

307

He can handle this particular problem and many others which might be similar to it in various ways. He can handle new problems because he understands. The first principle employed in appraisal interviewing is to allow, encourage, assist, and stimulate the employee to seek the relationships and understanding on his own.

Of course, the supervisor will have to present certain facts to his employees. It is quite a different matter however, to present two facts and then present as a fact the relationship between the two. This certainly differs from the procedure which presents the facts and then allows the employee to develop the relationship or implications.

Principle B. Self-initiated understanding is more likely to lead to emotional acceptance of the discovered relationship, solution, or objective than is understanding which is initiated and directed by another person.

Generating Will to Work

The will to work is often generated and maintained not only by solid, intellectual understanding of objectives, relationships, etc., but also by the degree to which emotional acceptance occurs on the part of the individual. It appears that worker participation in problem solving, self-development, etc., is more likely to lead both to understanding and to emotional acceptance of the result.

It might help at this juncture to reflect on experiences you have had when you were the employee being interviewed and really had ideas but were not permitted the opportunity of adequately expressing them. Even if the evaluation or solution given to you by your supervisor was exactly the one you had in mind, didn't you experience a bit of dissatisfaction that you had not been given the opportunity to show you could do some solid thinking too?

Again, note how the supervisor's attitudes and behavior will either facilitate or interfere with the employee's understanding and emotional acceptance of the matter under discussion. It is important to note also that understanding and acceptance are directly related to employee growth, satisfaction and productivity.

Principle C. Be yourself, but know yourself.

In other words, the actual words you use and/or the sequence of words you use are not as important as the spirit (attitude) you communicate. If you are genuinely desirous of helping your employees improve themselves, and if you really believe that this can best be accomplished through the individual expressing his ideas, then your interviews —almost despite your words—will communicate this attitude.

CONCLUSIONS

In summary, we by no means wish to imply that there aren't some stock techniques of phrasing questions, of encouraging employees' expressiveness, etc. Rather, we wish to emphasize that YOU are, or will be doing the interviewing, and your own style of expression will probably be better than any stock list of memorized phrases. Don't try to imitate or mimic some stereotyped idea you might have about interviewers. Be yourself.

In conclusion, successful interviews don't "just happen!" They reflect the use of techniques based upon an objective and realistic knowledge of one's values and attitudes about the employee.

41. Ground Rules for Appraisal Interviewers*

Robert Hoppock

Much of the current skepticism about the value of the appraisal interview has its roots in the simple fact that good managers are not necessarily good counselors. Most men to whom this particular responsibility falls have to learn how to handle it—and what proficiency they achieve generally is acquired only through the painful and sometimes costly process of trial and error.

This learning process is further complicated by the volumes that have been written about appraisal in general. Indeed it is not surprising that, confronted as they are by an apparently unending torrent of advice on the subject, many managers should now have the feeling that conducting an appraisal interview is some esoteric art that they will never be able to master.

In actual fact, any manager with a reasonable degree of sensitivity for the feelings of others and a genuine desire to help his subordinates develop can conduct an effective appraisal by following a few simple and straightforward principles. Here they are:

1. *Before you discuss the man, discuss the job.* You and he may have different ideas about the exact nature of his responsibilities. If you have a short, written job description, review it together to see if it needs revision. If you do not have one, ask him such questions as these:

What are *all* the things you do on your job?
Which do you think are the most important?
Which take most of your time?
Are there ways in which you think we could use your talents and your time more profitably?
Do we agree on what your job is?
Do we agree on the standards by which your performance should be appraised?

2. *Ask him before you tell him.* When you are ready to review a man's strengths and weaknesses, ask him to tell you what he thinks he has done well and what he would like to do better. He can criticize himself more readily than he can accept criticism from you. In fact, he may judge himself more severely than you would judge him.

You may find some of the following questions useful:

* Reprinted by permission of the publisher from *Personnel*, May/June, 1961. © 1961 by the American Management Association, Inc.

What do you think are your greatest strengths?

Where do you feel less competent?

Do you feel that you are growing more competent or less as time goes by? In what ways? How? Why?

Have you been doing anything that you hope will increase your competence in any way?

Is there any way in which you think that I, or someone else, could help you to make yourself more valuable to the company?

Do I do anything that makes your job harder?

3. *Listen.* The effectiveness of your interview will increase with your understanding of the man you are counseling. If you talk when he wants to talk, you may miss some of the best opportunities you will ever have to find out what makes him tick.

Of course, listening is more than a matter of just keeping silent while the other fellow talks. How you hear his words and how you respond to them do much to determine what he will say in the course of the interview. There are at least four levels of listening:

You remain silent but you ignore what he is saying because you are thinking what *you* will say next.

You pay attention but say nothing in response except "uh-huh."

You occasionally summarize in your own words what you think he has been trying to tell you. This gives him a chance to correct any misunderstanding. Moreover, by assuring him that you consider him important enough to listen to, it encourages him to go on talking.

You try to detect the feeling behind what he is saying. If strong feelings are present, you put them into words. Thus you might respond by saying, "You are a little anxious about what is going to happen to you" or "You feel pretty bitter about this" or "That gives you a real sense of achievement."

The more accurately you can recognize his feelings and the more calmly you can accept them, the better will be your chance of helping him tell you what is really of most importance to him.

4. *If the subordinate appraises himself more favorably than you appraise him, invite him to tell you why.* Then, if you still disagree, restate his self-appraisal. Be sure you understand it. Let him see that you want to consider his judgment as well as your own and that you think his feelings are important even if you must disagree. Review, and state, the points on which you do agree. Then discuss your differences.

5. *In appraising a man's mistakes,* consider the number of mistakes in proportion to the number of decisions he had to make; consider how much freedom he was given to act on his own judgment; and try to recall

his performance over a long period of time. In comparing the mistakes of two men, consider the relative difficulty of the tasks assigned to them.

6. *Try not to be unduly influenced by things that affect your feelings but not otherwise affect a man's value to the company.* Among these might be such sources of bias as the following:

You are a clean-desk man. His desk is always cluttered.

You and he share certain interests in work or recreation.

He has some mannerisms that annoy you though they do not seem to annoy anyone else.

You are always punctual. He is usually a little late, though he makes it up by working overtime.

You are aggressive. He is submissive.

Remember that you are trying to help men to develop *themselves*, so that they can give the company the best that *they* have to offer. You are not trying to remake your subordinates in your own image. Remember Billy Sunday's advice to parents: "If the Lord had wanted two of you, He would have made you twins."

7. *When you must criticize, criticize the man's performance, not the man himself.* He may be able to change his performance. It is doubtful whether he can do much about changing himself.

8. *If you are partly at fault, admit it.* He may become more willing to admit his mistake if you admit yours.

9. *Never discuss another employee with him.* Unfavorable comparisons cannot be kept confidential. They always leak.

10. *If you want cooperation, do not undertake a performance interview too soon after a disciplinary interview.*

11. *Do not discuss salary or promotion during the performance appraisal.* Such discussion may be interpreted as a commitment. Instead, focus on helping the man improve his competence in his present job.

12. *It is not necessary that you agree on everything.* When you cannot agree, try to state your position and his so that each of you understands the other. Then tell him that you will continue to think about what he has said, and ask him to think about what you have said.

13. *Be yourself.* Do not try to copy someone else's counseling methods if they do not make sense to you. Experiment until you find out how to conduct an interview in which both you and your subordinate can relax and be yourselves. You will get nowhere so long as you are both putting up a front.

14. *Don't try to do too much.* Unless you are unusually skillful or lucky, some goals will generally be beyond you. Four in particular are seldom attained:

You cannot make an unfavorable appraisal a happy experience.
You cannot make a suspicious man trustful.
You cannot make a belligerent man cooperative.
You cannot make a defensive man self-critical.

15. *If the subordinate is really deficient and must be corrected, here are four things you can do:*

Let him know exactly where he stands. Otherwise, he may suspect that your appraisal is worse than it actually is.

Point out that if you didn't think he could become a satisfactory employee you wouldn't be keeping him on the payroll.

Tell him what you think he can do to improve.

If he shows any desire to improve, offer him your help.

16. *For your good men, here are five things you can do:*
Identify the men that you feel sure are potential managers or top-level specialists, and put their identification on the record.

Let them know that you recognize and appreciate what they are doing for the company.

Invite each man to tell you how he would like to develop himself, and what help he would like from you.

Help him along these lines to the extent of your ability.

17. *It is more important to develop strength than to correct weakness.* Successful companies are run not by little paragons who have corrected all their faults but by well-balanced teams of able men, each of whom has his own weaknesses.

Your job is not to produce supermen. Your job is to discover talent and develop it.

42. Staff Evaluations: A Key to More Effective Performance*

Earl W. Wolfe

Evaluation of the worker in terms of his progress and in relation to the agency's standards of performance places upon the supervisor one of the most difficult responsibilities of his job.

The typical supervisor approaches the evaluation conference with dread and breathes a sigh of relief when it's over. He will be the first to affirm that the evaluation is an essential part of the supervisory process, but concurrently with his affirmation, he will deplore the experience itself. There is a wide range of reasons for such feelings—extending from the psychological conditioning which makes it hard for the supervisor to evaluate the work of another human being to uncertainty as to what the job really entails.

EXAMINING EVALUATION

What is it that makes evaluation different from other aspects of supervision? Are evaluations really necessary? How can evaluations be used constructively in development of the worker and performance of the job? What happens if the evaluation is made hastily and artificially? When should evaluations be made? What part should the worker play in his evaluation?

These and many other questions occupy the supervisor's mind as he examines this part of supervision. He may gain comfort in knowing that he is not alone in his dread and uncertainty.

Before public welfare programs appeared on the scene, the necessity for evaluating workers arose only rarely; when the occasion did arise, the evaluation was usually a subjective appraisal of the worker's personality and behavior. With the development of governmental responsibility for financial distance, the large number of workers employed and the accountability of the public agencies made it mandatory to make decisions on the quality of the workers' performance and usefulness to the agency.

Development of merit systems for recruiting, employing, retaining and dismissing staff insured values to both the agency and workers. However, it was necessary to measure qualifications, performance, and progress against some standards; otherwise, the merit system would have been weak and ineffectual, since subjectivity would have continued to be the decisive element.

* From *Journal of Rehabilitation*, July–August, 1960, pp. 19–22, 37. Reprinted by permission.

314

In recent years, practically all social agencies have integrated evaluations with other supervisory and administrative processes.

The evaluation process may be defined as that part of supervision which measures the quality of a worker's performance against the agency's requirements of the worker. It should not be confused with or separated from the supervisory process as a whole.

Evaluation of performance takes place continuously in the individual conference which is the primary medium for supervisory help. The evaluation conference is the summation of all the individual supervisory conferences over a stated period of time. It is an appraisal of the worker's performance on the total job over this period—where he was at the beginning, what progress he has made, where he is now—and a plan for the next steps in supervision.

The evaluation conference focuses on goals set for improving the worker's performance. Periodically, the supervisor and worker must take stock of the latter's progress, the supervisor's effectiveness in helping him, and what is necessary for future development.

Any progressive agency must continually ask itself: "Where are we now, and where do we go from here?" The services of an agency are no better than the staff through which they are administered. Therefore, it is mandatory that each staff member periodically undergo this inventory, keeping in mind that he exists as a worker for no other reason than to render effective services as an agency representative.

SUPERVISOR'S PURPOSE

The supervisor's purpose in evaluation is to take stock of the worker's performance over a stated period, to note the progress during the period, to point out areas where the worker needs help for future development, and to measure the supervisor's effectiveness and give him direction for future emphasis. The worker's purpose in evaluation is to see where he stands in relation to what is expected of him, and to point up where he needs to place more effort in the future.

Agencies must examine the quality of their services consistently. In doing this, the agencies must know the quality of performance of each worker, and what can be done to maintain or improve that performance. Agencies vary as to the time of evaluations, but there are distinct advantages in making them at regular intervals. This provides a framework within which the worker and supervisor can place their goals.

The worker must know that his performance will be measured, as well as the purpose of such evaluation. He must also know when such evaluations will occur and how they are related to other agency processes.

Some supervisors feel that an evaluation is too threatening for a worker until some experience with the agency is gained. However, the commencement of evaluation depends on what the supervisor thinks about evaluations, the agency's purpose in evaluating workers, and the methods used. If the agency has a negative attitude toward evaluations, it is likely that the supervisee, whether new or experienced, will also negate them.

Efficient administration of agency services necessitates realistic standards which are high enough to provide incentive, yet low enough to be attainable.

However, these standards can not be rigid or static. Rehabilitation counseling is a profession which is constantly learning, testing, re-formulating, discarding, and implementing ideas. As a result, thinking and practice change, and what is considered good practice today may be antiquated tomorrow.

This results in a fluidity of standards and change in content and method of the job. For this reason, workers must always know what the agency expects at any given time. A worker's performance must always be directly related to the standards, and both must be kept fluid and flexible in accord with the times.

Standard-setting and evaluation are complicated by the intangible components of feelings, attitudes, and relationships. It is a simple matter to measure the number of rehabilitations against a set figure, but quite another matter to measure the effect of a worker's attitudes in adminis-tering services.

ONLY THE BEGINNING

Understanding the standard on the part of the worker and supervisor is only the beginning. The supervisee's performance in the first month of work, even though excelling that expected of a beginning worker, is not adequate a few months later. His progress will be determined by many factors, such as effectiveness of supervision, his native ability, understanding of his job, motives in working at this particular job, and satisfactions obtained at each step in work performance.

An individual who has accepted responsibility for supervision must also accept the responsibility for evaluation of the worker. He may feel guilty about judging another person's work, or he may rationalize that evaluations are not worth the effort. He may paint a rosy picture of the mediocre performance, or he may excuse poor work on the basis of the worker's effort.

On the other hand, he may compensate for his insecurity by being overly critical, by denying the worker's right to participation, or by evaluating his personality and behavior. Still others may approach the process calmly and with confidence, feeling secure in the relationship to the worker, job knowledge, and agency standards.

If he cannot accept the full responsibility for evaluation there is reason to question his readiness for supervision, as one cannot be separated from the other.

It has been pointed out that evaluation is an integral part of supervision. Someone once said that evaluation is to supervision what diagnosis is to to casework. It must be continuous, purposeful, and based on mutual understanding. Every supervisory conference must contain some evaluative elements, as it is necessary to appraise the quality of work in every conference, with reference to how the job is being done.

Evaluations are often difficult for both supervisor and worker because they have not been adequately prepared for them. It is essential that both understand the purpose, method, content, and emotional aspects of evaluations. In addition, there must be sufficient time for preparation and agreement on method and content between supervisor and worker.

The supervisor who holds an evaluation "off the cuff" and the worker who is merely waiting to see what the supervisor has to say about him will often set up defense mechanisms to affirm the rightness of their actions. Although both should be sufficiently aware of the other's performance to discuss it at any time, the evaluation is too important to approach in a "hit or miss" fashion.

From the time he begins work, the supervisee must know how the evaluation will be used. There have been instances of workers being released in a period of staff curtailment when they were not aware that evaluations could be used for that purpose. The positive aspects of evaluations should be stressed, but this also requires positive *use* of them.

ACTIVE PARTICIPATION

The supervisor and worker must know how to make adequate preparation for active and purposeful participation in the evaluation conference. The supervisor will derive much of his information from case records, supervisory conferences, and statistical reports; if he cannot read all of a worker's cases, he should make use of a block reading plan.

Reading a number of cases helps the supervisor answer many evaluation questions, such as whether a certain attitude or method was typical or exceptional. Was the worker spending most of his time on a few interesting cases to the neglect of others? Did he transfer what he learned from one case to another? Were clients generally difficult or defensive?

If supervisory conferences have been concerned with the worker's performance and trends in his work, the conferences will have evaluative connotations. The evaluation conference then becomes a logical step in the supervisory process when the supervisor and worker can sum up the content of supervisory conferences during the period, determine progress made, consider where the worker is at the moment, redefine goals, and outline next steps.

There are varied opinions as to whether the supervisor should review the worker's past evaluations. However, this should present no problem to the mature and capable supervisor who has grasped the full implications of evaluations. Just as the case record reveals both the client and the worker, so evaluation reveals the supervisor as well as the supervisee. The supervisor who goes to the worker's past evaluations wants to know not only what has been the quality of his work, but what has been done to help him develop.

Preparation for the evaluation conference is also imperative on the part of the worker. Not only must he know the purpose, content, method, and emotional aspects of evaluations, but he must examine his own attitudes and motives, using previous supervisory conferences as a springboard to thoughtful and purposeful preparation.

If he is defensive, he will also have been defensive about previous case discussions. If he sees the evaluation only as a form of grade, it is likely that he has seen casework in terms of what values it has for him. If he is a worker who feels that his performance is top-notch, he will have indicated such feeling in previous conference participation.

If he has an excuse for every error, he will have tried to justify what he has done in each individual case. If he is bored with the evaluation, he is likely to have been bored with supervisory conferences.

How has the supervisor dealt with his attitudes and feelings prior to the evaluation conference? If he has avoided them, he bears a large portion of the responsibility for lack of progress and should do a little self-analysis of his own.

An outline of points to be considered in the evaluation is often helpful, since it is difficult for the worker to look at his total job objectively.

It is sometimes helpful for the worker to write down his self-evaluation, which requires provocative thinking, objectivity, and actual involvement in the evaluation process. This is revealing to the supervisor as to attitudes, areas of resistance, particular interests, help needed, and capacity for self-evaluation. The worker should share in selection of case material and method to be used in the evaluation conference.

The evaluation conference period should be confined to the evaluation, rather than being sandwiched in between regular conference material. Neither the supervisor nor the worker should feel rushed, for points which are of sufficient importance for evaluation are equally important for discussion. As in other aspects of the supervisory process, a professional relationship is essential here. Performance measurement is not based on whether a supervisor likes the worker, dislikes him, or feels sorry for him, but rather on an objective appraisal, with the supervisor using his best judgment in reference to standards. To determine how the conference can be most effective, the supervisor must use all he knows about a worker. If the worker is modest about his strengths, the supervisor will conduct the conference in a different way from one held with a worker who makes special efforts to avoid criticism. Remember, however, that regular supervisory conferences set the tone for the evaluation conference.

Supervisors and workers have varied feelings about evaluations. Some supervisors are afraid of the authoritative aspects of their job. Others are unable to internalize the agency's standards and thus cannot realistically and honestly measure the worker's performance against them. Still others may have a need to compete with the worker and feel that too high an evaluation is threatening them. The supervisor must have sufficient self-awareness to examine his feelings, attitudes, and motives, seeking help if it is needed.

WORKER'S FEELINGS

Equally important are the worker's feelings about evaluations. He may see the supervisor as the all-wise parent who can do no wrong. He may resist authoritative tones and see the supervisor as the punishing parent who has a need to find fault. He may hearken back to "report card" days when he proudly displayed his grades or cunningly contrived means to explain receipt of poor marks.

The supervisor must take into consideration the worker's feelings about evaluations, attitudes toward authority, desire for help, ability to participate, and also determine how he can be helped to perform more effectively. If agencies can enable staff members to see that authority is "authority of the job" rather than "authority of the person," they will have made giant strides toward constructive relationships.

Both supervisor and worker may be ambivalent about the evaluation, and both should be helped to realize and consider such two-way feelings.

Not only must the worker prepare for evaluation, but he must participate responsibly in the evaluation conference. The supervisor should help him to participate to the extent of his capacity. It may be destructive to expect him to participate beyond his ability, which imposes upon the supervisor a responsibility to know the maturity, capacities, attitudes, and needs of the individual.

Genevieve F. Miner has written a helpful article, "Techniques of Mutual Evaluation," which deals with worker participation. She points out that the worker should be helped to express his feelings about the effectiveness of supervision. In a healthy supervisor-worker relationship, the former will seek to determine wherein he has not been helpful and honestly examine the reasons. This may require changes in his methods, content, or even possibly his own attitudes.

The worker should be helped to express disagreements and opposing viewpoints, just as the supervisor will be articulate when he does not concur with the worker's opinion of his performance.

Some supervisors avoid hurting the worker and pass over difficult areas. Since there may be some pain in learning and growth, the supervisor may take comfort in facing such areas honestly with a desire to help. Opposing viewpoints must be brought into the open and discussed freely and objectively. If a point of agreement cannot be reached, the worker has a right to have his viewpoint entered in the evaluation report, along with that of the supervisor.

Although the content of the evaluation will depend on the particular job, certain items are basic to the evaluation in any social agency setting:

Capacity to be a responsible agency representative—knowledge of the agency, its functions and structure; and identification with the agency in the community;

Ability to work with people in such a way as to convey the worker's sincerity, warmth, and desire to help them;

Skills pertinent to the particular job, including capacity for interviewing, diagnosing, and recording.

The supervisor must establish an orderly relationship of the part to the whole. This requires that he approach each individual situation with a determination to learn from it all that it may reveal of total functioning.

Supervisors must learn to seek in each individual case implications of problems—existing or emerging—in the work of the supervisee, in order that such knowledge may be applied in training and supervision of the total load. It is necessary for supervisors to look for trends, rather than merely what happens in an isolated bit of performance.

One of the most important principles of evaluation is that the supervisor evaluates the work, not the worker. In earlier years, supervisors spent much time studying the personality and behavior of the worker as an individual. If personal problems are interfering with performance, the worker must decide what he wants to do in view of the fact that the total job is not being done. Evaluation must include the total job, with appropriate emphasis on both the positive and negative aspects.

Remember that the evaluation is not an end in itself; it is worthless unless it contributes to job performance. Furthermore, negative criticism should not be made unless accompanied by an attempt to help, or by suggested remedies.

Evaluation reports fall into three categories: oral, narrative, and chart. Some agencies use only oral reports, and others use only narrative. In still other agencies, it is considered essential to use a written evaluation and a chart in order for the agency to have some comparative basis for making salary increases, demotions, promotions, dismissals, etc.

A narrative alone cannot be used comparatively. Narratives are more conducive to subjectivity. Nobody has found a chart which is entirely satisfactory because it is hard to measure degrees of skill. The disadvantage of using a chart is that the worker thinks about score and fails to concentrate on strength and weakness. A chart plus a narrative are considered most effective by many agencies.

Evaluations should be based on present, rather than anticipated, performance. Because a worker is exerting unusual effort, a supervisor may be lax in measuring the present job. He is correct in recognizing the effort, but premature in determining that the goal has already been attained.

OPINIONS DIFFER

Conflicting opinions exist as to whether the worker should read the written evaluation. Although the written word is cold, nothing belongs in the report which cannot be discussed with the supervisee. Certainly, the worker gains confidence in the supervisor when he knows that all his cards are on the table. However, it is a bit fallacious for the supervisor to say or think that the worker knows everything which has been said about him, for in listening he may not have heard.

If an adjective description is formed from the total evaluation, the terms must be understandable by all concerned, and of such a nature as to approximate uniformity. For example, ten supervisors may have a different concept of the meaning of "excellent." Also the supervisor and supervisee may attach quite different meanings.

It is preferable to use such terms as "unsatisfactory," "approaching standard," "standard," and "above standard." These terms are easily understood when the standard is known.

There must be continuity of evaluations, with one related to the other. At times, it is helpful to compare all the evaluations to see where the worker was at the beginning and how far he has come. As evaluations ensue, there should be increasing capacity for self-evaluation on the part of the worker and continued focusing on next steps.

At each evaluation conference, the worker should know that he will have opportunities for further discussion, and there should be planning for follow-up on areas of needed help. This also means the supervisor may learn that he needs help in order to make his supervision more effective, and implies that he will take appropriate steps to obtain it.

Evaluations may be used as a force in the agency's knowledge of itself and as a basis of staff development plans. In most agencies, these evaluations are a contributing factor in salary increases, promotions, demotions, and dismissals. Reference letters are written from evaluation records that are retained by the agency, which means that the evaluation is not obliterated when the worker leaves the agency.

Of all the ramifications of the evaluation, the element of most value is the teaching-learning process which goes on between supervisor and worker. Principal goals are the supervisee's increased capacity for self-evaluation and ability to function more effectively on the job.

In this frame of reference, the supervisor and worker can approach evaluations positively and constructively, with less fear and dread, and keep their sights trained on the client and ways in which the agency can be of maximum service to him.

43. The Indispensable Man*

Irving Paster

The director of an advertising agency recently telephoned the writer to complain that:

His very best copywriter had taken three days' vacation and had not appeared for work on the morning when the vacation had ended. He did not call in until 3:00 P.M. that day—two hours before quitting time. Since the director was on the telephone when he called, the employee had relayed the message through a colleague. His excuse for his failure to report: He had been delayed by motor trouble and would be in the following day. The director was upset. He wanted to know why the employee had not called in the morning so that arrangements could be made to cover his work. Secondly, he wanted to know why he did not appear at 3:00 P.M.—since he was in town that day—to handle what work was left even if he had to work that evening to complete it. A discussion of the problem showed that first, the employee was an outstanding copywriter and secondly, he had frequently violated work rules in the past but had never been disciplined.

When asked why he had not disciplined the employee for previous violations, the director replied, "If I reprimand him, he'll quit and I can't afford to lose one of my best men."

Are there really indispensable men? Of course, there are many individuals of such high caliber and capacity that their contributions cannot be matched. They are unique. But indispensable?

Most employers will tell you that when their "best" men leave, the business continues to operate efficiently. Other men, they say, are found, although they may not perform at the same level as those they replaced.

A little probing, however, will show that many employers bend over backward to make exceptions for some of their employees whom they regard as irreplaceable. They allow them to break the rules, overlook temperamental outbursts and, in effect, discriminate in their favor. Although they know that uniform enforcement of personnel policies is vital to proper administration, exceptions are made because of the employees' outstanding abilities.

HOW DOES SUCH A SITUATION ARISE?

In many large organizations, top management is often unaware of situations in which lower levels of management discriminate in favor of the "indispensable man" until the problem becomes acute. Foremen, for

* From *Personnel Journal*, Vol. 49, No. 3 (March, 1970), 246–49. Reprinted by permission.

example, may hesitate to discipline the unusually high producers. They may permit such favored employees to violate rules either by ignoring such violations or justifying them. They may "bend" seniority and other labor contract provisions for their "favorite sons." Some managers have an unreasonable fear of disciplining or terminating an employee for violations of company rules. They prefer to live with the situation rather than face the employee and call him to account for his actions. This, of course, is an emotional problem of the manager, not to be confused with that of supervising employees.

If there is no formalized, effective recruitment policy, a manager is naturally hesitant about letting an exceptionally qualified worker go, even though he acts as though the rules were made for him to break. Then, again, a supervisor may not be certain about how far he can go in disciplining employees without running into trouble, or, if the company is unionized, because he doesn't know how the union will react.

The idea that if all but one of the employees obey a rule, then the rule must be a good one is open to question. Sometimes an unusually capable worker will flaunt a rule because it seems an unreasonable one —to the employee, that is, as the following illustration indicates.

You sit down for a talk with the office manager, Helen Smith. She has been on the job for some time and has mastered all of its intricacies. She's happy in her work, but there is one irritant: the problem of Marian, the telephone operator-receptionist. The rest of the office staff keeps the specified, regular hours of 9 to 5, but Marian doesn't think they apply to her. She likes to start her weekends early on Friday; when her dentist or doctor appointments conflict with her working hours, she comes in late; she's never available for overtime. When she's on the job, she's excellent: messages are always clear and concise and the customers find her efficient and pleasant.

After Marian had made a place for herself in the office and the company indicated it was happy about her performance, she announced to Helen that if her irregular hours were interfering with the office operations, she would gladly resign and train a replacement. She knew, of course, that it would be hard to replace her. Helen knows that the rest of the employees feel Marian is getting away with murder and they don't like it. She admitted that she didn't know how to act in this situation so she put off doing anything about it to the detriment of the office morale.

WHERE CAN SUCH A SITUATION ARISE?

This problem can be found almost anywhere in business and industry. The size of the enterprise may be something of a factor, however. If there are a large number of employees, one or two indispensable men may not be too important. The president's brother-in-law may irritate the people in his department, but the sheer number of employees in the enterprise minimizes his influence. But the brother-in-law who is argumentative and inconsiderate of fellow employees and throws his weight around in a small company can pose a real problem.

WHO IS INVOLVED?

The individual who regards himself as indispensable and lets it be widely known, can be a blue or white collar worker—an executive, a professional or the boss himself. For example, Mr. Walters owns and runs a small manufacturing plant. He has told his wife who is to take over the business when he departs this planet. She knows who will be responsible for factory management, sales, accounting, labor relations, etc. when Mr. W. is no longer there. And there is Mr. Jones who runs an enterprise for a major conglomerate. He has designated three key employees to run the business if anything happens to him. And he has notified the home office exactly what should be done and who should do it when he leaves.

Contrast these two men with another executive, Mr. Braun, who runs a branch plant. He keeps all the plant's decision-making responsibilities for himself. His key men are told that when any problems arise, he must be informed promptly so that he can decide what should be done. Although he realizes that he should have a second in command, after ten years of looking, he's failed to find anyone to suit him. He's young, intelligent, hardworking and filled with self-confidence, but has no confidence in other people. Top management is delighted with his performance now, but will it still feel that way if he leaves without having someone trained to take over his spot?

WHAT ARE THE EFFECTS?

Employees who watch the indispensable man "get away with it," resent what they consider unfair, discriminatory treatment. Their reactions may range from a drop in both quality and quantity of their work to outright sabotage. If nothing is done to correct the situation, these people are an excellent target for union organizers. One such organizer has succinctly stated the union position on such a matter. After having commented on how employers "protect" themselves against a union, he concluded by saying:

My next advice would be to terminate any foreman or supervisor who plays favorites with the employees under his jurisdiction. To punish one employee for an infraction of plant rules, and ignore violation of others; to require a full eight hours' work from one employee and allow some of his fellow workers to get by with half-hearted work, is to invite a labor union into the plant. Foremen who play favorites organize more employees for me than I could ever organize through my own efforts.[1]

Once a plant is organized, the union representative will move quickly if he feels there is an "indispensable man" in the bargaining unit. Such an employee becomes the subject of a grievance which may be carried through to arbitration unless something is done about it. The labor reporting services cite many awards by arbitrators who have directed employers who discriminate in favor of particular workers to cease such activities forthwith.

Indispensable men are costly and the employer should ask himself whether such people are worth it. Does the cost of permitting an employee to behave as he pleases offset what he contributes because of his unusually high productivity? How much is the productivity of the other employees affected? Will any of the other employees leave because one or more people are given preferential treatment? If the answers are in the affirmative, what are the alternatives?

Assuming that the indispensable man in question is one without whom the company can not get along, can't something be done to set him apart from his co-workers? A private office, a secretary, a title, for example? These and some other accoutrements" would tell the other employees that he is being given special treatment because he makes a special contribution to the success of the enterprise. He might also be assigned a special job or project. Obviously, his fellow workers must clearly understand the situation and accept the fact that he deserves special consideration.

Corrective discipline is another possibility—a stiff warning will sometimes work, but with many people it is not the answer. Take, for example, the case of Bill Walker, a fine tool and die maker who works for Harry Jones. Bill lives about sixteen miles away from his work and is frequently late. When he does show up, his work is of fine quality. Harry hates the thought of trying to replace him because good tool and die makers are hard to come by. But the other fifty employees are expected to get to work on time and they are disciplined when they are consistently late. Harry would like to do something about the situation, but feels that if he puts any pressure on Bill, he'd quit since he can easily get a job elsewhere. This problem was one discussed at a recent business administration seminar. As the meeting closed, Harry remarked, "I'm going to fire that guy!" But will he? And isn't there perhaps a better way to resolve the problem?

Ordinarily, discharging an indispensable man is difficult. To be sure

[1] Comments of a union organizer as quoted by S. Maynard Smith, Atlanta attorney, in a speech before the Southern States Industrial Relations Conference, Birmingham, Alabama.

of arriving at the right decision, an employer should ask himself the right questions. Here are some of them.

EMPLOYER CONSIDERATIONS

Have you discussed the problem with the favored employee?

Have you discussed the problem with the employees who are affected?

What are the alternative solutions and what problems would follow corrective action?

Have you given any thought as to whether you are handling this problem along the lines of Theory X or Theory Y?

Is there something wrong with your recruiting, selection, or training policies? Do you actually have such policies?

What is the reason for having delayed action so long? How did the situation develop and why did you allow it to develop? Will a similar situation develop again? What action should you take to prevent it from happening again?

What bearing do your behavior, personal opinions, and prejudices, have on the handling of this problem?

Have you established a personnel policy which is being administered consistently with this one exception?

Does your failure to enforce work rules consistently show a weakness in management? What is this weakness?

SITUATION FACTORS

How serious is the problem? Is it serious enough for action to be taken by the company?

Are the rules clear? Unambiguous? Do the employees know the effects of breaking the rules on employee morale and productivity? Do the rules fit the existing work and social environment? Are they expressed simply so that all employees understand them? Do the employees know the rules? Are the rules arbitrary or are they reasonably necessary for the operation of the enterprise?

Do the employees regard the employee's behavior as a threat or do they accept it without resentment?

Is there some situation in the organization framework which leads an employee, otherwise exceptionally capable, to flaunt the rules?

Should operations be changed so that the employee can adhere to the rules and thus, no exception to be made?

Are there circumstances in which the rules may be broken and the employee still be retained? What are these circumstances?

EMPLOYEE CONSIDERATION

Does the employee's performance and importance to the company merit favoritism?

Will allowing him to take certain liberties lead to his taking additional ones and thus make the situation worse?

Does the employee have an emotional problem which leads to the deviate behavior? Can it be alleviated? Cured? Is the employee aware of his problem?

44. Solving the Problem of Staff Turnover*

John E. Horejsi

Recently an administrator of public welfare remarked that it is inevitable that welfare offices will continue to be plagued with a high rate of worker turnover. "To say it's a symptom of the times in which we live or it's correlated with the economic cycle is not to offer useful advice. Yet the problem can be attacked, not merely accepted."[1] The fact is, if the worker cannot achieve and grow psychologically in the job he holds, he will go elsewhere. It is my contention that excessive worker turnover can be substantially reduced by emphasizing changes in administrative styles and by using enrichment and motivation techniques with welfare workers.

The challenge, as I see it, is to improve the effectiveness of people. In order to improve effectiveness, the welfare executive will have to develop new insights into what staff needs and wants. He will have to be willing to avail himself of new ideas and motivation techniques as a means of improving overall administrative effectiveness.

PARTICIPATIVE MANAGEMENT

The welfare leadership will have to discover, just as private industry managers have discovered, that, in many jobs, productivity can be increased by applying what is called "participative management" and "job enrichment." The ideas are so new that only a handful of companies have tried them. "Professor Douglas McGregor of M.I.T. developed the concept of 'participative management' which is based on Maslow's hierarchy of human needs. This advanced theory of leadership advocates giving workers greater freedom, greater responsibility, and giving more consideration to their nonfinancial needs."[2]

Worker participation in planning changes in their job routines and in deciding how they will perform their work vastly enriches worker morale. When the worker is given the opportunity to come up with his own answers instead of being told what to do, the results show an increase in production, better quality of work, and greater effectiveness of workers.

The executive must be willing to stake his agency's future on the belief that ordinary people have great potentiality for growth and will

* From *Public Welfare Journal*, Vol. XXIX, No. 4 (Fall, 1971), 455–61. Reprinted by permission.
1 Robert N. Ford, *Motivation Through Work Itself* (New York: American Management Association, Inc., 1969), p. 79.

2 Earl Nightingale, "Freedom Works Wonders," *Our Changing World*, The Earl Nightingale Program, March 25, 1971, Script 2803. KMOX Radio, St. Louis, Missouri.

perform far better if they are trusted with important responsibilities. The public welfare administrator needs to consider ways and means of involving workers and giving them greater responsibility. He must not be so autocratic that all sense of importance is denied except to those at the top. In most instances, workers want to be permitted to decide on matters in which they feel competent, and they want guidance or leadership in situations which make them feel insecure. For example, a worker found to be doing a job in an obviously inefficient and wasteful manner said, "We all know it's stupid, but they won't listen to us." Although it is impossible to allow everyone to work his own way, it should be possible to combine efforts to be more effective and productive with a certain amount of freedom.

CONTROL THE PROCESS, NOT THE WORKER

Ordway Tead describes the worker's plight when he says that the worker craves an opportunity to become enthusiastic about his work, but he has only a small job in a huge undertaking in which the supervisor wants to tell him how to carry out each step in a modest assignment. This, he said, can be the final blow.[3] Our present approach, which too often constitutes over-supervision, can be very devastating to worker morale. The use of consultants would considerably alleviate most serious problems associated with oversupervision. It would create an environment in which the worker could pursue his work free from unnecessary interference and controls. He would be allowed the fullest amount of discretion consistent with capabilities and then judged on the basis of his results. The welfare administrator would assume the role of controlling the process, not one of controlling and directing workers.

Essentially, the time has come for the welfare department to realize that it will be cheaper to enrich workers' jobs than to pay the price of excessive staff turnover. Failure to embrace new ideas, largely because of agency inertia, represents a costly proposition as workers become increasingly alienated from their jobs. The young person now entering the welfare agency as an employee is eager to become involved. Essentially, it is the leadership task of the administrative staff to create conditions in which the new employee is given a chance to become involved.

Time reports an interesting example of increased productivity in private industry where workers were involved and given a chance to participate: "When the workers asked for pay raises, management suggested that the money would have to be saved before this could be done. Within three weeks the employees found ways to save the company more than twice as much chiefly by cutting purchasing and material costs and

---

[3] In Felix A. Nigro, *Public Personnel Administration* (New York: Henry Holt and Company, 1959), p. 367.

altering production procedures to trim waste."[4] The welfare office with its seemingly endless number of forms, procedures, and manuals filled with expense-producing regulations, policies, and procedures represents fertile ground for workers to help make decisions about changes that would cut cost and improve effectiveness of production and quality.

We have unique examples of this involvement, hard work, and commitment of staff during disaster periods: when water pipes froze and burst at the Pruitt-Igoe Housing Compelx, a crisis occurred in which families lost all their food and furniture and were forced out of their apartments onto the street: during the teamster strike more than 90,000 persons were suddenly out of work and demanded food stamps for their families. The amount of food stamps issued more than doubled in a few short weeks. During both of these crises, staff had to work largely on their own (that is, without the usual direction and control) and were given additional responsibility. Through the use of group interviewing techniques and of the client's own involvement in filling out required forms, the workers became highly productive and committed. However, this productivity and commitment dropped off tremendously as the crisis came to an end and normal bureaucratic routines became reestablished.

From the motivation standpoint, Robert N. Ford says, in an emergency situation "the employee feels he is truly needed; he knows that the community needs him and his services. His chance of personal achievement is great and immediately measurable. (Service is desperately needed and it is provided by the worker.) Many day-to-day rules are laid aside during the emergency; employees typically have more freedom of decision. Individual responsibility is more clearly defined. These are the elements of any good job: a chance to be truly responsible and accountable, to achieve, and to be recognized for what one has done. The challenge for a supervisor is to transfer these motivating elements into the everyday job situation and to see that they are not lost completely when the naturally interesting situation is ended."[5]

The challenge is to find ways of putting responsibility, challenge, and involvement back into workers' jobs by providing the machinery and responsibility to question procedures, to influence decisions, and to help determine how the job will be performed. Chris Argyris reports that lagging production was corrected in one company by bringing the workers into the solution of the problem instead of the "management hatchet men," as some of the workers labeled them. "Changes in this direction led to marked increases in quality and productivity . . . as well

4 "The Blue Collar Worker's Lowdown Blues," *Time* (November 9, 1970), 74.
5 Robert N. Ford, *op. cit.*, p. 98.

as reduction in employee turnover from 18 percent to 6 percent a year and a lowering of absenteeism from 17 percent to 4 percent."[6]

HIGHER ORDER NEEDS

In order to realize enrichment goals, McGregor contends that Maslow's hierarchy of needs must be considered. Improved work effectiveness, motivation, and productivity must be derived from the satisfaction of what he calls "higher order" needs of self-esteem and self-fulfillment. Higher order needs are considered to be other than financial. Lower order needs are physical, financial, and social in nature. Workers attempt to satisfy lower order needs through their demands for pay increases, fringe benefits, seniority, improved working conditions, and so forth. The demands of the lower order are most vigorously pursued when administration fails to provide conditions in which the higher order needs are being met.[7]

When the welfare executive fails to consider the participation and involvement needs of his workers and overlooks enrichment possibilities, a long list of complaints usually develops. These complaints represent a plea for recognition that the individual has a contribution to make and is capable of assuming greater responsibility. According to Chris Argyris, "His thoughts are focused more on wages and working conditions than on self-realization. Once he accomplishes this, even increased benefits as a reward for productivity lose their power. Instead, they become mere compensation for his dissatisfaction."[8]

According to J. A. C. Brown, "constant demands for more money when wages are already adequate indicate either that the workers feel vague dissatisfaction without quite knowing why and think of money as an obvious solution, or else that they are aware of the causes of their discontent and are taking the attitude 'If you won't give us what we really need, you must pay us in the only way you seem to understand.' It is easily noted that, in the agency with poor morale, the workers continue to ask for more money. In other words, they feel that when conditions are unsatisfactory they deserve extra incentives to offset the disadvantages of their employment." In short, "administrators who neglect to consider the higher order needs of their workers pay a terrific price in low production, goofing off, absenteeism, high job turnover, and grievances."[9]

[6] Chris Argyris, "We Must Make Work Worthwhile," *Life*, Vol. 62 (May 5, 1967), 58.

[7] Douglas M. McGregor, "The Human Side of Enterprise." From *Adventure in Thought and Action.* Proceedings of the Fifth Anniversary Convocation of the School of Industrial Management, Massachusetts Institute of Technology (Cambridge, Mass.: Massachusetts Institute of Technology, June, 1957).

[8] Chris Argyris, *op. cit.*, p. 2.

[9] J. A. C. Brown, *The Social Psychology of Industry* (Baltimore: Penguin Books, 1958), pp. 202–203.

Frederick Hertzberg of Cleveland's Case Western Reserve University suggests that strikes are often welcomed by workers as relief from their mind-numbing jobs and could be drastically reduced. As Hertzberg puts it: "Administrators must get more men going home to their wives saying, 'Honey, do you know what I did today?' instead of 'Honey, do you know what they did to me today?' "[10] The most important consideration for the welfare executive to realize is that workers give less attention and energy to the satisfaction of lower order needs if the administrator addresses himself to the challenge of developing conditions in which the higher order nonfinancial growth needs of workers can be met.

"The importance of meeting nonfinancial growth needs of workers is supported by a study which identifies sources of job satisfaction and dissatisfaction which suggests that opportunities for growth and self-fulfillment are the essential requirement of both job satisfaction and high performance. It was found as reported by Hertzberg that the wants of workers divide into two groups. One group revolves around the need to develop in one's occupation as a source of personal growth. The second group is associated with fair treatment in compensation, supervision, working conditions, and administrative practices. The fulfillment of the needs of the second group of low order needs does not motivate the individual to high levels of job satisfaction and . . . to extra performance on the job. All we can expect from satisfying the second group of low order needs is the prevention of dissatisfaction and poor job performance."[11]

CONVENTIONAL VIEW

Excessive attention to the physical and security (financial) needs of workers stems from a conventional view of administration as to how to motivate workers (that is, get them committed to agency goals): they must be directed (that is, told what to do); they must be controlled (that is, made sure they do only what they are told to do); they must be rewarded (that is, offered praise, security, higher wages); they must be punished (that is, threatened, criticized, deprived of wage increases, discharged). Once control and restriction are begun, the need for extending them increases, and the situation gets worse rather than better.

Many of the welfare policies and practices reflect these assumptions. Certainly there is no better example than in the structure of the welfare office itself where by design, work is simplified and specialized so that it will be easier to plan, control, and direct. The responsibilities of workers involve carefully defined lines of command and subordination. The communication line is so long that information frequently becomes distorted

10 *Time, op. cit.,* 74.
11 Frederick Hertzberg, Bernard Mansner, and Barbara Block Snyderman. *The Motivation to Work* (New York: John Wiley and Sons, Inc., 1959), pp. 114–115.

before it reaches those who are in a position to take action, and, for the same reason, the workers' suggestions, grievances, and feelings on day-to-day matters come to be ignored. Too much emphasis is given to devising an organizational chart which defines and limits responsibility of the worker to a level well below his capabilities. The result is that administration by detail control and direction becomes a dominant pattern, and the agency becomes caught up in a defensive and compulsive type of administration that is considered unchangeable.

As a recent example, caseworkers without degrees who performed casework services very capably for several years were suddenly shifted to assistance payments assignments only. These workers were not permitted to be deployed to the service section when the duties of workers were separated by eligibility functions and services functions. It seems inconceivable that nondegree workers seeking goals to remain in services would be expected to further the goals of the agency after transfer to assistance payments work. The paradox is that so many of the degree workers forced into service had not wanted to transfer and had stated clearly they were not interested in service assignments. Under such circumstances, it is obvious that the performance of service staff and assistance payments staff will suffer to the detriment of the agency and its clients. Agency goals are given first consideration and if the workers' goals are considered at all, it is assumed that salary and/or promotion will satisfy them.

NEED FOR NEW FOCUS

The executive may ask, "Why are not people more productive? We pay satisfactory wages, provide decent working conditions, have good fringe benefits, and steady employment. Yet people do not seem to be willing to put forth more than minimum effort." McGregor contends this state of affairs continues to exist because the administrator continues to focus on financial security and physical needs.

What needs to be stressed here is that satisfied physical and security needs are not prime motivators of behavior. Salary, like air, has no appreciable motivating effect on the worker's behavior unless he is threatened with being deprived of it. For practical purposes, once lower order needs are met, they exist no longer. Trying to satisfy workers by meeting their lower order financial needs is not possible because of diminishing returns. When higher order psychological needs are met they continue to motivate and the law of diminishing returns will not apply.

As an example of diminishing returns as it applies to low order incentive, workers who get a higher rate of pay may be absent more because the need for money may have become secondary to the need for leisure.

When the physical security needs are met, the motivational shift of the worker will begin to focus on "higher order" social, ego, and self-fulfillment needs which have as their basis an altogether different set of assumptions about human behavior. These assumptions require that the administrator see his workers as representing a vast source of "untapped resources" and be aware that workers want to contribute, want to be consulted and recognized, and need to feel important.

In other words, social, ego, and self-fulfillment needs of workers must be viewed favorably as inducements for motivating workers. A good example is the administrator's alarm regarding closely knit work groups. There exists a tendency to overcontrol and direct them. This is unnecessary as studies have shown that tightly knit work groups are more effective than are the same number of separate workers. Under proper conditions, group tendencies of workers can work in favor of achieving agency goals.

EGO NEEDS

Just as important are the ego needs of workers that relate to the need for self-confidence, achievement, competence, recognition, respect, and appreciation. Attention to ego needs can result in a significant degree of effectiveness in eliminating dissatisfaction. Self-fulfillment needs, McGregor says: ". . . are the needs for realizing one's own potentialities, for continued self-development, for being creative in the broadest sense of the term."[12] McGregor stresses that self-fulfillment needs remain dormant unless lower order needs are reasonably satisfied. The desirability of creating a condition in which self-fulfillment needs can obtain expression and be dealt with by the administrator is unquestioned. However, the executive must be willing to accept the challenge that goes with it.

Basic to the challenge is that "it takes much delegation, job redesign, commitment to the concepts, and trust in what workers can really do, given the opportunity."[13] Careful study and evaluation of job content and attention to the better use of worker talent is required. The administrator will be faced with the choice of further fractionalizing the job to bring about greater efficiency or of putting the job together to provide greater challenge.

The real motivators of improved job performance and job satisfaction are centered in the work itself. The job can and should be restructured with the help and participation of the worker, so that the work can be improved and made more meaningful for him. Conditions of over-supervision and excessive controls are ineffective because both tend to limit performance.

12 Douglas M. McGregor, *op. cit.*, p. 276.
13 *Ibid.*

ENLARGE THE JOB

Agency leadership should not cut workers down to fit the job that needs to be filled; instead, jobs should be enlarged so that workers grow to fill them. Change the shape of the job and the level of worker satisfaction can be improved. If the worker is made to fit the job, the administrator can expect to perpetuate existing troubles and perhaps breed new ones. If the administrator decides that college level workers are actually needed, the job must be designed to challenge a college graduate's ability.

An excellent example of job fractionalizing occurs when the client, upon approval for public assistance by the intake worker, is transferred to the Work Incentive Unit, which assigns a Work Incentive Family Service Worker, an Assistance Payments Worker, an Employment Security Worker, and possibly a Day Care Worker. Consideration must be given to learning what this condition does to the worker as well as the client, to finding ways to change the traditional assembly line system and to putting complexity and challenge into the job by giving the worker responsibility for more aspects of the job.

The following four suggestions are only a few that Ford advocates to increase worker responsibility, learning, growth, recognition, and achievement:

1. Attempt to remove some controls without removing accountability.
2. Provide a worker with a whole unit of work.
3. Give the worker greater job freedom by giving him additional authority to decide.
4. Introduce new and more difficult tasks not previously handled.[14]

Perhaps the administrator should consider combining two or more related jobs. He will have to consider what happens before and after the worker does his part of the job. Ford suggests several ways to improve work itself:

1. See what the supervisor now does for the worker that he can do for himself once he (the supervisor) is sure the worker is competent.
2. Consider what steps that now precede his work should be part of his job if he is to have a more meaningful job.
3. Consider what steps that are now done after his work would make his job more meaningful and responsible.
4. Consider what tasks should be relocated to a job at a lower level.
5. Consider what the employee is permitted to do in an emergency or in the absence of his supervisor that he may be allowed to do all the time.
6. Consider whether there are any verifiers or checkers who might be dropped.[15]

14 Robert N. Ford, *op. cit.*, p. 208.
15 *Ibid.*, p. 29.

The "work itself" approach is an attempt to make workers' jobs as full as possible of responsibility and to provide a chance for achievement and for recognition. The theme is to build the worker's job so that it becomes more complete in its own right. Instead of relying only on his supervisor, the worker now has the authority to make decisions on his own. The changes in the work-itself approach, in addition to giving workers greater responsibility, provide the freedom and challenge necessary for self-development. More responsibility and control increase worker commitment to decisions and goals which in turn enhances the effectiveness of the agency. The commitment represents a personal challenge because it is the worker's own goals set for himself in such a way that the supervisor becomes a helping person to assist and support him in achievement of his goals.[16]

Implementation requires from the start that the executive and administrative staff attempt in their own work to apply the principle of participative management.

EVERYBODY IN THE ACT

Later, all supervisors must be included in a training program designed to break up old habits of distrust, secrecy, and noncooperation and to develop openness, trust, and active, joint solution to problems.

The entire agency must be taken through exercises in problem-solving through participative methods in groups with a view toward making such procedures a normal part of the management system of the agency. There must be a concerted effort to distribute responsibility and influence downward in the agency so that every person can have some significant part, however small, in the management of his own work.

Those who have experience with participative management stress that getting employees to participate in decision making must be gradual. Drastic, sudden shifts toward participation and shared responsibility provoke skepticism and often induce anxiety and uncertainty. Where people have been unfamiliar with the idea of participation for long periods, workers and other employees may interpret any sudden removal of the emphasis on authority as a sign of weakness.

In one organization the manager began to encourage employees to participate in problem-solving meetings. Soon after, there was a sharp increase in turnover. Investigation revealed that the workers had decided that if managers were so "ignorant" that they had to consult its employees, the company was badly managed and would fail. They quit to look for jobs with "well managed" companies that did not consult their employees, but told them what to do.

---

[16] *Ibid.*, p. 158.

EFFECTING A CHANGEOVER

Workers who have been denied involvement in their work will at first lack the skills needed for participation. Workers do not learn to work independently by being kept dependent. Only slow and careful re-education of workers can change deeply ingrained relationships with their supervisors, their bosses, and their work.

The introduction of participation may be difficult at one time or another for each person involved—and all must be involved. It may be difficult for supervisors and administrators to hold themselves back while workers perform many of the tasks which they themselves were accustomed to doing. There is much uncertainty about the results because the lack of confidence in workers is difficult to overcome.

One of the greatest demands connected with the participation approach is that placed on the executive and supervisory staff, especially during the time when changes are being implemented and restraints of the old approach are being overcome.

HOW IT WORKS

At the administrative and supervisory levels some may find it difficult to change, others may go through the motions of accepting the participation and involvement approach without being affected very much. The majority derive a great deal of satisfaction from the new participation and increased responsibility which accompanies it, as noted in the following example.

As a result of the assignment of increased responsibility and the evaluation of jobs to determine how workers are being used, it was discovered in our office that caseworkers were forced to spend too much time completing forms. It was decided by a committee of clerical and casework staff that it was time to train clerical staff to prepare forms for the workers. The result was that clerical staff did a better job in terms of accuracy, while the morale of both the casework and clerical staff improved because of the status and importance gained from preparing forms instead of just typing copy work. The workers gained importance and satisfaction from the fact there is now less paper work and more time to serve clients. This is not to suggest that there are not other aspects of jobs in public welfare where intensive review by staff may help to enrich the job and increase the worker's motivation.

Only when there is increased job responsibility will a job change occur which will reward achievement and bring about job satisfaction and more positive attitudes. Worker contribution through involvement and participation must be considered, in contrast to "the creation of a sense of participation." It must be stressed there is no room for a pseudo approach such as a decision made in advance by the administrator and employees then invited to talk about the decision, with the intention of making the employees feel they have participated and that the decision is theirs. Pseudo-participation will not achieve the type of employee involvement that will lead to commitment and effectiveness in carrying out the decision.

The administrator must be a practical-results oriented type of person who realizes that through his staff he can look at all aspects of the picture or problem. Through a deliberate effort to involve workers in decision making he encourages a growth approach and, furthermore, takes advantage of the experience of his workers. The workers of his agency have information based on experience and knowledge which will help him to make better decisions. The practice of participation and involvement will bring the experience and know-how of workers into the decision-making process in such a way that better decisions will result.

The goals of the administrative task of participation and involvement as outlined here need not be as overwhelming as they may seem. It is realistic to believe that a merging of the individual's goals with those which bring about the improved effectiveness and success of the agency are compatible. Goals geared toward the success of the agency can and must be made much more attractive for the worker. Administrators must create a proper climate where it is possible to develop and grow and where the worker voluntarily will choose to use his capabilities, his knowledge, his skill, his ingenuity in ways that will benefit the agency in its goals of providing services to welfare recipients.

Workers are capable of exercising self-direction and self-control in the direction of achieving agency goals, when agency policies and practices make it possible. This is not intended to deny the appropriateness of reasonable authority but it does refuse to grant that authority is appropriate for all purposes and under all circumstances.

The ideas developed in this paper are well stated by Robert E. Slaughter in his article, *Emerging Corporate Policies—A Look Ahead:* ". . . young people want involvement in Administration—genuine, subjective involvement. They want a genuine welcome for their ideas. They want a working environment, including human relationships, that will enable them to use their talents to grow and develop in their competence; to advance in their responsibility and income; to experience a real sense of self-fulfillment in their work; and to achieve self-respect."[17]

[17] Robert E. Slaughter, Executive Vice President, McGraw-Hill, Inc., *Emerging Corporate Policies—A Look Ahead.* From a speech given before the Administrative Management Society, St. Louis Chapter, November 19, 1970.

SELECTED READINGS

Books

Argyris, Chris. *Integrating the Individual and the Organization.* New York, John Wiley & Sons, Inc., 1964.

Blumberg, Paul. *Industrial Democracy: The Sociology of Participation.* New York, Schocken Books, Inc., 1969.

Caldwell, Lynton K. *Improving the Public Service Through Training.* Washington, D.C., Office of Educational and Social Development, Agency for International Development, 1962.

Cherrington, David J. *Supervisor Training Programs on Minority Employment: Suggested Concepts and Procedures.* Champaign, Ill., University of Illinois, 1972.

Eckstein, Otto. *Education, Employment, and Negro Equality.* Washington, D.C., Government Printing Office, 1968.

Hampton, David R., Charles E. Summer and Ross A. Webber. *Organizational Behavior and The Practice of Management.* Glenview, Ill., Scott, Foresman and Company, 1968.

Joint Commission on Correctional Manpower and Training. *Perspectives on Correctional Manpower and Training.* Washington, D.C., Government Printing Office, January, 1970.

Moan, Charles E., Jr. *Public Employee Training on the State Level in the United States.* Research Series No. 8. Kingston, R.I., University of Rhode Island, 1964.

Pateman, Carole. *Participation and Democratic Theory.* London, Cambridge University Press, 1970.

Stahl, O. Glenn. *The Personnel Job of Government Managers.* Chicago, Public Personnel Association, 1971.

————. *Public Personnel Administration.* New York, Harper & Row, Publishers, 1962.

U.S. Department of Labor, Manpower Administration. *Supervising the Hard Core: Some Management Guidelines.* Washington, D.C., Government Printing Office, 1969.

Articles

Allen, Keith. "Controlling the Costs of Recruitment," *Personnel Management,* Vol. 3, No. 12 (December, 1971), 28–30.

Argyle, M. G., and F. Cioffi Gardner. "Supervisory Methods Related

340

to Productivity, Absenteeism, and Labor Turnover," *Human Relations*, Vol. 11, 23–40.

Bell, Joanne I. "Appropriate Functions of Staff Development," in *Staff Development and Practice Supervision*, U.S. Department of Health, Education, and Welfare booklet. Washington, D.C., Government Printing Office, 1968, 7–11.

Boyd, Rex D. "Planning the Development of Managers," *Public Personnel Review*, Vol. 23, No. 2 (April, 1962), 90–93.

Burke, Ronald J., and Linda J. Kemball. "Performance Appraisal: Some Issues in the Process," *The Canadian Personnel*, Vol. 18, No. 6 (November, 1971), 25–34.

Butler, William N. "Supportive Communication and Performance Appraisal," *Personnel Administration*, Vol. 32 (January–February, 1969), 48–51.

Campbell, John P. and Marvin D. Dunnette. "Effectiveness of T-Group Experiences in Managerial Training and Development," *Psychological Bulletin*, Vol. 70, No. 2 (August, 1968), 73–102.

Clark, William. "How to Cut Absenteeism and Turnover," *Administrative Management*, Vol. 32, No. 3 (March, 1971), 64–65.

Day, R. C., and R. L. Hamblin. *Some Effects of Close and Punitive Styles of Supervision*, Technical Report 8, Contract N ONR 816 (11), Washington University, St. Louis, 1961.

Dill, R. William, Wallace B. S. Crewston and Edwin J. Elton. "Strategies for Self-Education," *Harvard Business Review*, Vol. 43, No. 6 (November–December, 1965), 119–30.

English, Joseph T. "Sensitivity Training: Promise and Performance," *American Journal of Psychiatry*, Vol. 126 (1969).

Falk, John A., Jr. "Orientation of New Personnel," *Public Personnel Review*, Vol. 21, No. 4 (October, 1960), 263–65.

Halloran, Daniel F. "Why Position Classification?," *Public Personnel Review*, Vol. 28, No. 2 (April, 1967), 89–92.

Indik, B. P., B. S. Georgopoulos and S. E. Seashore. "Superior-Subordinate Relationships and Performance," *Personnel Psychology*, Vol. 14 (1961), 357–74.

Johnson, Fred R. "Recruiting, Retraining and Advancing Minority Employees," *Training and Development Journal*, Vol. 26, No. 1 (January, 1972), 28–31.

Joure, Sylvia A., Roland L. Frye, Paul C. Green and Frank P. Cassens. "Examples of Over Use of Sensitivity Training," *Training and Development Journal*, Vol. 25, No. 12 (December, 1971), 24–27.

Kimble, Joseph P. "Daydreams, Dogma and Dinosaurs in Police Administration," *The Police Chief*, April, 1969.

"Management Training: An Act of Faith," *Dun's Review*, Vol. 92 (December, 1968), 46–49.

Millard, Kenneth A. "Has Your Training Been Validated?" *Public Personnel Review*, Vol. 33, No. 2 (April, 1972), 135–36.

Miller, Richard D. "A Systems Concept of Training," *Training and Development Journal*, Vol. 23, No. 4 (April, 1969), 4–14.

Oberg, Winston. "Make Performance Appraisal Relevant," *Harvard Business Review*, January–February, 1972.

Parsons, William W. "The Personnel Function in Public Management," *Public Administration Review*, Vol. 17, No. 3 (summer, 1957), 149–55.

Reeves, Elton T. "Management Development—A Conceptual Continuum," *Training and Development Journal*, Vol. 22, No. 9 (September, 1968), 29–35.

Scharinger, Dale H. "Performance Appraisal—A Means or an End," *Training and Development Journal*, Vol. 23, No. 4 (April, 1969), 52–53.

Scheer, Wilbert E. "A Practical Approach to Supervisor Training," *Personnel Journal*, Vol. 48, No. 5 (May, 1969), 369–71.

Schrank, Robert, and Susan Stein. "Sensitivity Training: Uses and Abuses," *Manpower*, Vol. 2, No. 7 (July, 1971), 2–7.

Seiler, Joseph. "Preparing the Disadvantaged for Tests," *Manpower*, Vol. 2, No. 7 (July, 1970), 24–26.

Sheblak, Vernon. "The Older Worker: Employment and Training," *Training and Development Journal*, Vol. 23, No. 3 (March, 1969), 4–8.

Steele, Fred I. "Can T-Group Training Change the Power Structure?" *Personnel Administration*, Vol. 33, No. 6 (November–December, 1970), 48–53.

Tissue, Thomas. "A California Study Looks at Expected Turnover Among Old-Age Assistance Social Workers," *Welfare in Review*, Vol. 8, No. 3 (May–June, 1970), 1–7.

Widop, F. R. "Why Performance Standards Don't Work," *Personnel Journal*, Vol. 47, No. 2 (March–April, 1970).

Wiggins, Thomas W. "Sensitivity Training: Salvation or Conspiracy?" *Educational Leadership*, Vol. 28 (December, 1970), 58–61.

Zalenznik, A. "Management of Disappointment," *Harvard Business Review*, November–December, 1967, 59–70.

SECTION IV: DIRECTING HUMAN RESOURCES

A man's personal philosophy, his way of looking at the world and the men and women around him, determines his success as a manager of things and people more than any other single factor. His basic attitudes are far more significant than the techniques he uses. . . . As we look ahead, we have reason to believe that this will be increasingly true. In short, the time may come when an evil man or one who has no clear sense of values simply cannot be an effective administrator.

DEAN STANLEY F. TEELE
Harvard Business School

The directing phase of management could properly be called the essential link between plans and performance. Its importance is such that some people have referred to it as management itself—telling people what to do and seeing that they do it. A manager must make plans which he hopes to have implemented, develop an organization that divides up the work to be done, and secure people capable of doing the work. Even after he has done these things as well as he can, he is still confronted with an all-important task—that of influencing his employees to carry out his plans to the best of their ability. *Directing*, then, may be thought of as the process of communicating plans, choices, and decisions to employees. The manager's action of directing sets the organization in motion, and his particular style of leadership tends to give it a continuing sense of direction.

Leadership styles and techniques differ widely from that of the authoritarian use of rewards and sanctions, sometimes characterized by the example of the "carrot and the stick," to the democratic principle of sharing decision making known as participative management. Most people strive for leadership, and the personal recognition and self-satisfaction that accompanies it, but a leader's job is not always a pleasant one. It requires the leader to assume responsibility and make unpleasant, sometimes unpopular decisions. Douglas McGregor's article "The Boss Must Boss" points this out. A good leader is strong and tough, when strength and toughness are required, yet humane and fair. Leadership implies creativeness and positive action even when such action is distasteful. Harry D. Hicker's article "Who Bosses Whom—Why and How," dealing with the abuse and misuse of authority, brings out the fact that the most successful leader is the one who is able to challenge his associates to give their best in cooperation and abilities to the enterprise not because he is the boss, but rather because he is their leader.

When we speak of directing the organization, and of leadership as the quality of that directing, we assume that the manager has the requisite authority and power to enforce his directives. Surendra S. Singhvi shows in his presentation "Authority and Power" that power and authority cannot be taken for granted. Frequently the organization fails to grant sufficient authority for managers to effectively direct, and often individuals fail to acquire the power that makes leadership meaningful. The author analyzes authority in terms of delegation and power in terms of will and capacity. Together, authority and power hold the key to successful leadership and the effective fulfillment of the directing function of management.

Employees may tend to accept the manager's right to issue directives because of his position. They may also understand that absence of direction would quickly result in chaos, particularly when various kinds of work must be coordinated. While acceptance of these facts may prove sufficient to prevent an open rebellion of employees in most organizations, it has never provided sufficient inducement to people to give their best efforts to their work. Successful directing is often determined by the extent to which the employees are motivated to follow orders. John W. Darr, in his article "Motivation and Morale: Two Keys to Participation," makes the case for participative management. If the employees identify their own personal objectives as closely related to those of the organization, motivation will be high and the resulting morale good, he postulates.

A most important element in developing motivation and good morale is found in the organization's system of communication. Edwin Timbers' article "Strengthening Motivation Through Communication" enumerates the principal roadblocks in organizational communication which are related to attitudes and status. He goes on to show how the supervisor can operate and communicate in a favorable climate of trust, and that that climate must be established at the top.

If a manager plans to accomplish anything worthwhile he must make use of the abilities and skills of others by delegating certain tasks to selected subunits and individuals and by delegating some of his own authority while continuing to be responsible for the task to his own superiors. Even when the manager understands the importance of delegation, he encounters many problems in mastering the art. Charles C. Gibbons feels that the problems of delegation center around a lack of clarity concerning the authority and responsibility to be delegated, an overestimation on the part of the superior of his ability to do the work with a minimum of delegation, and feelings of insecurity which hinder delegation. In his article "Breaking the Barriers to Delegation" he explores ways to overcome these difficulties. The article "The Art of

Delegating," by Dave Tver, discusses some of the questions that arise in delegation and offers some practical suggestions.

Much has been written concerning the importance of delegation in management, but little of it is of value to the practitioner. Management literature, for the most part, is silent with reference to the mechanics by which effective delegation is performed, and it is also lacking in information and techniques designed to help the manager keep up with progress in each delegated task. James C. Harrison, Jr., comes to our assistance with his article "How to Stay on Top of the Job." He provides us with a guide to styles of delegation and an auditing system by which the manager can gauge the progress of each activity delegated.

Some delegated tasks call for staff work, which may involve one person or several middle-management subordinates. The delegation may specifically include a request for recommendations. Such recommendations may deal with needed changes in policy or procedure offered for the consideration of the top executive. Some managers maintain such tight control over delegated staff work that delegates are hesitant to offer recommendations. Others expect the report to include not only the findings but also the recommendations for action. The brief article "Tell the Boss—Don't Ask," by Jack E. Grant, gives a checklist of questions to ask which will indicate whether the job is really completed before reporting back to a superior.

45. Authority and Power*

Surendra S. Singhvi[1]

History reveals that the terms "authority" and "power" have been used interchangeably by politicians, economists, sociologists, and scholars. Hannah Arendt writes, "The time has come to consider the importance of making distinctions between authority and power. To stress such a conviction seems to be a gratuitous truism in view of the fact that nobody has yet openly stated that distinctions are nonsense. There exists, however, a silent agreement in most discussions among political and social scientists that we can ignore distinctions and proceed on the assumption that everything can eventually be called anything else, and that distinctions are meaningful only to the extent that each of us has the right 'to define his terms'."[2]

What Hannah Arendt means is that it is useful to define the terms in the particular frame of reference in order to make sure that our maps and territories are the same. In order to define these terms, let us review the views of a few scholars.

Jacques Maritain, a great French philosopher of the 20th century, writes, "Authority and power are two different things. Power is the force by means of which you can oblige others to obey you. Authority is the right to direct and command, to be listened to or obeyed by others."[3] According to him, it is evident that the end to be achieved through the exercise of power and authority is the same—get the work done; however, the manner in which the end is to be achieved is different—in the case of power, influence or force is used, and in the case of authority, right or reasonableness is used.

According to Professors Eells and Walton, ". . . authority tends to reflect the common will, power all too frequently interposes the personal will."[4] This distinction points out that authority involves sanction from others and is impersonal by nature, while power does not possess any type of sanction from others and is personal by nature.

Running water produces power to run mills—but not authority; a

---

* From *S.A.M. Advanced Management Journal*, Vol. 34, No. 3 (July, 1969), 64–71. Reprinted by permission.

1 The author wishes to express his thanks to Professor Robert Albanese of Miami University for his helpful comments.

2 Hannah Arendt, "Authority in the Twentieth Century," *Review of Politics*, Volume XVIII (October, 1956), pp. 413–14.

3 Jacques Maritain, *Man and the State* (Chicago: University of Chicago Press, 1951), p. 126.

4 Richard Eells and Clarence Walton, *Conceptual Foundations of Business* (Homewood, Illinois: Richard D. Irwin, 1961), p. 340.

turbine involves power—but not authority. One of the most urgent problems of the business world of today is the relation of bargaining to value, and bargaining rests on power. He seems to get the best of the bargaining who has the greatest power—but not authority. These views evince that authority and power are two different terms not only in theory but in practice.

AUTHORITY

Authority is the character of a communication in a formal organization by virtue of which it is accepted by a member of the organization as governing his action. It is also another name for the willingness and capacity of individuals to submit to the necessities of cooperative system, i.e. the formal organization. One can classify authority in two broad categories:

Formal Authority

According to Max Weber, it is a legal, rational authority.[5] In other words, it is delegated from a superordinate to a subordinate on the basis of bureaucratic rules and regulations. Chester Barnard refers to it as the authority of position.[6] For example, an individual is promoted to a higher position because of his seniority. He has authority because of his new position, and not necessarily due to his ability, knowledge and skill. It is often recognized that though the officer may be of limited personal ability, his advice may be superior solely by reason of the advantage of his position. This type of authority is a formal sanction from the top person in the organizational hierarchy.

Informal Authority

One observes in day to day life that some people have superior ability. Their knowledge and understanding, regardless of their position, command respect. According to Chester Barnard, it is the authority of leadership.[7] It comes from the bottom, i.e. it rests on the acceptance or consent of subordinates. An individual accepts authority when four conditions are obtained simultaneously:

He understands the communication, i.e. the order.

At the time of his decision he believes that it is not inconsistent with the purpose of organization.

It is compatible with his personal interest.

He is mentally and physically able to comply with it.

In a formal organization managerial authority asks of workers three

---

[5] See Talcott Parsons (ed.), *Max Weber: The Theory of Social and Economic Organization* (New York: Oxford University Press, 1947), p. 328.

[6] See Chester I. Barnard, *The Functions of the Executive* (Cambridge, Massachusetts: Harvard University Press, 1938), p. 173.

[7] See *Ibid.*

responses—subordination, loyalty, and productivity. Subordination may be achieved through the authority of position, but other things may not be realized by it. Loyalty and high productivity will be achieved only when the authority of leadership is combined with the authority of position.

Sources of Authority[8]

A brief review of major theories of authority will provide useful insight regarding the sources of authority.

THE FORMAL THEORY OF AUTHORITY. According to this theory authority is referred to the right residing in a person to direct and command, to be listened to or obeyed by others. Authority under this theory comes "from above." The ultimate source of management authority, therefore, is taken to be the right of private property.

THE ACCEPTANCE THEORY OF AUTHORITY. According to this theory, the source of authority is in the subordinates. If one's subordinates do not accept the order, then one has no authority. In this sense, authority comes "from below." This theory refers indirectly to the effective authority. The ultimate source of authority, however, is the individual's ability to influence.

THE CONTRACTUAL THEORY OF AUTHORITY. The consent-of-the-governed theory is the basis of the contractual theory of authority. According to this theory, the authority of the manager has its source in the contract, written or implied, between the employer and the employee. The contract is the source of the manager's right to give orders and his right to expect compliance.

POWER

No word is used more carelessly than the word "power." No one has argued so far whether power is a good word or a bad word. According to Mary Parker Follett, "Power might be defined as simply the ability to make things happen, to be a casual agent, to initiate change."[9]

Three classes of variables are generally recognized by psychologists as determinants of power: resources, dependencies and alternatives.[10] A resource may be defined as a property of an individual which enables him to affect the rewards and costs experienced by another individual. A resource includes a possession, an aspect of his behavior, or merely his presence. The usefulness of such resources is not determined solely by the property of the individual, but also by the dependency of the other person on him.

[8] For an interesting and detailed discussion, see: Robert Albanese, "Substitutional and Essential Authority," *Academy of Management Journal*, IX (June, 1966).

[9] Mary Parker Follett, *Dynamic Administration* (New York: Harper, 1940), p. 99.

[10] See Paul F. Secord and Carl W. Backman, *Social Psychology* (New York: McGraw-Hill, 1964), p. 274.

For example, the technical education of an individual is a resource only in relation to those organizations which recognize the importance of such education and need such individuals. In situations where such education is unimportant, it is unlikely to be a resource. Resource and dependency are also a function of the availability of alternative sources of reward and means of reducing costs. The power of the individual with technical education to attract organizations where need for such individuals exists depends in part upon the availability to them of other qualified individuals, as well as the degree of sacrifice the organizations need to make to gain their favor.

One can classify power in two broad categories:

Realistic Power

Realistic power is here referred to as those attributes of an individual which he possesses, or are accessible to him, to influence others, such as knowledge of the job, leadership traits, interpersonal competence, monetary resources, physical strength, and the like. This type of power may also be defined as one's ability to mediate rewards and punishments for the other.[11] According to the late Professor Douglas McGregor of M.I.T., knowledge is power, primarily because it decreases dependence on the unknown and unpredictable.[12] All these views confirm that realistic power is an individual's ability, capacity, and knowledge to influence others.

Perceived Power

People perceive the situation differently because of the different desires, motives, values, and attitudes.[13] It is quite possible that people may over-estimate or under-estimate the realistic power of an individual. For example, a Negro is hired by a business firm. He has the capacity to work as a supervisor of a particular department in the organization, but he may not be given authority to do that job if his boss is preoccupied with racial prejudices.

DIFFERENCES BETWEEN AUTHORITY AND POWER

The above mentioned dimensions clearly differentiate the two terms —authority and power. In brief, the following are the main differences between these terms.

1. Authority is delegated, while power is acquired. Mary Parker Follett said, "I don't think that power can be delegated because I believe that genuine power is capacity."[14]

[11] See *Ibid.*, p. 275.

[12] See Douglas McGregor, "Conditions of Effective Leadership in an Industrial Organization," *Journal of Consulting Psychology*, volume 8, March, 1944, p. 59.

[13] See J. P. Chaplin and T. S. Krawiec, *Systems and Theories of Psychology* (New York: Holt, Rinehart and Winston, 1960), pp. 161–167.

[14] Follett, *op. cit.*, p. 109.

2. Authority accompanies responsibility, while power does not.

3. Authority tends to reflect the common will, while power tends to reflect the personal will.

POWER WITHOUT AUTHORITY

Power without authority means that an individual has comparatively more power than his authority. In some cases power can also exist without authority in absolute terms. This disequilibrium situation exists in numerous situations. For example:

Informal Leader

An informal leader of a group is an individual who has power or ability to influence the group, but he does not have formal authority to get work done from other individuals.

"Assistant-to"

Individuals carrying such title have power, i.e. knowledge about the job, but they do not have authority to get work done. In other words, these people can get work done through their influence, but they do not have formal authority to do so.

Staff Member

According to Melville Dalton, there exists a conflict between staff members and line personnel.[15] Staff members have power, i.e. ability and competence to make decisions, but they do not have authority to implement them. Increasing specialization in many situations has left staff members with more power than authority.

The King's Mistress

Laswell and Kaplan have given an example of power without authority.[16] According to them, the king's mistress does not have authority but she may have power over the king's subjects.

A Robber

An example of power without authority in absolute terms has been cited by Eells and Walton. The robber who holds a man at gunpoint will just as surely achieve compliance as a policeman armed with the same kind of weapon. In this case, the robber has power to get work done, but he does not have any authority.

REASONS

The above-mentioned example and many more which are not cited here, clearly show that power can exist without authority. Following are some of the reasons for such a situation in an organization:

[15] See Melville Dalton, *Men Who Manage* (New York: John Wiley and Sons, Inc., 1959), pp. 71–75.

[16] See Harold D. Lasswell and Abraham Kaplan, *Power and Society* (New Haven: Yale University Press, 1950), p. 85.

1. This type of imbalance occurs when the realistic power of an individual is under-estimated by his boss. The reasons for this under-estimation may be as follows:

a. Parkinson's Law. According to this law, every individual wants many competent subordinates, but not many competitors. Due to this tendency among human-beings, competent individuals are often kept as subordinates and are not given authority.

b. Lack of communication. Many times a subordinate's competence is not properly communicated to his boss. His realistic power is not truly perceived by his boss and, consequently, power remains without authority.

c. Pre-occupied notions of the boss. A Negro worker is not promoted or given authority, though he has capacity to work for higher position, because his boss has racial prejudices.

2. This type of disequilibrium can also take place when the bureaucratic procedures are strictly followed. A person with seniority is very likely to get promoted regardless of his capability.

CONSEQUENCES

1. According to Jacques Maritain, power without authority is tyranny.[17] Power exercised without authority constitutes a threat to freedom. Under this situation there will be an imbalance and the members of an organization will not contribute effectively in the system of co-ordination.

2. The individual having power without authority may use some kind of defensive mechanism, such as

a. He may form a sub-group and oppose the formal leader.

b. If this situation continues for a long period, he may become a passive contributor in the organization and slow down his work speed.

c. He may use horse-playing devices on the job.

d. He may begin to identify himself more with other groups, viz. unions rather than the formal organization.

e. He may quit the organization.

f. He may withdraw himself from the situation and begin to lose confidence in his abilities.

g. He may use his ability for some type of compensatory devices. For example, Dalton writes that staff members try to establish their relations with top management.

3. This situation creates obstacles in the self-actualization process of an individual. Differences exist in goals of individuals and the organization, and this creates a conflict-situation in the organization.

[17] See Maritain, *op. cit.*

AUTHORITY WITHOUT POWER

This type of situation exists when an individual has relatively more formal authority than realistic power. Authority without power exists in many cases, such as:

Dashman Company

In this company a new purchasing vice-president was appointed to centralize purchasing procedures of twenty plants. He wrote letters to all plant managers saying:

Dear ... (Plant Manager),

The Board of Directors of our company has recently authorized a change in our purchasing procedures. Hereafter, each of the purchasing executives in the several plants of the company will notify the vice-president in charge of purchasing of all contracts in excess of $10,000 which they are negotiating at least a week in advance of the date on which they are to be signed. ...

> Very truly yours,
> William Post
> Purchasing Vice-president[18]

Within two weeks after the letter was received, the majority of the plant managers had assured Mr. Post that he could count on their co-operation. The fact is, however, that they sent him no orders to process or review. This state of affairs lasted for a substantial period of time. This is an example of authority without power. Mr. Post had formal authority over the plant managers but he did not have influence or ability to exercise this authority over them.

Christopher Columbus

When Queen Isabella of Spain appointed Christopher Columbus "Admiral of the Ocean Sea,"[19] she granted him authority over a vast number of people. But the American Indians whom Columbus met continued to live in their own way, unimpressed by the Admiral's authority. Columbus had formal authority but lacked influence and power to back up his position.

Stockholders

Adolf Berle observes that power can exist without property.[20] The reverse of this statement, i.e. property can exist without power, is also true. Since property is one of the sources of authority, therefore it can be said that authority can exist without power. Stockholders in most of

18 E. P. Learned, D. N. Ulrich and D. R. Booz, *Executive Action* (Boston: Graduate School of Business Administration, Harvard University, 1951), p. 16.

19 William M. Newman and Charles E. Summer, Jr., *The Process of Management* (Englewood Cliffs, New Jersey: Prentice Hall, 1961), p. 199.

20 See Adolf A. Berle, Jr., *Power Without Property* (New York: Harcourt, Brace and World, 1959).

the corporations have more authority than their individual influence or power. While the board of directors, on the other hand, has more power than the authority.

EXAMPLES

Numerous examples of such disequilibrium can be cited here. These examples clearly show that relatively more authority than power can exist and does exist in the real world. The main reasons for this situation are:

1. In many cases, a hasty decision is made by a superordinate in delegating authority to an individual where capacity has not been developed. This can happen where:

a. The boss over-estimates the capacity or realistic power of his subordinate under wrong presumption or due to mis-communication regarding the subordinate's abilities; or

b. The boss favors his subordinate because of blood relation or friendly relations.

2. An individual may be given authority on the basis of one type of realistic power, i.e. skill, but lacks leadership or interpersonal competence. This happens when the boss cannot judge which power is more important in a given situation.

3. Bureaucratic procedures also create such situations many times. A person is delegated authority because he is senior in the organizational hierarchy and it is quite possible that he may not possess the qualities of leadership or ability to get work done.

4. This situation can also develop due to conscious efforts and it may prove beneficial. For example, the Goodyear Tire and Rubber Company appointed its first three presidents just because they could finance the firm to a great extent. They were given authority of presidential position, but they did not have capability to exercise that authority and consequently they all resigned within a short period.

CONSEQUENCES

1. The individual having authority without power will not be able to get full cooperation and active participation from his subordinates. Consequently, organizational goals are not likely to be achieved as planned and inefficiency and ineffectiveness are likely to result.

2. His subordinates will stop contributing to the system of coordination. In order to satisfy their need of belonging, they will identify themselves with sub-groups or unions, etc.

3. The individual having authority without power will have conflict with the informal leader. He will have a hard time in getting the job done in time. Under such a situation he may react as follows:

354

a. He may become aggressive and follow the policy of "be strong." He may fire some people and hire "yes-men" of his liking.

b. He may quit the job to get rid of this tense situation.

c. If this situation continues for a long time, he may develop his abilities to cope with his present authority.

4. This situation may prove good to the organization. For example, in a period of financial crisis, if the firm delegates authority to a person who is incapable of doing a managerial job, he can compensate his incapability by providing adequate finances and the organization can survive for a long period.

CONCLUSION

It is concluded that authority and power are two different terms and should not be used interchangeably. Power is necessary for successful implementation of authority, and authority is necessary for exercising one's power legitimately. Power can exist without authority and authority can also exist without power, and this creates disequilibrium in a formal organization. Authority without power is a relative term, and it means that a person has relatively more formal authority than his power. In modern bureaucratic organizations, there is a growing imbalance between ability and authority.[21]

By developing an index for measuring the magnitude of power and authority for each individual, one can hopefully establish an equilibrium in an organization. The development of such an index will require research by academicians in cooperation with practitioners. Such research will be useful to an executive in a formal organization in making decisions regarding hiring, firing and promoting individuals. Management should promote those individuals who have power but no corresponding authority, such as informal leaders and staff members.

If authority is delegated to those who possess power, it is referred to as the legitimate power or affective authority. The manager should find out the situations where an imbalance between power and authority exists, and then should try to eliminate these situations since the consequences of such imbalances are not desirable for the organization as well as for the individuals involved.

However, it should be recognized that the manager is faced with a dilemma. On the one hand, he is expected to delegate authority under a bureaucratic system to a senior person; on the other hand, the seniority does not necessarily mean that he is the best qualified person to do the required job. The manager should adjust the bureaucratic system to minimize imbalances between power and authority.

21 See Victor A. Thomas, *Modern Organization* (New York: Knopf, 1965).

46. Motivation and Morale: Two Keys to Participation*

John W. Darr

It is the firm belief of the writer, although many who are widely accepted and approved as being knowledgeable in this area may well disagree, that a firm's work force is by far its most important resource. Support for this belief derives from the presence of increased demands for more and better products, increased employee requirements stemming from more sophisticated production environments, and the need for increased productivity (better cost control, larger utilization of men, materials, machines, and the like), all of which conspire in such a manner as to emphasize the importance of the human resource in today's economy. But, if employees are positively and effectively motivated, if their morale is high, and if they are able and willing to personally identify with the affairs of the firm in a positive manner, then no limits may be placed upon their accomplishment. Accomplishment is, in fact, unlimited.

Fortunately, traditional management thought, which conceived the individual as an economic man working only for economic gain, is now being positively and importantly influenced by research findings in personnel, in sociology, and in industrial psychology. It can now be stated, without fear of organized reprisal, that employees can be motivated to higher productivity through securing their best efforts, but that the principal stimulus cannot be only higher pay. Rather, a combination of stimuli must be developed and applied in an environment which will permit individuals to realize a compelling sense of achievement on the one hand, and to develop a full and complete sense of their own individuality on the other.

MOTIVATION DEFINED

Dr. John B. Miner defines motivation as follows:

. . . motivation is largely an emotional phenomenon, and human behavior derives almost entirely from the interaction of positive and negative states, including—it is important to note—both those anticipated and those actually experienced. We act and talk as we do largely because we expect that we will achieve certain events and conditions which will provoke pleasant emotions within us.[1]

In light of this definition, it may be concluded that motivation is con-

* From *Personnel Journal*, Vol. 47, No. 6 (June, 1968), 388–97. Reprinted by permission.
[1] John B. Miner, *The Management of Ineffective Performance* (New York: McGraw-Hill Book Company, Inc., 1963), p. 72.

cerned with human interests, desires, and wishes; with impulses, intentions, wants, and drives; and with attitudes, as well as the impact of attitudes upon all of the foregoing. In short, motivation is concerned with the entire person, both on and off the job. Since motivation is concerned with behavior and since both on- and off-the-job behavior influences productivity, then management is inescapably concerned with motivation.

MOTIVATION—A BASIC NECESSITY

Motivation is of basic and fundamental importance to managing. In fact, successful managing today is impossible without it. Since motivation is concerned with creating and maintaining the desire and willingness of all persons in a business organization to achieve predetermined objectives in accordance with the requirements of predetermined plans, it follows logically that such persons must be willing to subordinate, if and when necessary, their own purposes to the group achievement of common goals. And it logically follows that motivation is also concerned with such indirect management areas as leadership, organizational behavior, education and training, communication, and the growth and development of personnel.

Motivation is, additionally, of utmost importance because it constitutes the base for the management functions of planning and organizing. Since the "typical" business organization today is one of ever-increasing size, requiring as it does more and more decentralization of responsibility and authority, especially as these relate to performance, the successful organization and operation of business enterprise will be more and more dependent upon the generation of power from the creativity, ambition, and achievement desires of people.[2] Thus, the direct relationship which exists between management and motivation cannot be denied.

THE ROLE OF MOTIVATION

A positive theory of motivation—if it is to be effective—must be based upon the premise that people differ significantly, each from the other, in a great many respects. Individuals differ, for example, in terms of skills, abilities, capacities, and basic mental abilities; in personality, motor abilities, available energy, and stamina; in education, training, experience, and cultural levels; and most important of all, in interests, levels of aspiration, aggressiveness, and drives. They also differ in their needs and wants and in their willingness to satisfy them. Therefore,

---

2 See Saul W. Gellerman, *Motivation and Productivity* (New York: American Management Association, Inc., 1963). Mr. Gellerman comments regarding people that ". . . nothing of any consequence happens until an individual wants to act. What he accomplishes depends to a considerable extent on how much and on why, he wants to act." In commenting on individual differences he concludes that "all men have purposes, and these purposes affect the way they work." p. 7.

motivation should be given primary emphasis, if proper consideration for the individual is to be achieved in such manner as to be beneficial both to the person and to the firm.

BASIC HUMAN NEEDS

What is now coming to be an accepted theory of motivation is that people have in common certain basic needs and that these basic needs are the origins of almost if not all human behavior. For this discussion, the identification of basic needs developed by Charles D. McDermid, consulting psychologist for the firm of Humber, Mundie & McClary, Evanston, Illinois, will be used.[3]

HIERARCHY OF NEEDS

There can be little doubt that "man is a wanting animal." This is to say that man wants, and wants, and wants: his wants are insatiable. Two further principles are of fundamental importance to understanding and accepting this concept: *First*, what a particular person wants at any given time depends almost completely upon wants previously satisfied. Satisfied needs do not motivate behavior; rather, it is ungratified needs which exert a compelling influence on behavior; *Second*, wants array in a hierarchy of importance and as wants on a lower level are gratified, those on the next higher level will emerge and demand gratification. The hierarchy of needs (wants) can best (especially for purposes of discussion and demonstration) be arranged in a five-level pyramid from physiological needs (or drives), to safety (or security) needs, to social needs, to esteem needs, and to self-realization needs.

The Physiological Needs

These needs include the need for food, drink, elimination, sexual gratification, oxygen, activity, rest and the like. Such needs constitute the basic behavior drives and they motivate behavior only to the extent that they are ungratified. Should an individual be deprived of any of these needs (except, perhaps, sexual activity), he will bend his entire efforts to their satisfaction. An overworked manager will yearn for rest, relaxation, and sleep; a person who is hungry will think mostly of food, including, of course, ways to obtain it; and a person who is drowning becomes frantic in his effort to obtain oxygen.

However, once such needs are satisfied, they do not control behavior. They are, in fact, largely taken for granted. When the physiological needs are gratified, they no longer stimulate goal-seeking activity and higher needs will emerge and demand gratification. It should be noted, however, that both the expression or gratification of most, if not all, of

[3] See Charles D. McDermid, "How Money Motivates Men," *Business Horizons*, Vol. III, No. 4 (Winter, 1960), pp. 93–100.

358

these needs are either socially determined or socially modified. For example, those activities associated with the securing and consuming of food as well as sexual gratification are controlled by many laws, customs, and taboos.

Safety Needs

Safety needs are next above the physiological needs in the hierarchy. Such needs include:

... protection from physical danger (fire, accidents, criminal assault, and so forth); for economic security (by means for example of various social insurances); for the familiar rather than the unfamiliar; and for a religious, philosophic, or scientific ordering of the chaotic into a meaningful whole.[4]

In our society, the well-adjusted, mature adult achieves at least a minimal satisfaction of the safety needs with a minimum of investment in time and effort on his own. As a result, such needs constitute a diminishing motivating force.

The safety needs no doubt give rise to individual and group desires for job security, a "living" wage, fair and considerate treatment by employers, and predictability of both employment and income because without such, the physical environment within which individuals and groups exist appears to be much more threatening than would otherwise be the case.

There may even be some overlapping of the physiological and safety needs. As an example, the need for shelter is, at one and the same time, both a physiological and a safety need.[5]

The Social Needs

Almost all human beings appear to have a compelling need to be able to relate to other people. Elton Mayo once said: "Man's desire to be continuously associated in work with his fellows is a strong, if not the strongest human characteristic."[6] So the individual need to relate to others exists in the work environment as well as in off-the-job environments. In fact, those who do not manifest this need are generally considered to be, to some degree, abnormal.

A compelling need for acceptance by various groups external to the family appears to be manifestly important to individuals, when prior family relationships have resulted in love and affection being experienced or when the individual finds it necessary to go outside the family to gratify such needs. Where the individual is deprived of either family,

---

4 *Ibid.,* p. 95.

5 See Wendell French, *The Personnel Management Process: Human Resources Administration* (Boston: Houghton Mifflin Company, 1964), p. 23.

6 Elton Mayo, *The Social Problems of an Industrial Organization* (Boston, Mass.: Harvard University Press, 1945), p. 11.

or friends, or both, he will feel the need for them just as intensely as a hungry person wants food, a drowning person wants air, or a tired person wants rest and sleep. But unlike those needs previously discussed,

... social needs are not readily satisfied in our culture. The flight from the family farm and small town community, often to impersonal urban centers, and our traditional taboo on tenderness have helped to prevent fulfillment of these needs. Consequently, social needs have become a dominant motivating force in the United States. Incentive workers who restrict output in accordance with group pressures are motivated by this powerful need to belong. For the same reason, some young people develop a loyalty to their gang that yields to no outside pressure.[7]

Clearly, it appears that social needs—especially those which are relatively unsatisfied—constitute a compelling influence on our behavior today.

Esteem Needs

While esteem needs may also overlap with social needs (i.e., belonging, love, affection, tenderness, and the like), all "normal," well-adjusted, mature persons need esteem. Esteem needs take two principal forms: self-esteem and the esteem of others. For example:

The need for self-esteem includes the desire for personal worth and dignity, for strength, for competence, achievement, and mastery, for independence and freedom. The need for the esteem of others includes desires for attention and recognition, for status, prestige, and reputation, for importance and power.[8]

While it is true that esteem needs are quite capable of being gratified in our society, a considerable investment in time and effort must be made by the individual to insure their satisfaction. Consequently, the goal-seeking activities of those attempting to satisfy esteem needs constitute a most important determinant of both individual and group behavior:

The very real need of "keeping up with the Joneses," of joining the best club, of getting the better office, of driving the right car, or of having a socially acceptable address—all of these are manifestations of needing the esteem of others. Self-esteem, too, takes various forms: for example, the need to feel the importance of one's work or to take a stand on some moral issue.[9]

Self-Realization Needs

Self-realization needs represent the ultimate in human achievement in the total hierarchy of needs. Such needs have been variously de-

---

[7] McDermid, *Op. Cit.*, p. 95.
[8] *Ibid.*
[9] *Ibid.*

scribed as "becoming," as "growth," and as "self-actualization," and are described by Maslow as

... man's desire for self-fulfillment, mainly the tendency for lives to become actualized in what he is potentially. This tendency might be phrased as the desire to become more and more what one is, to become everything that one is capable of becoming.[10]

While there is a tendency to emphasize "Einstein-types" of capacity and ability in our society (with such types being admittedly rare), it is the writer's belief that all persons are capable of fulfilling their self-realization needs, with the basic requirement being fulfillment of capacity, whether that capacity be large, intermediate, or small.

MOTIVATIONAL THEORIES

A number of schools of thought have recently been emerging as the result of a considerable increase in research activities conducted by academicians (in personnel, management, sociology, psychology, and the like) and by practitioners. Dr. Dalton E. McFarland summarizes the various schools of thought as follows:

Several schools of thought are emerging. . . . Among these are the participation theories, such as that promulgated by McGregor; the interaction theories advanced by Homans, Whyte, Chapple, Sayles, and others; the "management pattern" theory propounded by Ukert; the motivational constraint theory of formal organizations elaborated by March and Simon; and the achievement expectation theories.[11]

There is, as a consequence, a wide range of motivation concepts, and the manager's choice of vehicle (whether such choice represents a single vehicle or a combination of vehicles) becomes quite difficult. However, one conclusion is inescapable: it is every manager's *primary responsibility* to continuously concern himself with the development and application of ways and means designed to cause employees to *want* to perform more effectively. Therefore, the question is not whether to motivate, but *how* and *how well* subordinates will be motivated.

MORALE

Morale can be defined from many different points of view, depending on the interpretation and the concept which is to be demonstrated. One definition, which appears to be universal in nature, is that morale is a

---

[10] See A. H. Maslow, *Motivation and Personality* (New York: Harper & Brothers, 1951), pp. 91–99. In a later book Maslow suggests that the terms "becoming" and/or "growth" may be considerably more descriptive than "self-actualization." See A. H. Maslow, *Toward A Psychology of Being* (Princeton, N. J.: D. Van Nostrand Company, 1962), pp. iii–iv, and p. 146.

[11] Dalton E. McFarland, *Management: Principles and Practices* (New York: The Macmillian Company, 1964) p. 532.

mental attitude which causes both individuals and groups to subordinate willingly their own purposes to a common end; to cooperate willingly with their associates; to submit cheerfully to reasonable discipline; and to give their best efforts without pressure. In light of this definition, it may be concluded that a meaningful relationship exists between morale and motivation in so far as managers are concerned. McFarland describes the relationship as follows:

Morale . . . describes a state of the individual's or group's complex attitudes, judgments, and feelings about his work, his job, his company, his supervisor, and so on, whereas motivation describes a propensity for particular behavior patterns reducing or satisfying certain needs inducing tension . . . motivation is a function of drive and confirmed desirability estimates regarding various alternative satisfactions, whereas morale is freedom of restraint in action toward a goal. Thus an individual or group may be highly motivated, but unable to act. With freedom to act, the degree of morale may be related to the strength of motivation. Morale in a sense may be thus regarded as motivation demonstrated in overt action toward a goal.[12]

It may be concluded, therefore, that motivation appears to provide the potential for morale.[13] If so, then morale must be a resultant state which encompasses the willingness to cooperate (on the part of both individuals and groups) and expresses the degree of integration which exists between conflicting interests. Motivation, also must be considered to be an active force which affects behavior by causing individuals to seek to achieve goals which lie in the future.[14] Both motivation and morale, therefore, relate directly to productivity and are directly influenced, in so far as individuals and groups are concerned, by the superior (manager) in the execution of his delegated responsibility and authority.

THE MANAGER'S RESPONSIBILITY

Managers, occupying as they all do positions of leadership in the business organization, must invest considerable time and effort in planning for and achieving high levels of motivation and morale. For example, seldom are employees, either as individuals or groups, motivated to perform at a level of performance which is anywhere near the level of which they are capable in terms of skills, abilities, and capacities. Miner, for example, states that demonstrated performance generally never exceeds more than fifty per cent of the individual's ability to perform.[15] "Most individuals (either on their own or as members of groups) tend

---

12 *Ibid.*, pp. 520–21.

13 See Ralph M. Stogdill, *Individual Behavior and Groups Achievement* (New York: Oxford University Press, 1959), p. 213.

14 See Laurence Seigel, *Industrial Psychology* (Homewood, Illinois: Richard D. Irwin, Inc., 1962), p. 282.

15 Miner, *Op. Cit.*, p. 106; see also McFarland, *Op. Cit.*, p. 532.

to balance their efforts around an assessment of relative costs (time and energy) and benefits."[16] Motivation, therefore, is both a continuing and a fundamentally important management problem, and one which the manager cannot safely ignore, especially from the point of view of seeking a continuing solution.

The concept of motivation offered by the late Douglas McGregor represents one of the most if not the most, effective conceptualizations now available to permit the achievement of those higher and higher levels of performance which are so vital to the want-satisfying activities of business firms in securing the highest possible level of customer satisfaction. A climate of creativity,[17] which will result in positive cooperation by employees, must be developed and maintained by management. As a result, employees may be shown that their work and their association with a given firm represent a vehicle which will permit the simultaneous achievement of personal goals as well as the achievement of goals of the firm.

THE CONCEPT OF PARTICIPATION

The concept of participation is one of the most widely misunderstood and, as a result, one of the most widely misapplied ideas that has come from the field of employee-employer relations in recent years.

... it is now clear that the all-important climate of the superior-subordinate relationship is determined not by policy and procedure but by the subtle and frequently quite unconscious manifestations . . . underlying . . . (the manager's) conception of management . . . (and his) assumptions about people in general.[18]

In an attempt to eliminate some of the difficulties inherent in such misunderstandings, the following definition of participation will be used:

Participation is . . . an individual's mental and emotional involvement in a group situation that encourages him to contribute to group goals and to share responsibility for them.[19]

On the one hand there are those who accept and use this concept in such manner as to give those with whom they come in contact

... the distinct impression that it is a magic formula which will eliminate

---

16 Eli Ginzberg, "Perspectives on Work Motivation," *Personnel*, Vol. 31, No. 1 (July, 1954), pp. 48–49.

17 Maier and Hayes, for examples, say that "The optimal climate for creativity . . . is *whatever human condition is optimal for individual freedom and self-expression in social settings.*" Norman R. F. Maier and John J. Hayes, *Creative Management* (New York: John Wiley & Sons, Inc., 1962), p. 36.

18 Douglas McGregor, *The Human Side of Enterprise* (New York: McGraw-Hill Company, 1960), p. 141.

19 Keith Davis, "The Case for Participative Management," *Business Horizons*, Vol. 6. No. 3 (Fall, 1963), p. 57.

conflict and disagreement and come pretty close to solving all of management's problems. They give the impression that it is a formula which can be applied by any manager regardless of his skill, that virtually no preparation is necessary for its use, and that it can spring full-bloom into existence and can transform industrial relationships overnight.[20]

On the other hand, those who criticize, or reject, or both, the participation concept see it as a kind of managerial abdication of that unilateral responsibility and authority which are so necessary for effective direction and control. Still others see it as ". . . a manipulative device for getting people to do what they want, (and) . . . they tend to conceive of all participation as taking this form."[21] Neither of these extreme views is representative of participation. However, it can be said that "Participation . . . is inherent in the man-boss relationship; the skills of leadership and management include the ability to elicit effective participation in common enterprises."[22] Such conclusion can be justified by a careful consideration of McGregor's "Theory X" and "Theory Y."

"THEORY X"

"Theory X" is predicated upon the following assumptions:

1. Management is responsible for organizing the elements of productive enterprise—money, materials, equipment, people—in the interest of economic ends.

2. With respect to people, this is a process of directing their efforts, motivating them, controlling their actions, modifying their behavior to fit the needs of the organization.

3. Without this active intervention by management, people would be passive—even resistant—to organizational needs. They must therefore be persuaded, rewarded, punished, controlled—their activities must be directed. This is management's task—in managing subordinate managers or workers we often sum it up by saying that management consists of getting things done through other people.[23]

Behind this conventional theory of management, according to McGregor, are a number of additional beliefs which are perhaps less explicit, but which are widespread as evidenced by the philosophies and practices of too many managers today:

4. The average man is indolent—he works as little as possible.
5. He lacks ambition, dislikes responsibility, prefers to be led.

[20] McGregor, *Op. Cit.*, p. 124.
[21] *Ibid.*, p. 125.
[22] McFarland, *Op. Cit.*, p. 511.
[23] Douglas McGregor, "Adventures in Thought and Action," *Proceedings of the Fifth Anniversary Convocation of the School of Industrial Management*, Massachusetts Institute of Technology, Cambridge, Mass., April 9, 1957, as reprinted in Paul Pigors, Charles A. Myers, and F. T. Malm (eds.), *Management of Human Resources* (New York: McGraw-Hill Book Company, 1964), p. 56.

364

6. He is inherently self-centered, indifferent to organizational needs.

7. He is by nature resistant to change.

8. He is gullible, not very bright, the ready dupe of the charlatan and the demagogue.[24]

As a result, in far too many instances, it appears that the underlying management philosophy of human-resource utilization in business is predicated upon such propositions and beliefs. In fact, typical organization structures, as well as the conceptualizations of management objectives, policies, plans, programs, and practices by practitioners, appears to reflect such assumptions.

"THEORY Y"

This approach to resource utilization being, as it is, positively oriented, is based upon much more meaningful assumptions about people:

1. Management is responsible for organizing the elements of productive enterprise—money, materials, equipment, people—in the interests of economic ends.

2. People are *not* by nature passive or resistant to organizational needs. They have become so as a result of experience in organizations.

3. The motivation, the potential for development, the capacity for assuming responsibility, the readiness to direct behavior toward organizational goals are all present in people. Management does not put them there. It is a responsibility of management to make it possible for people to recognize and develop these human characteristics for themselves.

4. The essential task of management is to arrange organizational conditions and methods so that people can achieve their own goals *best* by directing *their* own efforts toward organizational objectives.[25]

Behind this theory are a number of additional beliefs which are also, perhaps, somewhat less explicit, but which are not as widespread as should be the case:

5. The expenditure of physical and mental effort is as natural as play and rest.

6. External control and the threat of punishment are not the only means for bringing about the effort toward organizational objectives. Man will exercise self-direction and self-control toward organizational objectives to which he is committed.

7. Commitment to objectives is a function of the rewards associated with their achievement.

8. The average human being learns, under proper conditions, not only to accept but to seek responsibility.

9. The capacity to exercise a relatively high degree of imagination, in-

24 *Ibid.*
25 *Ibid.*, p. 59.

genuity and creativity in the solution of organizational problems, is widely, not narrowly, distributed in the population.

10. Under the conditions of modern industrial life, the intellectual potentialities of the average human being are only partially utilized.[26]

THE NEED FOR PARTICIPATION

As can be seen from the foregoing discussion of "Theory X" and "Theory Y," two extremes of views and concepts are involved. However, as is usually the case when dealing with extremes, the two most widely separated concepts on the continuum are seldom, if ever, representative of the majority. The emergence and growth of numerous environmental pressures which tend to make managements more cost conscious, i.e., increased governmental participation in management decision-making (local, state, and national); increased labor-union participation in all phases of business,[27] and the general public insistence for evidence of more social consciousness on the part of management, have caused managers to look for new ways and means of effectively solving such problems and, at the same time, to seek new ways and means of improving relative competitive positions. Increased utilization of human resources offers fertile opportunity for the kinds of changes which result in meaningful improvements. The participation concept, if positively practiced as a management philosophy, can achieve significant benefit to the employer, to the employee, and to the public *if properly applied*.

The participation concept requires that management, in most cases, redefine the employee. In so doing, the writer suggests that the resulting redefinition give full consideration to the fact that an employee is:

1. *A unit of energy* that seeks to spend itself and, in the process, both possesses and exercises the choice of how to spend this energy; that is to say, whether to conserve it, waste it, or use it productively.

2. *An organism possessing the dynamic ability to grow and adjust and select quantitatively.* In other words, man has the power to extract from his environment the nourishment he needs to build more of himself, both physically and mentally. Because the environment . . . can be conditioned, growth may be accelerated or slowed down. . . .

3. *Purposeful* . . . the force that induces him to expend his energy to become more perfectly what he wants to become. This drive may be conscious or unconscious. . . .

4. *Unique.* Each human being has his own personality, and each has the capacity to direct his energies. Thus capacity . . . magnifies the effect of ex-

---

[26] McFarland, *Op. Cit.*, p. 532, summarizing McGregor, *The Human Side of Enterprise, Op. Cit.*, Chapter 16.

[27] As one example, the official release of the bargaining goals of the United Steelworkers of America ". . . talks strongest of 'total job security,' the new union goal. . . . A principal demand is for maintenance of income for 'longer service employees' during lay-offs or sickness and disability for as long as such periods might last." "Steel Union Asks Large Wage Rise and Job Security." *The Wall Street Journal*, December 3, 1964, p. 3.

perience upon his ultimate development. . . . Each . . . is . . . always in the process of becoming more and more different from his fellows.[28]

It is, therefore, important that management always view the employee —either as an individual, or as a member of a group, or both—as

. . . a unit of energy wanting to produce; having the dynamic ability to grow and adjust; being purposeful; and possessing unique capabilities to respond to experience. It is also apparent that side by side with these characteristics must be placed the fact that man cannot be separated from his environment and that his knowledge, attitudes and values largely derive from it.[29]

Thus, it becomes apparent that the traditional management concept as evidenced by "Theory X" does not contribute positively to the kind of human resource utilization which the increasing future requirements of business will demand. The inadequacy of the traditional approach and the justification of the participation concept may be shown in the following terms:

Any system set up to control people as though they were irresponsible, self-centered, and indifferent—must be so treated by the few who are responsible —is likely to encourage them to behave that way. You fit them into the system if you have the power to do so—and managers do have the power. Then, when people behave as they have been compelled to, you insist they were born that way and can't behave in any other way.

Management's troubles with high turnover, absenteeism, low productivity, featherbedding practices, strikes, poor quality, and other inadequacies that contribute to higher costs—all these are the result of the failure to deal competently with the human needs of employees and of false assumptions.[30]

CONCLUSIONS

"Theory Y" is not only compatible with the concept of participation, but represents a solid foundation upon which such a philosophy may be developed and applied. For example, McGregor comments that "This is a process primarily of creating opportunities, releasing potential, removing obstacles, encouraging growth, providing guidance."[31] It should also be noted that the acceptance and application of the participation concept does not in any way involve, as is oftentimes suggested, an abdication by management of authority and responsibility, or a reduction of either performance evaluation requirements or standards, or a diminishing of the importance of effective leadership, or in any way forcing

[28] Albert F. Walters, "Management and Motivation: Releasing Human Potential," *Personnel*, Vol. 39, No. 2 (March–April, 1962), pp. 8–16 as reprinted in Harold Koontz and Cyril O'Donnel, *Management: A Book of Readings* (New York: McGraw-Hill Book Company, 1964), pp. 382–83.

[29] *Ibid*.

[30] Alfred J. Morrow, *Behind the Executive Mask* (New York: American Management Association, 1964), pp. 63–64.

[31] McGregor, as reprinted in Pigors, *et al.*, *Op. Cit.*, p. 59.

employees and managers farther apart. Rather, such an approach will make possible a larger integration of interests, goals, and achievements between employees and management because it makes it possible for such interests, goals, and achievements to be common to both.

Significant, innovative ideas which are compatible and consistent with the successful organization and operation of business enterprise derive from the incorporation of participation into management theory, philosophy, and practice. Further, there is some evidence, though admittedly spotty, that such ideas are being applied in business firms with appreciable degrees of success. Among these, the following are deserving of being cited:

1. *Decentralization and Delegation.* These are ways of freeing people from too-close control, . . . giving them a degree of freedom to direct their own activities, to assume responsibility, and, importantly, to satisfy their egoistic needs.

2. *Job Enlargement.* This concept . . . encourages the acceptance of responsibility at the bottom of the organization; it provides opportunities for satisfying social and egoistic needs. Moreover, the economic and psychological results . . . have been substantial.

3. *Performance Appraisal* . . . has to do with performance appraisal within the ranks of management . . . the individual is encouraged to take greater responsibility for planning and appraising his own contribution to organizational objectives; and accompanying effects on egoistic and self-fulfillment needs are substantial.[32]

Such a conceptualization, self-evidently, emphasizes the satisfaction of those social, esteem, and self-realization needs which are compelling determinants of behavior in our society today.

BENEFITS OF PARTICIPATION

The concept of participation must be effectively integrated into the total management philosophy of organization and operation of business enterprise if the best results are to be achieved. This is to say, then, that participation is not a technique, nor is it a "gimmick"; rather it represents a most important part, and it may be, as some have inferred, the cornerstone of the basic foundation upon which a positive, constructive, and most useful philosophy may be erected. Such a philosophy must, of course, be long-run oriented. And if it is, acceptance and application of this concept by all who are associated with a particular firm should make possible such practical and developmental benefits as the following:

1. Better development of individuals in the company, by providing opportunity to test their skills and utilize their contribution.

---

[32] McGregor, as reprinted in Pigors, *et al., Op. Cit.,* pp. 60–61.

2. Improved attitudes by emphasizing participation of subordinates in matters that affect them and their work.

3. Fostering an integration of interests and abilities of organization members and a reduction of the "every man for himself" spirit.

4. A diffusion of the exhilarating experience of helping to solve problems and accomplish tasks.

5. Development of subordinates' sense of independence, self-direction, and confidence.

6. Provision of opportunities to demonstrate how subordinates may find ways of satisfying their own needs and drives through helping the company achieve its objectives.[33]

A practical example of the benefits of the positive utilization of the participation concept may be seen in the experience of the Lincoln Electric Company.[34] The impact of positive participation, as it pertains to the primary objectives achievements in production, sales, and finance, is so dramatic that no business executive can afford to ignore it. The astonishing success of Lincoln Electric, from a most insignificant beginning some fifty years ago to a position of unquestioned leadership in its industry today, was largely made possible, according to its president, by the incorporation of the participation concept into the firm's basic philosophy of management.

IN THE FUTURE

The participation concept, if properly understood and appreciated, can, through effective applications, permit a substantial increase in the utilized potential of employees at all levels in a given firm. Recall, if you will, Miner's conclusion that at best, rarely more than fifty per cent of individual potential is typically utilized on the job. Consider the impact of raising this figure to sixty, seventy, or eighty per cent on costs, on customer service, on want satisfaction, on standards of living, and upon derived job satisfaction. Nor can the off-the-job impact be ignored. As an example:

A worker spends most of his waking hours at his job. Whatever interferes with his sense of dignity as a man or his sense of justice, exerts a crippling influence upon those hours that he spends as a member of his family or society.[35]

In an on-going work environment, the manager must formulate objectives which are acceptable; organize present or prospective human

---

[33] McFarland, *Op. Cit.*, p. 512.
[34] See James F. Lincoln, *A New Approach to Industrial Economics* (New York: The Devin-Adair Company, 1961), especially Chapter 7.
[35] "Labor Looks at Industrial Engineering," *Advanced Management* Vol. 21, No. 1 (January, 1956), pp. 14–17, as reprinted in Herbert J. Chruden and Arthur W. Sheriman, Jr., *Readings in Personnel Management* (Cincinnati, Ohio: South-Western Publishing Co., 1961), p. 511.

resources; and develop and maintain levels of motivation and morale which will result in the achievement of a compelling sense of job satisfaction, with such satisfaction being derived from the opportunity to become a meaningful participant. This will permit the needs of the entire person to be carefully considered and satisfactorily gratified, and total group accomplishment may then, in fact, become unlimited. If it is the case, and surely it must be, that the participation concept provides for the encouragement of all who associate through employment with a business firm to direct their creative energies toward a better achievement of common goals (both those of the individual and those of his firm), and if such requires that the individual be granted a larger control over his own destiny if he is to become a meaningful participant in the firm's affairs, how could such a delegation be other than beneficial to us all?

David Sarnoff, President of Radio Corporation of America, once said: "Whether a man is a plumber or an artist, a musician or an industrialist, his mission on earth is to express the creative forces within himself."[36] The best vehicle for the highest possible creative contribution is to incorporate the participation concept into managements' working philosophy of organization and operation of business enterprise.

[36] *Saturday Evening Post* (February 16, 1963), p. 59.

47. The Boss Must Boss*

Douglas McGregor

It took the direct experience of becoming a line executive, and meeting personally the problems involved, to teach me what no amount of observation of other people could have taught. I believed, for example, that a leader could operate successfully as a kind of adviser to his organization. I thought I could avoid being a "boss." Unconsciously, I suspect, I hoped to duck the unpleasant necessity of making difficult decisions, of taking the responsibility for one course of action among many uncertain alternatives, of making mistakes and taking the consequences. I thought that maybe I could operate so that everyone would like me—that "good human relations" would eliminate all discord and disagreement. . . .

It took a couple of years, but I finally began to realize that a leader cannot avoid the exercise of authority any more than he can avoid responsibility for what happens to his organization. In fact, it is a major function of the top executive to take on his own shoulders the responsibility for resolving the uncertainties that are always involved in important decisions. Moreover, since no important decision ever pleases everyone in the organization, he must also absorb the displeasure, and sometimes severe hostility, of those who would have taken a different course. A colleague recently summed up what my experience has taught me in these words: "A good leader must be tough enough to win a fight, but not tough enough to kick a man when he is down." This notion is not in the least inconsistent with humane, democratic leadership. Good human relations develop out of strength, not of weakness.

* From *Leadership and Motivation* (Cambridge, Mass., M.I.T. Press, 1966). Reprinted by permission.

48. Who Bosses Whom—Why and How*

Harry D. Hicker

The use or abuse of authority can make or break any organization. Of course, there must be authority as the accompaniment of responsibility; decisions must be made and policies enforced. But in an organization like ours, with a staff of professional workers, all presumably mature, reasonable, and intelligent persons, I have always advocated minimum emphasis on "bossing" and maximum emphasis on all working together, consulting together, arriving at sound conclusions together, and consequently progressing together with the aid of each other toward a double goal—first, successful conduct of our worth-while program, and second, enjoying the work as we go along.

Also, I have always advocated the principle of delegating to each worker the maximum autonomy he is capable of exercising wisely. Degree of supervision should vary with the development of the supervisee in ability to stand on his own feet, to initiate and carry through sound planning, and—very important for all of us—to realize when aid is needed and in difficult situations have the grace and wisdom to ask for consultation and advice. In this happy situation post-review of action taken supersedes pre-approval; the supervisor ceases to worry about his responsibility, although it still exists, for the activities of his unit; and the case workers have the satisfaction of comparative independence and freedom of action.

Let no one think, however, that this democratic ideal of supervisory relationship develops automatically, or that it lessens the responsibility or the authority of the supervisor. The privilege of direct action with a minimum of supervision must be earned and its continuance justified by effectiveness. The supervisor is still responsible and retains full authority to enforce instructions. It is the degree to which he must exercise that authority that varies with the individual situation. While most of our staff work effectively on their own, there are others who require and must expect direction and close supervision. For example, there is the worker who, in his desire to do everything possible for the client, lets his heart rule his head. There is the one who is so allergic to paperwork that he neglects or even shortcuts necessary case entries. Another may be lacking in good judgment, or may act impulsively without due consideration of all the facts.

Nor is the supervisor perfect. He knows the principles of good super-

* From *Journal of Rehabilitation*, July–August, 1952, p. 2. Reprinted by permission.

vision, but may not always put them into practice. Or, one may tend to be too strict in his interpretations, another too liberal, another may be so concerned with the minutiae of case-checking as to lose sight of the fact that a very fine piece of counseling may have been done. All this calls for the attention of *his* supervisor, in the interests of harmony and of reasonable uniformity of operation.

Few things attain perfection in this world. It would be too much to expect perfection in personnel relationships, but we can aim in that direction. Improvement will result from self-evaluation, adoption of a cooperative attitude, and respect for the other's point of view. Let the case worker keep in mind that the supervisor has responsibility for acceptable program operation, has a duty to perform, and is expected by *his* supervisor to exercise authority to correct substandard work. Let the supervisor observe the principles of good supervision, and recognize the fact that the case worker's personal contact with the client is a factor lacking in his own paper review of a case. Let both remember that there is ample provision for review by higher authority if an impasse is reached after a dispassionate discussion and genuine effort to come to an agreement. Better an appeal than continued futile arguments. Every gain resulting from a wholehearted attempt to play the game and get along with co-workers will pay big dividends in satisfaction on the job as well as effective operation.

49. Strengthening Motivation Through Communication*
Edwin Timbers

One of the principal responsibilities of every supervisor is to put the "see" into his communications. The mere possession of communication media, however, will do little to accomplish this objective. Supervisors have all the communication tools they need to communicate information and ideas with great proficiency, but the fact remains, nevertheless, that they are not affecting attitudes and behavior as they should. Obviously, the answer to today's communication problems lies not in the media we possess, but in how we use these media.

THE CARROT AND THE STICK

Samuel Johnson, the great eighteenth-century British lexicographer, once said that "the two greatest movers of the human mind are the desire of good and the fear of evil." This can be restated colloquially as motivation by the carrot and the stick. Before collective bargaining became commonplace, employers were often prone to use the stick and did so with relative impunity. In 1935 the Wagner Act, however, gave labor a powerful stick with which to strike back, and management's stick lost much of its sting. The power of the carrot grew accordingly, and management began to focus its attention on improving communications as a means of promoting more harmonious labor relations.

Since fear has lost much of its potency in American industry as a primary motivator, management has no choice but to use the employees' desire of good. If supervisors correctly ascertain the good desired by their employees, direct their communication efforts to the satisfaction of such desire, and practice what they preach, their effectiveness as leaders will be greatly enhanced.

THE BASIC HUMAN WANTS OF THE EMPLOYEE AT WORK

What are the basic human wants that can be satisfied, at least in part, by a company communication program? Prominent in any list of job-related wants are recognition, communication, belonging, and emotional security:

Recognition

Possibly the most important want of any employee is to have others recognize his dignity and worth as an individual. This want can in some measure be satisfied merely by each supervisor making an effort to get

* From *S.A.M. Advanced Management Journal*, Vol. 31, No. 2 (April, 1966), 64–69. Reprinted by permission.

more than superficially acquainted with each of his employees. So important is that obvious step that it should be standard management practice at all levels in every company. This point is stressed for two reasons: First, the employee will be flattered by his supervisor's interest in him as an individual, and, from the inception of their relationship, rapport between supervisor and employee will be considerably strengthened. Second, in getting acquainted, the supervisor must listen. In listening, he develops the employee as a communication source, for the supervisor by listening implies that what the employee says is worth hearing. This implication usually flatters the employee and motivates him to increase his contacts with his supervisor. As a result, the upward flow of communication, the so-called "neglected half of communication," is stimulated.

Communication

The great majority of employees want their supervisors to keep them informed about what is going on and what is anticipated in the company. Conversely, they want to have the ear of their supervisors, want them to listen to their problems, complaints, and achievements with understanding. In satisfying this want of his employees, the first obligation of each supervisor is training them to do their jobs. With new or untrained employees, the four-step job instruction training approach is best, and every level of supervision should be carefully and thoroughly trained in the use of this instructional technique. Regardless of the employee's initial skills and preparation, his supervisor's training responsibility continues, for new and better ways of doing work, new equipment, and better materials are continually being developed. Furthermore, without training, workers tend to regress and become careless and sloppy. Training, consequently, is a continuing supervisory responsibility which should be based on the supervisor's first-hand knowledge of the skills, strengths, and weaknesses of his subordinates. Such knowledge can best be obtained by careful and frequent observation and listening.

After basic training, worker skills can be refined not only by formal coaching but also by frequent and apparently casual contacts between supervisor and worker. The virtues of such informal coaching are that it is natural and spontaneous; it enables the employee to keep abreast of the latest methods; and it motivates him to do his work better. Employees appreciate and welcome good coaching. In coaching employees some do's and don'ts should be mentioned:

TELL THE EMPLOYEE WHY THE JOB IS DONE IN A CERTAIN WAY AND WHY IT IS DONE AT ALL. Help him to see the importance of the job by understanding why it is necessary. Not only will he take greater pride and care if he sees its importance, but he will be able to work much more intelligently in a crisis if he is guided by the light of understanding.

AVOID OVERINSTRUCTING. This kills his initiative, dulls his creative edge, and denies him the pleasure of figuring it out for himself.

GET "FEEDBACK." Have the employee play back your ideas, information, or instruction in his own words. If he says what you meant to say, your communication effort was successful. But if he errs, there has been a flaw in sending, in receiving, or both. You then repeat this process until the employee sees what you see. This technique used in oral communication is a virtually foolproof method of putting the "see" into communication. It is standard operating procedure in the U.S. Army Infantry to get such feedback on all oral field orders, and there is no doubt that this procedure has saved many lives in battle. It can also save many dollars in industry.

SAVE THE EMPLOYEE'S FACE. When you criticize, do so privately. Make your criticism constructive by showing the employee a better way. Always direct your comments to the employee's work and not to him personally.

RECOGNIZE THE EMPLOYEE'S PROGRESS. Compliment him on his good work and, at the same time, encourage him to strive for even greater achievement.

A Feeling of Belonging

One of our strongest desires is to belong and to be accepted by a group or groups. Man is undeniably a social animal. Aristotle once said, "A man who lives outside society is either a god or beast." This feeling of belonging, however, is not acquired by mere nominal membership in a group. It is acquired by *participation*, by the individual's contributing something of value to the group's work, and by the group's recognizing the contribution as worthwhile.

Communication can do much to satisfy the desire to belong in two ways: First each supervisor should consult with his subordinates before instituting changes in processes, personnel, or equipment, a practice known as *consultative management*. Supervisors should make it a habit to ask their employees what they think, then listen and get their ideas. Whenever you ask someone, "What do you think?" you flatter him. You say to him, in effect, "I value your judgment." Not only does this approach raise employee morale and strengthen supervisor-employee rapport, but it often opens the floodgates to a flow of valuable ideas which can increase efficiency and cut costs. Every supervisor should be mindful of the fact that no one is quite so conversant with the details of a job as the man who does it daily. Many employees get good ideas from time to time about improving their jobs. These ideas should be tapped.

Consultative management is particularly important when changes are contemplated. Most of us tend to resist change. We have adapted ourselves, sometimes painfully, to the status quo, and we dislike having the pattern of our lives upset, especially when changes come abruptly and unexpectedly. To induce your employees to accept change cooperatively and to introduce it as smoothly as possible, get them to participate in planning and implementing it. If you do this, they will probably produce a number of valuable ideas that never occurred to you, ideas that will make the change better for all concerned. But, best of all, they will support the change because they had a hand in it. It is *their* change, a product of their efforts. In addition to their participation, it is important that all employees affected by an impending change clearly see how they will individually and collectively benefit from it. Satisfy their desire to know what is in it for them.

Second, each level of management should *make more frequent use of group problem solving*. Group problem-solving meetings have one merit, perhaps their greatest, which is often overlooked or glossed over. This merit is the tremendous lift which this method can give a group's morale, for this is participation at its best. In addition to the morale factor, such meetings provide an ideal milieu for horizontal communication, for the rapid exchange of ideas between supervisors across departmental lines. Such exchanges promote mutual understanding, enhance cooperation and coordination of effort, and knit the players of the company team more closely together.

Emotional Security

Few conditions contribute more to a sense of emotional security than being employed by a well-managed organization. All of us like order and predictability. We like to know what we can and cannot do. We like to know how we are doing. And we like to feel that we can predict fairly accurately where we are going. In companies having good communication between management and employees, the employees know these things, for, in such companies, employees are well trained and well informed; jurisdictional lines are carefully drawn; each employee knows what he is supposed to do, where, when, how, and why he is supposed to do it; penalties for poor performance are firm, fair, and clearly understood; and credit for good work is freely and promptly given.

In summary, communication is the conveyance of meaning designed to motivate people to take desired action. People act most readily to satisfy their wants. Communication is the principal means by which the supervisor can help his employees satisfy their job-related wants. Communication, therefore, is the supervisor's most important tool.

377

COMMUNICATION BEGINS AT THE TOP

Communication must be an integral and vital part of management's philosophy. As all management philosophies, it must originate with top management and be a continuing network for the exchange of information and ideas up, down, and across the company structure. It must be as much of part of management planning as production schedules, procurement of materials, and the maintenance of equipment. And it must function continuously, not just when a crisis occurs. Management, therefore, must be communication conscious at all times. This does not mean that supervisors should bare their souls to their employees or completely divulge every decision and plan, but it does mean that every supervisor should consider the advisability of complete disclosure with due regard to the limitations applicable to his situation. And, if something should be told, the supervisor must, of course, decide when, where, to whom, and how.

While any plant-wide or company-wide communication program must start at the top and radiate downward through every echelon of management, the first-line supervisor is the key in any continuing communication program. He is the king-pin who can unite or sunder the labor-management segments of the company team. To the worker, he personifies the company, and it is he who is the key link in most upward communication from worker to top management. Likewise, it is he who must interpret company policy to the worker, pass on information, and transmit orders and instructions.

Up to this point, we have considered only the vertical half of the communication function. It is equally important, however, that ideas and information be communicated across the company structure as it is that they be communicated up and down. This means that management personnel at each level must view themselves as links in a horizontal chain of communication. No matter how effective a company's verticle communication may be, if its supervisors are not communicating well with each other and if they do not know, understand, and accept each other's problems and needs, there can be only ineffectual teamwork and poor cooperation.

ELIMINATING COMMUNICATION ROADBLOCKS

How can interdepartmental barriers to communication and understanding be overcome? The best and quickest way is by frequent face-to-face discussions at each level of management, provided such discussions are approached with an open mind and a spirit of friendly helpfulness. Such interdepartmental discussions should be aimed primarily at exchanging knowledge, creating understanding, and gaining acceptance of each other's problems and needs. These meetings should take place as often as practicable until each supervisor is so thoroughly familiar with and appreciative of the needs and problems of his peers that he consistently and unhesitatingly coordinates his efforts with theirs.

A second, and equally formidable, communication roadblock is the barrier of status and position. It particularly inhibits the flow of upward communication. Some men "freeze up" in the presence of their superiors and experience mental blocks which prevent them from expressing themselves fully or clearly. Other men take the position that "what the boss doesn't know won't hurt him" and deliberately screen out all unpleasant information which might upset their superiors. Often these self-appointed censors screen out information that management urgently needs to function intelligently.

What can management do to "thaw out" its employees, to put them at ease, and get them to "open up?" The first and most important step is to establish by the daily example of top management a free and permissive climate favoring upward communication. Once this climate has been established at the top, it will quickly permeate the entire organization.

There are two intangible but essential elements in a good communication climate: an attitude that is people-centered rather than production-centered and an open door in fact as well as in word.

This is not an atmosphere that can be established by words, but only by deeds, by management's daily example on the job. Besides practicing what it preaches, management must make it clear to all supervisors that they should make time for communication. The driving insistence that every moment of a supervisor's time be spent on production is too frequently the preoccupation of some top managers. Such thinking has no place in modern management, for experience has abundantly demonstrated that the supervisor's job is handling people and that devoting enough time to communicating with them is an integral and inescapable part of that job.

Is there one best way of communicating? Not for all situations and messages, but face-to-face communication is preferable whenever it is practicable. It is personal and warmer than other media. It can convey more meaning than written or telephonic communication, because the parties can also communicate via gestures and facial expressions. It is quick and inexpensive. It permits immediate feedback and clarification. When each level of management communicates with the next lower level by meetings, three distinct benefits accrue:

1. Management's leadership at each level will be strengthened by regularly scheduled, face-to-face meetings.
2. The information conveyed at such meetings will usually be much more complete and accurate than that transmitted on the grapevine.

3. The workers will look increasingly to their supervisors rather than the union or the grapevine for company information.

SUMMARY AND CONCLUSION

Management is *man management*. As Lawrence Appley has said, "Management is personnel administration." The results managers get can be achieved only through people. Since the supervisor cannot slave-drive people for a prolonged period without having it backfire, he must motivate them affirmatively by the carrot rather than the stick. A good communication program is a powerful motivational influence, because it makes it possible for employees to satisfy many of their basic wants, such as recognition, communication, belonging, and emotional security. Communication activities contributing to the satisfaction of these needs are induction, training, coaching, counseling, listening, informational meetings, consultative management, and group problem solving.

The cardinal prerequisite for a successful communication program is a proper climate. This must first be established at the top-management level, from which it will radiate downward throughout the entire organization. To sustain this climate, management must be employee centered, keep an open door, listen, and allow time for communication. Finally, all persons in the organization with important communication responsibilities should be located and trained in the most effective use of communication skills.

Removing barriers to communication, establishing a favorable communication climate, and improving the supervisor's skills as a communicator are among the foremost challenges and opportunities facing modern management. One of the measures of an organization's success is the extent to which its management has recognized and met this challenge.

50. Breaking the Barriers to Delegation*

Charles C. Gibbons

Delegating is entrusting responsibility and authority to others who then become responsible to you for results. What you delegate essentially is the right to make decisions. The right to make decisions includes the right to make mistakes, for anyone who makes decisions will make a certain number of mistakes. The crux of the matter is how big a mistake are you willing to let your subordinates make?

Books on business management agree that it is highly desirable, even essential, for a manager to delegate a certain amount of authority and responsibility to his subordinates. Although there is general agreement on the desirability of delegation, I have observed that it is difficult for many managers to delegate to the extent they know they should.

HOW WELL DO YOU DELEGATE?

To appraise your own delegation you might consider such questions as the following:

1. Are decisions in your organization made at the lowest level at which they can properly be made?

2. Do your subordinates know what you expect them to do?

3. Do your subordinates have policies to guide them in making decisions?

4. Is your unit organized in a way that facilitates delegation?

5. Do you direct your subordinates to accomplish certain results rather than to perform certain activities?

6. Do you make the fullest possible use of staff?

7. Are your subordinates properly motivated so that they willingly accept more responsibility?

8. Do you exercise adequate control over your operations?

9. Do you spend most of your time on matters that are really important?

WHY IS IT SO HARD TO DELEGATE?

Many managers who answer these questions regarding their own delegation come to the conclusion that they do not delegate as well as they know they should. It may be worthwhile to consider why it is so hard to delegate.

* Reprinted by permission from the November, 1966, issue of the *Michigan Business Review*, published by the Graduate School of Business Administration, The University of Michigan.

In my opinion, there are three basic reasons why managers do not delegate as well as they should:

1. They do not understand clearly what their responsibility and authority are.

2. They overestimate the extent to which they can do the work themselves better than it would be done by their subordinates.

3. They feel insecure in their jobs and in their relationships with their superiors, their peers, and their subordinates.

Unless a manager understands clearly what his responsibility and authority are, he will not be a good delegator because he can delegate only those functions which have been assigned to him. When managers are uncertain regarding the content of their jobs, it is not surprising that they do not delegate properly.

The manager who fails to delegate may be an egotist who truly feels that he can perform the work better than any of his subordinates. It may actually be true that he can perform each task better than anyone else but it does not follow that the egotistical manager can get as much done as the entire work group could if their activities were properly coordinated.

Some managers feel they must do things themselves or they will not be done right. Although on the surface such a manager appears to be self-confident and egotistical, such behavior is really a mark of insecurity. Many managers fail to delegate because they are afraid that their subordinates will make some mistake for which the manager will be criticized. When you delegate, you become vulnerable to criticism for mistakes which your subordinates make. To delegate properly a manager must be secure and must be confident that he can solve any problem which a subordinate may create.

Men who feel insecure in their positions make poor delegators for a variety of reasons. They may fail to delegate because they are afraid of not being essential. They may feel more competent and comfortable performing routine duties rather than performing the work of a manager —planning, organizing, leading, and controlling. Finally, I would suggest that the insecure person often fails to delegate because he does not want to appear lazy. Many managers do not delegate as much as they should because they are afraid of seeming lazy to their superiors, to their subordinates, or even to themselves. It takes a secure person to run such a risk.

MAKING IT EASIER TO DELEGATE

Since delegation is regarded as a management virtue, but a difficult one to practice, there may be some value in considering what a manager can do to make it easier for him to delegate.

1. *Be sure you and your boss agree as to what your job is.* Unless you have a clear idea as to what your authority and responsibility are, you cannot delegate. In defining your job, you should take all the initiative you can without encroaching on the rights of others. A narrow definition of your job will be restrictive and will serve neither your purposes nor the purposes of the company.

2. *Be sure your subordinates understand what you expect them to do.* The simplest way to delegate to your subordinates is to tell them what authority you reserve for yourself and that all other authority is theirs. You should delegate somewhat beyond what the subordinate has proved he can handle. Challenge the subordinate to do a little more than he has yet shown he can do. He may well surprise both himself and you.

It may help for you to list for your subordinates those matters which you wish them to discuss with you before any action is taken. There may be a second group of responsibilities on which the subordinates can take action and then report later to you. Any activity or responsibility not falling into one of these two groups could be performed by the subordinate without any consultation with you, either before or after taking action.

Be sure each of your subordinates knows what you consider the signs of a job well done: i.e., what conditions will exist when he has performed his job satisfactorily.

3. *Prepare written policies which your subordinates can use to guide their decisions.* It is easier for you to delegate authority and for your subordinates to accept responsibility if policies are available to guide those making decisions.

A policy is a general, continuing answer to a recurring question. A soundly conceived and clearly understood set of policies permits subordinates to make decisions and take action with confidence.

4. *Be humble enough to admit that someone else may be able to do the job as well as you can.* It is important to recognize that even though you may be more capable than any one of your subordinates, you cannot perform all of the work better than the whole group of your subordinates can do it. The manager of a baseball team might be an excellent pitcher, catcher, and first baseman, but he cannot play all these positions simultaneously.

5. *In organizing your work group, have a large number of subordinates directly responsible to you.* By having a flat organization, you eliminate the necessity of having several levels between yourself and the rank-and-file employees.

Such a flat organization improves communication, decision-making, the taking of action, and the exercise of control. It is possible to have a flat organization only if you have capable, well-trained subordinates, and if you delegate real authority to them.

6. *Make your subordinates responsible for accomplishing certain results rather than for performing certain activities.* After a subordinate understands what results are desired, he should be able to choose for himself the methods he will use in accomplishing the desired results. The subordinate can make his fullest contribution only if he is free to exercise some initiative and ingenuity in carrying out the work. If you delegate effectively, your subordinates will understand that the real boss is the task to be performed.

7. *Reward the men who get things done.* You cannot delegate unless your subordinates will accept responsibility. They will accept responsibility and actively participate in accomplishing the objectives of the organization only if they feel that rewards go to the men who get things done. The rewards for being right must always be greater than the penalties for being wrong.

8. *Distinguish between the urgent things and the important things you have to do and try to spend more time on the important ones.* So much of a manager's working time may be consumed in performing the urgent tasks which clamor for attention that he has little time left to do the important things. The strongest argument, in fact, for more delegation of minor responsibilities is that it leaves the manager free to give attention to more important matters. Only if a manager frees himself from operating details will he have the time necessary for the management functions of planning, organizing, leading, and controlling the operations for which he is responsible.

SUMMARY

Those who speak and write on management practices are unanimous in saying that managers should delegate authority and responsibility to their subordinates. Furthermore, most managers themselves recognize that they cannot perform all the work for which they are responsible. What are the reasons then why managers find it so difficult to delegate?

Some of the major reasons why managers fail to delegate are: (1) they do not understand clearly what their responsibility and authority are; (2) they overestimate the extent to which they can do the work themselves better than it would be done by their subordinates; and (3) they feel insecure in their jobs and in their relationships with their superiors, their peers, and their subordinates.

Some suggestions are offered as to what a manager might do if he wishes to improve his delegation.

51. The Art of Delegating*

Dave Tver

The word delegate means many things to many people. It has caused more consternation, frustration and management dissatisfaction than any other word. It is the subject of meetings, seminars, training sessions and bull sessions. It is the word that has been perpetrated on management as a panacea for all problems.

Is it? What are we really talking about?

If you are looking for an easy definition or a simple explanation, there isn't any, any more than there is an easy answer to many other management problems. The answers look good on paper and they sound reasonable in speeches, but become difficult to carry out when you, as an individual, have to apply the principles.

Delegation is a delicate proposition. It requires one person to assign part of his authority to make decisions, but none of the final responsibility for those decisions, to another person. While the delegator doesn't take a direct part in such decisions, he's ultimately responsible for them.

The art of successful delegation requires great skill, insight and judgment from the delegator. He must strike an appropriate balance between over and under delegation so that he yields authority without losing over-all control. He must coach and otherwise train subordinates to exercise authority correctly. He must have courage to take risks, for he can't be sure how much authority any subordinate can manage until he's tried.

The need for delegation is much more than theoretical. Delegation enables the manager to manage, to oversee the work of his subordinates. In a recent study of why three hundred executives failed, eighteen general causes were uncovered. The Number One cause was the failure to delegate.

The manager or supervisor acquires his own authority through delegation. He must know how to use it and that includes redelegating part of it, in turn, to his subordinates.

That's delegation in a nutshell, and the crux of the problem. The problem is to crack the nut, to put this principle into practice! To delegate successfully, the manager must be able to answer seven basic questions.

The first is, to what extent should I consult my chief about using authority that he delegates to me?

When authority is delegated to you, try to resolve any problems by

* From *Oklahoma Journal* (Midwest City). Reprinted by permission.

yourself. Unless you operate on your own, you are not accepting the authority entrusted to you. Authority is delegated so that you'll use it to free your chief for other parts of his job. The more you depend on his help in solving problems, the less help you are to him.

Fear is the greatest obstacle to the successful use of delegated authority. When your superior delegates to you, you may assume that he has confidence in your abilities. Even so, it's often hard to decide whether to proceed on your own or to get help from your boss. Whenever you have a real problem, ask for help.

The longer you work with your boss, the more you'll know how he feels about your acting independently. For instance, a critical deadline may force you to decide a controversial issue by yourself, take some immediate action, and tell your chief about it later, but be sure to tell him as soon as possible. The first time you do this, his reaction will give you a clue to how you should proceed in the future. As we have stated before, there isn't any pat answer, it depends upon the individual you work for, his philosophy and temperament.

The second question is, what kinds of authority should the manager or supervisor delegate to his subordinates?

Since you can't delegate authority you don't have, start by finding out exactly what your authority is. To delegate a part of it, you may need your superior's consent, permission from a policy body, or other clearances.

Never delegate policy formulation, nor over-all supervisory duties. Without these, a manager cannot control his staff and, as a result, can lose his authority as chief. The manager must retain authority for major discipline, for promotions and for appraising subordinates.

In general, he can safely delegate the functions that remain, largely the technical ones of operating the department. Most managers automatically consider convenience so that, for example, they reassign duties that are time consuming or highly detailed.

A manager may even delegate some routine decision making, as long as the decisions don't involve the over-all objectives of his department.

The third question of delegation is, how much of his authority should a manager delegate?

Delegation can be a chain reaction. As a supervisor effectively exercises authority delegated to him, his superior, in turn, is freed to manage more authority than before. This releases still higher management, in succession, from some of its routine and gives them more time for long range planning.

Thus, it is in the company's interest that every manager handle as much authority as he can. The general rule is: Delegate as much as you can of your authority in technical matters, but always delegate in keeping with the ability of your subordinates. As they develop through the authority that you've granted them, you can delegate more to them, take on more yourself, and so on up the line.

The fourth question is, when is the right time to delegate?

Before you can delegate, the following conditions should exist. Delegation must fulfill a specific purpose. It is not enough to say, "This will streamline the operation." Instead, you should determine specifically what you're trying to achieve. Will delegation save you time? If not, what results do you expect?

You must have an immediate subordinate to whom you can delegate. If you don't, train someone.

The delegated function should be one that occurs reasonably often and is fairly time consuming. The time it takes to train a subordinate in the early stages of delegation may not be worth while unless it enables you to turn over to him a substantial amount of work. In other words, training should take less of your time than the function you're delegating.

Before a manager can delegate successfully, he must be willing to accept the decisions made by his delegates. You can't expect every job to be performed exactly as you would do it. If, for any reason, you find yourself unwilling to accept subordinates' decisions, something in your delegation picture is wrong. You may not have the proper attitude or the task may be too important to be delegated. Be realistic and face the facts. If you can't delegate them, do it all yourself and face the consequences.

The fifth question is, to whom should a manager delegate?

Delegate only to immediate subordinates. Delegating to someone who reports through a third person invites resentment or misunderstanding from the man in the middle, your immediate subordinate. If you sidestep him, he can rightfully feel either that you lack confidence in him or that you don't know how to run an organization.

Delegate only to people whom you can trust, who will use their authority with skill. Also, match delegation to subordinates' special abilities. Assign broad planning to the man with imagination. Give work that demands extreme precision to your most meticulous subordinate. Assign delicate matters to the person who is most diplomatic.

A decision to delegate is often a calculated risk, but so is business itself. If the facts and reasoning are adequate, most of the risks the manager takes will be to his advantage.

The sixth question is a thorny one, how should I delegate?

Delegation should be broad to give the delegate real responsibility and to enable the manager to manage his entire job with time left over to help his superior with special assignments. Therefore, delegate a function rather than a specific task. Authority should always be delegated clearly and concisely, in writing if necessary. State explicitly the results you require but let your subordinate work out his own way of achieving them. This is most important.

Having defined the goal, give the subordinate enough authority to achieve it. There's no use putting a man in charge of a work group unless that group knows that he's their boss.

You may have to tell him how to exercise his new authority, and the pitfalls. Be sure to tell subordinates the limits of their authority. If you don't, they invariably get in trouble with their superiors and a great deal of misunderstanding develops. Then the damage becomes twice as hard to undo.

There are some special "don'ts" in delegation. Don't delegate to one subordinate the authority that you have already delegated to someone else. In pointing out limitations of, or restrictions upon, delegated authority, be careful not to inhibit the delegate's use of his new authority or make him reluctant to tackle the job, as so often happens.

Don't delegate to the detriment of your proper staff and line balance, nor to the impairment of over-all morale.

The seventh and final question is, how can the manager or supervisor maintain control, once he has delegated authority?

If more managers knew the answer to this, they would delegate more authority more often. It's not always easy to control delegation but it is usually possible. The principal method is to keep in touch. It's your job to require the delegate to keep you informed on how he's using the authority you've granted him.

There are several ways to do it. First, and most important, establish the kind of working relationship that makes members of your staff want to keep you informed. This means that you should maintain a friendly atmosphere that encourages free discussion. It also means that your subordinates should have confidence in your ability to understand them and their problems.

Follow up. From time to time, ask subordinates how their projects are going. When it's suitable, ask them to submit brief reports, written or oral. Ask, especially after they have sought your advice or help, how the problem is turning out.

Establish deadlines. If you've delegated a man to investigate the best buys in machinery or equipment for a plant, tell him you'd like his suggestions within a month.

Establish performance standards too. Requiring answers to specific questions will keep you in control, and your delegate on his toes. If you delegate authority to sign letters, you might request at first that copies be submitted to you. This will keep you abreast of the delegate's activity, but only after he has acted, after he's signed and sent letters, and, therefore, should not interfere with his making independent decisions.

Don't check every piece of correspondence or every move he makes. Close supervision tends to make the subordinate feel he has no real authority. Occasional spot checks provide a progress report without diminishing the subordinate's sense of responsibility.

Keep him informed. Tell him of policy or procedural changes that may affect his work. Pass along any company information that he needs to know. Chances are that if you keep your subordinates informed, they will also keep you informed. As you discuss new information with them, they are likely to volunteer a quick report on their progress.

If your subordinate is reluctant to exercise authority, he may only be overcautious or playing it safe, but if he continues to return problems to you, the authority will soon be back where it started, on your desk.

You can improve his decision making ability by helping him, step by step, to make a few decisions, then putting him on his own. Later, if he still wonders what to do, ask him the kinds of questions that you consider when you make decisions, or begin by asking why he's bringing the matter to you, what is unique or troublesome about it? You may find that it's time for you to step in. If not, your questions should help him to decide and they certainly will demonstrate your position, that it's up to him to decide.

All right, what if a delegate makes a real blunder? Try to mitigate or change it, if you can. If the company, or your department, is made to look foolish by the delegate's action, it's occasionally legitimate to expect him to soften the outside impression by admitting personal responsibility. On the whole, however, it's better to help him save face.

In private, and let us stress in private, discuss the mistake, the reasons it occurred, and the steps that could have prevented it. Be sure to identify it as a mistake and let the subordinate realize that he shouldn't repeat it.

If, afterwards, the subordinate continues to fumble in exercising his authority, you may have to withdraw the authority you had delegated to him.

The requirements for successful delegation are stiff. Stiff as they are, though, the benefits are enormous. The manager acquires considerable freedom from routine, repetitive functions. As a result, he has more time to spend on his primary management duties, administering, supervising, planning and controlling.

Just as important, delegation gives subordinates invaluable experience in decision making. This leads to increased individual responsibility, greater pride in work, higher morale and strong initiative. Practiced throughout an organization, delegation becomes a source of vitality and progress.

52. How to Stay on Top of the Job*

James C. Harrison, Jr.

Think of four executives you know. How many of them delegate responsibility to a subordinate the same way you do? One? Two? More
than likely, *none* of them does.

Styles of delegation can range all the way from the executive who
turns over an assignment carte blanche to the executive who treats his
subordinate as an "assistant to," giving him a minimum of authority and
responsibility. To be sure, most executives are familiar with and probably share the common business tenet that "the delegation of responsibility for performance should never be conferred without the delegation
of authority for directing the performance." But what about the act of
delegation itself? Specifically:

How much responsibility can an executive delegate to a subordinate?

When delegation proves unfruitful, can an executive excuse himself
by placing the blame on the delegated-to subordinate?

Does the delegating executive have equal responsibility for the
failure?

If so, how can an executive use delegation to reduce the demands on
his time, develop his subordinates, and still keep on top of every job?

In sum, what do executives really mean by the word *delegation*?

The plain fact is that some executives are able to use delegation successfully and others are not. And the differences in practice that go to
make up delegation undoubtedly relate to the indication that there is a
good deal of confusion among executives as to exactly what delegation is.

TWO EXTREMES

Example I

Following the Presidential election [1960], an Associated Press dispatch, carrying the by-line of Jack Bell and bearing the dateline Washington, D.C., dealt with the question of whether the new Cabinet, under
the direction of John F. Kennedy, would imitate its predecessor's custom
of "calling turns and making policies." Bell doubted such would be the
case, after having evaluated the new President's past behavior: "He
hasn't tackled as mammoth a task as the presidency, but he has kept

* From *Harvard Business Review*, Vol. 39, No. 6 (November–December, 1961), 100–108.
ⓒ 1961 by the President and Fellows of Harvard College; all rights reserved. Reprinted by
permission.

personally *on top of jobs* he has filled as a member of the House and a member of the Senate."[1]

Example II

I happened to be present when a company president called a hurried conference with his staff following a meeting of the firm's board of directors. The board had been very critical of a recent decline in sales and profits, and had strongly intimated to the president that the fault lay not in the capabilities of the staff but in a lack of energetic application of their talents. The president concluded his post-mortem with this admonishment:

I don't intend to subject myself to such humiliation again. You men are paid to do your jobs; it's not up to me to do them for you. I don't know how you spend your time, and I don't intend to try to find out. You know your responsibilities, and these figures bear out that you haven't discharged them properly. All I can say, men, is that if the next report doesn't show a marked improvement, I can't guarantee that all of us in this room will be together when another conference of this nature takes place.

For the sake of mutual understanding, even at the risk of belaboring the obvious, permit me to compare these two events. In both situations, there was a "delegation of responsibility." The fact that President Kennedy kept "personally on top of jobs" is, by nature of the wording, indication that he was not the sole performer. The company president conveyed his delegation with the words, "You know your responsibilities"; for, given the hierarchical organization of a business, such responsibilities could exist for his staff only by his transfer of them from himself to the staff.

But there are great differences in the styles of delegation used by these two men. The key to these differences in practice lies in their interpretations of the word *delegation*. Thus:

President Kennedy's interpretation is to distribute jobs among his aides, and yet continue to keep on top of them. By maintaining surveillance over an assignment, he knows its approximate status at all times. He does not have to carry out the work himself, nor does he take away from his subordinates the freedom of action necessary for their personal development. Instead, his procedure enables him to delegate while keeping track of what is going on.

In contrast, the humiliated company president's interpretation does not include follow-up: "I don't know how you spend your time. I don't intend to try to find out." This is delegation in the extreme: interim relinquishment of participation. He interprets the word delegation to allow him to shed not only the burden of responsibility, by his manner of

1 *Chronicle*, Augusta, Georgia, January 22, 1961; italics added.

delegation, but also the mantle of leadership. He makes no attempt to stay on top of the job; he wants only to get out from under it.

Yet the company president undoubtedly does not believe that he is shirking his duties, and his personal sense of responsibility is, no doubt, equal to that felt by President Kennedy under his style of delegation. The difference between these two men, again, is not in their zeal or conscience; it lies in their *interpretation* of the word *delegation*—in a situation where interpretation is the key to the successful practice of it.

ROOT OF CONFUSION

Why are there such differences in interpretation and, consequently, differences in practice? All Americans have a common language, presumably, so where does the confusion in meaning originate?

The search for answers to such questions has given birth to the scientific study of the meaning of words, called semantics. Semantics has as a basis the idea that words are not things in themselves, but are symbols of things. Consequently, one's interpretation of a word is not as flawless as might be one's examination of the object represented by the word.

In effect, the meaning of the word is not more correct than the symbolization it possesses for the hearer or reader. In spite of Gertrude Stein's reiteration that "a rose is a rose is a rose," a rose is *not* a rose if the person reading or hearing the phrase associates the word rose with a peony. This same kind of confusion can arise with the word *delegation*. No matter what the intent of the speaker or writer, its meaning is what the hearer or reader receives.

The dictionary does not settle the matter. *Webster's New International Dictionary* defines delegation as the "act of delegating, or investing with authority to act for another." But what is meant by "investing with authority"? Here is the root of the problem.

The key semantic, and consequently behavioral, difficulty arises in defining what degree of authority and what type of behavior are to be invested. For the amount of power or the kind of power to be given is not an inherent or specified part of the written definition. *Rather, the degree of authority is dependent on the extent to which a person is allowed to substitute one behavior for another.* And this is usually—in daily business practice—a matter of subjective interpretation and operating behavior on the part of the delegator. Consider:

If, for example, delegation allows unrestricted substitution, then the company president is justified in the attitude he has adopted. Having invested his subordinates with authority (if such investiture can be unrestricted), he has unburdened himself of the particular responsibility.

On the other hand, if delegation allows only a restricted substitution, then President Kennedy's method is the only possible approach. Because his subordinates act with limited authority, he himself has to stay "on top of jobs," for he has to bridge the gap between the power they are given and the power necessary to complete the task at hand. That is, he has to participate with them in order to provide, when required, for the variance between the amount of authority delegated and the full power demanded in the final action.

Is the amount of substitution of behavior, the delegation of either unlimited or limited authority, merely a matter of personal choice? Can any executive divest himself of full authority in an action which comes within the sphere of his jurisdiction? Does the act of delegation have certain specific definable goals? Can styles of delegation be tailored to meet these goals?

SCOPE OF OBLIGATION

The decisive answer to these questions, and to the confusion over the meaning of delegation, is one word: *accountability.* An executive can delegate responsibility, that is, obligation. He can hold another person accountable to him as the delegator of responsibility to do a certain job. But this act by no means diminishes the measure of his own accountability to his own superiors. He can no more divorce himself from this liability than he can excuse himself from blame in the event of his subordinate's failure, or take full credit for the success. *The executive himself, not his subordinate, possesses the full obligation.*

Thus, in every single act of delegating there are two sets of correlative and equal responsibilities: (1) the obligations which the delegate has to his principal, and (2) the obligations for which the principal is accountable to those whom he represents.

The obligation in the principal's case is not solely that of setting action in motion, such as by assigning the work to his subordinate. Far from it. His responsibility is for final results, irrespective of the style or type of delegation he uses. The same holds true for his subordinate if the latter in turn delegates the job to his own assistant.

A president, for example, is a delegate of his board of directors assigned to the task of increasing sales and profits. He, in turn, since this assignment is no one-man job, delegates specific aspects of this responsibility to members of his staff. Because of this delegation, they are obligated to him to produce the desired results. However—and this is the emphatic point—he cannot delegate to them his accountability to the board; this is his and his alone.

Nor can his assistants delegate to their assistants their accountability to the president. The proper discharge of their responsibilities will pay off the obligation he imposed on them, but a failure on their part will not make the president blameless for the outcome as far as the board is concerned. His assignment may have been more than a one-man job, but his accountability for its successful completion is *a one-man burden*. Only the labors can be shared.

Keeping on Top

If one must delegate and yet retain full accountability for the results, then some sort of supervision is necessary. How can a busy executive keep on top of every job he must turn over to others? The ease that an executive will have in doing this job depends on the style of delegation he selects.

Many executives, such as the company president cited earlier, behave as if keeping on top means only that they should watch what is going on, as spectators. But in this guise a man is actually not an executive; he is not, as is demanded in his title, working through others. Rather, he has simply turned a job over to others. And he has all the confining characteristics of a helpless onlooker. He can really be an *executive* only when he works through others; only when they are extensions of himself; only when he is well enough informed of their efforts to protect his own accountability, to be certain of the outcome.

Many executives hold "orientation" sessions. Here the nature of the problem is spelled out, dissected, and apportioned among the potential solvers. Yet this practice merely justifies the role of the spectator. Such a procedure amounts to no more than the president's saying: "*Now* you know your responsibilities. . . ." His executives may have known their responsibilities, but, judging by the results, he certainly did not know his, or was more a gambler than an executive. Certainly, an orientation session is necessary; the problem has to be spelled out and apportioned. But the crucial error occurs when an executive divorces himself from further participation by regarding himself merely as the depository of the end result. Keeping on top of what is going on means more than simply knowing what is going on; it means keeping a hand in the actions as well.

Keeping a Hand In

But to delegate and at the same time remember one's own full accountability requires self-discipline. Let me give you a very personal example. At one time I headed an advertising agency. One day there came to our door an account which was very foreign to my experience: publicizing a series of evangelistic meetings conducted by Billy Graham. On the advice of his friends, he was making his first public appearance outside his adopted home of Charlotte, North Carolina. The account was placed with our agency by a committee of local citizens whose sole responsibility to Graham consisted of engaging advertising services, setting the dates of meetings, and stipulating the amount of money to be expended on the campaign.

I knew that the head of our art department was a running mate of the members of the sponsoring committee and, realizing my own inexperience with this type of account, "delegated" the task to the artist. I dismissed the matter from my mind until Graham's business manager (whose name I have since forgotten) came into the agency prior to the first evangelistic meeting. I sent for the artist, and he showed up with layouts far more suitable as illustrations for religious works than as a mass appeal to the audience that Graham hoped to reach. Well, shamefacedly, I banished the artist along with his works to their northern-lighted quarters, and begged for another day of grace. The business manager granted it, but with some memorable parting words:

"Mr. Harrison, may I give you a little advice? A good executive has to delegate, just as you have done in this case. And the power to delegate enables a man to multiply his abilities many times. But, in order to do this, he must learn one basic rule: *to keep his hand in* whatever he delegates."

Most executives *do* want to multiply their abilities by spreading the actual work to be done among subordinates. But to do this successfully requires that an executive remember that *accountability* cannot be delegated. In sum, an executive must select delegating behavior that will concurrently allow him to:

Spread the physical work among his aides.
See to it that the job is done correctly.
Have enough time to take corrective action should something go wrong.
Develop his subordinate's talents and abilities.

It is combining these four elements into practice that most executives find difficult. Yet only by selecting a style of delegation that includes these four elements can an executive keep his hand in sufficiently to protect his accountability.

AUDITING PROGRESS

But just how can an executive keep his hand in every job, considering the multiplicity of demands on his time and energies? Obviously, such limitations prevent a complete sharing of the assignment. However, time is not so short (and, in fact, cannot be) that it prevents an active participation in every delegated job.

Such participation is possible, not by supervising every detail of the job, but by periodic audits of what is going on. Though the captain of a ship has other duties that prohibit his steering of the boat himself, he still has to make intermittent comparisons between the ship's present position and planned destination. True, such checks do not guarantee constant, undeviating, continuous direction of the ship's course. They do, nevertheless, enable the captain to make corrections with a minimum of lost time, effort, and results.

However, *auditing*, like delegation, can denote many different kinds of specific activities. So rather than fall into semantic traps, let us define auditing by looking at some methods that successful executives use to audit progress. From time to time I have observed various styles of delegation which businessmen use to protect their accountability. Each of these methods has as a goal the four elements outlined above, and stresses active executive participation in the delegated activity, giving ample opportunity for correction before it is too late.

Now I confess that in only rare instances did I find uncompromising adherence to any single one of these methods for auditing delegation. Rather, the choice of a particular device depended on the nature of the responsibility delegated. The same executive would use several of them concurrently, each for different individual assignments. Conditions, not the executives, determined the selection of a specific plan of delegation. But more about this later. First, here are the methods of delegation.

1. PREVIEWING DIRECTION. In this method, an executive gives his subordinate the problem and asks him to submit in writing at a specified time a synopsis of his plan of action. By this process the executive receives at the very start his subordinate's interpretation of the problem, a definite and concrete line of attack, and a detailed plan of procedure that can be corrected or adjusted.

2. QUESTIONING ON PROGRESS. This is the most informal, the most revealing, and the most time-consuming style of delegation emphasizing executive participation. It requires that an executive send for or go to his subordinate at or during the most propitious stages of development for the project in question. This method requires deft timing and a clear attitude of friendly interest. The executive cannot risk the appearance of "checking up," lest he destroy his subordinate's self-confidence. This method is inconvenient because it requires an executive to stop work at the most inopportune moments, takes time to carry out, and interrupts the subordinate. Yet the executive does maintain a maximum grasp of what is going on.

3. DEMANDING REPORTS. This method requires that the subordinate submit periodic progress reports, with or without specific deadlines. It can be the most pleasant of all audits, since it saves the time of all concerned. Yet it can also be the least satisfying method because its effectiveness depends on the ability of the subordinate to express himself in writing, the inclusion in the report of all facts necessary for judgment of progress (usually making the report unwieldy), and mutually under-

stood measurements of development and progress which allow the accountable executive to be aware of deviations from an apparent pathway to the desired goal. In sum, this method relies heavily on the subordinate's talents and the executive's clarity in putting across his ideas originally. It may be doubly difficult to use if the project is complex.

4. SCHEDULING CONFERENCES. By scheduling oral reports or conferences for definite dates in the future, this style of delegation attempts to alleviate the complications of Method 3, while at the same time gaining the merits of the informal questioning used in Method 2. It is most useful when the project to be audited is one which has a series of events that can be planned and timed in advance. Success is contingent on a carefully planned chronology of developments, an assumption that the forecasts or scheduled events will actually materialize at the times anticipated, and a presumption that the original plan of attack decided on is the only feasible approach. The drawbacks consist of the pressure imposed by time, a blind conformance to a prearranged method of attack, and a prohibition of creative experimentation by the calendar-bound subordinate.

5. SETTING DEADLINES. This method of delegation sets a time limit for completing delegated assignments. It is fairer than scheduling conferences in advance, since it abolishes all of the drawbacks except for the pressure imposed by time. But it also entails a maximization of certain potential liabilities.

These include loss of all time and materials consumed in the event of an impractical or unworkable solution, denial of all possible interim help and advice the delegator could have given his subordinate, and setback in the morale of the work force if failure should result.

Against these must be weighed freedom of thought and action extended to the delegated-to person, development of the subordinates' talents through the thrust of full and unrestrained authority, and minimizing interruptions of the work of the delegating executive.

Obviously, the only difference between this method and that employed by the company president in our vignette is the length of time during which there is, for all intents and purposes, complete abandonment of executive control. Naturally, the shorter the period, the better. This style of delegation is warranted only when the subordinate has proved his ability to perform successfully, his mode of performance is identical to that of the delegating executive, or the task is so perfunctory that the path to its completion is unmistakable.

6. CHECKING RESULTS. This method, unlike #2, can be used only when the particular project has tangible results while in progress. It is the most accurate, the most convenient for all concerned, and the least trouble to the subordinate.

The real test in using this method is in the self-discipline of the delegating executive, since he must schedule and prod himself to witness the progress (or lack of it) firsthand. This style requires available time to travel to and make an inspection of the progress, a knack of showing interest in the progress instead of reflecting suspicion on the abilities of the delegate (as in Method 2), and an ability and temperament to make constructive suggestions, as well as to leave behind an aura of encouragement.

7. MEASURING BY CROSSCURRENTS. Few problems are separate entities. The solution of one problem is usually reflected in other phases of an enterprise. For example, relieving a bottleneck in filling orders will automatically minimize the number and vociferousness of the complaints from the shipping department. In fact, the great majority of business problems are made known, not by their noticeable presence, but by their hindrance to other activities.

These crosscurrents of work flow provide measuring devices and warning signals, if an executive is attuned to them. This style of watchful delegation is effective where there is no damaging delay due to time lags in the crosscurrent warning signals, and where there is a dependable and direct relationship between the warning sign and its designated cause, and isolation and control of all other factors that filter into the crosscurrent.

8. DELEGATING BY INTERDEPENDENCE. This method can be used when the start of one activity begins with the culmination of another, or when the solution of a problem in one department becomes a problem in another, much like a relay race. Though devoid of intermediate participation by the top executive and consequently subject to inherent dangers, this style of delegation redeems itself on the strength of the adage: "Two heads are better than one." In effect, the report of progress is automatically given by the start of the next phase in the sequence. The delegated subordinates check on each other, for any one's performance is dependent on the others.

Such chains are quite often the case in business, as when the production, sales, and advertising departments are charged with increasing the volume of goods sold. Production must come forth with a product which sales thinks it can merchandise successfully; sales must invent a strategy in its area of marketing which will lend the greatest support to advertising; and advertising must originate a campaign designed to promote the salability of the product and to accelerate the effectiveness of the sales strategy. The responsibility and compliance of one group are, under such an alignment, mutually dependent on and therefore limited by the efforts of the others. The top executive has a built-in audit of progress.

Naturally, delegating by interdependence relies for favorable outcome on a marked degree of departmental interdependency for final results, separate and distinct functional responsibilities for each department involved, and sharp lines of demarcation whose boundaries, while contiguously dependent, are mandatorily independent in that they circumscribe departments whose progress can be measured by their own results and not by the shortcomings of others.

9. DELEGATING BY CORRELATION. In contrast to the preceding method, this one depends on parallel activities: two or more departments predicate their plans on the fact that all the others will complete their roles successfully and simultaneously. The chief advantage over delegation by interdependence is a reliance on *concurrent* employment of efforts, so that all related (but departmentalized) goals will materialize at the same time. By the same token, the main disadvantage is that such a parallel relationship of results will end up in failure for all if there is a failure for one. This type of delegating arrangement can be employed whenever a successful conclusion can be pinpointed in time. For example:

A bakery might be faced, in its wrapping area, with the problem of adapting machines to the use of a new wrapping film. A deadline of three weeks is given. During this same interval, the sales department is to formulate merchandising plans to introduce the bread in its "new dress." The same length of time is granted to the advertising department to prepare, and have ready to go, a specific promotion and media plan. Thus, on a stated date, all three responsibilities must be fulfilled: the bread must appear in its new wrapper, the merchandising must begin, and the advertising must appear.

Obviously, delegating by correlation needs to take into account assurance of satisfactory results, assumption of scheduled performance, and willingness of the top executive to accept accountability in the event of failure in any or all departments.

Combining Methods

As must be clear to the reader by now, all these styles of delegation can be easily combined. For example:

Delegating by correlation can be supplemented by scheduling conferences in order to obtain reports.

Delegating by interdependence can also include demanding reports of the subordinates.

Measuring crosscurrents may be made more accurate by checking of results.

The method of previewing direction offers an effective start to setting deadlines.

The system of demanding reports may be improved by questioning on progress as well.

In many instances more than two of the methods may be combined. One successful method for delegating and still keeping a hand in might combine previewing directions, scheduling conferences, checking results, and also delegating by interdependence.

SELECTING A STYLE

As noted earlier, the successful executives I observed allowed the situation, the particular project, to dictate their choice of a style of delegation. In addition, they considered the effectiveness of any one method insofar as inherent advantages or disadvantages made the particular delegating process easier or more difficult. Finally, they made their selection with a view to the amount of time, money, and effort needed to keep on top of the job optimally, weighed against the value of perfect performance within a given span of time. In effect, they appeared to ask themselves, unconsciously, two sets of questions:

What do I need to know in order to check the progress of this particular job and when do I need to know it most? How effectively do each of the styles of delegation adaptable to this project give me the optimum information?

What compromise, if any, must I make between the optimum style of delegation and other effective methods because of limits of time, effort, or money? Or, in other words, how important is it to do this project perfectly?

Measuring Points

The terms of the specific information needed are usually defined by the project itself. These terms may consist of personal observations, physical measurements, or end results. They may be posed as general judgments or may refer to specifics such as manpower, sales volume, units, and so on—in sum, whatever measurements are applicable to the nature of the job.

In addition, however, there is the problem of when it is best to make these measurements. That is, the problem of finding those crucial times in the project which will indicate clearly the absence or presence of progress toward the desired end result. Obviously, a busy executive cannot check all aspects of any one job. If he could, then he would not need to delegate. Therefore, an executive must also narrow down these measuring points to only those areas and times which will give him a maximum insight into the project.

In any job, the natural place to find such measuring points is between the different phases or steps of the project. For example, the artist working under me in the Billy Graham promotion example had to work in stages. He would have developed his ideas in a number of steps: (1) general idea or theme; (2) rough layouts depicting the theme; (3) copy expounding the theme; (4) finished layouts; (5) finished artwork; and (6) pasteups for reproductions. I could have selected any one or all of these points for auditing his progress. And a correction at any early stage would have prevented wasted time and effort in the steps that followed. Each phase gave me the opportunity for corrective action, to keep my hand in and at the same time to protect my accountability.

In sum, I had to decide what I wanted to know as well as the optimum time for having this information and making my audit.

In many cases, the specific method to be used for participating in the delegated job is predetermined by the job itself. In the Billy Graham campaign, for example, the only measuring stick was my reaction to the ideas themselves. The only way I could make this measure was to go and look at the work in progress. A report could not substitute for my "seeing for myself," and only a method of auditing progress which allowed me to do this would have been suitable.

On the other hand, in many other kinds of business situations an executive could use quite different methods almost equally well. A written report giving product performance statistics could be just as good (if not better) as going to see the product in action. In such situations, the executive must rank the different methods according to the degree to which they provide the optimum amount of information about the project for purposes of keeping his hand in. But in making this evaluation an executive must not be beguiled by the method that appeals to him as most comfortable. He must evaluate the device according to the needs of the situation.

Necessity for Compromise

Three tentative evaluations will have now been made by an executive selecting a style of delegation: the specific terms of the information needed; the crucial measuring points; and the optimum method of auditing. Yet these three elements are not always harmonious, nor can the executive always be certain that he will have the time or money to carry them through effectively. The final selection of a method of auditing, then, is a matter of compromise, a matter of weighing the following five considerations and resolving them to a solution:

How important is this job? What are the costs of imperfect final results?

How much time and money will it take to make the optimum measurements and audit?

Do I have this much time? Must I make the time available?

Can I interrupt this project to make an evaluation? For how long? How important is the deadline for completion?

How much faith do I have in the man carrying out this project?

Such conflicts demand adherence to the principle of "first things first." For example, if the job is so important that the executive cannot risk failure, then, of course, control is his primary objective. In such a situation, a relatively time-consuming method giving good control may, in the end, be a small price for seeing to it that the job is completed successfully—may be cheap in light of the costs of failure. Even drawing time and effort away from other projects may be less costly in the long run.

In another case, the executive's primary goal may be to reduce his time on a particular project in order to spend effort elsewhere. To do this, he must select a method that will, with the least amount of time, still give him the optimum information needed to protect his accountability. The crucial point in making such a selection usually comes in deciding which measuring points can be bypassed with the least danger. That is, how long can the executive afford not to look into a given project?

Such a decision can best be made by considering each stage or part of the job in terms of the degree that this particular phase carries the project to an irreversible decision—i.e., a decision which could destroy the project or bring it short of its mark. Obviously, once such an irreversible phase is over, it is too late. The executive must decide how long before such an irreversible phase is reached he needs to make his audit. And this decision must certainly consider the costs of making changes at any given phase.

Though an executive's primary objective may be to minimize the amount of time spent in auditing delegation, his decision is not that simple. Rather, his objective should be to minimize the amount of time needed to gather the optimum information that he must have in order to protect his accountability. He does this by selecting the style of delegation that not only uses the least amount of his time, but helps him to keep his hand in the job most efficiently. The happiest compromise ensures that the executive is protecting his over-all accountability as completely as he can, even if this occasionally means that he has to spend more time than originally planned.

If an executive is constrained by the fact that the project cannot be interrupted for evaluation, then he must select a style of delegation that allows him to keep his hand in from the very beginning. At the least, he will have to devise a plan to get as much information as early as possible. In essence, he will have to adopt a style which is optimum within the restriction imposed by a crash project.

One final caveat: many times the strongest restriction on choosing a style of delegation does not relate to the job itself, but to the man delegated to carry out the job. If the project is one in which there are a number of inherent pitfalls, perhaps closer supervision is needed for one subordinate than for another. Similarly, the executive must consider the effects that any style of delegation on his part will have on his subordinate's morale and development. And many times the critical restraint on the executive will be his need to select a style that will best help him to train his subordinate to carry out delegation effectively.

Each of the five considerations, then, can serve as a constraint on the selection of a given style of delegation. These considerations, by dictating what is most important about the particular project, determine the direction of any compromise. As constraints, they serve as a center around which the executive can resolve all the considerations into a solution—that is, his own style of delegation for the project in question.

CONCLUSION

An executive can never delegate accountability. Though he vest his assistant with full responsibility and complete authority, the executive, nevertheless, cannot escape final full accountability for the results. His only recourse for seeing to it that things go right is through executive participation—maintaining enough contact with every job so that he is "on top of it" by "keeping his hand in."

This article suggests a number of styles of delegation which accomplish this goal. Their purpose is to advise the executive of the status of an assignment in time to take corrective steps before failure either renders success hopeless or becomes unnecessarily costly.

However, the selection of one style or a combination of them is not a matter of arbitrary choice. Rather, it is dictated, first, by the type of job to be delegated and, secondly, by the amount of time an executive can invest in protecting his accountability. The weighing of these two factors, resolved one against the other, determines the optimum style of delegation to be selected.

53. Tell the Boss—Don't Ask*

Jack E. Grant

It's easy to tell, although much more natural to ask, the boss. But you can tell him and he will like it, whether he is president or section head.

A good boss looks to his staff for solutions, not problems. All too often it seems easier to let the boss make the choice between proposed solutions. This places the burden for results on him, not you. Some bosses like it. If yours does, save your time, read no further.

Completed staff work is basic to modern management. Indoctrination of this concept throughout an organization will save many man-hours of nonproductive work. Amazing as it may seem, 12 out of 15 top business executives recently interviewed confessed ignorance of this term.

Completed staff work is simply defined. It is the presentation of reports to your boss in a manner that requires nothing more than his signature. By signing, and thereby expressing approval, he takes the only action necessary to establish a policy, set up a new procedure, or solve an existing problem. He does not have to resolve questions or make a choice between proposed actions.

When staff work is incomplete, the boss is wasting his time. This also builds an additional though unnecessary workload on his already overburdened staff. Time and attention are diverted from other pressing problems.

Poor and incomplete reports are the treadmill to inaction. They devour staff time, increase administrative overhead, and reduce profits.

A little more effort in preparing a report for the boss can result in telling the boss. You make the policy; let him approve it, easily. Here are the steps:

DEFINE THE PROBLEM

State it clearly and concisely. A problem clearly stated is either solved at once or is well on its way to solution.

HAVE ALL THE FACTS

Do not make any assumptions. Dig out those facts directly related to the problem. Above all do not ignore those facts that may have a collateral relationship to the problem. Cover the waterfront. Ignoring relationships or misunderstanding of the whole problem is no excuse. Time spent now will prevent rework later.

* From *Public Personnel Review*, Vol. 19, No. 2 (April, 1958), 133. Reprinted by permission.

DRAW CONCLUSIONS

Self-evident facts lead to positive conclusions. Point out each signifi-cant observation. Each must be considered in arriving at a conclusion.

MAKE A DECISION

Set forth a definite course of action. If it requires a change in the policy manual, the procedure manual, the organization chart, or merely a letter, prepare it in final form for the boss's signature. A completed job is easy to approve.

Granted all this sounds easy, and it is. As an added precaution, how-ever, after preparing a report, ask yourself the following questions *before* you tell the boss what to do:

1. Have I cleared and coordinated this paper with all interested organizations?
2. Do I have all the facts?
3. Are the facts supported by specific examples?
4. Are my conclusions logical?
5. If I were boss, would I make this decision?

Only five "yes" answers will qualify you to tell the boss; otherwise you will be wasting his time. You may have to do the job all over again or perhaps even look for a new job.

SELECTED READINGS

Books

Herzberg, Frederick. *Work and the Nature of Man.* Cleveland, World Publishing Company, 1966.

Likert, Rensis. *The Human Organization: Its Management and Value.* New York, McGraw-Hill Book Company, 1967.

————. *New Patterns of Management.* New York, McGraw-Hill Book Company, 1961.

Maslow, Abraham H. *Eupsychian Management.* Homewood, Ill., Richard D. Irwin, Inc., 1965.

McGregor, Douglas. *The Human Side of Enterprise.* New York, McGraw-Hill Book Company, 1960.

Articles

Appleby, Paul. "The Role of the Budget Division," *Public Administration Review*, Vol. 17, No. 3 (summer, 1957), 156–58.

Argyris, Chris. "The Individual and Organization: Some Problems of Mutual Adjustment," *Administrative Science Quarterly*, Vol. 2, No. 1 (June, 1957), 1–24.

Bennis, Warren G. "Leadership Theory and Administrative Behavior: The Problem of Authority," *Administrative Science Quarterly*, Vol. 4, No. 3 (December, 1959), 259–301.

Bidwell, Charles E., and Rebecca S. Vreeland. "Authority and Control in Client-Serving Organizations," *Sociological Quarterly*, Vol. 4 (1963), 231–42.

Brown, Davis S. "Importance of Understanding Objectives," *The Federal Accountant*, Vol. 13, No. 3 (March, 1964), 63–73.

Carey, H. H. "Consultative Supervision and Management," *Personnel Journal*, Vol. 18, No. 5 (March, 1942), 286–95.

Carlisle, Howard M. "Measuring the Situational Nature of Management," *California Management Review*, Vol. 11, No. 2 (winter, 1968), 45–52.

Day, Roscoe A. "Delegation of Responsibility: Some Notes on Behavioral Aspects," *Public Personnel Review*, Vol. 15, No. 2 (April, 1954), 85–89.

Hall, Milton J. "Supervising People: Closing the Gap Between What We Think and What We Do," *Advanced Management*, Vol. 12, No. 3 (September, 1947), 129–35.

Herzberg, Frederick. "One More Time: How Do You Motivate Employees?" *Harvard Business Review*, January–February, 1968, 53–62.

Jones, John Paul. "Leadership, Motivation and Communication," *Personnel Administration*, Vol. 33, No. 4 (1970), 5–7, 13–14.

Kirkpatrick, Forrest H. "New Dimensions in the Management Function," *Industrial Engineering*, Vol. 4, No. 1 (January, 1972), 10–13.

Knowles, Henry P., and Borje O. Saxberg. "Human Relations and the Nature of Man," *Harvard Business Review*, March–April, 1967, 22–40, 172–78.

Koontz, Harold. "Challenges for Intellectual Leadership in Management," *California Management Review*, Vol. 7, No. 4 (summer, 1965), 11–18.

Kriesberg, Martin. "The Use of Conferences in the Administration Process," *Public Administration Review*, Vol. 10, No. 2 (spring, 1950), 93–98.

Kuechle, David. "Participative Management Mania," *The Business Quarterly*, Vol. 36, No. 4 (winter, 1971), 22–29.

Livingston, J. Sterling. "Pygmalion in Management," *Harvard Business Review*, Vol. 47, No. 4 (July–August, 1969), 81–89.

McLeod, Ian H., and J. E. Bennett. "Why Participative Management Doesn't Work," *The Business Quarterly*, Vol. 36, No. 4 (winter, 1971), 80–87.

Mandry, W. J. "Participative Management: The CIL Experience," *The Business Quarterly*, Vol. 36, No. 4 (winter, 1971), 73–79.

Migliore, R. Henry. "Improving Worker Productivity Through Communicating Knowledge of Work Results," *Management of Personnel Quarterly*, Vol. 9, No. 2 (summer, 1970), 26–32.

Mitton, Daryl G. "The Dimension of Leadership Style," *Management of Personnel Quarterly*, Vol. 10, No. 4 (winter, 1971), 9–12.

Moravec, Milan, and Philip J. Schreiner. "Adjusting Managerial Acts to Behavioral Concepts," *California Management Review*, Vol. 10, No. 2 (winter, 1967), 31–34.

Murdick, Robert G. "Managerial Control: Concepts and Practice," *Advanced Management Journal*, Vol. 35, No. 1 (January, 1970), 48–52.

Nathan, Frederick M. "Staff Role in Communication," *Personnel Administration*, Vol. 32, No. 4 (July–August, 1969), 59–62.

Norton, E. Long. "Power and Administration," *Public Administration Review*, Vol. 9, No. 4 (autumn, 1949), 257–64.

Odiorne, George S. "Management's Motivation Muddle," *Michigan Business Review*, Vol. 16–17 (1964–65), 27–32.

Ondrack, Daniel A. "Attitudes Toward Authority," *Personnel Administration*, Vol. 34, No. 3 (May–June, 1971), 8–17.

Pajer, Robert G. "The Relationship of Morale to Productivity: What It Means Today," *Public Personnel Review*, October, 1970, 273–77.

Sorcher, Melvin. "Motivation, Participation, and Myth," *Personnel Administration*, Vol. 34, No. 5 (October, 1971), 20–24.

Stahl, O. Glenn. "Communicating Personnel Policy," *Public Personnel Review*, Vol. 20, No. 3 (July, 1959), 181–87.

It is essential that all functions and activities of an organization work together to accomplish its major objectives. This cooperation necessitates harmonious, effective, and economical performance on the part of each department, unit, and individual. To accomplish this performance, the organization must constantly appraise the results of its performance as a basis for the correction of deviation from plans. This function in management is known as control.

The manager may use a wide variety of methods and techniques to effect adequate controls, and it is essential that some of these involve personal relationships. They may also include such things as the use of committees and meetings, consultative management, communications, supervision, and a system of reporting and feedback. The techniques used should be those that prove most effective in providing the stimulation, restraint, or both necessary to develop and maintain the highest possible productivity of the entire organization. Admittedly, the goals of private enterprise, oriented to the profit factor, and those of government agencies, related to public service, are different; still, the major objectives, as well as the techniques used, are often equally applicable.

The extent to which the activities of an organization or agency are concentrated or dispersed will affect the system of control selected and the authority required to maintain that system. The determinants may be geographical or functional in nature. The organization may decentralize some of its operations through regional or district offices and at the same time maintain centralized control of such functions as financial accounting, purchasing, data processing, and research.

Control implies delegation of responsibility and authority and division of decision making at various levels. A requisite is a system of reporting which provides necessary information concerning such things as costs, production rates, performance progress against plans and forecasts, and feedback with reference to the organization's public image. Such control is a basic essential to program evaluation, which must be continuous. The word *control* is sometimes associated with maintenance of the status quo, connoting lack of movement or progress. On the contrary, an organization's control system, employing data processing and research, can be quite creative, resulting in dynamic change and necessary adjustment.

The article "Control in Modern Organizations," by Philip M. Marcus and Dora Cafagna, deals with the concept of control and its effect on the organization and its personnel. The article, the result of considerable research carried on at the University of Michigan, concludes "that with greater total control there is greater sharing in control at all levels, morale is higher, consensus regarding work is greater, and organizational effectiveness is facilitated." William A. Froehlich's article "Internal Control in Government" reviews two of the basic elements of sound internal check and control as they apply to government agencies. The emphasis here is on fiscal control measures needed to assure fiscal accountability and operational effectiveness. "Staff and Management Controls," by Herbert A. Simon, deals with various problems of control as they affect line and staff and illustrates these problems as they apply to the operation of the federal government. The very direct relationship between the planning and the control functions of management is brought out by Allen Weiss in "The Supervisor and the Budget." The author emphasizes the key role of the supervisor in planning, coordinating, and controlling operations of the organization.

An important aspect and function of control is that of coordination. In the article "Coordination as a Task of Management: A Review," by Robert C. Heide, the author deals with coordination as an activity and coordination as a condition of being and discusses some of the current methods and techniques in use. The term *coordination*, as used here, implies formal authority to enforce the internal coordination necessary in an organization. The constant expansion of government agencies, many with overlapping responsibilities, has stimulated the reorganization of such agencies into larger units and departments with the view of bringing about better coordination of all the functions involved. Such reorganization as that of the Department of Health, Education, and Welfare has triggered a continuous, similar reorganization in many of the states.

Along with the development of larger units of government, agencies whose primary responsibilities are often quite dissimilar are being urged to coordinate their services in the interest of more effective government performance. The word *coordinate*, as used in this sense, means to integrate services through cooperative agreements. This kind of coordination implies no formal authority except that given up by an agency in a formal agreement with another department of government.

54. Control in Modern Organizations*

Philip M. Marcus and Dora Cafagna[1]

Perhaps Cervantes' Don Quixote expresses a universal urge in his words, "I would have nobody to control me, I would be absolute." Never possible even in a feudal age, such aspirations today seem all the more unreal in the face of the pervasiveness of modern organizations. Yet control need not be exercised to bring misery to men, and recent research or organizational theory has examined the implications of control for the sometimes competing goals of individual adjustment and organizational performance.

In pre–World War II organization theory, efficiency was assumed to result from specialization of task and strict adherence to a hierarchic chain of command.[2] While much theoretical literature of this period contains broad and useful hypotheses on organization behavior, its propositions are often highly abstract and difficult to apply to specific organizational situations.[3] More recent investigations including those of the Organization Behavior Program at the Survey Research Center, have shown that greater initiative at lower levels, freer communication between levels, and less specialization may simultaneously provide an organization with a tighter control structure and a more competent and satisfied staff.[4] The research program at The University of Michigan has focused on control because of its central importance in coordinating diverse specializations and integrating groups into functioning units. After examining some of the theoretical aspects of control, we will dwell on some representative findings concerning the control structures of various organizations.

SOME THEORETICAL ASPECTS OF CONTROL

Coordination in an organization is effected by the organization's control structure. What must be coordinated includes not only the various

* From *Public Administration Review*, Vol. 25, No. 2 (June, 1965), 121–27. Reprinted by permission.

1 This article and much of the current research cited within it was made possible by a grant from the Carnegie Corporation of New York to the Survey Research Center, Institute for Social Research, The University of Michigan. We are indebted to Robert S. Friedman, Glenn Jones, Stanley E. Seashore, and Arnold S. Tannenbaum of The University of Michigan for critically reading our earlier drafts.

2 A thorough critical evaluation of the early organization literature can be found in James G. March and Herbert A. Simon, *Organizations* (Wiley and Sons, 1958).

3 Examples of these abstract propositions are Robert Michel's "iron law of oligarchy" and Max Weber's "routinization of charisma."

4 Some of these more recent theorists would include Rensis Likert, Chris Argyris, Douglas McGregor and W. F. Whyte. Georges Friedmann, writing of the industrial situation in Europe, has come to very similar conclusions about the more traditional approaches to administration.

organizational units representing division of labor, or specialization, but also the diverse capabilities, temperaments, and attitudes of the people employed. Control may be defined as "that process in which a person (or group of persons or organization of persons) determines, i.e., intentionally affects, what another person (or group, or organization) will do."[5] This definition is sufficiently inclusive to encompass unilateral control, whereby one person or group influences another, or bilateral control, whereby two parties mutually affect each other.

An attempt to clarify aspects of organizational control has been made by Arnold S. Tannenbaum and Robert L. Kahn in their development of the "control graph"[6] (see Figure 1), which depicts two aspects of control operative within an organization. The horizontal axis represents hierarchical levels in an organization. The vertical axis represents the amount of control that each level exercises.[7]

Plotting control in this manner provides a picture of the *distribution*, as well as the *amount* of control at various levels. The distribution of control is the amount of control exercised by *each* level in the organization. The sum of levels of control at all hierarchical levels may be considered the *total amount of control* operative in an organization. The *total amount* of control exercised in an organization is a variable frequently neglected in the literature. Control is most often viewed in terms of the position or person(s) exercising it.[8] Thus, there are analyses of "authoritarian" or "democratic" structures, or, in other words, analyses of the *distribution* of control. Such a conceptualization assumes that if control is redistributed and increased at the lower levels it is decreased at the top. But control removed from an upper level may result in a reduction of total control in the organization. For example, if executives, for some reason, issue fewer directives, it cannot be assumed that the discretion of lower echelons will necessarily be increased; it is more likely that fewer organizational demands will be met. Reducing the

[5] Arnold S. Tannenbaum, "Control in Organizations: Individual Adjustment and Organizational Performance," 2 *Administrative Science Quarterly* 236–257. (September 1962).

[6] Arnold S. Tannenbaum and Robert L. Kahn, *Participation in Union Locals* (Row, Peterson, 1958).

[7] The measure employed to derive these control curves is usually some variation of the following questionnaire item:
"In general, how much influence do you think the following groups or persons actually have in determining the policies and actions in (organization's name)?"
The question is asked for each group or level in the organization and the response categories range from "no influence" to "a very great deal of influence." "Total control" is usually derived by summing the amount exercised at all levels. The distribution of control is calculated by subtracting the control exercised by the upper echelons from that exercised by the lower.

[8] A few social scientists have begun to explore the possibility of social control as a non-fixed entity. It is quite explicit in Talcott Parsons, "On the Concept of Influence," 27 *Public Opinion Quarterly* 59–62 (Spring 1963). David Riesman implicitly makes a similar assumption in his analysis of the American power structure. David Riesman, "Who Has the Power?," in R. Bendix and S. M. Lipset (editors), *Class, Status and Power* (The Free Press, 1953), pp. 154–162. For a thorough discussion of control, see Rolf Dahrendorf, *Class and Class Conflict in Industrial Society* (Stanford University Press, 1959) pp. 157–240.

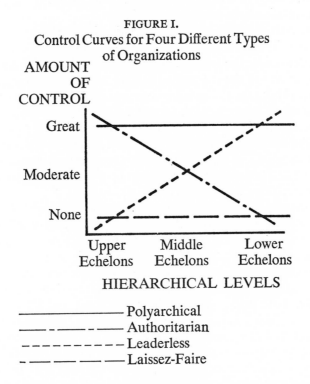

FIGURE I.

Control Curves for Four Different Types of Organizations

——————————— Polyarchical
— · —— · —— Authoritarian
— — — — — — Leaderless
— —— —— —— —— Laissez-Faire

amount of total control beyond a certain level may endanger the coordination and effective functioning of an entire organization.

Different types of organizational control structure may be depicted on the control graph. An authoritarian organization would be represented by a negatively sloped line; a democratic or laissez-faire organization by a low flat line; and a polyarchical organization by a high flat line. Obviously, no organization would conform perfectly to any curve.

Although the *total amount* and the *distribution* of control are conceptually independent, subsequent research has not clearly indicated their empirical independence. In the Center study of the League of Women Voters,[9] the correlation between total amount of control and distribution of control was very small and statistically insignificant. David Bowers[10] also found a very low correlation between total control and distribution of control in his study of insurance agencies. On the

9 Arnold S. Tannenbaum, "Control and Effectiveness in a Voluntary Organization," 68 *American Journal of Sociology* 33–46. (July 1961).
10 David G. Bowers, "Organizational Control in an Insurance Company," *Sociometry* 27, 2. (June 1964).

other hand, a study of a large delivery company revealed a high and significant correlation between the two variables.[11]

In an analysis of membership participation in four labor unions it was reported that the membership as a whole exercised more influence than their presidents, i.e., the control curves tended to be positively sloped.[12] But when officers of the two most effective unions were compared with those of the other two, the membership reported that the more effective officers exercised more control. Members also reported that they exercised more control in the effective unions than in ineffective ones, thus affirming the assumption that effectiveness is related to the total amount of control exercised in an organization. Generally, all other organizations studied had negatively sloped control curves, i.e., officers were perceived as exercising more control than employees.

Self-ratings by the rank and file as to control they exercised showed variations among organizations.[13] On a five point scale of influence, for example, the lower skilled workers in a national delivery company felt they exerted the least control of the four hierarchical levels. League of Women Voters' members and insurance salesmen rated the amount of influence they exercised in their respective organizations about equally, and slightly above mid-points for the scale. Rank and file union members estimated their total influence to be very near the top of the scale.

In several studies respondents were asked to rate the amount of influence they *should have* (ideal control) in their organization as well as the amount of influence they did possess (actual control). The distributions of *ideal* and *actual* control responses for these studies have been plotted on control graphs and compared. A comparison of 32 stations in the delivery company showed negatively sloped curves for both actual and ideal control, i.e., workers felt they had and should have less than their superiors. The workers' ideal curve also indicated they felt both they and their superiors should have more control.

In the League of Women Voters study, the ideal control curve was higher than the actual control curve; the actual and ideal slopes also differed in that members reported, on the one hand, that their officers had more control than the rank and file, and on the other hand, that members ought to have more control than either the president or the board. The amount of control the members thought the board should exercise was much greater than the amount they would grant the president, suggesting that League members see the role of president primarily

[11] Clagett G. Smith and Ogus Ari, "Organization Control Structure and Member Consensus," 69 *American Journal of Sociology* 623–638. (May 1964).

[12] Tannenbaum and Kahn, *op. cit.*

[13] When making cross-organizational comparisons such as these self ratings, one of the limitations of the control graph should be kept in mind. The horizontal axis on the control graph representing the hierarchical levels varies for each graph since it depends upon the structure of each organization.

as expediter, or representative to outside groups. In conclusion, it should be reported that most respondents of the organizations studied want more control, not only for themselves, but for others within the organization.

CONTROL AND INDIVIDUAL ADJUSTMENT

Distribution of control significantly affects individual behavior and adjustment to organizational life. Several studies made by the Center test the hypothesis that *morale* and *loyalty* to an organization and *participation* in it are high for those who desire to exercise control and are able to do so. Two experimental programs were set up in a clerical organization.[14] One was patterned after a *democratic model*, i.e., responsibility was increased and greater authority delegated to lower level personnel. At group meetings, decisions were made as to work distribution, length of recess, right to leave department during working hours, etc. The other experimental program was established along more *autocratic* lines, i.e., the clerks' routines were regulated more rigidly by "scientific management" principles, and decisions were made by upper level company officials. Results indicated that more clerks preferred the democratic model. However, there were persons in both programs who would have been more satisfied with the other type of control structure. What is needed is the integration of personality predispositions with the organizational pattern of control.

In the study of the League of Women Voters, loyalty to the League was measured by two questionnaire items concerning the degree of effort the respondent would make to prevent local leagues from failing from membership apathy or community opposition.[15] The amount of influence and control exercised by League members was measured by a question concerning the influence exercised by members and officers. When the loyalty index was related to the control measure, it indicated that the more control League members exercised, the more loyalty they felt toward the organization.

Employees of 32 delivery stations were asked to rate the level of morale in their stations.[16] The mean of their responses regarding morale was computed for each station and was found to correlate with the measure of employee influence. Total control (i.e., the total amount of influence exerted within an organization) is also related to loyalty and morale. The delivery stations study showed that stations with more total control had higher employee morale. But this was also true for the four

14 Nancy C. Morse and Everett Reimer, "The Experimental Change of a Major Organizational Variable," 52 *The Journal of Abnormal and Social Psychology* 120–129. (January 1956).

15 Clagett G. Smith and Arnold S. Tannenbaum, "Organizational Control Structure: A Comparative Analysis," *Human Relations* 299–316. (in press, 1963).

16 Bernard Indik, Basil Georgopoulos, and Stanley E. Seashore, "Superior-Subordinate Relationships and Performance," 14 *Personnel Psychology* 357–374. (1961).

labor unions studied. No such relationship was found in the League study.

CONTROL AND ORGANIZATIONAL EFFECTIVENESS

Because goals vary from organization to organization and are often intangible, development of adequate measures of organizational effectiveness has been very difficult. Data on productivity, turnover, and absenteeism do not provide entirely satisfactory indices.[17] Measures of organizational effectiveness were related to measures of control in a number of studies. For example, in the study of the delivery stations, productivity records and ratings from questionnaire responses concerning the degree of intraorganizational strain and flexibility were used to determine effectiveness. Scores were assigned to each station. These scores correlated with scores on total control, but were found to be unrelated to the distribution of control.

In the study of the League of Women Voters, judges were asked to rate the individual leagues on a number of matters, e.g., success in fund-raising, quality of League publications, impact on the community, etc. Both total control and the distribution of control were found to be related to organizational effectiveness. The more influence exerted by lower levels of the League, the greater the effectiveness; the more reciprocal influence among all organizational levels, the greater the effectiveness.

In both studies, total control was related to organizational effectiveness; the distribution of control was found related to effectiveness only in the League study. This suggests that the total amount of control exercised in an organization is more crucial than the distribution of control.

The League however, must substitute psychological remunerations for the financial and status rewards offered to members of other organizations. The exercise of influence and control in League affairs is perhaps a major factor in maintaining the interest and activity of the membership and the effectiveness of the League as an organization.

Data from a nationwide survey of 30 automobile dealerships—highly competitive and reliant "individual enterprise" among their salesmen—suggest that the amount and distribution of control are more important in an organizational structure which emphasizes cooperation and coordination of its parts than in one which stresses competition and individual initiative.[18] Using sales records as a measure of effectiveness, it was discovered that there was no correlation with measure of total control or distribution of control.

[17] Basil Georgopoulos and Arnold S. Tannenbaum "A Study of Organizational Effectiveness," 22 *American Sociological Review* 534–540 (1957).

[18] Martin Patchen, Stanley E. Seashore, and William Eckerman, "Some Dealership Characteristics Related to Change in New Car Sales Volume," Unpublished report (Institute for Social Research, 1961).

Size may be another factor affecting the relationship between control and effectiveness. When the units of an organization are small and scattered, as are automobile dealerships, there is less likelihood of close personal ties. Group cohesiveness built upon these ties would not be enhanced, nor would norms governing production be sustained as motivating forces for the participants. Consequently, lower organizational effectiveness may result. In contrast, larger work units allow small subgroups to form among individuals with shared values and attitudes. Overlapping membership in small groups provides links with the larger organization and promotes greater member morale and loyalty, which, in turn, increases organizational effectiveness.[19]

CONTROL AND CONSENSUS

Consensus may be defined as uniformity in perceptions and attitudes.[20] Members of an organization may agree, for example, upon what jobs need to be done and the best ways of doing them. Such agreement among organizational participants produces judgments as to appropriate behavior and application of sanctions against those who do not conform. Consensus gives rise, then, to shared norms which govern the behavior and activities of members of an organization. Consensus should thus be positively related to organizational effectiveness.

A number of areas of consensus have been identified as relevant to work groups, including work group standards, morale, adequacy of supervisory planning, general work group consensus, and amount of influence desire for various levels. In the stations of the delivery company, no significant correlations were found between *the distribution of control* and these variables. However, another variable, degree of trust and confidence in the supervisor, was significantly related. Even when the averages of these items were computed across hierarchical levels, they did not yield a relationship to the distribution of control. When the measures of consensus were correlated with *total amount of control* within each station, a different picture emerged. Four of these measures were found to be significantly related to total control: morale; trust and confidence in the supervisor; adequacy of supervisory planning; and general work group consensus. No relationship was found between work group standards or the influence desired for various levels and total control. When the amount of consensus *between* levels was analyzed, it was found that work group standards and morale were correlated with

19 The relevance of work group size and its implications for social activity is explored in S. M. Lipset, M. A. Trow, and J. S. Coleman, *Union Democracy* (The Free Press, 1956), pp. 150–175. Stanley E. Seashore (*Group Cohesiveness in the Industrial Work Group*, Institute for Social Research, 1954), however, found a curvilinear relationship between size and group cohesiveness; small groups tended to have very low or very high cohesiveness scores. It is clear, then, that more research is needed to clarify this important point.

20 Clagett G. Smith and Ogus Ari, *op. cit.*

total control, while influence desired for various levels was not. Further, a general measure of consensus was found to relate to total control, but not to the distribution of control.

This indicates that total control, or the composite of mutual influence within a station, is related to the amount of consensus both between levels in the hierarchy and within the work group. Consensus, is necessary to the coordination and attainment of the goals of large scale organizations. Consensus makes possible a greater amount of decentralization of responsibility and delegation of tasks and, for this reason, is crucial to the effective operation of an organization.

Findings concerning control and consensus in the delivery company stations are consistent with those of the study of four labor unions. Twenty-four different items were used to measure union norms, including the willingness to do picket duty, the international's role, various passive and active sanctions, attitudes of member's friends, spouse, etc. In general, active members of the union showed a higher consensus on most of these norms than inactives. The four locals were ranked on their overall uniformity in nine content areas (representing a categorization of the 24 original items) and there was a very high correlation among the areas. Locals high in one area of uniformity tended to be high in others. A strong positive relationship was found when these measures were correlated with amount of total control in each local.

RESULTS FROM EXPERIMENTAL STUDIES

While some of the studies described yield findings of interest and potential value, it may be argued that the practical application of these findings is somewhat limited, that it would be an extremely difficult task to introduce new patterns of control into organizational settings. However experimental studies are available which demonstrate that control variables and some of their correlates are capable of being implemented.

One such study conducted in a large white-collar organization has already been mentioned. In both the democratic and the autocratic experimental divisions, attempts to change the level of control and decision making, albeit in different directions, were successful. Along with the delegation of decision making, the amount of job involvement and company loyalty increased among members of the participative groups. The experimenters also reported that these employees continued to perform their jobs even in the absence of supervisors, and attitudes toward company management and high-producing workers became more favorable. The reverse was found among members of the hierarchically-controlled groups. These employees reported a decrease in job involvement, less loyalty to the company, and less feeling of job responsibility in the absence of their supervisors. Turnover also increased as did negative attitudes toward management and high-producers.

Yet productivity increased among both groups. In fact, the amount of increase was greater in the hierarchical groups than in the participative groups. While it is difficult to judge what the long run effects will be, it is suggested that effectiveness will decrease in the hierarchical groups because of the hostility and resentment developed toward high producers and management. ". . . [T]urnover and the adverse attitudes created by the hierarchically-controlled program tend typically to affect productivity adversely over a long period of time."[21]

Another experimental study cited earlier was conducted in a large manufacturing plant over a three-year period. Results of measures taken just prior to induced change indicated that all plant departments which had been selected to undergo no change, scored higher than the experimental departments on eleven independent variables. These variables involved various aspects of employee participation in decision making, peer interaction and influence, supportive behavior, and emphasis on the work group.[22] Measures taken at the end of the study revealed that all but one of the initial differences in variables reversed themselves. The experimental departments showed substantial improvement on ten of the variables,[23] while the others experienced negative change on seven variables.[24]

An analysis of the dependent variables in this study revealed a more or less consistent pattern with that of the independent variables, i.e., generally favoring the experimental departments. An increase in measures of machine efficiency and employee satisfaction was found for the experimental groups, and a decrease in both variables was found for the control groups. While both the experimental and control departments increased in absentee rates, the increase was greater in the control groups.

CONCLUSION

The research described in these pages suggests that the concept of *total control* must be closely considered in a study of organizational behavior. Whether the criterion of a good organization is that of productivity or the intelligent utilization of human resources, the findings indicate that with greater *total control* there is a greater sharing in con-

---

21 Rensis Likert, *New Patterns of Management* (McGraw-Hill, 1961), p. 68.

22 Of the eleven independent variables, only five differences between control and experimental departments were statistically significant. See Seashore and Bowers, *op. cit.*, Tables 3 and 4, pp. 73–74.

23 Of these ten independent variables, eight were found to be statistically significant.

24 Of these seven independent variables, four were found to be statistically significant.

trol at all levels, morale is higher, consensus regarding work is greater, and organizational effectiveness is facilitated.

It is virtually impossible for upper echelons to integrate and coordinate the lower levels in organizations characterized by increasing specialization, because persons in the upper echelons lack sufficient technical understanding. In fact the subordinates who carry out the directives are often in a better position to make wise decisions.

In short, both organizational characteristics and humane considerations require that some control be delegated to the lower echelons. A greater amount of total control, whereby subordinates can actually influence their supervisors, will heighten, not lower, the organization's performance. However, when subordinates obtain a measure of expertise but are given no control, morale and willingness to contribute to the organization decrease. Dissatisfactions manifest themselves in high turnover and absentee rates, and in lower efficiency and production.

The comparisons made earlier between actual and ideal control curves showed that subordinates do not want more control and influence for themselves at the expense of higher levels in the organization. Rather, they desire more control for all levels over job activities, so that individuals know what is expected of them and what rewards or punishments they may receive. As society becomes increasingly dependent upon organization services, it needs also to become increasingly sensitive to the critical implications of control for individual adjustment and organizational performance.

55. Internal Control in Government*

William A. Froehlich

The definition of the term *internal control* is well recognized as being a plan of organization with methods and measures adopted within a governmental entity to safeguard its assets, to check the accuracy and reliability of accounting data, to promote operational efficiency, and to encourage adherence to managerial policies.

Two of the basic elements of sound internal check and control are:

1. A system of authorization and recordkeeping procedures adequate to provide reasonable accounting control over assets, liabilities, revenues, and expenditures.

2. Appropriate segregation of functional responsibilities both at the departmental level and individual employee level. This segregation of responsibilities is based on the principle that no one person or department should control all phases of a transaction without the interrelated functioning of some other person or persons which affords a cross-check.

Let us review these two basic elements as they apply to municipal, provincial and state governments, both large and small.

In regard to the first basic element—authorization and recordkeeping procedures—we can best demonstrate the purpose of this element by illustrating the origination and flow of a transaction through the desired divisions of responsibility.

This excellent illustration is quoted from a paper presented by Mr. Joseph M. Lowery at the October 23, 1962 meeting of the Finance Officers Department—League of California Cities:

1. The *Legislative Body* authorizes the appropriation through the adoption of the budget.
2. The *Department Head* requests the purchase.
3. The *Purchasing Agent* issues the purchase order after the *Chief Accounting Officer* approves it for proper budget authorization.
4. The *Vendor* delivers the item to the *requisitioning department*, who notifies the *Chief Accounting Officer* of its receipt, condition, weight, quantity, etc.
5. The *Vendor* bills the *Chief Accounting Officer* who matches the invoices with the purchase order copy and the advice of goods received and prepares the voucher for payment.
6. The *Chief Accounting Officer* has recorded the transaction in its entirety and also exercised budget control over the transaction.

* From *Municipal Finance*, Vol. 36, No. 2 (November, 1963), 86–88. Reprinted by permission.

It is recognized that the larger governmental units have departmental structures which readily permit such division of transaction responsibility. However, even in the smaller governmental unit sufficient breakdown of responsibiilty can be had on a practical basis, so as to attain the highest degree of internal control under the circumstances.

Also under basic element number one, it is important to note that legal structures and/or requirements have endeavored to obtain a degree of internal control through the election of certain officials whose duties and responsibilities in this connection are set forth by statute. While the intent of such statutes was by design or otherwise to provide a measure of internal control, in certain instances the resulting system has produced cumbersome arrangements.

The second basic element of internal control places its emphasis upon the proper segregation of duties and responsibilities between people and departments. By proper segregation of duties we mean a distinct separation between asset control functions and recordkeeping functions. Let us illustrate a hypothetical situation in which a separation of duties does exist, but the separation violates the principle of good internal control.

Mary is the bookkeeper for the City of X. Her duties are to post water consumers' charges and payments in the books of account, but she also prepares and banks the daily deposit. Alice is the cashier who receives remittances through the mail and over the counter, but, in addition, also has access to the water consumers' accounts receivable ledgers for the purpose of making adjustments, refunds, etc., and so originates such transactions.

One can readily see the dangers inherent in such a division of duties; however, the officials of the City of X might be completely oblivious to the weakness in their system and, possibly, they might even feel "secure" in the mistaken belief that they have a "segregation of duties" in the finance office. The foregoing illustration is not necessarily fiction, for such conditions have been found to exist in many governmental units, and not necessarily confined to the smaller units.

To further illustrate this area of internal control, let us presume that Province Y desires to strengthen its control over incoming mail receipts by having an employee separate and distinct from the cashier pre-list all receipts in duplicate for subsequent independent checking to the bank deposit slip or receipt. An obvious question arises immediately: "Who checks the individual assigned to pre-list the mail receipts?"

The answer to the question is, of course, that it is neither practicable nor feasible to have a checker check a checker, ad infinitum, for the entire system of internal control must be practicable and feasible, designed to accomplish a high degree of control commensurate with costs required to attain such control.

It is an established fact that upon the development and implementation of a well designed system of internal control, continuous reviews, together with auxiliary guides and activities, are required to insure that the system is operating as originally planned.

The auxiliary guides and activities can be summarized as follows:

1. Procedural manuals
2. Internal auditing
3. Services of Chartered Accountants or Certified Public Accountants

Let us review each of the auxiliary helps.

PROCEDURAL MANUALS

A procedural manual which defines the duties and responsibilities of each job or position provides a permanent record which is invaluable for subsequent review of operations and also for the training of new employees.

Too often, when turnover of employees takes place, the new employee either is partially trained by the out-going employee, if at all, or is "trained" by others in the department who might not necessarily be familiar with the required procedures. In addition, planned procedures can be innocently altered by employees voluntarily assisting others, done in the spirit of "being helpful," whereby in many instances, the temporary assistance offered has resulted in a permanent shift of duties.

INTERNAL AUDITING

The governmental unit, whether large or small, can and should initiate some form of internal review of its fiscal transactions and general operations. The larger units can more economically establish a formal internal audit program, staffed by well-trained personnel, who are wholly independent of departments and operations subject to review. A properly developed internal audit program would include a review of the system of internal control, not only as it relates to financial transactions and recordkeeping, but also as to the accountability and safeguard of assets, such as physical inventories of water meters, automotive parts, movable personal property, etc.

Through the periodic and cyclical review of all facets of the governmental operation and the implementation of resulting recommendations of the internal auditors for constructive changes and improvements, the likelihood of serious deficiencies or irregularities should be lessened or brought to light before reaching substantial proportions.

As to the smaller governmental units, it generally would be uneconomical for them to establish a formal internal auditing department; however, this should not preclude the appropriate elected officials and administrative employees from instigating periodic checks or surprise examinations of cash and securities, bank reconciliations, physical inventories, current procedures followed, etc. Accordingly, in the smaller governmental unit, greater vigilance is generally required of "management" to insure that operations are being conducted in a manner which affords adequate protection of the assets of the government and that the compilation of financial transactions is reliable.

SERVICES OF CHARTERED OR CERTIFIED PUBLIC ACCOUNTANTS

The services of the qualified outside accountant complements the foregoing auxiliary control guides and activities, without necessarily duplicating the work of others. In the larger governmental units the activities of the internal audit group and the outside auditor are so coordinated that overlap of activities is eliminated, with the end result that the governmental unit and the internal auditors benefit from the reviews of the outside accountant and the latter is afforded a broader review coverage of operations of the unit. In addition, under such an arrangement, the outside auditor can incorporate such benefits in the normal audit of the new unit, which in many cases results in a financial benefit to his client.

In regard to the smaller governmental unit, the services of the outside accountant can be of immeasurable value to the elected officials and administrative employees. Many of the elected officials cannot, or are in no position to devote full time to their governmental responsibilities and accordingly, would find it difficult to undertake periodic reviews or accounting assignments, of the nature previously discussed.

The outside accountant is qualified and capable of making unannounced examinations at dates other than at fiscal year-end and to review the system of internal control and accounting practices then in effect. If deficiencies exist or deviations from planned procedures are noted, the report from the accountant would set forth such deficiencies with appropriate recommendations for correction. Similar benefits would accrue to the governmental unit, as was cited previously, in that more frequent assurances would be had that the system of internal control and accounting practices are operating in accordance with planned procedures and that operating and financial information can be read with confidence.

In conclusion, it is apparent that *Internal Control* is not a mysterious force at work as an espionage activity, but rather is a common sense approach in the definition and segregation of duties and responsibilities as between employees and in the development of proper accounting practices to insure reliable financial information, all for the primary purpose of safeguarding assets of the governmental unit and to provide the citizens of such unit with services at realistic and efficient cost values.

56. Staff and Management Controls*

Herbert A. Simon

. . . Large-scale organization inevitably creates problems of control. In every organization in our society there is always some person or group of persons whom we regard as having the legitimate right to determine the organization's program and the way the program is carried out. In business concerns, the legitimate right of control rests with the stockholders; in government, with the citizens. The problem of control is the problem of implementing that right. The board of directors in business concerns and the legislature in governments are formal devices whose main concern is the implementation of the right of control, and these are supplemented by many other devices, formal and informal—political parties are an example.

The problem of control is a serious one in large-scale organization because of two related facts: (1) those who legitimately control it simply cannot cope with its size—they have time neither to find out in detail what is going on nor to decide what should go on; (2) the employees in the bureaucracy may use this absence of accountability to further their own purposes, which may not be the purposes of the legitimate controllers. There is nothing about this situation that is peculiar to government. The executives of any large business spend most of their time dealing with these same problems: securing adequate motivation of manual workers and middle-level executives and supervisors, securing co-ordination of goals and activities, combating the venality of employees who are tempted to steal tools or accept bribes from vendors.

The phenomena we call "corruption," "confusion," and "inefficiency" in large-scale organization are the symptoms of the inadequacies of the control process. And the phenomena we call "red tape" are largely the unintended effects of our attempts to strengthen the controls by formalizing the procedures for co-ordination, communication, and review. "Red tape" is, so to speak, the secondary reaction produced by the sulfa drugs we have prescribed for the primary infection of lack of control.

CONTROLS OVER RESOURCES: THE BUDGET

Every military commander knows that when he has committed his reserves, he has had his say—he retains painfully little control over the subsequent course of the battle. It would be only mild exaggeration to say that, similarly, when the budget has been approved and resources

* From *Annals of the American Academy of Political and Social Science*, Vol. 292 (March, 1954), 95–96, 98–103. Reprinted by permission.

allocated to programs and departments, the top level executives in large organizations have had their say. Control devices can help them ascertain that the resources have been used for the general purposes intended, but can have little detailed effect on the precise way in which they are used.

The budget is essentially an expenditure plan for a specified period of time, usually a year. Two basic kinds of decisions have to be reached in order to establish a budget; and to understand the budget process it is essential that they be distinguished clearly. First, there are decisions as to the objectives to be reached—the kinds of services and the quality of service to be provided. Second, there are decisions as to how much money, if it is spent efficiently, is required to meet these objectives. Much of the confusion that surrounds public discussion of "economy in government" can be traced to a failure to distinguish these two aspects of the problem. When we demand governmental economy do we mean that we want fewer and poorer services, or do we mean that we think the same services we now have, and the same quality of service, can be provided for less money?

A simple analogy with our household budgets will illustrate the distinction. If a husband asks his wife to economize on the food budget, does he mean that meat should be on the menu less frequently or that she should shop for the meat more carefully? The first is a question of *service levels*, the second a question of *efficiency*. And I am sure that any husband who supposes he can accomplish substantial economies in the food budget by improving efficiency, without affecting quality, will find a very unreceptive audience in his wife.

It is easy to cut a budget, governmental or otherwise, simply by refusing to appropriate more funds. But to cut a budget without reducing service levels—that is, by increasing efficiency—is an extremely difficult feat in a large organization. It is accomplished, if at all, by a painstaking re-examination of specific administrative operations—an examination that can be undertaken only with the help of the members of the bureaucracy whose efficiency is to be improved.

Here, as elsewhere in large-scale organization, control from above and without is a poor substitute for motivation from within. High-level review of budgets is an important tool for determining what services shall be provided, and at what levels. But the road to control of efficiency lies in a different direction: in the direction of a bureaucracy that is professional in its attitude towards its management tasks and that is technically equipped to find efficient ways of doing its work. Such a bureaucracy can be assisted in its search for efficiency by specialized units, but the function of these is more in the nature of "consultation" than in the nature of "control." . . .

427

AGENCIES OF CONTROL: "LINE" AND "STAFF"

We have said that the problem of control in a bureaucracy arises basically because the controllers cannot cope with its size and complexity. The budget reduces this complexity to some sort of order, but hardly to a scale where it can be handled effectively by a President and a Congress. "The President needs help," said the 1937 President's Committee, and cries for help for both President and Congress have been frequent and strident.

Specific proposals for providing this help most often take the form of new agencies—"staff agencies" they are usually called—designed to share with the executive and the legislature the responsibilities of control. In the federal government, for example, we have a Budget Bureau, a Civil Service Commission, a Comptroller General, and a General Services Administration, all of which are involved in one or another aspect of the control process.

But does not this solution contain a fundamental paradox? The federal government is too large and complex to be controlled effectively by the President. We will remedy this by creating a new agency, thus increasing its size and complexity. Instead of having his dozen department heads to deal with, the President will now also have a Director of the Budget.

Are Staff Agencies "Different"?

Those who recommend the proliferation of staff agencies as a solution to the problem of control deny this paradox by arguing that staff agencies are "different"—both in their relation to the controller and in their relation to the controlled. They are "different," it is said, in their relation to the chief executive because they "represent him," they "act for him" or "in his name," they are "a part of him." They are "different," it is said, in their relation to the bureaucracy because, unlike the chief executive himself, they do not "actually exercise authority," they "only advise and inform"; when they give orders, they exercise "the chief executive's authority, and not their own."

I must confess that this kind of language has always baffled me—as it must baffle laymen who have not grown accustomed to its constant use in the literature of administration. The President needs help to control the Department of Agriculture, say, because in the absence of such help he cannot be sure that the Department will accept his purposes, and those of the Congress. The Bureau of the Budget is to give him that help. But what guarantees that the Bureau will not develop its own bureaucratic purposes, will not implement these instead of the President's? The steward guards that the servant serve the master. But who guards that the steward serve the master?

428

Stripped of its metaphysical clothing, the argument for the staff agency is based on the premise that a relatively small administrative agency not possessed of special responsibilities of its own will be more likely to identify with the President, and less likely to develop its own bureaucratic purposes, than will a large operating agency. Stated thus, the proposition is not without plausibility, and has perhaps even some empirical evidence in its favor—although the evidence has really never been examined in a systematic and scientific way.

But if this is the reason that the staff agency helps in control, we should expect its effectiveness to be in inverse relation to (a) its size and (b) the degree of internal specialization within it. If the staff agency is large (and even the Budget Bureau numbers its employees in the hundreds), it has its own internal problems of bureaucratic control. And if there is much specialization within it, the over-all viewpoint identified with the Presidency will gradually yield to the partial viewpoint of specialized goals and objectives. When the Civil Service Commission has a disagreement with the Secretary of Agriculture—the one preoccupied with the problems of governmental personnel, the other with the problems of agriculture—which one "represents" the President and the will of the Congress?

What about the relations of the staff agency with the bureaucracy it is supposed to control? Again, the idea that "the staff agency does not really exercise authority, but only speaks in the name of the President" must be treated as myth rather than reality. If the President acts on the recommendations of a budget examiner for a reduction in a request from the Department of Commerce, the authority is, in some legal sense, the President's, but the judgment is the examiner's. The Secretary of Commerce, at least, will be under no illusions as to the authority exercised over him by the Budget Bureau. He will realize that only a small fraction of the disagreements that arise between him and the budget examiners can be appealed to the President—that the function of the Bureau is precisely to relieve the President of this burden of decision.

The Price of Control

In summary, we see that the processes of control can be strengthened by creating agencies whose primary function is to provide an "independent" review of the action of the administrative departments. But we see also that a price must be paid for these additional controls. The price is made up of several components: (1) the actual salary and other costs of operating the control agency, (2) the development of goals within the control agency that are not identical with the goals of the executive and legislature, and (3) the limits that are placed on the operating departments by the control agencies, which restrict the discretion of the department executives in discharging the responsibilities that are placed on them.

This last category of costs—costs arising from the limits placed on operating departments—leads us to the subject of "red tape." The summary report of the Hoover Commission contained this analysis, full of unintended humor, of the problems of control in the federal government:

Definite authority at the top, a clear line of authority from top to bottom, and adequate staff aids to the exercise of authority do not exist. Authority is diffused, lines of authority are confused, staff services are insufficient. Consequently, responsibility and accountability are impaired.[1]

What the Commission did not point out—or see—was that the staff services, whose "insufficiency" it deplored, were a primary cause for the confusion in lines of authority that the Commission equally deplored. Let us cite a concrete example. One of the important functions of the Department of Commerce is to gather a wide range of statistics about the operation of the American economy. The notion of a "clear line of authority" would imply that the Secretary of Commerce and his subordinates should make the decisions involved in carrying out these statistical functions, and should be judged by the results. But before any federal agency can send a questionnaire to a business firm, the questionnaire must be approved, in its complete detail, by the Division of Statistical Standards of the Bureau of the Budget. The DSS is charged with the responsibility of eliminating duplication in federal questionnaires and ensuring the technical adequacy of statistical studies. Under these organizational arrangements, who is to be held responsible for the quality of the statistical services of the Department of Commerce? And how many review steps, over what period of time, must a questionnaire undergo before it is employed by the Department?

In spite of the delays and the ambiguities in responsibility that are inevitably created when such a review process is established, the advantages of the review may well outweigh its costs. But in assessing its value, it is important that we try to measure the *net* benefits, after all these extra costs have been deducted, and that we not delude ourselves into thinking that we have gained something for nothing. The staff agency can be a valuable device for solving difficult problems of control in large-scale organization, but it is a device that needs to be used sparingly and with discretion. It is a real question in my mind, and in the minds of other observers of large-scale organization, whether further improvement of control in the federal government calls for a greater, or a more restricted, use of this device. . . .

[1] *The Hoover Commission Report on Organization of the Executive Branch of the Government* (New York: McGraw-Hill Book Company, Inc., 1949), p. 3.

The same issues as those discussed earlier apply as we move down the administrative ladder to organizations of smaller size and lesser complexity. Units specialized for control functions can make a contribution at all these levels, but generalization is hardly possible as to how many are desirable or at what specific levels.

But as we move down the structure, mechanisms of control other than specialized units take on increasing importance. In administrative organizations having a fairly cohesive purpose, and drawing their professional staffs from a relatively homogeneous background, "internal" mechanisms take on more and more of the burden of control. The United States Public Health Service, for example, draws the largest part of its professional staff from the medical profession. In so doing, it is able to use the whole structure of controls which that profession impresses on its members. I do not refer to the official pronouncements of the American Medical Association, or to "professional ethics"—although both of these are important—but to the whole set of values, techniques, and standards of professional competence that the members of the profession have in common, and that are enforced through the constant interaction of practitioners and the significance they attach to the approval of their peers.

Professional standards do not guarantee conformity with the values of society or of its political mechanisms. Librarians may want more libraries, public health practitioners more clinics, fire chiefs more equipment, than citizens want or are willing to pay for. Hence, professional standards do little to simplify the resource allocation process that is the central purpose of budgeting. A budget process and top-level political review of budget allocations are still absolutely necessary to mediate the claims of the various professions, each with its own conception of the public welfare.

But if professional standards help little to solve the problem of service levels, they help a great deal to solve the problem of efficiency. Efficiency must start at the "grass roots" of the bureaucracy; it must permeate each small part of the mass of activities performed by a large-scale organization. And we have seen that the available techniques for control from the top are particularly ineffective for the task of detailed day-to-day supervision. The motivation toward efficient administration must derive primarily from the bureaucracy itself— from the professional standards it imposes on its members and the desire it instills in them to do a good job as judged by their fellows.

Although no careful comparative study has ever been made of the efficiency of government agencies, it appears to the casual observer that there is a high correlation between managerial efficiency and the degree of professionalization of a particular agency. The Forest Service, with its close parallel development of the federal agency and of university programs in forestry, is a case in point.

Government and Business Compared

Much has been made of the absence of the "profit motive" as an explanation of why government agencies are less efficient than business organizations. Even if we accept the assumption, which seems to me somewhat doubtful, that government agencies *are*, across the board, less efficient, I am not sure that the explanation holds water. In the first place, in any large business concern there are many activities whose contribution to profit cannot, in fact, be assessed in any very accurate way. In the second place, in the absence of a profit criterion, a professional group motivated to do a good job will develop score cards for excellence to take the place of the profit criterion. Much remains to be done, in both government and business, to develop and improve such score cards, and to relate the criteria of the smaller component units to the over-all goals of the organization. If the work on performance budgeting is carried ahead with sufficient vigor and imagination, it will in time contribute to the development of such criteria.

CONCLUSION

We have seen that the problems of control in large-scale organizations can be made to vanish only by doing away with large-scale organizations—something unlikely to occur in the modern world as we know it. Short of making the problems vanish, there are some things we can do to make them manageable, but only after a careful assessment in each case of benefits and costs. One such way is to develop, along the lines already projected, a budget process that would assist in the intelligent allocation of society's resources to the many governmental services that compete for them.

A complementary line of approach is the careful and judicious development at various levels within the bureaucracy of units whose primary function is to assist in the control process. In order to do this intelligently, we shall need to be more realistic than we have been in the past as to just how such units operate, what consequences they have in terms of authority, responsibility, and "red tape," and how far their values outweigh their costs. With the rapid growth of "staff" agencies over the past generation, the immediate need is probably more for reflection and consolidation than for multiplication.

Finally, the control of governmental efficiency will make its progress primarily through the developing professionalization of the bureaucracy itself. Careers in governmental service must become more respectable and respected—an item in which our progress has been mostly backwards since the war. The examples of the professional corps and the university-profession-agency relationship that characterize some of the most efficient governmental operations need to be extended over a wider range of governmental functions, and over such time-honored municipal activities as fire, police, and public works administration.

In one sense these goals are nonpolitical—they can be accepted by Democrats and Republicans alike. In another sense they are intensely political. The rate at which they will be attained will depend critically upon public attitudes toward government. If the public accepts the common stereotype of the lazy, venal "bureaucrat," it will not expect efficient, responsible government, and it will not get it. To the extent that the public recognizes that the problems of efficiency in government are as serious as, but no more serious than, these problems in other large-scale organizations, we can expect substantial progress toward these goals.

57. The Supervisor and the Budget: Part 1: The Purpose of a Budget*

Allen Weiss

Sooner or later, most supervisors find themselves involved in preparing a budget—especially if they are set on climbing the management ladder. Even those who do not get directly involved in budget preparation often must gather statistics on costs and other information to be used by their superiors in preparing the budget.

The reason that so much time and effort is devoted to the preparation of budgets is that they are the basis for two essential functions of management: planning and control. Just how management makes use of budgeting is the subject of this first article in a series.

PLANNING

In business, as in traveling, you must pick a destination before you can plot a course. So the management of a company must have a set of long-range objectives in financial terms before it can properly allocate costs along the way. If, for example, a company is to bring out three new products in the next five years, what equipment will it need? How many people will it have to hire or train? What will be the cost of these investments in capital goods and staff? Intermediate goals or budgets help keep the enterprise on course financially so that its expenditures won't be substantially greater than it had planned for. The short-term annual budget is constructed according to financial plans for longer periods.

Of course, objectives vary from business to business. One distributor, which wants to expand into new regions, may allocate funds to develop sales and warehousing organizations in these regions. Another one, which would like to manufacture more of the items it sells, will probably allocate funds to develop and promote its own line of products.

COORDINATING ACTIVITIES

Another major purpose of financial planning is to coordinate the activities of the different departments so that they all work toward a common goal. Through the mechanism of a budget, departments are tuned in to the same objectives, the same markets, the same volumes.

Budgets also help avoid the embarrassment and other consequences of repeated crises. When, for example, materials and supplies are budgeted for early enough, they will be available to the production line when needed. Skilled people, having been hired or trained beforehand, will be ready to operate machines when they are scheduled to produce specific

* Reprinted by permission of the publisher from *Supervisory Management*, May, 1971. © 1971 by the American Management Association, Inc.

parts. Assembly lines will not have to shut down for want of an essential item for which no money had been allocated.

On a more complex level, productive capacity will be available to make sufficient quantities of the company's products to meet sales targets on which advertising and promotion expenditures are based. Still more sophisticated financial planning calls for allocating the limited resources of the company in such a way as to derive the greatest benefit from them.

Sophisticated or not, budgets provide a general framework for the planning of specific operations. Moreover, effective budgeting reaches into the details of every phase of the business. Just as every department is involved in the conduct of the whole business, so every department must be involved in planning the whole operation.

BUDGETING AS TRAINING

How far down the organization will people be asked to contribute to the budgeting process? That depends on several factors: the complexity of operations, the organization structure, the philosophy of management. In general, management has good reasons for involving as many people as it can: budgeting is a form of training in supervisory responsibility and a source of motivation as well. Before submitting his departmental budget, a department head is likely to ask the supervisors reporting to him to prepare segments that he can consolidate.

In the usual situation, budgets are prepared annually and revised at intervals—every four or six months, for example. Sales volumes are forecast, and production requirements are calculated. Based on these levels of activity, departmental operations are estimated: units to be produced, machine-time requirements, material and supplies requirements, direct and indirect labor needs, power use, and so on.

Statistical records of past requirements and costs are often helpful in assembling the data behind budget calculations, and much information may be available from the budget and data-processing departments. It is important to the supervisor to know what goes into the budget calculations for his department and where to get additional information needed.

CONTROL

When the planning phase is over and the budget is completed, it is used to help control operations. Basically, the budget provides a standard against which performance is measured and any variances analyzed. Were departmental labor costs for April higher than called for in the budget? The difference between the budget figure and the actual figure is called a variance. Those that reach a stipulated level—say, 5 percent—must be explained in a variance report. The costs may have been higher, for example, because absenteeism in the department necessitated the hiring of temporary help. Here, the variance is unfavorable; if April labor costs had been lower than the budgeted figure, the variance would have been favorable.

Because variances must be charged up to those who can control them, departmental expenses are usually segregated into controllable and uncontrollable portions. A supervisor cannot properly be held accountable for fixed expenses such as depreciation charges on equipment or space charges allocated to his activity because there is nothing he can do to reduce these costs. They fall into the uncontrollable category. But he can do something about the use of supplies, so this item is deemed controllable.

Other items that are usually uncontrollable by the supervisor are price rises in supplies when he doesn't do the purchasing, and changes in production mix. Changes in production mix would occur where there are several different processes or products, each requiring different quantities of material, supplies, labor, or machine time. A top-level decision to make more of product A and less of product B would change these quantities, but such changes are obviously not the supervisor's responsibility.

OFFICE BUDGETS

The terms *processes, products,* and *production* are not intended to refer exclusively to manufacturing. Office workers process paperwork. They produce letters, invoices, vouchers, checks, and a variety of other documents, records, schedules, and reports. Their output quantities are frequently called *production volumes.* And their activities are properly planned and controlled with the aid of budgets.

The purposes of budgeting, then, are to plan, coordinate, and control operations. To a greater or lesser extent, supervisors can expect to be involved in some aspects of the budget process.

58. Coordination as a Task of Management: A Review*

Robert C. Heide

Organizations and management are dynamic viable creations and must continue to be so if they are to keep pace with changing social needs and new programs. The challenge is a formidable one to meet. Old programs are being retreaded and new innovative services launched each day. The multiplication of numbers of organizational relationships, further complicated by increased specialization of staff and departmentalization of services, already taxes the structure and threatens to overwhelm the administrator. Informational systems, data processing, and functional forms of organization rise to meet some of the challenge. However, the administrator will still need to rely to a large extent on tested traditional principles of management to fulfill his role in the organization. Such principles and techniques should receive repeated review, adaptation, and reinforcement if they are to continue to be workable tools of the administrator.

One such element of management warranting review is that of coordination, a task which may take on ever-increasing dimensions for the middle manager of a public welfare program. Although much writing has been devoted to the importance and need for coordination at all levels of management, a review of the literature leaves the neophyte hanging somewhere between "so what else is new?" and "exactly what is coordination?"

Popular belief in the importance of coordination almost takes on the aura and dedication awarded to motherhood and the flag. Yet, we use "coordinate" and "coordination" so loosely that in this day of rapid communication the meaning to the listener is fuzzy, and the true essence is all but lost. In addition, "coordination" is applied to almost any human endeavor, whether of a physical, social or scientific basis, making it almost impossible to apply a universal definition. For purposes of clarification, and because coordination is presumed to be a task of considerable importance to the manager, it would seem appropriate to examine its usage and variety of meanings, and to review techniques for its use.

One of the earliest recorded uses of the word "coordinate" (c 1641) was in its application to church organization, indicating equal rank among churches.[1] Its use in modern grammar suggests members of

---

* From *Public Welfare*, Vol. XXVII, No. 3 (July, 1969), 279–83. Reprinted by permission.
1 Cf. *"The Oxford Universal Dictionary on Historical Principles* (London: Oxford University Press, Amen House).

equal rank, such as coordinate clauses in a compound sentence. In mathematics it may be used to determine position, by the use of points in common on a plane. The use of "coordinate" in military operations adds the essential element of appropriate timing to the usual interrelationships. The juxtaposition of the parts, the synchronization of their functioning, and a common goal are the ingredients of the meaning of the word in its general use today.

COORDINATION AS AN ACTION

In addition to its use in terms of equal (balanced) and spatial relationships and timing, "coordination" should be perceived in two other dimensions, namely, as an action, and as a condition of being.

A cursory review of recent history of governmental operations discloses that the concept and use of coordination was seen first as "an action," and applied earliest to the function of control, specifically in the area of budgeting for a multidepartmental organization. Interdepartmental coordination "arose as an essential factor from the demand for strengthened executive responsibility . . ."[2] Coordination was applied in an attempt to centralize expenditure control by delegating appropriate authority to an agency attached to a central public office. On a Federal level this took place in the early 1920's, following a similar innovation at the state level by the Illinois Legislature in 1917.

Coordination assumed increasing importance in the Federal government operations during World War II, specifically in the assignment of this task to the Office of War Mobilization. This office was charged with the duties to "unify the activities" and "resolve or determine controversies . . ." and "issue directives on policy. . . ."[3] In addition, this assignment appeared designed to relieve the Executive Office of handling details and avoid becoming involved with problems directly. An earlier attempt at coordination during the 1920's and the early 1930's involved a number of interdepartmental committees which were "collected" under the Federal Coordinating Service for the purpose of promoting good management practice and to achieve high level production. As might be expected in an era reflecting but emerging from the classical theory of organization, the answer to the lack of functional coordination was to devise reporting systems and central planning bodies.

In more recent times, "coordination" has become a byword, and in the thinking of at least one expert, the essence of management. Gulick described the functions of management as "Planning . . . Organizing . . . Staffing . . . Directing . . . Coordinating (that is the all important duty of interrelating the various parts of the work), Reporting . . . Budget-

2 Fritz M. Marx, *Elements of Public Administration* (Englewood Cliffs, N.J.: Prentice Hall, Inc., 1963), p. 177.
3 *Ibid.*, p. 179.

ing."[4] Other authorities have proposed that coordination is included in each of the parts described by Gulick and others, insisting that none of these tasks by management is without coordination as an essential element in its functioning. The importance of this element has grown so that few job descriptions or program plans are written today without emphasis being placed on coordination as a major task of the manager, director, or coordinator. It is difficult to perceive how and where further importance can be attached to it. This may explain in part why in very recent years there have been suggestions to see coordination in a different perspective, as a "condition of being," that has a nature or properties. It is suggested that coordination may be seen as something that exists and is built of substance, as well as an action that can be taken. It might be superfluous to note that one without the other portends only limited success for the organization. Nor does the presence of one ensure the natural inception and promotion of the other. It may be posited that both need to be worked on, consciously and deliberately by management, if high level achievement is to be realized throughout the organization.

COORDINATION AS A CONDITION OF BEING

Considering first the aspect of coordination as a condition of being, one might ask "what makes for its existence?" "what properties lend themselves to identification, examination, and planning?"

Likert emphasizes the importance of human resources and relationships. In a recent publication he devotes an entire chapter to recognizing problems and suggesting solutions for the development of coordination in a highly functionalized organization.[5] The framework and concepts of traditional organizational theory, such as manifested in large governmental agencies and industry, compound problems in the promotion of coordination. Solutions appear to lie in promoting coordination and formulating channels for decision-making along more than one line in the operation, as well as in a departure from the usually conceived hierarchal table of organization.

One of the bases of Likert's thesis stresses the importance of the relationship between the superior and the subordinate, concerning which he urges the use by the manager of the principle of supportive relationships. The definition of this term closely follows that applied in social work, and parallels the ends sought for a client by his caseworker. As such, it is not new to the manager of a social service agency. Yet, its significance may often escape one in the everyday operation and the

---

4 Luther Gulick, as quoted by Bertram M. Gross, *The Managing of Organizations* (New York: Free Press of Glencoe, 1964), Vol. I, p. 144.
5 Rensis Likert, *The Human Organization: Its Management and Values* (New York: McGraw-Hill, Inc., 1967), Chapter 10, pp. 156–188.

professional interactions of the staff. It would seem obvious that meaningful relationships are key indicators of and contribute much to the
nature of the organization and its functioning. Staff relationships are
built upon interactions, vertically and horizontally, between people,
albeit they may usually be seen as positions. People inside as well as
outside of formal organizations have personal needs which respond to
ego-building relationships and satisfying experiences.

A second contributor to a "condition of being" is the existence of
defined and understood goals of the organization that are needed to
provide the framework within which the employee can seek realization
of personal objectives.[6] Clear purpose, aided by defined staff patterns
and specific objectives, is basic to organizational planning and functioning. It is just as basic to another organism, man. Without these
important guideposts for the individual to relate to and identify with,
activity would tend to become random, relatively dysfunctional and
productive of anxiety.

The third substance, and closely interrelated with the first two, is the
potential and means for free-flowing, candid, and multidirectional communication. Obviously, interdependence of personal and organizational
goals, and assurance that would come from supportive relationships
would have little value and *raison d'etre* without means for communication. Together, *supportive relationships*, *shared purpose*, *and communication* make for the substance or essence that builds coordination.

Let us turn then to examine techniques for coordination through
action by administration. One of the first questions posed in literature
has to do with the proper degree of central authority in effecting coordination. Does management coordinate employees? Most if not all authorities agree that coordination cannot be accomplished *ad dictum*, but
rather, only facilitated by administration. Coordination more often
occurs, one might conclude, as a result of administratively promoted
and directed interaction among staff, whose goals are compatible with
the climate and purpose of the organization.

ACTION BY ADMINISTRATION

In describing principles of collective planning or coordination of industry on a national scale, Follett contributes a unique viewpoint of
coordination, which may be applicable at any level within any one
hierarchy, as well as in the relationships of superior-subordinate organizations. Follett contrasts coercion—the imposition of arbitrary plan-

---

[6] Definitions of organizational goals vary from what may be otherwise thought of as missions, or projected levels of program effectiveness, or work plan objectives. Is the purpose of
the goal statement to impress, inspire, give direction, or provide bases for measurement? If the
employee is a high priority target for involvement, he might relate even more meaningfully to
statements that include or are supplemented by the administrator's individualized professional
philosophy as well.

ning, with coordination—the voluntary adjusting or the reciprocal relating of all factors to each other within a situation. "But the process of adjusting is not one which can be imposed from outside—it is essentially, basically, by its very nature, a process of auto-controlled activity. No one can issue a fiat by which I am adjusted, I can only be helped to adjust myself."[7]

As a test to evaluate national planning as well as to assist the process of coordination, Follett suggested four principles of organization:

1. co-ordination by direct contact of the responsible people concerned;
2. co-ordination in the early stages;
3. co-ordination as the reciprocal relating of all the factors in a situation;
4. co-ordination as a continuing process.[8]

Follett continues on to make the point that coordination is more than placing components in proper and harmonious relationship to each other, but that "interpenetration" of its parts must also occur. If the individual elements have not changed because of their reciprocal relationships, then coordination has not taken place.

In addition to the application of the principles stated above, how otherwise can coordination, hopefully with interpenetration, be promoted by management? Some of the following methods illustrate a variety of impositions by administrative direction.

METHODS

Long-distance action by a central authority to bring about coordination in a field office may be attempted through definition and design in a number of ways: "Increased uniformity in . . . boundaries and . . . offices; incidental coordinating responsibilities of service and control agencies; reliance on informal coordination; appointment of regional coordinators; and the use of committees and commissions."[9]

Each of the five carries with it a different degree of "coordination by order." No one method may have higher hopes for success than the others. "Informal coordination" and "committees and commissions" depend much upon personal factors, e.g. common concerns and interrelated problems, mutual accessibility, authority and compensation level and status, so the "sitting down together" may have varied results.

Common boundaries and shared office buildings are obvious and direct methods to employ, and an appointed coordinator at least provides some definition of the need and degree of local authority to promote efforts. The degree of authority delegated to the local coordinator

---

7 Mary Parker Follett, *Dynamic Administration*, Edited by H. C. Metcalf, and L. Urwick (New York: Harper and Brothers, 1940), p. 296.

8 *Ibid.*, p. 297.

9 Fritz M. Marx, *op. cit.*, p. 266.

may vary widely, from one empowered to act as an agent of top administration to one who merely encourages harmony and cooperation. One advantage of a local coordinator is that the task is fixed at the local level, which should promote consonance with the uniqueness of that office and level of operation.

SHORT RANGE AND LONG RANGE GOALS

Another means for coordination through long distance direction, and something basic to all functioning at the local level, is the structure of the organization itself. Built into the framework, hopefully, is the grouping together of efforts seen as being necessary to accomplish the organization's purposes. The very proximity of the elements enhances their integrated functioning, and the authority necessary to ensure the success of the operation carries the means to develop relationships through which would flow coordination.

Coordination may be promoted at short range within any organization through a variety of means used for a variety of purposes. A common method is that manifested in the role of supervisors, who may not be explicitly coordinating several staff members, but nevertheless ". . . employ directional devices, teach principles of coordination, illustrate their application, and apply tests to determine the quality of synchronized effort."[10] Common directional devices and means to teach and illustrate principles may include any type of written communication, as well as the use of the individual conference and group staff meeting. Successfully administered, the group process in such conferences and meetings epitomizes the purpose of the functioning of the whole organization, which came into existence, in part at least, as an expression of collective needs for social relationships.

A long range goal of the efforts for coordination by management is the sensitization of each element to the potential of meaning of particular things and interdependency with another. All of the devices, techniques, and structures will have failed if the individual does not become a link in a reciprocating, interpenetrating chain of relationship and reaction. He will not perceive this role in the process until he senses the significance and interdependence of himself with others and within the organization.[11]

The essence of coordination as part of the role of the administrator was aptly expressed many years past by Reynolds in writing about the group aspect of administration. "Organization to administer any enter-

---

[10] Harold Koontz, and Cyril O'Donnell, *Principles of Management* (New York: McGraw-Hill Book Company, 1964), p. 43.

[11] Another reminder may be in order to emphasize that as in the case of staff relationships, coordination may take place vertically as well as horizontally. Perhaps the concept of a grid would be more apt than the illustration of a chain in describing a circuitry for organizational interaction.

prise or service calls for a group of people working together, with their individual functions coordinated into a smoothly working whole. Since they are human, they will require help at times in relating themselves to the whole, and seeing themselves as important but not isolated, significant only as others are significant too. Skill in administration consists not only in building organizational machinery which is adapted to the work to be done, but also in so dealing with the human parts of the machine that they all work at their individual and collective best."[12]

Coordination will not just happen, but can result from conscious appreciation of the needs of man, and efforts by administration to provide a climate that encourages harmony, interdependence and teamwork, through supportive relationships, understood goals, and freedom of communication. Directed interaction will best come about with a clear definition of roles, an integrated organizational structure, and face-to-face and supporting directional devices. Within such a climate and with these aids of administrative direction, man has the opportunity to fulfill his social needs and personal achievement goals. In providing such a climate, administration is manifesting a major achievement commensurate with its assumed lofty station in a hierarchy.

[12] Bertha C. Reynolds, as quoted by Gertrude Wilson and Gladys Ryland, *Social Group Work Practice* (Cambridge, Massachusetts: The Riverside Press, 1949), p. 618.

SELECTED READINGS

Articles

Day, Robert C., and Robert L. Hamblin. "Some Effects of Close and Punitive Styles of Supervision," *American Journal of Sociology*, Vol. 69, No. 5 (March, 1964), 499–510.

Einstein, Kurt. "The Management Audit," *Personnel Administrator*, Vol. 15, No. 1 (January–February, 1970), 16–23.

Murdick, Robert G. "Managerial Control: Concepts and Practice," *Advanced Management Journal*, Vol. 35, No. 1 (January, 1970), 48–52.

Roman, Daniel D. "The PERT System: An Appraisal of Program Evaluation Review Technique," *Journal of the Academy of Management*, April, 1962, 57–65.

Simmons, Roberta G. "The Role Conflict of the First-Line Supervisor: An Experimental Study," *American Journal of Sociology*, Vol. 73, No. 4 (January, 1968), 482–95.

Tannenbaum, Arnold S., "The Concept of Organizational Control," *Journal of Social Issues*, Vol. 12, No. 2 (1956), 50–60.

———. "Control in Organizations: Individual Adjustment and Organizational Performance," *Administrative Science Quarterly*, Vol. 7, No. 1 (June, 1962), 236–57.

SECTION I: EMPLOYEE RELATIONS

It is frequently stated in management literature that "management is getting things done through people." If this concept is true, it must follow that a most important managerial responsibility at any organizational level is that of promoting good employee relations. While this responsibility has always existed to some extent, current trends indicate that this task will take on increasing importance in the immediate and foreseeable future.

On every side can be perceived the "signs of the times"; that is, the factors and conditions that affect relations between the employer and the employee. Some of these are increased and increasing employment in government agencies in general, and in state and local government in particular; the need for improved administration at all levels; the tremendous turnover in employment in most government agencies; the need for expanded and continuing training in management and supervision; a manpower shortage that threatens to become worse in the immediate future; and generation and cultural gaps that tend to aggravate the problems of establishing and maintaining amicable and effective relations between management and its employees.

The marked increase in collective bargaining in public-supported programs, with such employee groups as public school teachers, postal workers, garbage workers, and others, is in itself evidence of the need for better employee relations in all of these fields. Therefore, what a government agency chooses to do about employee working conditions and

445

complaints may very well determine the character of its relations with its employees as well as its effectiveness as an organization.

All of this may tend to raise certain questions in the mind of the manager in a public-supported program about his possible and probable course or courses of action in the future. Should he assume that any legal bars to collective bargaining in the public sector will prove effective in preventing strikes? Or, should he assume that he inevitably must deal with the union? If the demand for collective bargaining arises out of poor employee relations, what can and should he do to improve the relations? We believe that the two articles in this section will prove helpful in finding answers to these and other questions. "Unions for Local Government? One Man's View of a Complex Problem," by Richard Dunsing, deals with these questions in some depth. Dunsing's idea and emphasis, simply stated, is prevention. Know your employee's needs and endeavor to improve your management so that these needs will be satisfied as far as possible, thus obviating the need and demand for collective bargaining. A second question, and one that inevitably must be asked and answered, is dealt with by David T. Stanley in "What are the Unions Doing to Merit Systems?" Stanley sees a rapid weakening of "management by itself," or the unquestioned sovereignty of the organization. While unionism will not necessarily harm the merit system, it will bring about the kind of participation between management and rank-and-file employees that has become common in the private sector.

59. Unions for Local Governments? One Man's View of a Complex Problem*

Richard Dunsing

My view is simple: Any organization which now has a union has earned it. Employees are seldom able to articulate exactly what it is that drives them into a stance where they respond well to a union pitch. The reasons can be readily identified, however.

Intense frustration relating to many unsatisfied needs has developed in employee groups. Long-standing and deeply imbedded, these frustrations are beginning to surface. The employees are looking to their leaders for guidance, support and understanding and yet the responsible people never seem to see these frustrations. If by chance the pent-up feelings *do* become apparent, managers deny them, white-wash them and soft-soap them. They almost never *respond* to them.

It is a long-championed American principle that people are unique. We are a country of differences yet we seldom run our organizations to draw on the resources inherent in these differences. We need to understand the irreplaceable value of differences today, and change our management approach accordingly.

The differences between younger and older are wider and more basic than ever in our history. The "over-30" employee operates on a pattern of values, interests and needs that is exhibited by respect for authority, obedience, rule compliance and unquestioning acceptance of their roles. Government policies and procedures anticipate employees behaving and thinking this way. They are designed to be followed by "good" employees. Now we are finding a large segment of younger employees who resist traditional approaches. Employees in the younger range have entirely different sets of these human needs, values and interests. From this widening gap grow the seeds of discontent that improve the appeal of unions.

HUMAN NEEDS ON THE JOB

Abraham Maslow has given us an easy way to look at the differences in human needs.[1] He ranks them into a hierarchy of levels. He begins with basic needs at the bottom of a hierarchy, and lists them upward as the human being grows from level to level (see illustration).

THE HIERARCHY OF NEEDS

While many levels may operate for a person in the course of daily activities Maslow saw a *single* need level as being dominant at any given

* From *Virginia Town and City*, October, 1970, pp. 5–8. Reprinted by permission.
1 Motivation and Personality, A. H. Maslow, Harper and Bros., 1954, pp. 80–106.

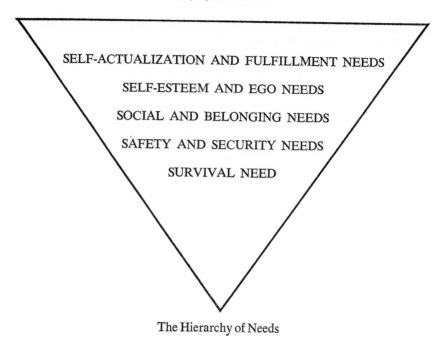

SELF-ACTUALIZATION AND FULFILLMENT NEEDS

SELF-ESTEEM AND EGO NEEDS

SOCIAL AND BELONGING NEEDS

SAFETY AND SECURITY NEEDS

SURVIVAL NEED

The Hierarchy of Needs

time. Each person must basically satisfy the needs at lower levels before he can move to the next higher level. This is true each time a person "grows" to a new higher level. Until dominant needs are satisfied a human being is unable to operate or even recognize his needs at the next higher need level. The key point is that a satisfied need no longer motivates a person.

Let's look at an example. Many of us were raised in the depression years, or by parents who were. Countless people in the U.S. today are still hung-up at the safety and security need level, engaged in the saving-for-a-rainy-day philosophy of life. They are concerned that they may not have a job, a place to live, and enough food to eat. For this reason, they have not moved beyond the second need level.

They have raised their children in an era of great affluence. These children, never having experienced a depression, have moved rapidly through the first three need levels. By the time they begin to think about college they are already operating at the fourth or fifth need level. The hard work of the parents has freed young people, and in so doing the parents have created the gap themselves. The parents are dismayed that their children are not afraid of losing a job.

It is not so much a generation gap as it is an experience gap. It also explains why the older mid-level manager is unable to relate to the younger manager or employee on the job. They speak a different language, come from different worlds and see things through different lenses.

The union movement in this country grew out of second-level need psychology. It is basically there that unions still make their pitch. They emphasize security, basic benefits such as insurance and pension, fairness and job protection. They are most concerned that people be promoted on a seniority system—that employees be protected from the arbitrariness of man and manager.

GOVERNMENT MANAGEMENT STYLE CONFLICTING WITH EMPLOYEE NEEDS

Managers in government place their emphasis on rules, regulations, procedures and guidelines and other structured methods of guiding human behavior. Employees who don't step out of line are rewarded with steady jobs, fringe benefits and security. These methods were essential to put order into chaotic management systems years ago. Today they are in extreme conflict with growing numbers of non-depression bred employees. Overemphasis on structured approaches to operating government units is disastrous. The traditional methods were comforting to people at the security and safety level (i.e., you and I who were raised in the depression era). Such policies and procedures are seen as a huge stumbling block by the younger generation.

While the older government employer is interested in protecting himself from a mistake and finds assurance in rules and regulations the younger person is interested in achievement. The younger person is willing to take the risks that are necessary for innovation and achievement. The younger person wants to express himself, to try his talents, and to utilize the long and arduous education we have forced upon him as a prerequisite to entering society. He has been promised that he *can* make a contribution to a significant world. He wants that to happen *now*.

Younger people are intense, free-swinging, curious and questioning about ways of operating we have long taken for granted. They want to accomplish and they want to do it now. While they seem a threat to the "system" to many people in government, it is their genius that can solve the massive problems erupting today.

THE APPEAL OF UNIONS

Actually, union propaganda and approach appeals more to the older generation. Like management, unions emphasize safety and security. In fact, probably the union's largest failing in the 1970's is to continue to beat the same dead horse. As someone once said, what we need to do is to call the union and say "Hey, you won! The war is over, now let's get on with more important things."

There is another appeal that reaches deep into younger ranks, too.

This is the protection for expression that a union not only promises but *guarantees*.

Needs that are blocked from fulfillment generate frustration. People who are frustrated exhibit a great deal of anger, hostility, and animosity. There is no better vehicle for displaying this than through the use of union power. A government unit that continues to hack away with the same old tired solutions to new and more complex problems is setting the stage for a high degree of employee frustration (to say nothing of frustration on the part of citizens).

Unions seek out these frustrations and are highly creative in fanning sparks into roaring flames.

SYMPTOMS OF DISCONTENT

A number of employee statements are often heard which are symptoms of problems. However, because of the high level of distrust in many government units, the boss is the last to hear them. The attitudes are there; they simply never surface. Examine them and begin to listen more intently.

FRUSTRATION LEVEL STATEMENTS BY EMPLOYEES

1. I'll take it up with the boss.
2. It's not in the budget.
3. Everything takes forever around here.
4. The only time I hear about my performance is when a mistake has been made.
5. There are two ways my boss sees to do things: his way and the wrong way.
6. I never get in to see my boss.
7. There are things *worse* than being fired.
8. Why is it that when there is a budget crisis we employees must subsidize it by losing a pay raise.

The employee sees himself as put-down and put-off. He is treated as an insignificant lifeform with little control over the world in which he lives. He has little opportunity to make a real contribution. The boss takes on an image of having all the right answers and knowing what is best for people without ever checking with them. The boss is seen as pro-budget but seldom pro-employee. A union will at least allow the employee a safe platform for being heard.

PRECRISIS ACTION

Reacting to the new perspectives that this article may suggest takes a radical change in management operation. A change of such nature and magnitude requires much time, planning, and competent guidance. Let me suggest a few points that may begin the process.

1. Try to collect some unbiased information about whether or not you have a problem. Attitude surveys done by outside people in universities or consulting organizations can give ample feedback. Caution: Don't try to construct your own form and do it yourself. The results are always radically distorted management's way. The employees slant their answers because they distrust your motives and are afraid the information will be used against them.

2. Begin moving to a participative-involvement style of management. Simple beginnings can be made in this direction by including hourly rated and clerical people as well as lower managers in the basic tasks of planning, goal-setting, and problem-solving, and in the operation of task forces working on major projects.

3. Set a management style of not only listening, but of responding. Set yourself a new yardstick that any employee complaint will be answered within 24 hours. Add one other dimension to that: when you are wrong, when unfairness has been done, you will correct it immediately.

4. Emphasize fairness. Often this means going beyond and or making exceptions to the rules. Rules have a way of becoming mechanical but people are not mechanical. They are made of living flesh and blood and seldom fit into the rules and regulations created in the abstract. In fact, most human problems fall in the cracks between the rules which are supposed to apply to them.

5. Appoint a committee made up of all levels of people to condense, eliminate, and rewrite all rules and regulations. Cross out all that are unduly restrictive and unnecessarily complex. Rewrite rules and regulations so that people can begin to achieve within them and make some decisions for themselves.

6. Begin to deal with reality. Stop pretending that everything is just fine and dandy and quit sweeping the key issues under the rug. You have problems just as I do. Until we admit, not only to ourselves but to those around us, that we have problems they will never be dealt with. In such an atmosphere, the union alternative gains favor quickly.

HOW DO UNIONS WIN?

Unions win by default. They out-hustle the government leaders in their promotion of the wrong motivators. Union organizers and government leaders wear themselves out battling over the wrong issues. In the end, unions can indeed *promise* more than the responsible leaders can deliver. With no channels in the existing system for expression, growth or achievement, even young people see the union as an outlet.

When a union has made its pitch and the pitch has been bought it often marks the beginning of years of disruptive, divisive conflict. Power faces power. A win-lose stance is taken. Each side tries to punish the other,

451

and the citizen finds himself even worse off—he is in a lose-lose position (no one even considers a win-win point-of-view).

A WIN-WIN STRATEGY FOR ACHIEVEMENT

Building a team commitment requires ability to meet organizational needs and people needs (workers and managers both) at the same time. Going this synergistic route is inevitable. Actually, it is more a matter of "What are the penalties we will pay later for not starting now?"

Most people have the capacity to grow and contribute important talent. Releasing this talent can be achieved. By releasing the pent up energy of employees, government wins two ways: frustrations are reduced, and the real problems of the organization are undertaken and solutions actually pursued.

Management is best equipped to meet the broad range of employee needs. Unions meet needs narrowly but loudly and aggressively. To earn the commitment and the creative energy of employees a manager has to provide an environment for achievement. Only a manager has control over the system, supervisory style and design of jobs. Redirected, these can provide the kind of team orientation that will cause employees to disregard the passionate pleas of a union organizer.

The question is: Who will respond to emerging higher level needs first; unions or management? At stake is government's prime essential resources; human talent, energy and commitment. By being first, government managers can create a "win-win" situation for us all.

60. What Are Unions Doing to Merit Systems?*

David T. Stanley

As unions of public employees grow in numbers and influence the question naturally arises, "What are unions doing to merit systems?" The question may have a tone of alarm for long-term practitioners, advocates, and beneficiaries of civil service systems. The gains of civil service, now nearing its century mark in this country, have been won and maintained with difficulty; alternatives are understandably dismaying. This question has been explored in the past by expert and interested persons in this journal and other publications.

We now have some preliminary results from a study of the impact of unions on public administration that throws further light on this question as it applies to local governments. Our raw material comes from about ten days of interviewing and document-grabbing in each of fifteen cities and four urban counties. (Cities: Binghamton, New York; Boston, Massachusetts; Buffalo, New York; Cincinnati, Ohio; Dayton, Ohio; Detroit, Michigan; Hartford, Connecticut; Milwaukee, Wisconsin; New Orleans, Louisiana; New York, New York; Philadelphia, Pennsylvania; San Francisco, California; St. Louis, Missouri; Tacoma, Washington; and Wilmington, Delaware. Counties: Dade, Florida; Los Angeles, California; Multnomah, Oregon; and New Castle, Delaware.)

The localities studied all have merit systems, but differences in strength, competence, and age of these systems were very obvious. There is great variety also in the state laws governing the conditions under which public employees may unionize and bargain. All these variations make it hard to generalize from the experience of these nineteen governments, but we can present some of the patterns we found. We do not contend that these cities and counties are truly representative of all local governments, only that they show what is going on in a variety of places where unions have been active.

A mixed and moderate report results from the study. Civil service is not disappearing, nor is it fighting unions to a standstill, nor is there beautiful collaboration everywhere. In general, unions, bargaining, and contractual provisions are invading more and more precincts previously

* From *Public Personnel Review*, Vol. 31, No. 2 (April, 1970), 108–13. Reprinted by permission. This is one of five studies on unions, collective bargaining, and public employment, sponsored by the Brookings Institution with the aid of the Ford Foundation. The other four concern: (1) the nature and types of unions; (2) laws governing labor-management relations; (3) structure of collective bargaining, including recognition, representation and impasse resolution; and (4) effects of unions on the wages of unionized workers in the public service. All relate only to local government, and except for the fourth, exclude school systems. All five are to be published as Brookings books.

occupied only by civil service commissions or personnel offices. How good or how bad this is depends upon the value systems of the beholder.

What do we mean by merit systems? We should distinguish them from the merit principle under which public employees are recruited, selected, and advanced under conditions of political neutrality, equal opportunity, and competition on the basis of merit and competence. Public employee unions do not question this principle in general and have done little to weaken it, as yet. When we say merit systems, however, this has come to mean a broad program of personnel management activities. Some are essential to carrying out the merit principle: recruiting, selecting, policing of anti-politics and anti-discrimination rules, and administering related appeals provisions. Others are closely related and desirable: position classification, pay administration, employee benefits, and training. Unions are of course interested in both categories.

What unions are we talking about? We refer particularly to the American Federation of State, County, and Municipal Employees; the Service Employees International Union, the International Association of Firefighters, the various police associations, the nursing associations, the International Brotherhood of Teamsters, the unions of licensed practical nurses.

This article will speak rather generally of union attitudes and pressures. Some are expressed through the collective bargaining process, with the results embodied in a formal agreement; some are stated as representations to the boards of local government. Or the pressure may be more informally applied, as when a union delegation meets with a department head or a steward meets with the first-line or second-line supervisor.

THE IMPACT IN GENERAL

The major and most distinct effect of union activity is a weakening of what might be called management-by-itself. The era of unilateralism, of unquestioned sovereignty, is about over. The age of bilateralism—consultation, negotiation, and bargaining—is already here. The "independent" civil service commission, responsible over the years for rule-making, for protection of career employees from arbitrary personnel changes, for adjudication of appeals from employees, still exists but is losing functions. Civil service commissions may not go out of business, but more and more of their vital organs will be removed by the bargaining process until, whether officially in existence or not, they are husks of their former selves. This change is occuring not because employes are clearly dissatisfied with existing merit systems but because they feel that unions will get more for them—more pay, more benefits, more aggressive protection against possible arbitrary management actions.

454

At the same time management is becoming more careful, more responsible, and more responsive. The fact that management at all levels is prodded, observed, objected to, and reasoned with by union stewards and business agents means that management must watch its step. Another effect is that this change from unilateralism to bilateralism brings transitional difficulties. First-line and second-line supervisors in government are not used to dealing with unions, and the unions have many inexperienced stewards who are busy fumbling hot potatoes. The passage of time and the application of effort and good will should reduce these problems.

ORGANIZATION FOR LABOR RELATIONS

Each of the governments we studied has had to provide organizationally for dealing with unions. In Hartford and Philadelphia, for example, the function has been clearly lodged within the city personnel office. This contrasts with Detroit and New York where a separate labor relations office operates in cooperation (and some competition) with civil service commission. In other governments labor relations are handled by some different administrator: a fiscal executive in Buffalo; the assistant to the mayor in Binghamton; the chairman of the Board of County Commissioners in Multnomah County, and the county manager in Dade County.

These varied patterns of organization result from both tradition and personality. It is much too early to say that any one system works better than another, and indeed, our findings may reflect personalities rather than organization schemes. It seems natural to predict, however, that the longer labor relations functions are separated from personnel functions, the more trouble we are going to have in the future. The activities of "independent" civil service commissions intensify the diffusion of managerial authority and make union negotiations more difficult. Even more important, it is impossible for a personnel officer (or civil service executive secretary) to be both an impartial defender of employees' rights and an adversary of unions as a management negotiator. It is perfectly possible to foresee governments adopting the industrial pattern: a department of labor relations headed by a vice-mayor or assistant city manager for labor relations who will supervise not only bargaining and employee relations, but also selection and training activities.

HIRING

We have already noted that unions accept the merit principle, and our field research shows that they are inclined to accept most of the qualification requirements and examining methods that are customarily part of the civil service system. Here and there we found some union resistance to the lowering of qualification standards, such as height requirements for policemen, high school graduation for custodians, or college degrees for caseworkers. There are various motives for such resistance: the wish to work with well-qualified associates (or with people like themselves) and the wish to argue that higher qualifications deserve higher pay.

On the whole unions have shown little interest in examining methods except where they have taken up the cause of citizens whose educational experiences do not prepare them to excel on pencil-and-paper tests. In those cases unions would naturally prefer performance tests to examinations which involve verbal aptitude. The civil service office discussing this should be in a position to show that the tests used are valid for their intended purposes. Unions have also affected selection by pushing management to shorten probation periods. Such a change clearly limits management's freedom to discharge unsatisfactory employees.

When the government runs special recruitment and training programs for disadvantaged citizens of the cities, the unions are put in a somewhat difficult position. Union leaders support such programs both because of altruism and because they see the new recruits to city service as potential union members do not want to see these less privileged citizens occupying a preferred position in selection and training in comparison to themselves. ("I had to take a civil service examination to get that job. Why doesn't he?" "We had to have high school diplomas before we could have such a job. Why don't they?") So acceptance depends on whether those recruited under the "new careers" and other comparable programs are regarded as allies or as threats to employees who are the real backbone of the union membership.

More important than all of these factors is the increased adoption of the union shop. Four of our localities (Hartford, Philadelphia, New Castle County, and Wilmington) provided this form of union security. The effect is that employment is limited to citizens willing to join unions —who may or may not be the best-qualified candidates. The effect is slightly less for the agency shop (Dayton, Detroit, and Boston) under which employees, if not willing to be union members, must pay fees in lieu of union dues because they presumably benefit from union services.

PROMOTIONS

The unions' naturally strong interest in promotions is expressed in support of measures that favor inside candidates for jobs and limit management's freedom of selection. When a job above the usual entrance level is to be filled, they strongly prefer that promotion lists be used ahead of open competitive lists and departmental promotion lists ahead of service-wide promotion lists. These policies are reflected anyway in many civil service laws and procedures, perhaps to excess, so the union influence reinforces some preexisting rigidities. In some cities promotion lists are limited to the union bargaining unit. This provision may be another wave of the future.

Another point of emphasis, clearly consistent with the others, is insistence on "rule-of-one" certification. Even in some places where "rule-of-three" prevails, union pressures are directed toward selecting the top person certified unless there is some extremely compelling reason for not doing so. In effect, management has to show cause why the top eligible on the list should not be appointed.

In rating candidates for promotion, unions have rather consistently opposed the use of oral examinations and performance ratings, at least arguing for a reduced weighting to be given such factors, and for increased weight to be given to seniority. They would prefer promotion by strict seniority among those basically qualified for the higher job. Thus far, however, this last provision has been negotiated in only a few contracts. Where we did find it, the promotions were not to supervisory positions but to higher-rated nonsupervisory jobs (laborer to truck driver, truck driver to bulldozer operator) within the bargaining unit. In these respects unions are still supporting the merit principle but maintaining that senior employees have more merit.

TRANSFERS

There is little union interest in interdepartmental transfers except in cases where the union helps an employee move to another department because he is facing disciplinary action or is involved in a personality conflict in his present department.

The situation is different, however, with respect to transfers to new locations or to other shifts within a department. Unions would like to have assignments to preferred places or times made on a basis of seniority among those who request such assignments. We found this policy in a few contracts, but in general management has full freedom to assign employees where they are needed.

TRAINING

Unions have had two kinds of impact on employee training programs. First, they urge or even arrange training to help their members gain promotions, such as on-the-job training in operation of more complex equipment or group training to prepare for promotion examinations. In Detroit, for example, the Teamsters Union in cooperation with the civil service commission has arranged for drivers to learn heavy equipment operation. The Service Employees International Union in California is pressing for training of psychiatric technicians to meet new state licensure requirements. Second, management has had to train its supervisors in labor relations, sometimes with the aid of university professors. In general, however, training continues to occupy an unfortunately low position in the unions' scale of values, as in that of management.

GRIEVANCES AND DISCIPLINARY APPEALS

One of the clearest patterns to emerge from our field research is the trend in grievance procedures. Most of the governments studied use negotiated procedures, usually going through four or five steps and ending in third-party arbitration, which is more often binding than advisory. This pattern replaces the usual grievance procedure which advances from lower to higher levels of management, ending with the civil service commission as the final "court of appeal." The arbitration provided in the new pattern may take various forms. A single arbitrator may be chosen from a list supplied by an impartial source. Or there may be a panel of arbitrators of whom the aggrieved employee (or his organization) appoints one member, management appoints a second, and the two agree upon a third, sometimes using nominations, again from an impartial source.

When we speak of grievances covered by these procedures, we are referring to grievances on supervisory relationships or working conditions. Work assignments and eligibility for premium pay are frequent subjects for such appeals. We are not referring to appeals of adverse personnel actions such as suspensions, demotions, or discharges. In most of the governments studied such adverse actions are still handled through civil service channels. A trend is beginning, however, to administer them like other grievances, and it is only a matter of time before adverse actions will be subject to arbitration in unionized urban governments. Without this change unions will continue to maintain that civil service decisions are made by pro-management bodies.

CLASSIFICATION

The position classification process—sorting jobs by occupation and level—is still a management activity but it is under several kinds of pressure from employee groups. Unions may claim that some jobs are undervalued in relation to others and urge, sometimes successfully, that they be upgraded. Unions also press for new job levels (e.g., supervising building custodian, senior caseworker) which will provide promotion opportunities for their members. Such claims and pressures may be expressed in the bargaining process. In Detroit and New York, for example, union and management bargainers have agreed on joint recommendations to civil service authorities.

A related problem arises from the insistence by unions that employees be paid at the proper rate for out-of-classification work. Sometimes there are difficult management determinations as to whether the employee really did work out of the classification, and for how long. Unions

458

contend that differences over such matters should be resolved through the grievance procedure. In one of the cities we studied, however, the civil service authorities went to court to insist that such cases be settled under management's classification authority, not through the grievance procedure. Civil service lost this one.

PAY

In all but a few of the localities studied, pay changes are made as a result of collective bargaining. In one of the remaining cities (New Orleans) only part of the local government is covered by collective bargaining procedures. In still others (San Francisco and St. Louis) the urges of employees to have fatter paychecks are expressed through group pressures on the civil service commission and more intensively on the legislative body. This form of pressure may be just as effective as bargaining. In all these bargaining-for-pay situations the end result is resolution of a complex group of factors: surveys of prevailing pay levels; the skill and influence of the chief executive; the political and economic power of the unions; the responsiveness of the city council to all sorts of pressures; the attitude of the state government, and many others.

It is terribly hard to say whether unions are getting more for employees through bargaining or other pressures than less organized employees might have obtained for themselves. Another study will undertake to demonstrate statistically the extent to which effective unionization correlates with salary increases. Our own data are not conclusive on this point. We know, of course, that both union and non-union pay have risen impressively. Looking at our nineteen governments as a whole (and it is very hard to generalize) pay rose seven to ten per cent on the average in each of the last two years, when the consumer price index was going up only four or five per cent a year. In a couple of these local governments where employees had not been given a raise for quite a time, they "caught up" with something like a 20 per cent increase. There are also the special cases of underpaid groups like some laundry, food service, and custodial workers who have been compensated so poorly for so long that union pressure results in a significant jump in their incomes.

FRINGE BENEFITS

Fringe benefits too show great variation in local governments, depending upon charter provisions, management attitudes, and priorities of union objectives. The clearest trends are those toward increased leave allowances and more generous financing of health benefits.

LOOKING TO THE FUTURE

It is clear that unions are here to stay, to grow, to become involved in more and more public personnel activities. Their influence is exerted now in many different ways but will increasingly be felt through formalized collective bargaining ending in written agreements.

In general unions do not quarrel with the merit principle although their definition of merit may be a little different from that of management. They are inclined to question the ability of management to determine who is the best of a number of employees or candidates, particularly if there are rating differences of only a point or two. Unions will resist such fine distinctions and will favor seniority as a basis for assignment and promotion.

It is clear also that pressure from unions brings increases in pay and fringe benefits which will at least keep up with and may outrun the advances in the cost of living and perhaps in prevailing wages. The time will come, however, when unions will have won the major gains that are possible in this area, and at that point one can expect them to turn their attention more aggressively to the make-up of work crews, and the conditions of assignment to shifts, and other aspects of work assignment and supervision.

Public personnel jurisdictions will have to give a great deal of thought to the way in which they are organized to meet the evergrowing strength of employee organizations. It is clear that the "independent" civil service commission is waning in power and influence and that personnel departments (whether or not subservient to a civil service commission) will also decline in influence unless they can take on the labor relations functions, as they have done very satisfactorily in some places.

I am inclined to predict that ultimately governments will establish strong labor relations departments, part of whose work will be the personnel function as we have known it in the past. With or without such a change in organization, public personnel systems need strong and experienced hands to conduct collective bargaining, to deal with grievances, and to be management's voice in matters which go to arbitration.

In general, the relationship between unions and merit systems is dynamic and immature. We are only beginning to learn the lessons that private commerce and industry learned more than a generation ago. Urban administrators would be well advised to ponder some of these lessons, notably those which concern management's freedom to organize the work and to select employees for promotion to supervisory positions. Finally, management people at all levels should somehow take the time and summon the energy to consult systematically with and listen sympathetically to union representatives.

SELECTED READINGS

Articles

Anderson, Arvid. "The Changing of the Establishment," *Kansas Governmental Journal*, February, 1971, 63–65.

Bakke, E. Wight. "Reflections on the Future of Bargaining in the Public Sector," *Monthly Labor Review*, Vol. 93, (July, 1970), 21–25.

Catlin, Robert E. "Should Public Employees Have The Right to Strike?" *Public Personnel Review*, Vol. 29, No. 1 (January, 1968), 2–6.

Cohany, Harry P., and Lucretia M. Dewey. "Union Membership Among Government Employees," *Monthly Labor Review*, Vol. 93, No. 7 (July, 1970), 15–20.

Douds, Charles T. "The Status of Collective Bargaining of Public Employees in Pennsylvania," *The Economic and Business Bulletin*, Vol. 21, No. 4 (summer, 1969), 28–31.

Dunsing, Richard. "Unions for Local Governments?" *Virginia Town and City*, October, 1970. 5–8.

Hamilton, Drayton N. "Labor Relations in the Public Sector," *The Alabama Municipal Journal*, October, 1970, 14–25.

Hazard, William R. "Teachers and Collective Bargaining: A National Dilemma," *Public Personnel Review*, Vol. 29, No. 3 (July, 1968), 130–35.

Hemskey, Jay E. "Collective Bargaining for State Employees: The Potentials of Pennsylvania's Public Employee Relations Act 195 of 1970," *Public Personnel Review*, Vol. 33, No. 1 (January, 1972), 37–43.

Hill, George E. "Collective Bargaining for State Employees," *Connecticut Government*, Vol. 24, No. 2 (winter, 1970), 1–5.

Horgan, Robert J. "Unions for Local Government?" *Virginia Town and City*, Vol. 5, No. 11 (November, 1970), 7–9.

Johnson, Aubrey P., Jr. "Can Municipal Governments Serve the Purpose for Which They Were Created if Their Employees are Unionized?" *Virginia Town and City*, Vol. 6, No. 6 (June, 1971), 5–6.

Kator, Irving. "Ombudsman for the Federal Government?" *Civil Service Journal*, Vol. 9, No. 3 (January–March, 1969), 16–19.

Kleeb, Robert H. "Preventing the Public Employee Strike," *Horizons for Modern Governments*, Vol. 18, No. 9 (November, 1970), 16–18.

Nigro, Felix A. "Labor Relations in the Public Sector," *Personnel Administration*, Vol. 33 (September–October, 1970) 34–38.

————. "Labor Relations in State and Local Governments," *Personnel Administration*, Vol. 33 (November–December, 1970), 42–47.

————, ed. "Collective Negotiations in the Public Service: A Symposium," *Public Administration Review*, Vol. 28, No. 2 (March–April, 1968), 111–47.

"Public Employees and the Right to Strike," *Senior Scholastic*, Vol. 93, No. 13 (December, 1968), 4–6, 22.

Ross, Anne M. "Public Employee Unions and the Right to Strike," *Monthly Labor Review*, Vol. 92, No. 3 (March, 1969), 14–18.

Shils, Edward B. "Collective Bargaining Can Strengthen the Merit System," *Public Employee*, Vol. 32, No. 10 (October, 1967), 11.

Snell, William. "Collective Bargaining—Its Impact on the Management Function," *The Municipality*, July, 1972, 135–48.

Stanley, David T. "What are Unions Doing to Merit Systems," *Public Personnel Review*, Vol. 31, No. 2 (April, 1970), 108–13.

"The Theory of Cruciality," *American Labor*, Vol. 2, No. 3 (June, 1969), 32–40.

Van Olinda, Patricia. "When the Natives are Restless," *Today's Secretary*, Vol. 70, No. 1 (September, 1967), 29, 67, 68.

White, Sheila C. "Work Stoppage of Government Employees," *Monthly Labor Review*, Vol. 92, No. 13 (December, 1969), 29–34.

Wurf, Jerry. "Trend Toward Collective Bargaining," *Public Management*, Vol. 51, No. 10 (October, 1969), 11–13.

Zeidler, Frank P. "An Overview of Labor-Management Relations in the Public Service," *Public Personnel Review*, Vol. 33, No. 1 (January, 1972), 2–5.

————. "Public Servants as Organized Labor," *Personnel*, Vol. 46, No. 4 (July–August, 1969), 44–55.

Both the individual and the various institutions in which he holds memberships are experiencing continuous change and disequilibrium. Events keep occurring which few would have imagined possible a short time ago. Evidence of institutional change is clearly seen in the picture of employment. Service organizations in the United States have become not only the largest category of employment, but also the fastest-growing category.

While some predict that the development of computer technology will lead us toward an increasingly rational, bureaucratized form of organization,[1] others assert that the modern organization is moving away rather than toward the highly routinized, rational organization postulated by Weber.[2] We believe that bureaucracy as an essential to organization and management will remain. However, with the younger, more highly educated employee challenged to find solutions to our complex social problems, and with a populace recognizing there are other than hard dollar costs that society must consider in its policy making, a more creative, innovative, responsive, and flexible bureaucracy is of necessity going to come about.

Erich Fromm, in "Thoughts on Bureaucracy," deals with the idea of bureaucracy not as an organizational problem but as a human problem. Fromm questions the assumption that a preestablished harmony exists between man and management. He shows how people have been dealt with as things in the past but how in the future a nonbureaucratic, humanistic, man-centered form of management will have to replace the bureaucratic form.

In his article "Post-Bureaucratic Leadership," Warren Bennis postulates a need for a new model of leadership. This need comes about from the breakdown of bureaucracy. Bureaucracy is breaking down because of rapid and unexpected change, growth in size of organizations compounded by ancient rules and tight controls, complexity of modern technology, and the shift in managerial values occasioned by a strengthening of our democratic culture. The model he proposes is an agricultural model. It ecompasses an active method for producing conditions wherein people and ideas and resources can be seeded, cultivated, and integrated to optimum effectiveness and growth. The inner-directed

---

1 Harold Leavitt and Thomas Whisler, "Management in the 1980's," *Harvard Business Review*, November–December, 1958.
2 Warren Bennis, "Beyond Bureaucracy," *Trans-action*, July–August, 1965, pp. 31–35.

will be supplanted by the other-directed, and collaboration rather than conflict will be a necessity if organizations are to cope with their uncertain environments.

61. Thoughts on Bureaucracy*

Erich Fromm

The problem I want to deal with can in a way be expressed under the heading, "The Human Side of Management." You are perhaps aware that one could express the same problem in a different way and speak of the "managerial problem of humanity." That sounds quite unusual, because most work in this field has been expressed in the former terms. For instance, Mayo's book is titled, *The Human Problems of an Industrial Civilization,*[1] rather than "The Industrial Problem of Man." The question is obviously what is the subject. Is man the subject and the aim of all social arrangements, including those of management? Then we should speak of the industrial-managerial problem of man. If management and production are the subject and the end of all social arrangements, then, indeed, we should speak of the human problem of management.

There is a good deal of literature in the field of industrial psychology which seems to assume a kind of preestablished harmony between man and management; the assumption is that *what is good for management is good for man, and what is good for man is good for managed institutions.* In saying this I am by no means minimizing the importance and great merits of the literature on industrial psychology. I am sure you are familiar with it, and I do not have to quote any names or titles. And, indeed, I believe that in the field of industrial psychology a great deal has been found that is very valuable, and not only valuable but important in making it possible to further the understanding of what managers call "the human problem." But I should still like to propose that the assumption of a preestablished harmony between man and management is not necessarily correct; that by making this assumption we are really evading the issue. We have to ask ourselves: *What if the interest of management and that of man are not harmonious?* What would we decide if something were better for man but worse for the process of production from the standpoint of maximal profit and the expansion of the enterprise?

I do not think we can evade this choice. As things are, the vast majority of Americans, not only in managerial groups but people in general, believe that what matters most is production, profit and efficiency; that if certain humanitarian measures are good for man without adversely

* From *Management Science*, Vol. 16, No. 12 (August, 1970), B-699–B-705. Reprinted by permission.

1 Elton Mayo, published by The Macmillan Company, New York, 1933; reprinted by Division of Research, Harvard Business School, Boston, Massachusetts, 1946.

affecting these highest goals, then one might employ such measures. But if there is any conflict, one should stress the side of efficiency, rather than that of man. If one takes this position then, indeed, one narrows considerably the range of one's thinking, and the possibility of creating alternative styles of management. What I am suggesting is the necessity of recognizing the potential conflict between the two interests, hence the existence of a choice.

The great problem is: *What is "good" for man?*

The terms self-expression, spontaneity, and expression of potentialities have become very fashionable; these are all words which have a meaning, but they are generally used vaguely, and they have become clichés. We must go beyond the clichés in popular literature and conversation and try to be precise; i.e., to know what is meant by these words in the context of our knowledge of man.

I contend that man is a system that can be studied like any other system. That is true whether we speak of man's body or whether we speak of his mind; and even this division is wrong, because we are really referring only to two different aspects of the same system. I need not remind you that if we speak of a living system we speak of something that is coherent, where the whole determines the part, where every change in one part implies a change in every other part; that system-thinking is not a linear form of thinking relating to cause and effect, but thinking about a totality, about a dynamic process; that the question "what is *the* cause" is meaningless, because there is no single "cause"; that one has to understand the whole system, with its hundreds of different aspects and its subsystems; that one has to go around it and look at it from all sides; that one has to find out in what particular way this system dysfunctions, and only then can one determine whether the dysfunction is still curable.

I might add that in speaking of systems we also speak of forces that move, and not of static entities put together in a mechanical way which can be changed as, let us say, parts of a machine can be changed. Such a science dealing with the "system man" is developing. Perhaps it started with Spinoza. It was greatly advanced by Freud. To be sure, it still is only a crude model of a system, but I believe that only to the extent that managers or, in general, people who try to understand society or a large enterprise, take the System Man as seriously as they take the system economics, the system technology, and so on, can they meaningfully talk about *human* ends in relation to the aims and ends of the managerial process.

I should like to mention one example, one of many that could be given. I choose this example because it constitutes one of the crucial aspects of our managerial society and, I believe, embodies one of the options we have. And that is the problem of bureaucracy, the problem of the bureaucrat. What is bureaucracy? What is a bureaucrat?

We know in the first place that bureaucratic management exists today in practically all large organizations, whether they are in industry or government, whether they pertain to education, health, or religion. All large organizations are managed in a bureaucratic way. And that is true not only for the so-called capitalist countries, but it holds true just as well, or more so, for the so-called communist countries—especially the Soviet Union, where the bureaucratic method is heavier and more old-fashioned, more conservative than it is in a highly-advanced capitalist country like the United States. But basically I think one can define contemporary capitalism and what the Russians call "socialism" as *bureaucratic-technological industrialism*, although they differ with regard to certain political and economic features.

It is obvious that bureaucracy is by no means a new discovery; one need only think, for example, of the bureaucratic system as it existed in ancient Egypt. Lewis Mumford pointed out in his splendid book *The Myth of the Machine*, that the technical achievements of the Egyptian society would not have been possible without their bureaucratic organization, which was so thorough and so complete that Mumford speaks of it as a "megamachine." That is to say, not in the usual sense of a machine, but in the sense that society itself is made into a machine of which each person becomes a part. Another old bureaucracy is the Roman Catholic Church; one finds at the present time that the oppositionist movement within the Church is to a large extent a protest against bureaucracy. Clearly, in speaking about bureaucracy we are referring to a phenomenon that is not new; it is not a phenomenon of the nineteenth or twentieth centuries, but one which has adapted itself to the particular requirements of our society and its own needs for management in a bureaucratic way.

What would be a general definition of the bureaucratic method? There are many definitions and much has been written about bureaucracy. I remind all those who are interested in this especially of the work of Max Weber, which gave a great impetus to the study of bureaucracy in the United States. Let me suggest a very simple definition: *bureaucracy is a method of managing in which people are dealt with as if they were things*.

I do not have to dwell on the obvious advantages of bureaucratic management from the standpoint of economic efficiency. All text books and the popular literature are full of praise for bureaucratic management to such an extent that most people believe that there is no other possible way of managing a highly complex human system. Obviously the advantages of bureaucratic methods are very great (even though the disadvantages are seldom recognized) and I take them very seriously. And I *have* to take them very seriously if I suggest the possibility that one could have an industrial society that is not built on the bureaucratic form of management.

But what I want to speak about mainly is not bureaucracy as a problem of organization but as a human problem. The question is whether we can speak of bureaucracy as a character trait, a mentality or an "attitude"? We do speak about a pedantic or stingy character, and we know what we mean by that. Can one speak also about a bureaucratic character, of a bureaucratic way of behaving, relating, and being? I hope you will not mind if I now speak very much as a psychoanalyst about an empirical problem of characterology about the problem, *what is the bureaucratic attitude as a character trait?*

Perhaps I should begin with a preliminary remark. When I speak about the bureaucratic attitude I am referring to character, rather than behavior. This difference itself is an important one, but it would require a detour to really explain the difference between a *behavior trait* and a *character trait*. However I should like to give one example, at least, to explain what I have in mind.

If you see a man who is behaving in a courageous way you might say "he has courage." That is a description of behavior. This behavior can be defined in the sense of a man's risking life and freedom for the sake of a certain aim in which he believes. But if you ask what the various possible motivations behind courage are, then you find that the motivations can be entirely different. What we usually like to think of as courage is the courageous behavior of those people who are so dedicated to an ideal and so free of egotism that they are willing to risk their lives for the sake of a fellowman, an ideal or a group. There are quite a few of whom this can be said, but there are many others who behave courageously for different motives, e.g., out of vanity, the desire to be admired. Others behave courageously because they have—consciously or unconsciously —suicidal tendencies and they do not care whether they live or die; in fact unconsciously they may want to die. And there are others who behave courageously simply because they lack the imagination to see danger. Now all this behavior is usually classified in terms of "courage" as a *behavior* trait; but if you compare the man who has a deep faith and dedication to an aim and the suicidal man, and the vain man, and the stupid man, then you can see that underneath this overt behavior trait you deal with entirely different forms of character. In fact, if you study the behavior more exactly you will find that even the behavior is not the same. For instance, a "suicidal" officer will be excellent in a certain situation in which reckless tacts are useful. But in general he would be very dangerous for his troops because he would not be sufficiently interested in life to avoid actions that a responsible officer should not initiate. The same holds true for the vain man, etc. In other words, an analysis of the behavior would show that in accordance with different unconscious motivations, the behavior differs also.

If you ask how one can discover the differences in motivations, especially the unconscious ones, then I will have to refer you to the science of man, and particularly to psychoanalysis. It is possible to discover these unconscious data from dreams, one can discover them from facial expressions, from the minute observation of what is said, from the language that is used; people do not have to be put on the couch in order to discover what character type they are. In fact, any good observer of men—which certainly applies to most effective managers—knows a great deal, not about the behavior but about the character of another person, simply by observation. One does not have to be a psychologist in order to be interested in perceiving more than just how the other person behaves at the moment, but in what is behind his overt behavior; that is to say, in the question, how will this man behave not only now, but tomorrow?

Let us be still more specific and describe what goes on between two people and how they relate to each other. Take as an example the situation between a teacher and a student. Compare the teacher while he is teaching with the same teacher while he is examining his students. These are two entirely different human situations. When I am teaching a student I am related to him; I am in tune with him. He is not an object sitting over there while I put something in him. I am in the process of teaching; I am sensitive to him; I am responsive to him; and if I am not, then I am not a good teacher. If the same student comes to me in the situation of an examination I am transformed into a mixture of policeman, judge, and bureaucrat. Because at that moment my duty is no longer that of responding to him, teaching him, being his ally, but that of watching him—even suspiciously, even to the point of finding out his tricks, finding out how he tries to deceive me. Suddenly the human relationship as it existed while I was teaching is transformed into an inhuman relationship in which he becomes an "object" to me. I watch him as I would watch a machine, or an instrument. I am no longer giving. I myself become a machine over here, and he is a machine over there; the machine *I* tries to find what goes on in the other machine. In fact, you could have two machines watching each other in that way—but this is not a human relationship. You find the same problem in the attitude of an executive to his employee. It is not a question of being "nice" and "friendly," or harsh and cruel, but the fact that due to the bureaucratic structure of the relationship the employee is a "thing," an object like any other part of the enterprise, and he is experienced like a thing, in an impersonal alienated and essentially inhuman fashion. Another example of bureaucrats are judges; they are people who act in a bureaucratic fashion, and if a judge were not to act thusly, how could he ever tell a man "I determine that you shall be executed on this or that day"? No human being fully related to another human being could ever say this except in hate. But if the defendant is not experienced as a human being but as an object of the judicial machine, then, of course, it is easy to say it.

Another interesting example of bureaucratic attitudes are nurses, who often relate to the patient as a "case," a thing they control—even with the best of intentions—but not to a person. The patient *is* an appendectomy, or a neurotic, or whatever the case may be. There are a number of investigations which show that the nurse's attitude makes a significant difference in the patient's chances of recovery. Studies have been made of post-operative patients who have been taken care of by "regular" nurses, and others who have been taken care of by nurses with special talent for an affectionate, responsive attitude to the patient as a *person*. The number of those who had post-operative complications were about three times as great with the "regular" nurse than they were with the "special" nurse. This is not a sentimental story from the Reader's Digest about "the good nurse," but a very well-documented study which simply shows what a difference it makes for a sick person if he is handled bureaucratically or humanly.

Many psychoanalysts and psychiatrists act bureaucratically. One of the favorite expressions of a bureaucratic response by a psychiatrist is the word "hmmm." The patient is "encouraged" to continue, the analyst wants to show that he is listening and not asleep; the word "hmmm" is deeply noncommittal, it does not even commit the analyst to much of an effort; it is, as I see it, a bureaucratic stimulus with no particular response expected.

The essential point of bureaucratic behavior is that the other person becomes a thing, and in watching him in a detached attitude, I become a thing myself. A technical philosophical expression for this is: the person becomes *reified*. He also becomes petrified; that is to say, deeply frightened, even though he may not be aware of the degree of this fright. In this bureaucratic, non-responsive situation the person involved becomes very lonely. This loneliness leads to deep suffering—again without the suffering being necessarily conscious. Man is not made to be without genuine human contact with his fellowman. And if he puts himself in the position of the "observer" or the "object" (and do not forget that the words "object" and "objection" have the same root), an inhuman relationship is established even if superficially it is a friendly one; it is manipulative, as many courses in "human relations" teach it.

We can differentiate between two kinds of bureaucratic attitudes which I am sure you will all identify immediately. One is the *friendly bureaucrat*. His "friendliness," nevertheless, does not alter the fact that the other person is an "object" to him, just as he can be friendly to his car and to other things he uses. These friendly bureaucrats usually have a friendly disposition, or they fake it, because it is in the nature of their particular position and method of management that they have to appear to be friendly.

Quite different from the friendly, though indifferent bureaucrat is the *authoritarian-sadistic bureaucrat* who is somewhat more old-fashioned. I had an experience with one such individual the other day—I still travel by train, as my last-ditch battle against the American railroad companies. I went to Pennsylvania Station to buy a ticket to Mexico, and the man behind the ticket window told me that as of the end of that year the Pullman service from St. Louis to Laredo would be discontinued, and he said, "*I'm glad about it*. I'm really glad about it." Then he added, "All that work, such a difficult ticket to make out!" (The difficult work is caused by not having a printed ticket, but having to write a ticket from here to St. Louis and from St. Louis to Mexico City.) This is the sadistic-authoritarian bureaucrat. Here was a man about 55 years of age; so he has been working for the railroads for 30 years. By discontinuing passenger travel his own job will be slowly abolished. He has grown up in this activity, and yet he is glad about its destruction. He is also so passive that even the small amount of activity involved in writing out a more difficult ticket than the usual ones is to him only a disagreeable chore. Another example is the face of the man behind the ticket window when three customers are still waiting and he puts his shade down and you can sometimes observe that slightly sadistic smile: this smile makes it clear that the man is not merely acting according to the rules, but that his *character* is that of a sadistic bureaucrat. If that same man were in a Fascist regime he might commit acts of great cruelty because he has a sadistic-authoritarian character that is satisfied by having other people submitted to his power and being able to see them being hurt, humiliated, and frustrated.

The friendly bureaucrat is the more modern type of bureaucrat, the one who has learned how to "oil" people so that they work with less friction. The older type of bureaucrat, the authoritarian character, is more often to be found in conservative enterprises like railroads, shipping, post offices, law courts, etc.

But in spite of these differences between the "friendly" and the "authoritarian-sadistic" bureaucrat, they have one important quality in common: that they relate themselves to be other person as to a thing, as

471

to an object—that they do not experience the other as a person and hence relate themselves to him without empathy or compassion.

I want to add that one must consider that the way people behave in their work situation, whether it is in business, in a hospital, or in a university, carries over to the way in which they behave in the other spheres of life. The often discussed idea, that work will very soon be more or less abolished is, I think, rather fantastic; we will continue to live with work—even though much less—for a long time to come; the way in which people relate to their fellowman in work will determine the way in which they relate to their fellowman outside of work. Therefore the work relationship itself will remain of utmost importance for the character of the relationships they have to other people.

The question is whether a non-bureaucratic, humanistic, man-centered form of management is possible.

This is a very complex and difficult question which I cannot discuss here. (I have discussed it at length elsewhere.)[2] I only want to state this: first, I believe that non-bureaucratic humanist management is possible. Second, the methods of such management are not easy to find, but the problem is not more difficult than space travel. Third, such methods will be found only if one is convinced (a) that the present bureaucratic spirit is inhospitable to life, joy, independence, love, compassion, meaningful human relations, real intimacy and sharing between people, and (b) that if one does not change the bureaucratic methods into humanist ones, the result will be increasing loneliness, boredom, aggressiveness, competition, consumption—from cars to sex, liquor, and drugs—and cruelty as the result of a lack of compassion. Fourth, that one can convince oneself of the real damage caused by bureaucratic behavior by studying the "System Man," and what it is that increases or decreases his optimal functioning as a human being. Economic and social planning is blind if the Science of Man is not integrated into the science of management and social planning.

[2] For instance, in *The Sane Society*, Holt, Rinehart & Winston, 1955; and *The Revolution of Hope*, Harper & Rowe, 1968.

62. Post-Bureaucratic Leadership*

Warren G. Bennis

In an early issue of this magazine (*Trans-action*, June–July, 1965), I forecast that in the next 25 to 50 years we would participate in the end of bureaucracy as we know it and in the rise of new social systems better suited to the 20th century demands of industrialization. The prediction was based on the evolutionary principle that every age develops an organizational form appropriate to its genius, and that the prevailing form today—the pyramidal, centralized, functionally specialized, impersonal mechanism known as bureaucracy—was out of joint with contemporary realities.

This breakdown of a venerable form of organization so appropriate to 19th century conditions is caused, I argued, by a number of factors, but chiefly the following four: (1) rapid and unexpected change; (2) growth in size beyond what is necessary for the work being done (for example, inflation caused by bureaucratic overhead and tight controls, impersonality caused by sprawls, outmoded rules, and organizational rigidities); (3) complexity of modern technology, in which integration between activities and persons of very diverse, highly specialized competence is required; (4) a change in managerial values toward more humanistic democratic practices.

Organizations of the future, I predicted, will have some unique characteristics. They will be adaptive, rapidly changing *temporary systems*, organized around problems-to-be-solved by groups of relative strangers with diverse professional skills. The groups will be arranged on organic rather than mechanical models; they will evolve in response to problems rather than to programmed expectations. People will be evaluated, not in a rigid vertical hierarchy according to rank and status, but flexibly, according to competence. Organizational charts will consist of project groups rather than stratified functional groups, as is now the case. Adaptive, problem-solving, temporary systems of diverse specialists, linked together by coordinating executives in an organic flux—this is the organizational form that will gradually replace bureaucracy.

Ironically, the bold future I had predicted is now routine and can be observed wherever the most interesting and advanced practices exist. Most of these trends are visible and have been surfacing for years in the aerospace, construction, drug, and consulting industries as well as professional and research and development organizations, which only shows

* From *Trans-action*, Vol. 6, No. 5 (July–August, 1969), 44–61. Reprinted by permission.

that the distant future now has a way of arriving before the forecast is fully comprehended.

A question left unanswered, however, has to do with leadership. How would these new organizations be managed? Are there any transferable lessons from present managerial practices? Do the behavioral sciences provide any suggestions? How can these complex, ever-changing, free-form, kaleidoscopic patterns be coordinated? Of course there can be no definitive answers, but unless we can understand the leadership requirements for organizations of the future, we shall inevitably back blindly into it rather than cope with it effectively.

Accepted theory and conventional wisdom concerning leadership have a lot in common. Both seem to be saying that the success of a leader depends on the leader, the led, and the unique situation. This formulation—abstract and majestically useless—is the best that can be gleaned from over 100 years of research on "leadership."

On the other hand, any formulations may be inadequate and pallid compared to the myths and primitive psychological responses that surround such complexities as leadership and power. Our preoccupation with the mystiques of the Kennedys is sufficient reminder of that.

Thus, leadership theory coexists with a powerful and parallel archetypal reality. But in what follows, we shall see that it is the latter myth that is threatened—the aggressive, inner-directed 19th century autocrat. For the moment, though, I want to quickly review some of the key situational features likely to confront the leader of the future.

The overarching feature is change itself, its accelerating rate and its power to transform. The phrase "the only constant is change" has reached the point of a cliché, which at once anesthetizes us to its pain and stimulates grotesque fantasies about a Brave New World with no place in the sun for us. Change is the "godhead" term for our age as it has not been for any other. One has only to recall that the British Parliament was debating in the last part of the 19th century whether to close up the Royal Patent Office, as it was felt that all significant inventions had already been discovered.

SITUATIONAL FEATURES

But what are the most salient changes affecting human organization, the ones with most relevance to their governance? Foremost is the changing nature of our institutions. In 1947, employment stood at approximately 58 million and now is at about 72 million. According to V. K. Fuchs, "Virtually all of this increase occurred in industries that provide services, for example, banks, hospitals, retail stores, and schools." This nation has become the only country to employ more people in services than in production of tangible goods. The growth industries today, if we can call them that, are education, health, welfare, and other professional institutions. The problem facing organizations is no longer manufacturing—it is the management of large-scale socio-technical systems and the strategic deployment of high-grade professional talent.

There are other important correlates and consequences of change. For example, the working population will be younger, smarter, and more mobile. Half of our country's population is under 25, and one out of every three persons is 15 years of age or younger. More people are going to college; over half go to college in certain urban areas. The United States Postal Department reports that one out of every five families changes its address every year.

Most of these changes compel us to look beyond bureaucracy for newer models of organizations that have the capability to cope with contemporary conditions. The general direction of these changes— toward more service and professional organizations, toward more educated, younger, and mobile employees, toward more diverse, complex, science-based systems, toward a more turbulent and uncertain environment—forces us to consider new styles of leadership. Leading the enterprise of the future becomes a significant social process, requiring as much, if not more, managerial than substantive competence. Robert McNamara is a case in point. Before he came to Washington, he was considered for three Cabinet positions: Defense, State, and Treasury. His "only" recommendation was that he was a superior administrator. Chris Argyris has concluded that success or failure in the United States Department of State depends as much or more on one's interpersonal and managerial competence as one's substantive knowledge of "diplomacy." It can also be said that leadership of modern organizations depends on new forms of knowledge and skills not necessarily related to the primary task of the organization. In short, the pivotal function in the leader's role has changed away from a sole concern with the substantive to an emphasis on the interpersonal and organizational processes.

MAIN TASKS OF LEADERSHIP

One convenient focus for a discussion of leadership is to review the main problems confronting modern organizations, and to understand the kinds of tasks and strategies linked to the solution of these problems.

Contributions and Inducements

A simple way to understand this problem is to compute the ratio between what an individual gives and what he gets in his day-to-day transactions. In other words, are the contributions to the organization about equivalent to the inducements received? Where there is a high ratio between inducements and contributions, either the organization or the employee gets restless and searches for different environments, or different people.

There is nothing startling or new about this formulation. Nevertheless, organizations frequently do not know what is truly rewarding, especially for the professionals and highly trained workers who will dominate the organizations of the future. With this class of employee, conventional policies and practices regarding incentives, never particularly sensitive, tend to be inapplicable.

Most organizations regard economic rewards as the primary incentive to peak performance. These are not unimportant to the professional, but, if economic rewards are equitable, other incentives become far more potent. Avarice, to paraphrase Hume, is *not* the spirit of industry, particularly of professionals. Professionals tend to seek such rewards as full utilization of their talent and training; professional status (not necessarily within the organization, but externally with respect to their profession); and opportunities for development and further learning. The main difference between the professional and the more conventional, hourly employee is that the former will not yield "career authority" to the organization.

The most important incentive, then, is to "make it" professionally, to be respected by professional colleagues. Loyalty to an organization may increase if it encourages professional growth. (I was told recently that a firm decided to build all future plants in university towns in order to attract and hold on to college-trained specialists.) The "good place to work" resembles a super-graduate school, alive with dialogue and senior colleagues, where the employee will not only work to satisfy organizational demands, but, perhaps primarily, those of his profession.

The other incentive is self-realization, personal growth that may not be task-related. I'm well aware that that remark questions four centuries of an encrusted Protestant ethic, reinforced by the indispensability of work for the preservation and justification of existence. But work, as we all must experience it, serves at least two psychic functions: first, that of binding man more closely to reality; and secondly, in Freud's terms, "of displacing a large amount of libidinal components, whether narcissistic, aggressive, or even erotic, onto professional work and onto human relations connected with it."

It is not at all clear as to how, or even if, these latter needs can be deliberately controlled by the leadership. Company-sponsored courses, sensitivity training sessions, and other so-called adult education courses may, in fact, reflect these needs. Certainly attitudes toward "continuing education" are changing. The idea that education has a terminal point and that college students come in only 4 sizes—18, 19, 20, and 21—is old-fashioned. A "dropout"' should be redefined to mean anyone who hasn't *returned* to school.

Whichever way the problem of professional and personal growth is resolved, it is clear that many of the older forms of incentives, based on the more elementary needs (safety-economic-physiological) will have to be reconstituted. Even more profound will be the blurring of the boundaries between work and play, between the necessity to belong and the necessity to achieve, which 19th century mores have unsuccessfully attempted to compartmentalize.

The Problem of Distributing Power

There are many issues involved in the distribution of power: psychological, practical, and moral. I will consider only the practical side, with obvious implications for the other two. To begin with, it is quaint to think that one man, no matter how omniscient and omnipotent, can comprehend, let alone control, the diversity and complexity of the modern organization. Followers and leaders who think this is possible get trapped in a child's fantasy of absolute power and absolute dependence.

Today it is hard to realize that during the Civil War, "government" (Lincoln's executive staff) had fewer than 50 civilian subordinates, and not many executives at that, chiefly telegraph clerks and secretaries. Even so recent an administration as Franklin Roosevelt's had a cozy, "family" tone about it. According to his doctor, for example, Roosevelt "loved to know everything that was going on and delighted to have a finger in every pie."

"Having a finger in every pie" may well be an occupational disease of presidents, but it is fast becoming outmoded. Today's administration must reflect the necessities imposed by size and complexity. In fact, there has been a general tendency to move tacitly away from a "presidential" form of power to a "cabinet" or team concept, with some exceptions (like Union Carbide) where "team management" has been conceptualized and made explicit. There is still a long-standing pseudo-masculine tendency to disparage such plural executive arrangements, but they are on the increase.

This system of an "executive constellation" by no means implies an abdication of responsibility by the chief executive. It should reflect a coordinated effort based on the distinct competencies of the individual. It is a way of multiplying executive power through a realistic allocation of effort. Of course, this means also that top executive personnel are chosen not only on the basis of their unique talents but on how these skills and competencies fit and work together.

Despite all the problems inherent in the executive constellation concept—how to build an effective team, compatibiilty, etc.—it is hard to see other valid ways to handle the sheer size and overload of the leader's role.

The Control of Conflict

Related to the problem of developing an effective executive constellation is another key task of the leader—building a climate in which collaboration, not conflict, will flourish. An effective, collaborative climate is easier to experience and harder to achieve than a formal description of it, but most students of group behavior would agree that it should include the following ingredients: flexible and adaptive structure, utilization of individual talents, clear and agreed-upon goals, standards of openness, trust, and cooperation, interdependence, high intrinsic rewards, and transactional controls—which means a lot of individual autonomy, and a lot of participation making key decisions.

Developing this group "synergy" is difficult, and most organizations take the easy way out—a "zero-synergy" strategy. This means that the organization operates under the illusion that they can hire the best individuals in the world, and then adopt a Voltairean stance of allowing each to "Cultivate his own garden." This strategy of isolation can best be observed in universities, where it operates with great sophistication. The Berkeley riots were symptomatic of at least four self-contained, uncommunicating social systems (students, faculty, administration, regents) without the trust, empathy, and interaction—to say nothing of the tradition—to develop meaningful collaboration. To make matters worse, academics by nature, reinforced by tradition, see themselves as "loners." They want to be independent together, so to speak. Academic narcissism goes a long way on the lecture platform, but may be positively dysfunctional for developing a community.

Another equally pernicious strategy with the same effects, but different style (and more typical of American business institutions), is a pseudodemocratic "groupiness" characterized by false harmony and avoidance of conflict.

Synergy is hard to develop. Lack of experience and strong cultural biases against group efforts worsen the problem. Groups, like other highly complicated organisms, need time to develop. They need a gestation period to develop interaction, trust, communication, and commitment. No one should expect an easy maturity in groups any more than in young children.

Expensive and time-consuming as it is, building synergetic and collaborative cultures will become essential. Modern problems are too complex and diversified for one man or one discipline. They require a blending of skills and perspectives, and only effective problem-solving units will be able to master them.

478

Responding to a Turbulent, Uncertain Environment

In the early days of the last war when armaments of all kinds were in short supply, the British, I am told, made use of a venerable field piece that had come down to them from previous generations. The honorable past of this light artillery stretched back, in fact, to the Boer War. In the days of uncertainty after the fall of France, these guns, hitched to trucks, served as useful mobile units in the coast defense. But it was felt that the rapidity of fire could be increased. A time-motion expert was, therefore, called into suggest ways to simplify the firing procedures. He watched one of the gun crews of five men at practice in the field for some time. Puzzled by certain aspects of the procedures, he took some slow-motion pictures of the soldiers performing the loading, aiming, and firing routines.

When he ran those pictures over once or twice, he noticed something that appeared odd to him. A moment before the firing, two members of the gun crew ceased all activity and came to attention for a three-second interval extending throughout the discharge of the gun. He summoned an old colonel of artillery, showed him the pictures, and pointed out this strange behavior. What, he asked the colonel, did it mean? The colonel, too, was puzzled. He asked to see the pictures again. "Ah," he said when the performance was over, "I have it. They are holding the horses" (Elting Morison, *Man, Machines and Modern Times*, 1966).

This fable demonstrates nicely the pain with which man accommodates to change. And yet, characteristically and ironically, he continues to seek out new inventions which disorder his serenity and undermine his competence.

One striking index of the rapidity of change—for me the single, most dramatic index—is the shrinking interval between the time of a discovery and its commercial application. Before World War I, the lag between invention and utilization was 33 years, between World War I and World War II, it was 17 years. After World War II, the interval decreased to about nine years, and if the future can be extrapolated on the basis of the past, by 1970 it will be around five to six years. The transistor was discovered in 1948, and by 1960, 95 percent of all the important equipment and over 50 percent of *all* electronic equipment utilized them in place of conventional vacuum tubes. The first industrial application of computers was as recent as 1956.

Modern organizations, even more than individuals, are acutely vulnerable to the problem of responding flexibly and appropriately to new information. Symptoms of maladaptive responses, at the extremes, are a guarded, frozen, rigidity that denies the presence or avoids the recognition of changes that will result most typically in organizational paralysis; or, at the opposite extreme, an overly receptive, susceptible gullibility to change resulting in a spastic, unreliable faddism. It is obvious that there are times when openness to change is appropriate and other

479

times when it may be disastrous. Organizations, in fact, should reward people who act as counterchange agents to create forces against the seduction of novelty for its own sake.

How can the leadership of these new style organizations create an atmosphere of continuity and stability amidst an environment of change? Whitehead put the problem well:

The art of society consists first in the maintenance of the symbolic code, and secondly, in the fearlessness of revision . . . Those societies which cannot combine reverance to their symbols with freedom of revision must ultimately decay.

There is no easy solution to the tension between stability and change. We are not yet an emotionally adaptive society, though we are as close to having to become one as any society in history. Elting Morison suggests in his brilliant essay on change that "we may find at least part of our salvation in identifying ourselves with the adaptive process and thus share some of the joy, exuberance, satisfaction, and security . . . to meet . . . changing times."

The remarkable aspect of our generation is its commitment to change in thought and action. Executive leadership must take some responsibility in creating a climate that provides the security to identify with the adaptive process without fear of losing status. Creating an environment that would increase a tolerance for ambiguity and where one can make a virtue out of contingency, rather than one that induces hesitancy and its reckless counterpart, expedience, is one of the most challenging tasks for the new leadership.

Clarity, Commitment, and Consensus

Organizations, like individuals, suffer from "identity crises." They are not only afflictions that attack during adolescence, but chronic states pervading every phase of organizational development. The new organizations we speak of, with their bands of professional problem-solvers, coping within a turbulent environment, are particularly allergic to problems of identity. Professional and regional orientations lead frequently to fragmentation, intergroup conflicts, and power plays and rigid compartmentalization, devoid of any unifying sense of purpose or mission.

UNIVERSITIES SURPASS BUSINESS IN SUBTERFUGE

The university is a wondrous place for advanced battle techniques, far surpassing their business counterparts in subterfuge and sabotage. Quite often a university becomes a loose collection of competing departments, schools, institutes, committees, centers, programs, largely noncommunicating because of the multiplicity of specialist jargons and interests, and held together, as Robert Hutchins once said, chiefly by a central

480

heating system, or as Clark Kerr amended, by questions of what to do about the parking problem.

The modern organizations we speak of are composed of men who love independence as fiercely as the ancient Greeks; but it is also obvious that they resist what every Athenian, as a matter of course, gave time and effort for: "building and lifting up the common life."

Thucydides has Pericles saying:

We are a free democracy. . . . We do not allow absorption in our own affairs to interfere with participation in the city's. We regard men who hold aloof from public affairs as useless; nevertheless we yield to none in independence of spirit and complete self-reliance.

A modern version of the same problem (which the Greeks couldn't solve either, despite the lofty prose) has been stated by the president of a large university:

The problem with this institution is that too few people understand or care about the overall goals. Typically they see the world through their own myopic departmental glasses; i.e., too constricted and biased. What we need more of are professional staff who can wear not only their own school or departmental "hat" but the overall university hat.

Specialism, by definition, implies a peculiar slant, a skewed vision of reality. McLuhan tells a good joke on this subject. A tailor went to Rome and managed to get an audience with his Holiness. Upon his return, a friend asked him, "What did the Pope look like?" The tailor answered, "A 41-regular."

Having heard variations of this theme over the years, a number of faculty and administrators, who thought they could "wear the over-all university hat" formed what later came to be known as "the HATS group." They came from a variety of departments and hierarchical levels and represented a rough microcosm of the entire university. The HATS group has continued to meet over the past several years and has played an important role in influencing university policy.

There are a number of functions that leadership can perform in addition to developing HATS groups. First, it can identify and support those persons who are "linking pins," individuals with a psychological and intellectual affinity for a number of languages and cultures. Secondly, it can work at the places where the different disciplines and organizations come together (for example, setting up new interdisciplinary programs), in order to create more intergroup give and take.

The third important function for leadership is developing and shaping identity. Organizations, not only the academic disciplines, require philosophers, individuals who can provide articulation between seemingly inimical interests, and who can break down the pseudospecies, transcend vested interests, regional ties, and professional biases. This is precisely what Mary Parker Follett had in mind when she discussed leadership in terms of an ability to bring about a "creative synthesis" between differing codes of conduct.

Chester Barnard in his classic *Functions of the Executive* (1938) recognized this, as well as the personal energy and cost of political process. He wrote, "It seems to me that the struggle to maintain cooperation among men should as surely destroy some men morally as battle destroys some physically."

The Problem of Growth and Decay

For the leader, the organization has to take a conscious responsibility for its own evolution; without a planned methodology and explicit direction, the enterprise will not realize its full potential. For the leader, this is the issue of revitalization and it confronts him with the ultimate challenge: growth or decay.

The challenge for the leader is to develop a climate of inquiry and enough psychological and employment security for continual reassessment and renewal. This task is connected with the leader's ability to collect valid data, feed them back to the appropriate individuals, and develop action planning on the basis of the data. This three-step "action-research" model sounds deceptively simple. In fact, it is difficult. Quite often, the important data cannot be collected by the leader for many obvious reasons. Even when the data are known, there are many organizational short circuits and "dithering devices" that distort and prevent the data from getting to the right places at the right time. And even when data-gathering and feedback are satisfactorily completed, organizational inhibitions may not lead to implementation.

In response to the need for systematic data collection, many organizations are setting up "Institutional Research" centers that act as basic fact-gathering agencies. In some cases, they become an arm of policy-making. Mostly, they see as their prime responsibility the collection and analysis of data that bear on the effectiveness with which the organization achieves its goals.

Fact-gathering, by itself, is rarely sufficient to change attitudes and beliefs and to overcome natural inertia, and unnatural resistance to change. Individuals have an awesome capacity to "selectively inattend" to facts that may in their eyes threaten their self-esteem. Facts and reason may be the least potent forms of influence that man possesses.

Some progressive organizations are setting up organizational development departments that attempt to reduce the "implementation gap'" between information and new ideas and action. These "OD" departments become the center for the entire strategic side of the organization, including not only long-run planning, but plans for gaining participation and commitment to the plans. This last step is the most crucial for the guarantee of successful implementation.

NEW CONCEPTS FOR LEADERSHIP

In addition to substantive competence and comprehension of both social and technical systems, the new leader will have to possess interpersonal skills, not the least of which is the ability to defer his own immediate desires and the gratifications in order to cultivate the talents of others. Let us examine some of the ways leadership can successfully cope with the new organizational patterns.

Understanding the "Social Territory"

"You gotta know the territory," sang "Professor" Harold Hill to his fellow salesmen in *The Music Man*. The "social territory" encompasses the complex and dynamic interaction of individuals, roles, groups, organizational and cultural systems. Organizations are, of course, legal, political, technical, and economic systems. For our purposes, we will focus on the social system.

Analytic tools, drawn primarily from social psychology and sociology, are available to aid in the understanding of the social territory. But we need more than such tools to augment and implement these understandings. Leadership is as much craft as science. The main instrument or "tool" for the leader-as-a-craftsman is *himself* and how creatively he can use his own personality. This is particularly important for leaders to understand, for, like physicians, they are just as capable of spreading as of curing disease. And again, like the physician, it is important that the leader heed the injunction "heal theyself" so that he does not create pernicious effects unwitingly. Unless the leader understands his actions and effects on others, he may be a "carrier" rather than a solver of problems. Understanding the social territory and how one influences it is related to the "action-research" model of leadership mentioned earlier: (1) collect data, (2) feed it back to appropriate sources, and (3) action-planning. The "hang-up" in most organizations is that people tend to distort and suppress data for fear of real or fancied retaliation. . . .

The Concept of "System-Intervention"

Another aspect of the social territory that has key significance for leadership is the idea of *system*. At least two decades of research have been making this point unsuccessfully. Research has shown that productivity can be modified by what the group thinks important, that training effects fade out and deteriorate if they do not fit the goals of the social system, that group cohesiveness is a powerful motivator, that conflict between units is a major problem in organizations, that individuals take many of their cues and derive a good deal of their satisfaction from their primary work group, that identification with the small work group turns out to be the only stable predictor of productivity, and so one.

The fact that this evidence is so often cited and rarely acted upon leads one to infer that there is some sort of involuntary reflex that makes us locate problems in faulty individuals rather than in malfunctioning social systems. What this irrational reflex is based upon is not altogether clear. But individuals, living amidst complex and subtle organizational conditions, do tend to oversimplify and distort complex realities so that people rather than conditions embody the problem. This tendency toward personalization can be observed in many situations. In international affairs, we [have blamed] our troubles with France on deGaulle, or [have talked] sometimes as though we [believed] that replacing Diem, or Khanh, or Ky [would] solve our problems with the Saigon government. Other illustrations can be seen when members of organizations take on familial nicknames, such as "Dad," "Big Brother," "Man," "Mother Hen," "Dutch Uncle," etc. We can see it in distorted polarizations such as the "good guy" leader who is too trusting, and his "hatchet man" assistant who is really to blame. These grotesques seem to bear such little resemblance to the actual people that one has to ask what psychological needs are being served by this complex labeling and stereotyping.

One answer was hinted at earlier in the Freud quote. He said that work provides an outlet for displacing emotional components onto professional work and the human relations associated with work. If there were no "Big Daddys" or "Queen Bees," we would have to invent them as therapeutic devices to allay anxieties about less romantic, more immediate mothers and fathers, brothers and sisters.

Another reason for this tendency toward personalization is related to the wounded narcissism leaders often suffer. Organizations are big, complex, wondrous—and hamstrung with inertia. Impotence and alienation imprison the best of men, the most glorious of intentions. There is a myth that the higher one goes up the ladder, the more freedom and potency one experiences. In fact, this is frequently not the case, as almost any chief executive will report: the higher he goes the more tethered and bound he may feel by expectations and commitments. In any case, as one gets entrapped by inertia and impotence, it is easier to blame heroes and villains than the system. For if the problems are embroidered into the fabric of the social system, complex as they are, the system can be changed. But if the problems are people, then the endemic

484

lethargy can be explained away by the difficulty—the impossibility—of "changing human nature."

If management insists on personalizing problems that arise from systems, serious repercussions must result. In the new organizations—where roles will be constantly changing and ambiguous, where changes in one subsystem will clearly affect other subsystems, where diverse activities have to be coordinated and integrated, where individuals work simultaneously in many different jobs and groups—a system viewpoint must be developed. Just as psychotherapists find it difficult to treat a "problem child" without treating the entire family, it will be more difficult to influence individual behavior without working with his particular subsystem. The leader will be compelled to intervene at the system level if the intervention is to last and serve its purpose.

An Agricultural Model of Leadership

I have not found the right word or phrase that accurately portrays the concept of leadership I have in mind—which can be summarized as follows: *an active method for producing conditions where people and ideas and resources can be seeded, cultivated, and integrated to optimum effectiveness and growth.* The phrase "other-directedness," unfortunately, has taken on the negative tone of "exclusively tuned into outside cues." For awhile I thought that "applied biology" might capture the idea, for it connotes an ecological point of view; a process of observation, careful intervention, and organic development. I have also noticed that many biologists and physicians (particularly those physicians who either have no practices or went into public health, psychiatry, or research) are excellent administrators. Socrates used a close and congenial metaphor to symbolize the role of the tackler, the "midwife," someone who helped others to give birth to creations.

The most appropriate metaphor I have found to characterize adaptive leadership is an "agricultural" model. The leader's job, as I have stated, is to build a climate where growth and development are culturally induced. Roy Ash, an astute industrialist and chairman of Litton Industries, remarked recently, "If the larger corporations, classically viewed as efficient machines rather than hothouses for fomenting innovation, can become both of these at once, industrial competition will have taken on new dimensions." I think Ash captures exactly the shift in metaphor I am getting at, from a mechanical model to an organic one. Up until very recent times, the metaphor most commonly used to describe power and leadership in organizations derived from Helmholtz's laws of mechanics. Max Weber, who first conceptualized the model of bureaucracy, wrote, "Bureaucracy is like a modern judge who is a vending machine into which the pleadings are inserted along with the fee and which then disgorges the judgment with its reasons mechanically derived from the code."

The language of organizational dynamics in most contemporary writings reflects the machine metaphor: social engineering, equilibrium, friction, resistance, force-field, etc. The vocabulary for adaptive organizations requires an organic metaphor, a description of a *process*, not structural arrangements. This process must include such terms as open, dynamic systems, developmental, organic, adaptive, etc.

All of these strategic and practical considerations lead to a totally new concept of leadership. The pivotal aspect of this concept is that it relies less on the leader's substantive knowledge about a particular topic than it does on the understanding and possession of skills summarized under the agricultural model.

This new concept of leadership embraces four important sets of competencies: (1) knowledge of large, complex human systems; (2) practical theories of intervening and guiding these systems, theories that encompass methods for seeding, nurturing, and integrating individuals and groups; (3) interpersonal competence, particularly the sensitivity to understand the effects of one's own behavior on others and how one's own personality shapes his particular leadership style and value system; and (4) a set of values and competencies which enables one to know when to confront and attack, if necessary, and when to support and provide the psychological safety so necessary for growth.

It is amusing and occasionally frustrating to note that the present view of leadership which I have referred to as an agricultural model, is often construed as "passive," and generally dismissed with the same uneasy, patronizing shrug one usually reserves for women who try, however clumsily, to play a man's game. The fact is that the role of leadership described here is clearly more demanding and formidable than any other historical precedent, from king to Pope.

It may be that the common tendency to give this new leadership role such passive and effeminate names betrays the anxiety that many must feel at the final downfall of that distant, stern, strict Victorian father, whose surrogate has led us so often as teacher, military commander, and corporation president. Perhaps that is the only kind of authority we have experienced first hand, or know intimately, or even consider legitimate. But if this new man of power—other-directed and interpersonally competent—takes over the dominant role, as he now seems to be doing, then not only will new myths and archetypes have to substitute for the old, family ones, but new ways—perhaps new legends—will have to be developed to dramatize the rise of new heroes. Let us hope that this new tradition of leadership is not only more potent, but in the long run more gratifying.

SELECTED READINGS

Books

Bennis, Warren G., and Philip E. Slater. *The Temporary Society*. New York, Harper and Row, 1968.

Blake, Robert R., and Jane Mouton. *The Managerial Grid*. Houston, Gulf Publishing Company, 1964.

Katz, Daniel, and Robert L. Kahn. *Social Psychology of Organizations*. New York, John Wiley and Sons, Inc., 1966.

Likert, Rensis. *The Human Organization: Its Management and Value*. New York, McGraw-Hill Book Company, 1967.

McGregor, Douglas. *Leadership and Motivation*. Ed. by Warren G. Bennis and Edgar H. Schein in collaboration with Caroline McGregor. Cambridge, Massachusetts, M.I.T. Press, 1966.

————. *Professional Manager*. Ed. by Caroline McGregor and Warren G. Bennis. New York, McGraw-Hill Book Company, 1967.

Marini, Frank. *Toward a New Public Administration*. San Francisco, Chandler Publishing Company, 1971.

Vroon, Victor Harold. *Work and Motivation*. New York, John Wiley and Sons, Inc., 1964.

Articles

Argyris, Chris. "The Individual and Organization: Some Problems of Mutual Adjustment," *Administrative Science Quarterly*, Vol. 2, No. 1 (June, 1957), 1–24.

Bennis, Warren G. "Organizational Developments and the Fate of Bureaucracy," *Industrial Management Review*, Vol. 7, No. 2 (spring, 1966), 41–55.

————. "Organizational Revitalization," *California Management Review*, Vol. 9, No. 1 (fall, 1966), 51–55.

————. "Organizations of the Future," *Personnel Administration*, Vol. 30, No. 5 (September–October, 1967), 6–19.

————. "The Coming Death of Bureaucracy," *Management Review*, Vol. 56, No. 3 (March, 1967), 19–24.

Bergey, John M., and Robert C. Slover. "Administration in the 1980's," *Advanced Management Journal*, Vol. 34, No. 2 (April, 1969), 25–32.

Borgese, Elisabeth Mann. "The Promise of Self-Management," *The Center Magazine*, Vol. 5, No. 3 (May–June, 1972), 54–60.

487

"The 4-Day Week," *Texas Town and City*, December, 1971, 18–19.

Harris, Louis. "Seeking and Resisting Change," *The Conference Board Record*, Vol. 5 (May, 1970), 14.

Lingle, Kendall I. "Crucibles of Change," *Public Personnel Review*, Vol. 30, No. 1 (January, 1969), 2–8.

Mulrooney, Keith F. "The American City Manager: An Urban Administrator in a Complex and Evolving Situation," *Public Administration Review*, Vol. 31, No. 1 (January–February, 1971), 6–46.

Musjgerd, Robert D. "Needed: Tolerance for Change," *Administrative Management*, Vol. 32, No. 6 (June, 1971), 69–70.

Smith, Michael P. "Alienation and Bureaucracy: The Role of Participatory Administration," *Public Review*, Vol. 31, No. 6, 658–64.

INDEX

The paper on which this book is printed bears the watermark of the University of Oklahoma Press and has an effective life of at least three hundred years.

41-400